The Life and Teachings of Hillel

The Life and Teachings of Hillel

Yitzhak Buxbaum

ROWMAN & LITTLEFIELD PUBLISHERS, INC.
Lanham • Boulder • New York • Toronto • Plymouth, UK

The author gratefully acknowledges permission to quote from *If I Am Only for Myself* by Aaron Blumenthal. Copyright © 1973 The United Synagogue of America.

ROWMAN & LITTLEFIELD PUBLISHERS, INC.

Published in the United States of America
by Rowman & Littlefield Publishers, Inc.
A wholly owned subsidary of The Rowman & Littlefield Publishing Group, Inc.
4501 Forbes Boulevard, Suite 200, Lanham, Maryland 20706
www.rowmanlittlefield.com

Estover Road
Plymouth PL6 7PY
United Kingdom

Copyright © 1994 by Yitzhak Buxbaum
First Roman & Littlefield edition 2004. First Rowman & Littlefield paperback edition 2008

British Library Cataloguing in Publication Information Available

Library of Congress Cataloging-in-Publication Data:

Buxbaum, Yitzhak.
   The life and teachings of Hillel / by Yitzhak Buxbaum.
      p. cm.
   Includes bibliographical references and index.
   1. Hillel, 1st cent. B.C. / 1st cent—Teachings. 2. Rabbinical
literature—History and criticism. 3. Rabbinical literature—
Translations in English. 4. Hillel, 1st cent. B.C./1st cent.—
Legends. 5. Legends, Jewish. I. Title.
BMS502.3.H55B89 1994
296.1'2'0092-dc20   93-5617

ISBN-13: 978-1-56821-049-0 (cloth : alk. paper)
ISBN-10: 1-56821-049-3 (cloth : alk. paper)
ISBN-13: 978-0-7425-6337-7 (pbk. : alk. paper)
ISBN-10: 0-7425-6337-5 (pbk. : alk. paper)
eISBN 13: 978-0-7425-6587-6
eISBN 10: 0-7425-6587-4

Printed in the United States of America

Contents

Acknowledgments

I would like to express my appreciation to my wonderful mother, Jeanette Buxbaum, and to my good friend Professor Herb Levine for reading the manuscript and providing invaluable suggestions regarding language, style, and arrangement of the material. I would also like to gratefully acknowledge the gracious assistance I received at the Hebrew Union College Library in New York City, from Dr. Philip Miller, head librarian, and from Mr. Henry Resnick, library assistant.

I

Ascent to Leadership

The Lost Teachings of Hillel

A GENTLE MODEL FOR OUR GENERATION

Hillel is one of the greatest rabbis of the Jewish tradition, yet even knowledgeable people usually know only the same few stories and sayings of his – about his teaching the Golden Rule to the gentile standing on one foot, his saying "If I am not for myself, who will be for me, and if I am for myself alone, who am I?" and so on. I became intrigued with Hillel when I came across some less familiar but fascinating stories about him and wondered why I had not been aware of them earlier. After some investigation I found that for various reasons many facets of Hillel's teaching and activity had been neglected and virtually "lost." I also discovered that he was a more interesting character than many people might have thought, more hasidic (pious) and radical. (Hasidic generally means "pious" and *hasid* a "pious person," but both terms can also refer specifically to the later hasidic movement of the Baal Shem Tov.) As I proceeded with my research, I was surprised to learn that no comprehensive book had ever been published about Hillel in English or in Hebrew. The only two books available – both written for young adults – were *Hillel the Elder*, by Nahum Glatzer, a brief treatment of a mere 100 pages, and *If I Am Only for Myself*, by Aaron Blumenthal, also of very modest size. Neither comprehensively treats all the stories and sayings of Hillel. Since no complete book about Hillel was available and I was inspired by what I had learned about him, I decided to fill the need.

Aside from curiosity about such a great figure in the Jewish tradition, another compelling reason for a book about Hillel is that he has a particular attraction for our generation, representing the gentler, more loving side of Judaism that so many people are searching for today. When looked at properly, the rabbinic tradition actually offers two contrary ideals, represented by Hillel and by his contemporary and adversary, Shammai. It not only recommends the softer one most modern people favor, but judges the rigid one critically. The tradition itself preferred the loving and flexible *hasid* to the severe and intolerant ascetic. The struggle and choice between these two ideals and types is still with us today. One purpose of this book is to reinforce those committed Jews who value openness, and to reconcile those who are alienated from their heritage, by showing them that Judaism seeks to draw them in, not push them away. I hope this study of Hillel will help to recover something precious that has been lost and, without distorting the texts, support a side of the tradition that needs to be reinvigorated.

This book has not been written as a biography of Hillel, recording in order the stages and events of his life and his career as a religious leader. There is hardly enough material for that. What I have done is weave together the various stories about Hillel with his own sayings and teachings, in order to reveal the interconnections between the parts and the integrity of the whole. The order and arrangement of the material is only roughly chronological, mostly for the beginning and end of Hillel's life.

But although *The Life and Teachings of Hillel* is not a biography, it does try to create a spiritual profile of this great teacher. Its goal is not only to offer new information about a radiant religious figure, but to show the reader something even more important: that Hillel's teachings can speak to his or her heart. I expect that many people will be charmed and fascinated by what can only be described as Hillel's fiery gentleness.

HOW COULD HILLEL'S TEACHINGS HAVE BEEN LOST?

Considering Hillel's fame, it might seem strange to suggest that his teachings have somehow been lost. This did not occur in the obvious way, however, but in many subtle ways.

In general, Hillel's teachings (and those of his School, his "House") have been "lost" due to their having been transmitted thoroughly mixed in with the contrary teachings of the opposing school, the House of Shammai. The tradition treasures and preserves both. Its striking judgment is: "Both these and those are the words of the living God." But although it originally presented them as two conflicting ideals, they were eventually combined and their mutual contradictions obscured. Jewish law (*halachah*) is always decided according to the views of the lenient Hillel, not the strict Shammai. But in matters of religious attitudes and values, in modes and patterns of observance, the tradition often works to reconcile the two camps, ending up with something in between. The two streams are poured into one cup. As a result, the particular dynamism of Hillel's way vanishes; the clarity of his religious position disappears from view. It is usually assumed that Hillel represents what came to be considered "normative" Judaism. But when his teachings are set apart and looked at by themselves, their distinctively hasidic leaning soon becomes apparent.

It was never part of the ancient rabbinic tradition to focus on a single man, no matter how great he was or how profound his influence. The sayings and stories of Hillel are never collected in one place. They are scattered here and there throughout the enormous rabbinic literature. Consequently, they do not coalesce in our consciousness either; they never attain a form and shape as a whole. But it is not only the unity and interconnectedness of the teachings that have receded into obscurity. The living personality of the man himself has faded in our collective memory; his image in our minds remains vague and ill-defined. The goal of this book will be to do the work of restoration that will return his portrait to its first form, to see the entire picture once again, and in its original bright colors.

To do so, it will be necessary to consider Hillel in the context of those who went before and those who followed – both his teachers and his students. We will also pay careful attention to the words of sages who lived in the generations after Hillel and who were deeply influenced by him. Aside from the rabbis of the Talmud and the *Midrash*, however, another valuable source of information will be found in the sayings and stories of the hasidic rabbis of the last centuries, who, though far from Hillel in time, are often close to him in character and sentiment. By using these traditional teachings from other sources to provide the setting, we will be able to fully appreciate

Hillel's words and the stories about him. We will see them not only in relation to each other but in relation to the rich world of Jewish religious wisdom. When we have finished this work of restoration and have recovered Hillel's portrait for our contemplation, I hope the reader will agree that it presents to us a man whose saintly character and remarkable deeds are worthy of his fame.

We live in changing times, when traditional religious verities need to be recast and reformed. Hillel, the man and his teachings, has much to offer our generation, for he accomplished a similar feat long ago. The rabbis said that when the Torah was forgotten in Israel, Hillel reestablished it, restoring the crown of the Torah to its former glory and rescuing the Jewish people from a religious decline. Hillel lived according to the urgent and stirring words of the Psalms: "It is a time to act for the Lord – they have made void Your Torah!" He taught: "Where there are no men, try to be a man!" and "If not now, when?" In a time of crisis, when many people were falling away from their faith, he drew them back with Torah teaching that was sweet and all whose ways were pleasant. He searched the Torah for its essence and found love of God and love of fellowmen.

Hillel reestablished the Torah when it had been forgotten. Now his own teachings have been forgotten and must be recovered. The intention of this book is not to be "about" Hillel so much as to let his words and example speak to us today. The rabbis tell us that when someone utters a traditional saying in the name of a teacher, he should see that teacher as if he were standing before him. May the words of Hillel in this book, and the stories about him, have the merit to call to mind his living example.

*   *   *

A Note about My Approach to the Sources

My basic approach to the source texts is religious, not historical. My attention to the historical context of Hillel's teaching and activity is modest, not because that perspective is unimportant, but because this study has a different focus. The people who originally told the legends about Hillel were usually not interested in his biography or in history. They recounted his various deeds and sayings for religious reasons. And each story about him stood on its own. No one in those days concerned himself with creating a continuous narrative of Hillel's life from beginning to end. Neither did any single person produce all the various stories; each came into being by itself, with no necessary relation to the others. We do not possess a movie, but isolated snapshots. And they are, of course, legends; we have no guarantee of their historical accuracy. Nevertheless, I do not share the view of those academic scholars who are uniformly and rigidly skeptical about the veracity of such traditions.

I have not embellished the sources novelistically or linked them into a narrative to make connections where none exist–by "filling in the blank spaces"–because I appreciate the authenticity that comes with evaluating texts as they are, without additions. Rather than trying to produce a "movie" of Hillel by splicing together the individual photos, of which there are far too few, I have chosen to collect them all in one album and provide explanatory captions to demonstrate how they relate to one another.

Although this book is scholarly and based on extensive research, it does not meet the rigorous standards of academic scholarship. I admit this without apology, since it is a religious book that does not pretend to analyze the legends about Hillel from an objective standpoint. They are occasionally considered critically, but more often they are accepted at face value for their religious message. But from a religious point of view, the issue of their historicity is not paramount. My own attitude to the stories is not very different from the people who created and first told them My foremost interest is: What can they teach me religiously? From that perspective, they have much to offer.

We cannot know with any certainty how the Hillel of legend compares with the real man, since there are no other sources that could be used as a basis for such a comparison. In this book I consciously adopt a naive religious view and usually accept the legendary Hillel along with the legendary history of his time that the tradition recounts.

To give merely one illustration of the difference between a religious and a historical approach: I occasionally interpret Hillel from the perspective of later developments in Judaism, such as the hasidic movements of the Baal Shem Tov. Academic scholars of religious history are usually constrained to interpret texts and events in the context of their time. Nonacademic religious scholars, on the other hand, may feel freer to interpret what went before from their own contemporary perspective. Their concern is not only to determine, for example, "what Hillel thought." Their relation to a great Jewish teacher is like that of an art critic to an artist: Once the work of art has been created and is in the world, its "meaning" depends on the critic's interpretation as well as on what the artist himself originally intended. But while a religious scholar's view of an earlier teacher might be weak in its historical sense, it might also provide insights not available from an objective, academic viewpoint because a religious scholar may (or may not) more closely share the same spirit as the teacher who is the subject of study and may understand him from a perspective essentially similar to his own. When the Baal Shem Tov, the founder of Hasidism, teaches about Moses, for example, his objective historical understanding is meager, but that does not invalidate his view! Far from it! Religiously, it is actually primary and essential, because it draws on what went before not just for study or intellectual curiosity, but to continue the living tradition. This hardly means, however, that a religious author today – when academic scholarship has produced a scientific viewpoint not available in earlier times – can abandon objectivity. The more an interpretation deviates from known historical fact, the less credibility it will have for intelligent people. On the other hand, a historical study of a religious subject can often be totally devoid of spiritual significance. Obviously, then, religious writing must seek a creative tension between scholarly objectivity and religious subjectivity – although the boundary can legitimately vary, depending upon the purpose of the work. I hope that readers will judge this book by the standard it chooses as its own and will appreciate perspectives that may depart from the strictly objective viewpoint.

Note to the Reader

See Appendix 1, "Editorial Collections of Sayings," for the reasons I analyze individual sayings of Hillel rather than editorial collections, and the nature of those collections. See also Appendix 2, "From Which Hillel Are the Sayings in *Avot* 2:4–8?" for a discussion of that issue.

Abbreviations

ARN = *Avot d'Rabbi Natan*. *ARN-A* and *ARN-B* = the two versions of *Avot d'Rabbi Natan*. When the title is written out, version A is understood.

Pirke Avot is the full name of the text usually cited as *Avot*.

2

Historical Setting and Family Background

BABYLONIA AND ISRAEL, POLITICS AND RELIGION

Hillel was born in Babylonia, that great exile community of the Jewish people, in the early part of the first century B.C.E.[1] In the Land of Israel, this was the time of the last Hasmonean (Maccabean) kings and, following them as rulers, the Herods, a family descended from Edomite converts. During this period the Romans were steadily extending their empire and their sphere of influence and had also insinuated themselves into Israel, where they became the dominant power. Herod the Great, a contemporary of Hillel, allied himself with that growing empire, slaughtered his way forward, and rose to be King of Judea, ruling by the grace of his Roman patrons. Sharing the Romans' taste for Hellenistic culture and having little interest in Judaism, he pursued what can only be called a paganization program, building gymnasiums, theaters, temples to alien gods, and whole cities for non-Jews. Although "Great" in terms of power, to most Jews he was small and despicable, a cruel and vicious despot who acted as an agent of the foreign empire.

Four religious sects or parties existed in Israel at that time: the Pharisees, Sadducees, Essenes, and Herodians. The most prominent were the Pharisees and Sadducees. The democratic Pharisees were the most popular sect by far, representing the huge mass of the people. Their main focus was on the primacy of the Torah, and their leaders were the expert interpreters of Torah, the rabbis. (During

9

Hillel's time, the sages and scholars were not yet called "rabbis" and Hillel, for example, is never called "Rabbi Hillel." But for ease of discussion we will use "rabbis" throughout this book to mean the Pharisaic Torah scholars of Hillel's time, the rabbis of the period after Hillel, and their predecessors who were at an earlier period before Hillel called "scribes.") The more conservative Sadducees, who represented an older establishment of priests, aristocrats, and wealthier merchants, had less influence on the religious views of the larger community, but they dominated the Temple worship and the Sanhedrin, the central religious council based in the Temple.[2] The other two sects were the Essenes, a pious brotherhood of separatists, who lived in isolated monastic communities in the desert, and the Herodians, a religious party allied to Herod the Great.[3]

These were the political and religious conditions in Israel then. But it is unlikely that any of these religious sects of Israel existed in the Babylonian Jewish community, where Hillel was born and grew up.[4] And while Israel was in the Roman sphere of influence, Babylonia was under the sway of the great Parthian Empire, Rome's eastern adversary.

FAMILY AND NAMES

Hillel's name goes back to the Torah: the judge who preceded Samson was called Avdon the son of Hillel.[5] The names of Hillel's parents are not known. However, certain names reappear in the line of his male descendants, all of whom were leaders in Israel. These are the names, generation after generation, beginning with Hillel himself: Hillel, Simon, Gamaliel, Simon, Gamaliel, Simon, Judah, Gamaliel, Judah, Gamaliel, Judah, Hillel, Gamaliel, Gamaliel.[6] By the names repeated in the family one can surmise that his father's name might have been Simon, Gamaliel, or Judah. Once, we find Hillel remarking to someone about the *tefillin* (phylacteries) he was wearing, "These are the *tefillin* of my mother's father."[7] That he wore these *tefillin* suggests a good deal of reverence for his maternal grandfather and for his piety. The last detail we have of his parents' family is that he had a brother named Shebna.[8] As to Hillel's own family, we are also short on names. His wife's name is not known. But he had at least one son, the Simon mentioned in the preceding list.

LINEAGE

His lineage was unclear to the rabbis, who at one point ask, "What was Hillel's ancestry?" The best answer that could be provided was that given by Rabbi Levi (c. 300 C.E.) who reported that "a genealogical scroll was found in Jerusalem, and in it was written: 'Hillel was descended from [King] David.' "[9] Rabbi Levi lived long after Hillel. We do not know when or where the scroll was found, nor what credence to give it.[10] It seems that Hillel himself had some interest in genealogy, as the Talmud reports that "Hillel taught: Among those who went up [to Israel] from Babylonia [with Ezra], there were ten genealogical classes."[11] It is not inconceivable, then, that he had an interest also in his own origins and knew that he was descended from David. Of course, it could be that a glorious lineage was somewhat naturally and spontaneously generated for Hillel, who was the founder of a dynasty of Jewish leaders.[12] On the other hand, someone as great as Hillel does not necessarily spring up out of the ground like a mushroom. A cultural "product" such as he is likely to have been the result of generations of development and refinement in families of the most intensely religious people. Although many Jews are not aware of it, such family lines of religious aristocracy exist even today among the Jewish people, and more than a few Jewish families can trace their lineage back to King David.

Hillel, then, probably was brought up and had his early religious training in a Babylonian Jewish family of the most intense and thoroughgoing piety.

3

Shebna

As a young man Hillel gave himself over, heart and soul, to the Torah. But he was still determined to provide for his own support, even if that meant he would live on a minimal subsistence. We have one tradition about Hillel's family, about him and his brother Shebna, that touches on this.

PARTNERS

First some background: It was the custom in those days that sometimes one brother devoted himself full time to business and supported another brother who was then able to give himself full time to Torah study. There was a partnership, both material and spiritual. The idea was that the two shared in both realms: the one who studied shared in the this-worldly wealth of his working brother; the one who labored, by his help in making it possible, shared in the merit of the other brother's Torah study and in its reward in the World-to-Come. The famous legendary example of this in the Torah was that of the two brothers, sons of Jacob, Yissachar and Zebulun, who according to the rabbis were such "partners." Yissachar was said to have occupied himself full time with Torah study and did not engage in earning a living; Zebulun, who occupied himself full time with business, supported his brother.

HILLEL AND HIS BROTHER

Here is the Hillel story, which, it would seem, probably took place in Babylonia:[1]

> Hillel and Shebna were brothers. Hillel devoted himself to Torah, while Shebna involved himself in business. Later on, Shebna said to his brother, "Come, let's be 'partners' and split everything evenly." But a heavenly voice was heard in answer, [echoing the words of the Song of Songs and] saying, "If a man were to give all the wealth of his house for love, he would be utterly despised" (Song of Songs 8:7) (*Sotah* 21a).

From this tradition about Shebna's offer (where we learn in passing that Hillel had a brother), we can perhaps conclude that their father was either deceased or financially unable to support his son's study. If the former, it seems that they did not inherit significant wealth from him. Shebna was not quite as devoted as Hillel and was involved mainly with business rather than with Torah, yet he was still pious enough to want to support his brother's Torah study and perhaps even saw that Hillel was destined for greatness. More important, we learn that Hillel could have allowed his brother to support him, but refused. Although the story does not say so explicitly, it is understood that he rejected his brother's money. While Hillel remained silent, the heavenly voice answered on his behalf and, as will become clearer later, rejected Shebna's offer.

We are not told in so many words why Hillel refused Shebna's offer, but it is not hard to understand.[2] In fact, a number of motives can be surmised, some from Hillel's own teachings of later years. On the one hand, it is likely that he did not want to make things easy for himself.[3] Hillel was ready and willing to contend with adversity in pursuit of the Torah, knowing that the spiritual reward gained thereby would be commensurate with the trouble.[4] Indeed, it was held by the rabbis that resorting to the Yissachar-Zebulun sort of partnership offered to Hillel by his brother was not the ideal and did not lead to the highest levels of spiritual attainment, for a person whose actions are motivated solely by love of God gives no thought to any hardship involved, while he who accepts such a partnership, at least to some degree, seeks to avoid suffering and difficulties that might come in the service of God. So Hillel was ready to undergo any hardship because of his great love of God.

We also know that later in life Hillel taught that a man should not "put the crown to a profane use,"[5] by exploiting his knowledge of the Torah for personal benefit.[6] This same perspective might have led him to avoid using his Torah study as a device to provide himself with a living, even if a Yissachar-Zebulun partnership was generally accepted as a necessary way to foster Torah learning.

The unstated corollary of Hillel's decision to refuse his brother's offer was that he was choosing for himself and his family voluntary poverty, for it was impossible for him to devote himself fully to Torah study and still make anything but the most meager living. We will see shortly how Hillel supported himself by working as a lowly day laborer.

On the most basic level, Hillel rejected a Yissachar-Zebulun partnership with his brother because he cherished his independence and did not want to rely on someone else. The spiritual aspect of this is that he did not want to depend on a man, on flesh and blood, even if it was his own brother.[7] Total reliance on God alone is a sign of great trust. And we know from a teaching of his that Hillel's attitude of trust in God was encapsulated in a phrase from Psalm 68:20, "Blessed is the Lord day by day."[8] So although he studied Torah in poverty, working as a laborer, he made do with the minimum and blessed God each day for all the goodness he received that day, not worrying about the next.

But having to rely on God day by day, with no other source of help, is itself a blessing, as the Torah teaches in the story of the manna in the desert. Some rabbis taught that even in later generations "the Torah is not given except to the eaters of manna"; that is, the full spiritual transmission is only to those who throw themselves completely on God for their material support. So Hillel was not tempted by his brother's offer. He was content to forgo his help and rely, in complete trust, on God.

The verse of Songs of Songs 8:7 echoed by the heavenly voice in the story is the final clue to a full understanding of Hillel's attitude. Song of Songs 8:7 reads: "If a man were to give all the wealth of his house for love, men would utterly despise him." The simple meaning of this is that if a man throws away all his money because of his infatuation with a woman, people think him a fool. But the tradition tells us that the love poetry of the Song of Songs is symbolic of the love between God and Israel and between God and every Jew – and so was it interpreted. The verse used by the heavenly voice means, then, that Hillel's love of God and His Torah was on the very highest level – it was like the fiery and passionate love between man and woman, an exclusive love in which another can have no share. Shebna's offer was "utterly despised" (in the language of the verse) not through any fault of his,[9] but because his brother's love of God was of the kind in which money cannot buy a share in partnership. Beyond the other motives already mentioned, this, the story tells us, was the deepest – that Hillel himself could not think of selling a share of his love.

As often in the tradition when a heavenly voice (*bat kol* in Hebrew) is heard, it quotes a verse from the Torah, here Song of Songs 8:7.[10] The use of this verse by the heavenly voice not only expresses divine recognition of Hillel's love for God, but is also a sign of God's great love for him. Hillel chose poverty out of his devotion to God and the Torah. That a heavenly voice praised his love is proof it was returned.

But the heavenly voice that answered Shebna and refused his offer only indirectly praised Hillel. Later we will discuss a story from the period of Hillel's fame that recounts more direct praise, when a heavenly voice was heard to say that he was worthy that the holy spirit rest on him as it did on Moses.

In later years Hillel would praise his own disciples with the words of a Torah verse where personified Wisdom says: "I will cause those who love Me to inherit richly, and I will fill their treasuries" (Proverbs 8:21). The same verse could certainly be applied to Hillel himself, and his "treasuries" were to become filled with all kinds of Torah knowledge. But to achieve that he had to go up to Jerusalem to learn from the sages of the Land of Israel.

4

Hillel on the Roof

About 60 B.C.E., as a young man, Hillel went to Jerusalem[1] – the heart of the Jewish people – to continue his Torah studies with the Pharisee sages Shemaya and Avtalyon. Later, he would call them "the two greatest teachers of the generation."[2] Another contemporary, Judah ben Durtai, echoed this when he spoke of them as "those two great men of the generation, Shemaya and Avtalyon, who were great sages and great Torah interpreters."[3] Shemaya and Avtalyon were the dual leaders of the Sanhedrin,[4] of the Pharisees, and of the popular religious community in Israel, Shemaya being the *Nasi*, the "Prince," and Avtalyon the *Av Beit-din*, the Head of the Supreme Religious Court.[5] Every day Hillel attended their lectures at their *Beit Midrash*, their House of Torah Study. And just as he had endured hardship and poverty for the sake of the Torah in Babylonia (refusing his brother's help), so too did he endure hardship and poverty in Israel. This story is told:

> Our rabbis taught: When a poor man who had neglected the Torah shall appear before the Divine Judgment he will be asked: "Why did you not occupy yourself with Torah study?" If he answers, "I was poor and overwhelmed with the need to earn a living!" they will say to him: "Were you then poorer than Hillel?"
>
> Because when Hillel the Elder was a young man, he went out to work every day and earned just one *tarpik*-coin. Half of it he gave to the doorkeeper of the House of Study, for the

admission fee, and with the other half he supported himself and his family. Once, being unable to find work for the day, he had no money and the doorkeeper would not allow him to enter. So he climbed up on the roof and swung himself over to the skylight, where he sat down to listen to the words of the living God from the mouths of Shemaya and Avtalyon. This happened on a Friday, before the Sabbath, and during the winter month of *Tebet*. Snow started to fall, but Hillel was so absorbed in what he was hearing that he did not even notice. Before long, though, he was covered over with a blanket of snow and lost consciousness. He lay there all through the night.

On Sabbath morning, when learning resumed in the House of Study, Shemaya said to Avtalyon: "Brother, every day the hall is well lit by this time. Why is it still dark? Is it such a cloudy day today?" They raised their eyes and saw the figure of a man on the skylight. When they went up they found him covered with a layer of snow fully four feet thick. After removing the snow, they took him down, washed and rubbed him over with oil, and placed him before a fire. When they became aware of what had happened and why Hillel was on the roof, they remarked, as they attended to him: "Someone like this is truly worthy that the Sabbath be violated for his sake" (*Yoma* 35b).

Jewish law places saving life above all else, and the Sabbath prohibitions against work—such as what the two teachers did to revive Hillel—are disregarded if there is even the slightest doubt of a risk to life. The rabbis would have done the same for anyone; their comment meant that a person of such self-sacrificing devotion and holiness as Hillel was most worthy that the holiness of the Sabbath be desecrated for his sake.

Hillel was, then, very poor at this time of his life—a day-laborer.[6] Every day men would gather on a certain street corner or other known place, and wait until an employer came to hire them.[7] Sometimes, as happened to Hillel, a man would not be able to find work for a day. An average daily wage for a laborer was one or two *dinars*.[8] A *tarpik*, the coin that Hillel earned, was only half a *dinar*. Perhaps he went to the House of Study in the early hours and worked only during the latter half of the day.[9] Regardless, this small coin indicates his poverty; he was so poor he could be held up as an example to other needy people, who, the rabbis said, would be asked: "Were you as poor as Hillel?" And of the half wage he did earn, half of that went for admission to the House of Study, and all he was left with, for the support of himself and his family, was what remained – half of a half-wage.

In its present context, this story serves as a lesson to the poor. The Talmud says that no poor man should think to use his poverty as an excuse – for was not Hillel desperately poor, and yet look how devoted he was to the Torah, see what he attained![10] If we forget about the "frame," the lesson to the poor that the rabbis provided for the original story, we see the focus shift more to an interest in Hillel himself, to "someone like this," as Shemaya and Avtalyon put it.[11] It is a story that explains why Hillel rose to greatness, by showing us his outstanding qualities even as a young man. We also see how this special young man first came to the attention of his great rabbis. Certainly, after this incident, Shemaya and Avtalyon made sure that Hillel would no longer have to listen from the roof.

The story also shows us Hillel's unquenchable thirst for the words of Torah, as the rabbis say: "Sit amidst the dust of the sages' feet, and drink in their words with thirst."[12] He had come all the way from Babylonia to hear these words of Torah; for their sake he would endure poverty and go to the lengths of self-sacrifice described in this story.

It is no accident that the phrase "the words of the living God" is used here. In later years, Hillel taught: "The more Torah, the more life."[13] For him, these words of Torah gave life, they were the life of the soul, and he could not be kept away – not by the doorkeeper and not by the snow (which was, by the way, a rare occurrence indeed in Jerusalem).

There is a religious abandon in Hillel's action here that was an essential part of his character. Sitting on the roof, he was completely distracted by the sweetness of what he heard. He was hardly aware of the outside world and probably did not even notice that it was snowing.[14] The rabbis traditionally related this state of religious transport to Proverbs 5:19 – "be ravished always with love of her," which they interpreted as being about the most intense love of the Torah. In the story of Hillel and his brother Shebna, the heavenly voice quoted Song of Songs 8:7 in praise of Hillel's love for God and His Torah, a love as intense and passionate as that between man and woman. In this story of Hillel on the roof, that is what we see – his rapturous love, even to distraction, for the words of the living God.

But how can we not be dismayed when seeing that even in those times people were kept away from Torah due to a lack of money! One can easily imagine that in the light of his own experience, Hillel did not favor this institution of the "doorkeeper."[15]

If we consider what is lost in the rabbinic presentation of this story, we find that the frame, which supplies its context–that the poor should not use their poverty as an excuse–of necessity almost tames the story in its attempt to provide a lesson for ordinary human beings. We are not told: Follow Hillel's extraordinary example; accept poverty willingly to acquire Torah; stop at nothing and overcome all obstacles for her sake. Instead, the message is restricted to the poor, those already poor, not from choice but from circumstance, who are asked: How can you excuse yourselves from Torah study–was not Hillel terribly poor? But though the rabbis were understandably interested in applying the lesson of this story even to the average man, we can look at what it says about Hillel, who was anything but average, and consider the lesson it has for those who share the fire that Hillel felt.

5

His Great Torah Knowledge

During the many years (forty, according to legend) he attended on the sages, Shemaya and Avtalyon among them, Hillel acquired prodigious Torah knowledge. In a tradition where the greatness of Yohanan ben Zakkai's learning is praised, he attests to the superior greatness of his own rabbi, Hillel:

There was no part of the Torah that Rabbi Yohanan ben Zakkai had not mastered. He knew Scripture and *Targum*, *Midrash*, *Halachah*, *Aggadah*, and Parables too; he had studied every branch of Torah and learned everything there was to learn. He once exclaimed, "If the whole sky were parchment and all the trees on earth pens, and all the seas ink—it would not suffice to write down all the wisdom I learned from my rabbi. But what was I able to receive from the wisdom of the sages, compared to what they knew? It is like a fly dipping in the ocean to bathe and then flying off; how much does it carry away?"

And from whom did Rabbi Yohanan ben Zakkai receive his Torah knowledge?—from Hillel and Shammai.[1] There was nothing of the sages' words that Hillel had not learned. He had even learned the languages of all the peoples of the world; as well as the speech of mountains, hills, and valleys; the speech of trees and grasses; the speech of wild and domestic animals, the speech of demons. He was expert in parables too.

Why was all this necessary? Because it is said, "God desired to make Israel worthy, so He expanded the borders of the Torah and made it glorious" (Isaiah 42:21)[2] (*Soferim* 16:9).

It was this extraordinary knowledge of Torah that, as we will see, would later win for Hillel the office of the *Nasi*.

6

Hillel Becomes Nasi

A FATEFUL VISIT

The next glimpse we have of Hillel's life is the story in the Talmud that tells how he came to succeed to the mantle of his masters Shemaya and Avtalyon, although this did not happen right away. After having attended on them for many years he returned, it seems, to his native Babylonia. Why? We can only speculate: perhaps the unstable political conditions in Israel then, involving the internecine struggles among the Hasmoneans or the conflicts between the Hasmoneans and Herod, became too difficult to bear; perhaps he left to bring the traditions of Israel back to his fellow Babylonians, for undoubtedly Hillel returned to his homeland as an accomplished rabbi and teacher.

At some point, when Shemaya and Avtalyon had passed away, they were followed in the leadership of the Sanhedrin by two members of a prominent family known as the Sons of Bathyra. But it was Hillel and not they who was the true disciple of those two great Torah sages and that he could say in his teaching of traditions, "So I heard it from Shemaya and Avtalyon," became precious to the Torah community. We will see why. The setting of the story is some period of years later, when Hillel, as a mature man, had returned to Jerusalem, most likely on a pilgrimage to celebrate the Passover festival but also to take advantage of his visit to clarify some halachic issues (of Jewish religious law) with the scholars in Jerusalem.[1]

PASSOVER AND SABBATH

One year the fourteenth day of the month of *Nisan*–the day before Passover–when the Passover lambs are to be sacrificed, fell on the Sabbath. It was already the thirteenth of *Nisan* and the Sons of Bathyra could not recall the halachic tradition as to whether the labors involved in the Passover sacrifice were prohibited on the Sabbath or not. Should the sacrifice be performed on the Sabbath or postponed? They asked the sages, "Is there anyone who knows this?"

Some among those present said, "There is a man who has come up from Babylonia,[2] called Hillel the Babylonian,[3] who attended on the two greatest men of the generation, Shemaya and Avtalyon. He would probably know whether the Passover sacrifice supersedes the Sabbath or not. Perhaps we can get some help from him."

They sent for him, and when he arrived they asked, "Do you ever remember hearing whether the Passover sacrifice overrides the Sabbath?"

Hillel replied, "Have we only one Passover in the year that overrides the Sabbath? There are more than two hundred Passovers a year that override the Sabbath!"

By this striking remark Hillel meant that two hundred other sacrifices offered during the course of a year on the Sabbath are similar to the Passover sacrifice in one way or another.[4] He then developed this argument by applying a number of rules of Torah interpretation and concluded that the Passover sacrifice also takes precedence over the Sabbath.[5] There are two versions of this story, one in each of the two Talmuds (the Babylonian Talmud originated in that great Jewish community; the Jerusalem Talmud, in the Land of Israel). In the Babylonian Talmud (remember that Hillel was a Babylonian) the Sons of Bathyra are convinced by Hillel's arguments and are so impressed by the profundity and scope of his learning that they immediately make him their leader. Ideally, leadership was based on Torah knowledge and, since Hillel had demonstrated his superior expertise in an important matter, they resigned in his favor. The text says:

On the spot they sat him in the chief seat and appointed him as
the *Nasi*. And Hillel lectured that whole day on the laws of
Passover.

But in the Jerusalem Talmud, the story takes a different turn.
They refute each of his arguments that are based on the rules of
interpretation and even remark sarcastically:

Didn't we say before, "How can you expect anything from a
Babylonian?"

This comment of theirs is not found in the Babylonian Talmud, which, it seems, toned down the anti-Babylonian aspects of
the story in a number of ways. In the Jerusalem Talmud the story
continues:

Although he sat and lectured the whole day, trying to prove
that the Passover sacrifice takes precedence over the Sabbath,
they continued to reject his arguments based on rules of Torah
interpretation, until, exasperated, he said to them, "I swear to
you! May heaven punish me if I did not also receive this
halachah as a tradition from Shemaya and Avtalyon!" Upon
hearing this they stood up and appointed him as *Nasi*.

However, after sitting in the *Nasi's* chair, Hillel began to
reproach the assembled sages, the Sons of Bathyra among
them, and asked them sarcastically, "Why were you forced to
seek help from a Babylonian and make me your *Nasi*? Isn't it
because you were lazy and negligent in not attending on the
two greatest sages of the generation, Shemaya and Avtalyon,
who were right here at your elbow?"

Afterward, having learned from Hillel that the Passover
sacrifice indeed was performed on the Sabbath, a related question arose and they asked him: "Master, what is the law if a
man forgot to bring the slaughtering knife in advance to the
Temple Court on Friday before the Sabbath? May he bring it
on the Sabbath or is that carrying prohibited as work?"

He said to them: "I know that I've heard this *halachah*, but
I've forgotten it. Leave this to the people of Israel themselves,
for although they are not prophets they are sons of prophets
and will surely know in practice what to do."

The next day [some individuals did forget and] those who were bringing a lamb as their Passover sacrifice and leading the animal along had the knife entangled in the thick wool of its neck, and those bringing a kid of the goats had the knife inserted between its horns. Thus they did not have to carry the knife on the Sabbath day, for the animal itself carried it. When Hillel saw what they had done, he recollected the *halachah*, which taught just that, and said: "Such is the tradition that I received from Shemaya and Avtalyon"[6] (combined version: *B. Pesahim* 66a, *Y. Pesahim* 6:1, 33a).[7]

SUDDEN ELEVATION

This story describes the abrupt and unexpected elevation of Hillel to leadership. One moment he is a virtual unknown, the next moment the *Nasi*. What gained him this dramatic promotion? It was his outstanding Torah knowledge, particularly of traditions he received from Shemaya and Avtalyon.

In view of the fact that the story of Hillel on the roof showed how Shemaya and Avtalyon became aware of their extraordinary student and of his self-sacrificing love for Torah, it is not farfetched to think that they finally recognized him as a leading disciple. If so, they would not have been surprised by his succeeding them.

HOW COULD THEY HAVE FORGOTTEN?

The Jerusalem Talmud adds after the story a comment by Rabbi Abun, who wondered how the Sons of Bathyra and the other sages could have forgotten whether to sacrifice the Passover on the Sabbath, since this situation recurs every fourteen years. "Rabbi Abun said: 'Isn't it true that two seven-year periods cannot pass without the fourteenth of *Nisan* falling on the Sabbath? How could they have forgotten the *halachah*?' "

A modern scholar remarks:

"Rabbi Abun, who lived many years after this confrontation, asks the obvious question. How is it possible for everybody to forget the law? Our calendar is so arranged that the fourteenth of *Nisan* must fall on the Sabbath at least once every fourteen years. It is incredible that of the seventy members of the Sanhedrin, not one of them had been alive fourteen years earlier and therefore could testify out of personal memory. Certainly the priests should have known. Furthermore, if the people knew what to do with their knives, would they not also know whether the Passover supersedes the Sabbath? Even Hillel, who was a mature man at the time, does not say that he remembers how the law was observed fourteen or twenty-eight years earlier, but 'I remember that this is what Shemaya and Avtalyon taught.' No matter how we try to explain it, this element in the story is impossible."[8]

Rabbi Abun, however, answered his own question, "How could they have forgotten the *halachah*?" by saying: "This event was brought about [by divine providence] in order to give the leadership to Hillel." He was forced to resort to the suggestion that God intervened miraculously, making them all forget in order to transfer the leadership to Hillel.

Rabbi Abun's comment is found in the Jerusalem Talmud. The Babylonian Talmud also adds a comment after the story, where the interest is not in how the Sons of Bathyra could forget, but why Hillel also forgot (about the knives). This will be discussed more fully later, but the basic point made there is that Hillel's intemperate sarcasm (when he accused the sages of having neglected to learn from Shemaya and Avtalyon) caused him to forget, since it is a law of spiritual psychology that pride and anger lead to forgetfulness.

RULES OF INTERPRETATION

In both Talmud versions Hillel uses specific rules of Torah interpretation to argue his case. In the Babylonian Talmud the sons of Bathyra are immediately won over by his genius and appoint him *Nasi*. In the Jerusalem Talmud, on the contrary, they find his interpretative methods unacceptable and are not persuaded, until he tells them that the position he has been trying to establish by argument is identical to what he had received as a tradition from Shemaya and Avtalyon (this latter element is absent in the Babylonian Talmud version). In either case, though, the rules of interpretation are presented as something new. The same conclusion can be gathered from another ancient rabbinic source that does not recount the story–where three rules are mentioned–but states that Hillel used seven rules in all:

> Hillel the Elder employed seven rules of Torah interpretation with the Sons of Bathyra. And these are they: inference from minor to major; inference from a similarity of phrases; deduction from one verse; deduction from two verses; inference from general and particular; inference from particular and general; similarity elsewhere; deduction from context. These are the seven rules of Torah interpretation that Hillel the Elder made use of with the Sons of Bathyra (*Avot d'Rabbi Natan*, chap. 37).

From early times Torah sages had used interpretation to formulate laws in cases where the Torah gave no explicit instruction or where they had no previous oral tradition.[9] But Hillel and other rabbis wanted to expand the use of interpretation. On the one hand, they believed that for the Torah to function as a guide and manual for living, it had to be constantly interpreted and applied to changing conditions and circumstances. On the other hand, they also wanted to extend the Torah's influence to all aspects of life.

But any interpretation inevitably inspires questions as to whether it is correct. If every rabbi could deal with the text as he pleased, he could easily make the Torah say whatever he wanted it to say. This problem was particularly acute in regard to *halachah*, where matters of practice were involved. So Hillel introduced specific rules of interpretation–based on common sense and logic–to invest this process with some order.

Not all the rabbis were equally enthusiastic about determining *halachah* by Torah interpretation. The rabbis in the Land of Israel had strong oral traditions about halachic matters, and if they needed to know how something was to be done, they most likely had an authoritative tradition that gave them the answer. But the rabbis in Babylonia, from whence Hillel came, were farther removed from the original source of the traditions in Israel and more frequently confronted questions of religious law to which no one had a relevant tradition.[10] And living among a gentile majority outside Israel, they more frequently faced circumstances never previously encountered that required a religious response. In such cases they relied on Torah interpretation, *midrash* as it is called, to determine the Torah's position by arguments based on a careful analysis of one or more verses. The difference between Israel and Babylonia in this regard was still only a matter of emphasis, the scholars in Israel being more conservative in relying on traditions and the Babylonians more ready to turn to Torah interpretation. But there was a struggle around this issue and something of that struggle is reflected in the story of Hillel the Babylonian's encounter with the Sons of Bathyra. The exact nature of the issue, however, remains unclear.[11]

We have to ask about the Jerusalem Talmud's version (that seems original on this point):[12] If Hillel had a tradition from Shemaya and Avtalyon (which he knew would convince the Sons of Bathyra) why did he resort to it only at the end? Why did he first try so hard to persuade them by arguing from his rules of interpretation? This procedure seems to make no sense, and requires an explanation. The answer that suggests itself, and makes his approach logical, is that Hillel was attempting to win their assent to his rules as a valid basis for halachic decisions.[13]

Hillel is said to have used seven rules of interpretation in his session with the Sons of Bathyra. Was he just a master at their application or had he been involved in their formulation?[14] We do not know, although it is relevant that his teachers, Shemaya and Avtalyon, are called in the tradition "great interpreters" of the Torah, that is, masters in the use of *midrash*.[15] Regardless, it is unlikely that any one person "created" these rules. Some are common sense, others are already found in the Torah itself. What probably happened is that many scholars had always used various "rules" unconsciously, so to speak, and Hillel, perceiving the need for systemization, searched the Torah and reviewed the many oral traditions to extract and list those rules that were most acceptable among the many that already existed.

Hillel's association with the development of the rules of interpretation is also significant because it indicates his activist orientation. Formalizing the rules not only enhanced their authority, but increased the rabbis' authority to act as interpreters. While the rules were restrictive and prevented chaos in interpretation, they also expanded the rabbis' freedom to adapt Torah laws to changed conditions, especially in situations where there were no relevant traditions or there were contradictory ones. Although this suited activists such as Hillel,[16] it was opposed by conservatives, who wanted to base the *halachah* almost exclusively on traditions.

NEGLECT

Hillel rebuked the Sons of Bathyra and the other sages for not having attended on Shemaya and Avtalyon. "Attending" on a sage means coming into intimate contact with him (which might involve personal service) to get the full benefit of his Torah knowledge – not only learning from him in formal classes, but observing his conduct in all life circumstances and at close range.

When we see that Hillel had been willing to go to the greatest lengths to hear the words of the living God from Shemaya and Avtalyon, we can understand his distress at the way others, who should have known better, neglected his great teachers. In later years Hillel taught:

> Whoever does not attend upon the sages deserves death (*Avot d'Rabbi Natan*, chap. 12).

Although this typical rabbinic hyperbole should not be taken literally,[17] it indicates the severity with which Hillel viewed such negligence. By complaining that the Sons of Bathyra and the other sages were lazy and neglected Shemaya and Avtalyon, he seems to be criticizing them for the fact that whereas he, who grew up in faraway Babylonia, came all that great distance to be with those giants of Torah, the targets of his reproach lived in Jerusalem right with them and did not bother to seek the benefit of their vast knowledge and wisdom. A story that we will discuss later on casts some light on his attitude: A common man, a donkey-driver, jokingly asserted his superiority, as a native Jerusalemite, over Hillel, who was a Babylonian. Hillel responded, also humorously, that, on the contrary, his efforts in coming to Jerusalem from so far away would win him a greater reward.

HILLEL'S RARE ANGER

Hillel's rebuke of the sages can be considered from various perspectives. The rabbis teach that a person's anger reveals his character, and this is especially true for someone like Hillel, who so rarely lost his temper. In this exceptional instance, where he succumbed, his anger and its causes should be carefully considered.

Although he might have had a long-standing resentment at the way some scholars ignored his masters and failed to honor them as they deserved, the most obvious source of his irritation would have been at the Sons of Bathyra refusing to accept his method of Torah interpretation and rejecting his arguments one after the other. Hillel was already exasperated when he finally swore that his position was the same as the tradition he had heard from Shemaya and Avtalyon. Even though the Sons of Bathyra then resigned in his favor, he still vented his earlier frustration by taunting them.

It is also probable that Hillel lost his temper because he was unhappy at being forced into a leadership position he did not desire, something necessary only because others had forsaken *their* responsibility. A famous saying of Shemaya's instructed his disciples to "hate lordship."[18] A saying of Hillel's own may help explain his reticence to assume a high position:

A name made great – is a name destroyed (*Avot* 1:13).

Certainly the power and honors associated with leadership are a temptation and a snare for many. Perhaps, paradoxically, Hillel's uncharacteristic outburst of anger was a result of his ingrained humility.

That the Sons of Bathyra had resigned their office to install an unknown person (Hillel), who demonstrated his superior Torah knowledge, shows their noble character and humility. In the Jerusalem Talmud version of the story we are considering, an added comment at the end says: "There are three who by giving up their crowns in this world inherited the life of the World-to-Come." "One" of these three is said to be the Elders of Bathyra. (The Jerusalem Talmud refers to them as the "Elders," rather than "Sons," of Bathyra.) None other than Hillel's own descendant, Rabbi Judah the Prince, further comments that they were indeed uncommonly great, for: "The Elders of Bathyra voluntarily resigned from the office of *Nasi* and appointed Hillel in their place."

In a related tradition in the Babylonian Talmud,[19] Rabbi Judah the Prince refers to them as "exceptionally humble men," although other rabbis wondered whether they did not simply see the obvious – that Hillel was greater than they were in Torah – and had no choice but to resign, for when they would be asked questions about laws and traditions in the House of Study and could not answer,

Hillel would answer, and they would be embarrassed publicly. Their motive, then, was not humility but fear of humiliation. However, Rabbi Judah likely knew, through a family tradition, the circumstances in which his famous ancestor had become *Nasi* and whether the motives of the Sons of Bathyra were praiseworthy or not. And he says that they were.

On the other hand, this incident, as recorded in the Jerusalem Talmud, also shows the disdainful attitude of the Sons of Bathyra at Hillel's not being native born, but being a Babylonian Jew. Their somewhat natural prejudice made them unhappy at having to turn to an outsider. Hillel, for his part, said to them, "Why were you forced to seek help from a Babylonian and make me your *Nasi*? Because you were lazy!" We can hear in his sarcasm a reaction to their prejudice against his Babylonian background.

When, as mentioned earlier, a common man, a lowly donkey driver, felt entitled to tease the great Hillel about his "inferior" status as a Babylonian Jew, Hillel answered with a joke. On another occasion, when some farm laborers rudely called him a "stupid Babylonian," he became angry at their bad manners,[20] as he did here with the Sons of Bathyra.

To summarize our thoughts on Hillel's angry rebuke of the sages: It can be taken at face value as expressing his attitude to their laxity in not having attended on Shemaya and Avtalyon (along with resentment at a slight to his masters). But behind this was his frustration at the sages not accepting his method of Torah interpretation, his distress at a sudden and undesired elevation to the leadership, and his reaction to local anti-Babylonian prejudice.

As mentioned briefly earlier, the Babylonian Talmud has following the story an additional comment that suggests that Hillel forgot the law about carrying the knives to the Temple because he allowed himself to become angry when he rebuked the sages. Hillel is given as an illustration of the teaching that "if a sage becomes arrogant, his wisdom departs." A parallel saying here (although without reference to Hillel) says: "If a sage becomes angry, his wisdom departs." The lesson is derived from the fact that immediately after Hillel became angry and spoke sarcastically to the sages, the story continues that when he was asked the question about the knives he said, "I know I've heard this law, but I've forgotten it." Although Hillel was very humble, and he chastised the sages from religious motives, even a trace of pride or anger disrupts the soul's balance. When either of them enters, wisdom departs. It is note-worthy that although Hillel became famous for his humility and for being almost immune to anger, the rabbis did not protect his reputation by removing this contrary incident.

DEFICIENT KNOWLEDGE AND FORGETTING

Hillel became *Nasi* primarily because of his vast storehouse of traditional knowledge. He was asked two halachic questions and finally answered both with traditions he had received from Shemaya and Avtalyon, although in one case he first tried to prove his position about performing the Passover sacrifice on the Sabbath by using rules of Torah interpretation and in the other his memory had to be jarred by seeing the people's custom of having the sacrificial animals carry the knives to the Temple. But note that both cases involved instances of deficient knowledge of oral traditions: first, that the Sons of Bathyra had never heard the *halachah* about a Passover on the Sab-bath, and then that Hillel had heard but forgotten about the knives. In the next chapter we will see that forgetting oral traditions was a major problem for the rabbis, and for Hillel.

7

The Nasi *as Scholar*

THE ORAL LAW AND FORGETTING

Traditional Judaism is based on two sources: the scriptural Written Law, and the commentary developed over centuries to explain it, the Oral Law. Once one appreciates the inherent difficulties of an oral tradition, the story of Hillel's elevation to *Nasi* becomes much more understandable. Chief among these difficulties is the insidious ease with which laws and teachings are forgotten.

The rabbis were very conscious of the problem of forgetting Torah that had been heard and memorized. This was something of an occupational hazard for them. The story of Hillel's rise to become *Nasi* has two instances of this inability to recall a tradition: first, when the Sons of Bathyra (and the other sages present) forgot, and then when Hillel himself forgot. The rule still held then that the oral tradition must not be written down.[1] That is why constant attendance on the sages was so necessary, for if you were out of your rabbi's presence at any time, who knows how many important teachings you might miss hearing or how many of his actions, based on Torah knowledge, you might miss seeing in performance? Hillel was diligent not to be absent for even one session at the House of Study (even if he had to listen from the roof) and considered failure to attend upon the sages unforgivable negligence. And once traditions were learned they had to be constantly repeated orally until they were fixed in one's memory. Elsewhere, Hillel said that you could not compare someone who repeats his lesson one hundred times to someone who repeats it one hundred and one times:[2] the latter's devotion to the Torah is such that he goes to the limits and beyond. Surely this was self-description. Hillel, who climbed on the roof to hear, also repeated one hundred and one times to remember.

THE HIGH PRIEST'S CLOTHES AND THE RED HEIFER

But even Hillel had his lapses. When asked about the knives, he said: "I've heard this *halachah*, but I've forgotten it." Another story tells how, as the *Nasi*, he was asked a halachic question about which clothes the high priest must wear during the ceremony of burning the red heifer after it was sacrificed (Numbers 19). He answered according to the tradition he remembered having heard. When that tradition was disputed, he went on to support his position by telling what he remembered having seen years earlier, when this rare sacrifice was performed in the Temple. But others present responded that they too were there and they remembered having seen something else. Furthermore, they convincingly supported their view from the Torah story that tells of the first such sacrifice, which was performed under the supervision of Eleazar, the son of Aaron (Moses's brother). At this point, Hillel realized that he was wrong. Here is the text:

Hillel was once asked a question about the Temple ritual of the sacrifice of the red heifer: "What garments does the high priest wear when the heifer is burned?" He answered: "[The tradition says:] The gold garments." They said to him: "No, [the tradition we received is that] he officiates at its burning while wearing the white garments." Hillel said: "When Joshua ben Perahya[3] was *Nasi*, I myself saw how a red heifer was burned under his supervision with the high priest wearing the gold garments." They answered: "No, you're wrong again. We saw that too and it was done in the white garments." "You're basing your position on his authority and so am I," came back Hillel, "How shall we decide?" One of them said: "Let's go to the Torah. Who supervised the burning of the first red heifer?" Hillel said: "Eleazar." "Would Eleazar," they continued, "wear the gold garments of the high priest while his father Aaron was alive [as he was – and still the high priest[4]]?" Hillel [realizing now that he was mistaken – he had not correctly remembered the tradition he had learned about what clothes were to be worn and he had not even remembered what he had seen] exclaimed: "Don't hold a man in contempt because of his forgetfulness! And if I could forget what my eyes saw, surely I could forget what my ears heard!"[5] (*Sifre Zutta,* Hukkat, beg., on Numbers 19:3).

Hillel had forgotten the tradition about what to do with the knives when Passover fell on the Sabbath, and here he forgot the tradition about what clothes the high priest was to wear at the burning of the red heifer.

With the normal fallibility of human memory and the awkward fact of opposing traditions, it was necessary to turn to the Torah and decide some matters by Torah interpretation. That was Hillel's own method, and here he himself was not only caught forgetting, but was corrected by means of Torah interpretation.

SCHOLARLY CONTEMPT

The prime interest in this story, however, is in Hillel's words at the end. He pleads with them not to hold him in contempt because of his forgetfulness and says that if he could forget what he saw, he could certainly forget what he heard. Forgetfulness might be lamented, but it was an unavoidable reality. Hillel asked for understanding for his own weakness, an understanding he surely gave to others. Compare the rabbis' saying found elsewhere: "A sage who has forgotten his learning for reasons beyond his control should not be treated with contempt."[6] If Torah sages disdained their colleagues' forgetfulness it would have at least two bad effects. First, scorn for a fellowman is always wrong, and in this case it is only the reverse side of an arrogance in knowledge to which learned people are naturally prone. Such arrogance is not only ugly but spiritually damaging in the worst way, as is all pride. Hillel himself was accused of a rare exhibition of this fault in his sarcastic words to the Sons of Bathyra. But the second negative effect of contempt for others' forgetfulness is that the more this bad trait contaminates the world of Torah discourse, the more it produces the kind of embarrassment and shame that lead people to conceal their lack of knowledge. Such hypocrisy and dishonesty are as spiritually corrosive as the arrogance and contempt of those who foster it. What then is the lesson of the story before us? It is that if the great Hillel can forget and can plead for understanding, certainly others should not be overly embarrassed, or looked down on by their fellows, for this most common failing.

Contempt for Torah sages who forget is just an example of the common tendency of people to judge others harshly and treat them with disdain. The rabbis, however, taught: "Have contempt for no man."[7] We will see later that Hillel strongly opposed that most human disease of judging our fellowmen for ill.

8

The Nasi *as Judge*

A story tells about Hillel's wisdom as a judge in a case that came before the Sanhedrin when he was *Nasi*.

> Jewish men in Alexandria, Egypt would betroth women, but [sometimes] before they took the women to the bridal canopy to wed them, others came and snatched them away [to marry them]. The sages wanted to declare the children of such marriages illegitimate. But Hillel the Elder said to the Alexandrians: "Bring me your mother's marriage contract." When they brought it, he found written therein: "When thou shalt enter under the bridal canopy, be thou my wife, according to the law of Moses and Israel."[1] And they did not declare their children illegitimate (*Baba Metzia* 104a).[2]

At that time a Jewish marriage had two stages, which might be separated by almost a full year. First, the groom betrothed the bride and gave her a marriage contract (*ketubah*), making the relationship binding, so that a betrothed couple had to be divorced if they did not want to proceed with the wedding. Second, and later, the actual wedding ceremony took place under the bridal canopy (*huppah*). In Alexandria, however, a man sometimes wed a woman betrothed to another man, without her getting a divorce, and this seemed to make the children of that union illegitimate (*mamzers*), having been born through adultery.

Being declared illegitimate was not only a humiliation and a disgrace, but it had serious practical disadvantages, since the Torah prohibits a *mamzer* from marrying most other Jews, and his or her children are also illegitimate.

When some children of an Alexandrian Jewish marriage – where a man had married a woman betrothed to another – brought their case to the Sanhedrin,[3] the sages wanted to declare the children illegitimate. But the wise Hillel was not hasty to decide and, standing against all the other judges, he asked to see the *ketubah* their mother had received from the man to whom she was originally betrothed. In it he found an unauthorized addition to the traditional rabbinic formula, stating that she would become his wife not at the betrothal but only after the marriage ceremony under the *huppah*. It is likely that these added words were not exceptional, but were standard or common in Alexandria. And even though this local custom tampering with the prescribed formula had not been authorized by the rabbis, Hillel ruled that it was valid and that their mother had never in fact been married to the first man. Thus Hillel freed these individuals and their families from the stigma of illegitimacy, and not only them, but also the children and families of all such Alexandrian Jewish marriages.

Although the other sages were unanimously agreed on declaring the children illegitimate, Hillel's trust in the people's proper conduct saved the situation. Hyman[4] remarks that Hillel "realized that the Children of Israel are holy and would not publicly engage in such unworthy behavior [as marrying an already married woman], for if they are not prophets they are the sons of prophets." The allusion is to the story about Passover sacrifices on the Sabbath, where Hillel considered the people's practice concerning the knives authoritative and called them "sons of prophets," meaning that their customs had divine inspiration. There, Hillel had temporarily forgotten the *halachah* that supported the custom. Here, he was willing to validate even an improper custom – of unlearned people who added a clause to the *ketubah* without rabbinic approval – so as not to cause unnecessary suffering. He was as lenient as possible and did everything he could to spare the people and their families from the stigma of being declared illegitimate.

The Talmud cites this story in a context listing a number of rabbis who made rulings based on laypeople's unauthorized forms of speech or writing. It introduces each example with a similar statement, here, that "Hillel the Elder interpreted, and based rulings on, the unauthorized language of common people." We can suppose that Hillel was astute not only in discovering the added clause in the original marriage contract, but in being able to convince his fellow judges to accept the irregular procedure of "interpreting" unauthorized language. Since Hillel is the first rabbi known to have followed this unusual procedure, it may be his innovation. In any case, this story shows us his wisdom, flexibility, and compassion as a judge.

9

Hillel's Views on Leadership

SONS OF PROPHETS

Hillel rose to become *Nasi* largely because of his genius in Torah. But scholarship alone is never enough to be an outstanding leader in Israel: A great rabbi must also live what he teaches. The story of how Hillel became *Nasi* contains hints of other aspects of his character, such as his reverence and esteem for the People of Israel. He was a remarkable man and leader but he did not look down on those he led and, as in the phrase of the sages, "his greatness was matched by his humility."

When he forgot the tradition about what to do with the knives when the Passover sacrifice is on the Sabbath, he relied on what the people did by habit and custom, and called them "sons of prophets."[1] In one version of the story he says: "The holy spirit is on them: If they are not prophets, they are the sons of prophets."[2] In other words, God protects the People of Israel, directing their ways, and even their customs, through the action of the holy spirit. A similar idea is expressed in the saying of the rabbis: "A custom of Israel is Torah."[3] When he ruled that the Alexandrian Jews whose parents had married under unusual circumstances were not illegitimate, Hillel was even willing to rely on their unauthorized local custom of inserting an added clause in their marriage contracts.

The significance of calling the Jewish people "sons of prophets" can best be appreciated by comparing it with similar phrases. Thus, the rabbis reverently praise all the Jewish people, even the poorest, as "sons of Abraham, Isaac, and Jacob."[4] They also say: "All of Israel are the sons of kings."[5] To Hillel and those who followed his ways, all the people of Israel, even the least and the poorest, were precious. Far from having an elitist contempt for the common people, Hillelite Judaism's tendency is thoroughly democratic. Thus, the great rabbi Hillel admitted his fallibility and told them to see what the people's custom was in the matter of the knives. His reaction reflects a strong egalitarian sentiment that holds all Jews in esteem, for they are all "sons of prophets."

SAMUEL AND SAUL

Hillel had a high regard for those he was called to lead. One of the few midrashic comments we have from him on a story in the Torah provides some insight into his views about leadership. The Torah tells of two grievous sins committed by King Saul: First, he disobeyed the explicit divine command from the prophet Samuel to slay all the Amalekites in retribution for their merciless attacks on Jewish stragglers in the desert during the Exodus, and he spared Agag, the Amalekite king. Second, after Samuel's death, when Saul was terrified before an impending battle with a superior Phillistine army, he transgressed the divine prohibition against recourse to sorcerers and secretly went to the witch of Endor, asking her to call up Samuel's spirit from the dead, for he desperately wanted Samuel's advice. In that Torah story, Samuel's spirit says to Saul that God has rejected him and will "*also* deliver Israel *with him* to defeat at the hands of the Phillistines" (italics added).[6] Hillel midrashically paraphrased, expanded, and explained these words.[7]

> Hillel the Elder said: The prophet Samuel said to King Saul: "It is not enough that you disobeyed the word of God that I spoke to you, and did not execute His wrath against Amalek – but you also went and asked help from a necromancer who calls up the spirits of the dead! Woe to the shepherd and woe to his flock! For it is because of you that the Holy One, blessed be He, has given Israel into the hand of the Phillistines" (*Pirke d'Rabbi Eliezer*, chap. 33).

Saul not only disobeyed the prophetic command from God, but he later turned to *avodah zarah*, a forbidden channel of connection with spiritual forces.[8] Hillel viewed the people's punishment as caused by the sins of their leader: When it is "woe" to the shepherd, it is also "woe" to his flock. That is how he interpreted the Torah text where Samuel says that Israel will "also" be defeated "with" Saul. We can only wonder whether this midrashic comment about Saul might in any sense have been a veiled condemnation of Herod, the sinful king of Hillel's time. Was Hillel blaming Herod for the Jewish people's suffering and their subjection to the Romans?

Hillel used the proverb "woe to the shepherd, woe to his flock" to teach the dire consequences for the people of a sinful leader and his responsibility for their suffering. Certainly he would have applied this proverb not only to others, but to himself as well, and as such it casts light on his concept of Jewish leadership. This is one of many proverbs in the ancient Jewish tradition that metaphorically compares a leader to the shepherd of a flock. Hillel's use of it shows his appreciation of that tradition and suggests that the ideal of the leader as a tender and caring shepherd guided him in his attempt to be a good shepherd of the people of Israel.

10

Years and Dates

STAGES OF LIFE

Up to this point we have discussed Hillel's early days and how he rose to become *Nasi*. A tradition summarizes the stages of his life:

Hillel the Elder came up to Israel from Babylonia
when he was forty years old,
and he attended upon the sages forty years,
and he was a leader of Israel for forty years (*Sifre*
Deuteronomy 357).

It is hard to know what information we can garner from this. Undoubtedly, the three "forties" are round figures, each meaning "an extended period." Hillel may have been a leader for forty years, but it is unlikely he first came to Israel when he was forty, or attended upon the sages forty years. The story of Hillel on the roof is about a fiery young man, and a forty-year tutelage seems exaggerated. According to this timetable, Hillel was already eighty when he became a leader in Israel. Perhaps he was forty when he visited Jerusalem a second time and became *Nasi*. That is, it refers not to his traveling to Jerusalem to study, but to his later journey, when he became *Nasi* and settled permanently in Israel.[1] Otherwise, the "message" of this tradition (regardless of its historical veracity) seems to be that although Hillel, an ideal leader, was already a mature man when he came to Israel, he continued his studies under

43

the sages for a very long time and was fully prepared for his
momentous task of leading the Jewish people, which he did for
many years.

The same text also says that Hillel was one of four who lived
to the age of one hundred and twenty years:

> There were four who died at the age of one hundred and
> twenty: Moses, Hillel the Elder, Rabban Yohanan ben Zakkai,
> and Rabbi Akiba (*Sifre* Deuteronomy 357).

The three greatest rabbis of the tradition—Hillel being the
first—are here associated with the original "rabbi": Moshe Rab-
beinu—Our Teacher (Rabbi) Moses—as he is customarily referred to.
(Yohanan ben Zakkai was a disciple of Hillel and Akiba was a
Hillelite.) Needless to say, Hillel's lifespan of one hundred and
twenty years is hyperbolic. We can take it for granted, however,
that he lived to a ripe old age, and that, together with his unques-
tionable greatness, suggested the comparison with Moses.[2]

DATES

We can roughly date Hillel's rise to the position of *Nasi* from
another tradition:

> One hundred and eighty years before the destruction of the
> Second Temple, the wicked State, Rome, extended its control
> over the Land of Israel. . . . It was taught: Hillel and Simon,
> Gamaliel and Simon, held the position of *Nasi* during the last
> one hundred years before the Temple's destruction (*Shabbat*
> 15a).

Hillel's son, grandson, and great-grandson succeeded him in
leadership of the Pharisees and the popular religious community, the
tenure of the four spreading over a century. The fourth, Hillel's
great-grandson, Simon ben (son of) Gamaliel, was followed as *Nasi*
by Hillel's disciple, Yohanan ben Zakkai; but after him the office
returned to Hillel's descendants, to continue a remarkable dynasty of
Torah leadership.

If we combine the traditions (of *Sifre* Deuteronomy and *Shabbat*) we can calculate that Hillel was the *Nasi* for the first forty of those one hundred years before the Temple was destroyed, and this latter event occurred, as we know, in 70 c.e. Thus, the years of his being *Nasi* were 30 b.c.e. to 10 c.e.[3]

Another tradition allows us to place Hillel in relation to the reign of Herod the Great:

"After the Second Temple was built, the Kingdom of Persia controlled Israel for another thirty-four years [The Persian king Cyrus allowed the conquered Jews to rebuild the destroyed Temple.]; then came the rule of the Kingdom of Greece for one hundred and eighty years; then came the Kingdom of the Hasmoneans (Maccabees) for one hundred and three years; then the Kingdom of the House of Herod for one hundred and three years; then came the destruction of the Temple. After that you can calculate the years of all that happened following the destruction."[4]

The House of Herod began one hundred and three years before the Temple's destruction, with the ascendance of its founder, Herod the Great, as king. Hillel's ascendance as *Nasi* took place one hundred years before the destruction of the Temple. Therefore, Herod came to power three years before Hillel became *Nasi*. This is a near coincidence worthy of note.

11

Hillel the Pharisee

Hillel was a Pharisee and a leader of the Pharisees,[1] who were undoubtedly the most popular religious party at that time. But there was a difference between being a member of the sect (a *haver*) and simply being in sympathetic agreement with its principles. Actual members numbered a mere six thousand. Nevertheless, many lay-people were members; although most rabbis were Pharisees, most Pharisees were not rabbis.

The information we have about the Pharisees comes from the rabbinic tradition, Josephus, and the Christian scriptures. The rabbis rarely refer to the Pharisees by that name, although they occasionally mention disputes the "Pharisees" had with the Sadducees and other sectarians. Otherwise they refer (and only infrequently) to those who were "associates" and belonged to an "association" (*havurah*). The basic conditions for membership in a Pharasaic association were a commitment to special ritual purity in food and meals and strict adherence to the laws of tithing.

Although Josephus nowhere mentions Hillel,[2] he speaks of Shemaya and Avtalyon, Hillel's masters, as Pharisees.[3] The Christian *Acts of the Apostles*[4] refers to Hillel's grandson, Gamaliel, this way: "But a Pharisee in the Sanhedrin named Gamaliel, a teacher of the Law [Torah] held in honor by all the people. . . ." Josephus[5] also mentions Gamaliel's son, Simon: "This Simon was a Jerusalemite of a very noble family [Hillel's] of the sect of the Pharisees, who are considered to excel others in their accurate knowledge of the laws of their country [the Torah]." Although it is not explicitly stated in any

46

source, rabbinic or otherwise, Hillel was certainly a leader of the Pharisees. However, so little is known about their internal organization that it is hard to determine what that leadership involved. In fact, the limited sources do not even offer any insight into what significance Hillel's identity as a Pharisee had for his religious life or for his work as a religious leader.

12

Hillel, Menahem, and Shammai

The greatest Torah sages in Israel then – such as Shemaya, Avtalyon, and Hillel – were all Pharisees. A rabbinic text gives a summary
of the line of Torah leadership and the transmission of the Torah
from Moses onward. After listing the names of Shemaya and
Avtalyon, it says: "Hillel and Shammai received the tradition from
them."[1] Thus, Hillel and Shammai – also a Pharisee – followed this
other pair of Torah sages in the dual leadership that was customary
at the time. It does not necessarily mean that Shammai was a
disciple of Shemaya and Avtalyon as Hillel had been, although that
is a distinct possibility.[2]

Hillel was elevated to the position of *Nasi*. Although the
traditional view is that this title means he was head of the Sanhedrin, there is reason to doubt the historical accuracy of that claim.[3] It
may rather indicate that he was the highest authority among the
Pharisees and the sages of Jerusalem and was the leader of what we
can call the popular religious community.[4] Otherwise, leadership of
the Sanhedrin seems to have been in the hands of Sadducees – the
high priest and his associates, who controlled the Temple. But there
were always Pharisees in the Sanhedrin, and Hillel was certainly an
influential member of that body.

Shammai, the other of the leader pair, was the head of the
supreme court, his title being *Av Beit-din*. Regardless of the exact
nature of the positions held by the *Nasi* and the *Av Beit-din* – which
are sometimes translated as "president" and "vice president" – the
former is the superior office.

Typically, however, Hillel is not called Hillel the *Nasi*, although in one story someone says to him, "Aren't you Hillel, who they call the *Nasi* of Israel?"[5] His common title, and the way he is usually referred to in the texts, is Hillel the Elder[6] (*zaken*).[7]

Shammai is also generally referred to as Shammai the Elder, which may indicate this was an honorary title granted to each of the pair, the *Nasi* and the *Av Beit-din*; or it could be that the bearer was a member of the Sanhedrin, or just that he was a leading authority among the Pharisees and the sages of Jerusalem. There are scholars who hold each of these views.[8]

At first, Hillel had been joined in the leadership by one Menahem. But then Menahem was replaced by Shammai. The tradition that reports this is found in a context that gives the positions of the successive leadership pairs on a halachic matter of historical contention. Certain sacrifices required the one bringing the offering to lay his hands on the head of the animal and press down. The issue in dispute was whether or not it was permissible to do this on a festival day. Some held that it was allowed; others considered it a kind of work forbidden on festivals. Hillel's ruling was that it was permissible. Four successive leadership pairs had split over this issue, until Hillel and Menahem agreed. But then Menahem was replaced by Shammai, who opposed Hillel and said that laying on of hands was forbidden. The language describing the change in leadership is:

> Hillel and Menahem did not disagree. Menahem went out and Shammai entered (*Hagigah* 2:2).

Although a long story describes how Hillel came to succeed the Sons of Bathyra as *Nasi*, we know very little about Shammai's replacing Menahem as the head of the court. But this brief note in the *Mishnah* about Menahem leaving office has been filled out somewhat in the Talmud. The Babylonian Talmud reports:

> Menahem went into the service of the King [Herod] and eighty pairs of disciples, all dressed in silk robes, went with him (*Hagigah* 16b).

The parallel tradition in the Jerusalem Talmud says:

> He stalked out of his [Hillel's] presence, along with eighty pairs of sages clothed in gold-embroidered silk robes (*Y. Hagigah* 2:2, 77d).

Even if Menahem left his office as Hillel's co-leader to enter the
service of King Herod,[9] we are not told why he did so or what
significance it had. However, the mention of the grand clothing
worn by Menahem and his followers seems designed to direct our
attention to their class status and wealth, or to their arrogance – or
both.[10] It might also indicate that their pursuit of position, power,
and money led them to attach themselves to Herod. Presumably,
Menahem and his followers formed or joined the Herodian party
we mentioned in a previous chapter.[11] Although the matter remains
clouded, one aspect of this event is clear, that Herod was thoroughly
despised and that entering his service was not something well
received by the religious community as a whole. That Menahem's
association with Herod seems to have involved a split with Hillel
("He stalked out of his presence") indicates the strained relations
between Hillel (who represented the larger religious community)
and the king.

Throughout the course of our story about Hillel, we will hear
much about Shammai. The tradition weds the two in opposition;
one can hardly mention Hillel without thinking of Shammai. Although antagonists, they have become an almost inseparable pair,
like David and Saul. A hasidic teaching states that the adversaries of
great men are born with them and are heavenly ordained.[12] Perhaps
that was the case with Hillel. But the opposition between Hillel and
Shammai was not only personal, although certainly it was that too.
It seems that the dual leadership gave permanent representation to
two different tendencies in the religious community and these
tendencies had different social bases. To oversimplify: Shammai and
his wing represented the rich, and Hillel and his wing represented
the poor. However, some commentators of the last generation
overdid this valid insight by interpreting every religious dispute as
motivated by class interests.

In his struggling youth, when he acquired his spiritual perfection, Hillel had been very poor, subsisting on the meager sum he
could earn as a part-time day laborer. At a later time, he was able to
afford generous charity to the needy; we will discuss a story that
tells how he once even bought a horse and hired a servant for
someone as an act of charity. Where did he get the money for this?
There is no evidence of any business activity on his part and he did
not teach Torah for money. A midrashic tradition comments on
Psalm 15:5, understanding "silver (money)" of the verse to mean

Torah: " 'He that putteth not out his silver on interest'—such as Shammai and Hillel, who did not teach Torah for money" (*Midrash Psalms* on 15:5). Hillel had a dim view of the urge to accumulate wealth, and was against a person's having a large household with many servants, since many possessions only lead to increased anxiety (*Avot* 2:8).[13] Perhaps once Hillel became *Nasi* the religious community as a whole generously provided for their leader. Or perhaps he was not wealthy at all and used gifts from wealthy supporters to give charity.[14] But considering Hillel's compassionate instincts and ideals, as well as his background of self-imposed poverty, we can understand how he became a champion of the poor and lower classes.

13

The Prosbul

Hillel's religious leadership was not restricted to his personal example or to his teaching. His position as *Nasi* enabled him to influence affairs and events in society as a whole, in economic and civil matters, as well as in the "purely" religious.

He could do more to help the poor than simply contribute his personal charity or encourage others to give. The most well known example of his direct involvement in economic and social matters is his famous ordinance called the *prosbul*, which he enacted to benefit the poor. In the typical ancient agricultural society, small farmers usually relied on loans from their prosperous neighbors to survive hard times. But high interest rates and increasing indebtedness caused them gradually to lose more and more of their land to the wealthier farmers. Ultimately, a sharp class division developed between the few wealthy landowners and a large number of dependent small farmers. To prevent this deterioration in the economic basis of social equality, the Torah prohibited payment of interest on loans and canceled all unpaid noninterest loans at one time every seventh year, that is, the final year of the seven-year Sabbatical cycle.

But this Sabbatical release of debts, designed to relieve the poor, worked to their detriment as the release approached, for then many rich people refused to make any loans at all, knowing that before a loan could be repaid the release would come, the debt would be canceled, and the money lost. Clearly, this problem is inherent in the nature of the institution of the release, and the Torah itself already warns about it (Deuteronomy 15:9). However, it should be remembered on behalf of the rich that when they extended loans they did so purely for religious reasons, since the Torah prohibited charging interest.

By the time of Hillel, the problem must have become acute. Since the days of the Torah, commerce had developed in Israel and a reluctance by the rich to make loans now affected both agriculture and commerce, so that not only farmers, but artisans, shopkeepers, and small businessmen who needed credit were placed in grave difficulty.[1] The situation was also exacerbated by the desperate poverty that gripped the people during periods of Herod's reign.[2] Since the *Nasi* was responsible for the welfare of the community, Hillel took the radical step of abrogating the cancellation of debts altogether by means of a legal device called a *prosbul*. Hillel's ordinance allowed the creditor to avoid the cancellation of debt by transferring its collection to the court, which, being a corporate body, was not bound by the commandment of the release. He could simply make a written declaration – a *prosbul* – before the court that he intended to collect his debt even during the Sabbatical year, and then he could collect it himself. The term *prosbul* is taken from a Greek word that means "before the council." This accommodation to reality and seemingly to the rich was actually intended as an emergency measure to save the poor by ensuring their ability to secure necessary loans.

As we have said, the Torah was already aware of the intrinsic problem in the debt release. Deuteronomy 15:9 reads: "Beware that there not be an unworthy thought in your heart, thinking, 'The seventh year, the year of the release of debts is at hand,' and you act selfishly with regard to your poor brother and you give him nothing. . . ." The text that describes the situation that led Hillel to enact the *prosbul* shows it was this problem, and Hillel's reflection on this verse, that forced him to take action. Here is the tradition in the *Mishnah*:

> A loan for which a *prosbul* is made is not canceled during the Sabbatical year. This is one of the things that Hillel the Elder instituted, for when he saw that people refrained from making loans and were transgressing the Torah injunction, "Beware that there not be an unworthy thought in your heart, etc.," he established the *prosbul*[3] (*Shevi'it* 10:3).

We get further insight into Hillel's motives when we see that elsewhere[4] the *prosbul* is included among those ordinances that were "for the welfare of the community" (*mipnei tikkun ha'olam*), a category that justified remedial action when a religious rule was not working in practice and was causing serious harm to the community.

What the *prosbul* tells us about Hillel is that when confronted with a pressing need, he was willing to circumvent and, in essence, annul even a biblical command. He was an activist, and the plight of the poor spurred him to take radical action. Regardless of the particular arguments he might have used to justify the *prosbul*, he clearly believed that in an extreme situation a religious leader must sometimes set aside a single commandment in order to preserve the community. When the rich ignored the Torah's warning about refusing to make loans as the year of release approached – and presumably also ignored the appeals of Hillel and the other sages – Hillel saw that it was necessary to abrogate the Sabbatical-year remission of debts, by means of the *prosbul*, in order to save the poor from ruin.[5]

Hillel's Torah greatness led him to look for the principles and purposes behind the commandments.[6] Although the Torah ordered the release of debts, the actual situation put that commandment in direct conflict with another that was its underlying purpose – the commandment of charity. If one of these had to make way for the other, Hillel knew which to choose. He may even have been the first to formulate the bold principle expressed in the phrase *mipnei tikkun ha'olam* that was used in later times also to cut through legal knots that impeded the "welfare of the community."

Hillel's decisive action to help the poor by means of the *prosbul* shows that his activity was not limited to his religious teaching or his personal deeds. But although Hillel was able to affect economic and social affairs, his political influence was probably severely circumscribed, as we will see in the next chapter.

Hillel and Herod: Religion and Politics

BABA BEN BUTA, HEROD, AND THE TEMPLE

We know little about Hillel's views on political matters or of any political involvement by him. Herod the Great did not tolerate opposition. Legend tells that when he feared resistance from the rabbis, he had many of them murdered. Then, after having one of the few remaining rabbis, Baba ben Buta, tortured and blinded, he found out in a conversation with him that the sages were not the zealots he had thought they were, and would not challenge him politically by supporting violent rebellion. When he better understood their religious perspective, Herod realized he had misjudged them: They were no threat to his power and could be depended upon to exercise prudence and counsel peace.[1]

Regretting now his massacre of the rabbis, he asked Baba ben Buta how he could repent and was told to rebuild and restore the Temple, which he did in a spectacular way.[2] Aside from the religious motive given in this story in the Talmud, Herod's restoration of the Temple also served his political interest to regain some credibility with the religious community and the populace at large, after his brutality. In addition, it was the crowning part of an ambitious building program throughout the country, that won him prestige in the Roman Empire.

Josephus tells us that Herod began the rebuilding of the Temple in 20–19 B.C.E., the eighteenth year of his reign, and that the work lasted for almost ten years.[3] Hillel became *Nasi* three years after Herod became king, and he held that office for forty years. Thus, this restoration of the Temple took place in the middle of Hillel's tenure as *Nasi*.

Herod must at least have acquiesced in Hillel's ascendancy. Perhaps Hillel's rise to the office of *Nasi* was due in part to the disaster that had befallen the religious community and its leadership at Herod's hands. Many scholars believe that the Sons of Bathyra were only provisional leaders in a time of turmoil and disarray.[4] It is understandable that the Torah might have been "forgotten" in such circumstances. Hillel had returned to Babylonia after studying with Shemaya and Avtalyon and was not in Israel during the turbulent and brutal period before and after Herod's conquest of Jerusalem. He went back to Jerusalem some years later and, as the rabbis said: When the Torah was forgotten in Israel, Hillel the Babylonian came up and reestablished it.

But Herod's impact on the religious community was not only negative, for the rebuilt Temple provided a focus for a renewed devotion and aided Hillel's activity to revive the religious life of the Jewish people. Possibly – in a peculiar sense – Herod's work on the Temple and Hillel's in reconstituting the religious community went hand in hand. After having enforced his firm control by ruthless repression, Herod began to rebuild the Temple, which was the physical focus of the religious community, and also allowed the rebuilding of the community itself and its leadership, the rabbis.[5] Conceivably, Baba ben Buta, who advised Herod about the Temple, also played some part in Hillel's emergence into leadership. Indeed, Baba, who was later known as a follower of Shammai, at one pivotal moment publicly supported Hillel on an important issue, as we will see further on.

THE TEMPLE AND PILGRIMAGE

Baba ben Buta's goal of making the Temple the centerpoint for a renewed religious community was certainly shared by Hillel. Hillel once taught in the Temple courts, on the pilgrimage festival of Sukkot:

To the place that my heart loves,
    there do my feet lead me.

If you will come to My House,
   I [God] will come to your house;
and if you will not come to My House,
   I will not come to your house,
As it is said, "In every place where I cause My name
      to be mentioned,
   I will come to you and bless you" (Exodus 20:21)
   (*Tosefta Sukkah* 4:3).

This teaching of Hillel, that God recognizes the people's devotion expressed by their attendance at the Temple, should be seen in its relation to his attitude to pilgrimage. In a pastiche distinctive of his own style, Hillel links a proverb, a parabolic image based on social etiquette, and a Torah verse. The proverb says that when a person loves a place he goes there again and again, his feet "carrying him there." Thus, the people's frequent attendance at the Temple is a sign of their love for the Temple and for God. Next is a parable of social etiquette, involving the principle of return visits: If someone pays a call at a person's home, the host is socially obligated to call at the home of his visitor. Thus, God will return visits to His House, the Temple. Last, a Torah verse provides scriptural support and completes the thought: Since the pilgrim has shown his love by going to God's House, God will return in kind by going to his house and blessing him. In this context the verse means that if a person visits the Temple, alluded to by the "place where I cause My name to be mentioned," then "I," God, "will come to you," to your house, "and bless you." This continues the metaphor of the etiquette of house calls, for customarily a guest blessed his host upon arrival at the house. Since the people blessed God when they were at His House, the Temple, He would visit their houses and bless them. People who made pilgrimage to the Temple in Jerusalem, especially from afar, were understandably concerned about the welfare of their homes and possessions in their absence.[6] Hillel's words reassured them that not only would no harm come to them or their property because of their visit to the Temple, but God would bless them and their houses for good.

   The rebuilding of the Temple, instigated by Baba ben Buta and accomplished during Hillel's tenure as *Nasi*, naturally brought about a heightened focus on the Temple as the center of the people's religious life. Quite possibly, Hillel, himself inspired by the rebuilding, led the way in a reaffirmation of devotion to the Temple. Clearly, this teaching of his encouraged a renewed commitment to pilgrimage.

Some evidence of a peculiar sort indicates that exceptionally large numbers of people made pilgrimage to the Temple in Hillel's time.

> Our rabbis taught: Although the crowds in the Temple were immense during the Passover season, no one was ever crushed to death in the Temple court except one time, in the days of Hillel, when an old man was indeed crushed to death. And they called that Passover: "the Passover of the crush" (*Pesahim* 64b).

Further evidence that Hillel encouraged pilgrimage can be found in the previously mentioned long-standing dispute between the leadership pairs about whether laying of hands on a sacrifice was permitted on a festival day. Hillel and Shammai disagreed about this, Hillel saying it was permitted, Shammai that it was forbidden. In a related matter, the two also disagreed about whether or not burnt offerings were permitted on a festival day, Hillel saying yes, Shammai no. One aspect of these issues is that Hillel's views encouraged people to visit the Temple on a festival, while Shammai's discouraged it. Indeed, it seems that some Shammaites even physically prevented people from bringing such offerings.

Hillel himself once went to the Temple with a burnt offering on a festival day and had laid his hands on the animal, when he was accosted by some zealous Shammaites who surrounded him and spoke to him in a threatening manner. However, he was then supported by the venerable Baba ben Buta, who, although he had allied himself with the Shammaite party, sided with Hillel in this important matter. Baba, who must have been a wealthy man, immediately had a tremendous number of animals brought to the Temple and publicly invited people to sacrifice according to Hillel's view. As a result of Baba's support and the *fait accompli* of many people having acted according to his and Hillel's direction, Hillel's position was accepted.[7] One version of this tradition says of Baba:

"When he once came into the Temple court on a festival and found it almost empty [since Shammaites prevented people from bringing burnt offerings], he said: 'As for those who have made the

House of our God a waste, may their houses be wasted!' He then
sent people to bring to the Temple three thousand sheep of the flock
of Kedar,[8] etc."[9]

Clearly, at least one of Baba's motives for supporting Hillel
was to ensure that the Temple would be occupied and bustling
during a pilgrimage festival. Baba had advised and encouraged
Herod to rebuild the Temple and he understandably wanted it to be
full. It is also likely that one of Hillel's motives – in permitting burnt
offerings on a festival – was similar to Baba's: for Hillel too wanted
to foster pilgrimage and encourage people to visit the Temple so its
courts would be crowded and lively. Baba's words in the aforementioned scene are in fact basically a negative parallel to what Hillel
said when teaching in the Temple, that if you come to God's House
and praise and bless Him, He will bless your house. Baba's angry
words were not a blessing, but a curse against those who kept others
away from the Temple: If they did this to God's House, he said, let
their houses be wasted! In fact, the Hebrew of Baba's imprecation
seems to contain a play on words that alludes to his fellow Shammaites as the object of his scorn (yashomu *bateihen shel eilu* she-
heishamu *et beit eloheinu*).

Hillel's position as *Nasi* of course gave him an exceptional
opportunity to lead a religious revival among the people. Encouraging pilgrimage to the Temple, aside from being good in itself, had
the additional benefit of extending his influence beyond Jerusalem.
One of the purposes of pilgrimage, the rabbis taught, was to bring
people from all over the country to Jerusalem, where they would be
near the great sages in the holy city, to be inspired and to learn from
them.[10] So by encouraging pilgrimage, Hillel was able to draw the
people to himself and to the Torah.

TWO SEPARATE WORLDS

After decimating the rabbinic leadership, Herod "repented" by
rebuilding the Temple. When Baba ben Buta convinced him that he
did not have to fear the rabbis, he accepted their religious activity, so
long as they posed no threat to his political power. Herod probably
tolerated Hillel's vigorous religious activism because of his prudent
respect for Hillel's popular support and because of Hillel's own
adherence to a basically nonpolitical religious view.

One of Hillel's central sayings, which we will shortly discuss, speaks of "loving peace and pursuing peace." Although this saying relates to much more than politics, its application to that area should be noted.[11] The peace-loving Hillel did not challenge Herod politically, but vigorously and diligently built in his own sphere: the religious.

Comparing these two men—one a cruel king, the other a saintly religious leader—is like comparing night and day. Herod, a ruler hungry for power and glory, had his eyes turned to Rome. As head of the state, his authority was based on a ruthless use of force. Hillel, on the other hand, was the humblest and gentlest of men and hated lordship. As head of the freely formed religious community, his authority was based on the popular sentiment and will of the people. In a symbolic and nonpolitical way, many Jews probably considered Hillel—their beloved Nasi ("Prince") who was descended from the House of David—their secret counter-king, their legitimate ruler, as opposed to Herod the usurper.[12]

Herod, who was descended from Edomite converts to Judaism, tried to link himself with the royal family of the Hasmoneans through his marriage to Mariamne (Miriam), a princess of that House. But the rabbis mocked his pretensions, saying that he was an Edomite servant of the Hasmoneans who had slaughtered his masters and seized the throne.[13] Herod was hated by the people and his putative dynasty disappeared after a mere three generations. But Hillel's influence on the Jewish people, and the impression he made on them, were so extraordinary that they made his line into a dynasty of religious leaders that held the office of Nasi for a remarkable fifteen generations and that lasted for more than four hundred years, until the first quarter of the fifth century C.E.[14] The Talmud[15] even interprets the prophetic promise to Judah that the kingly scepter would not depart from between his feet (Genesis 49:10), as referring to "the descendants of Hillel, who teach Torah in public to the multitudes."[16]

What is striking about the separation of the two men—Hillel and Herod—and their two worlds, is that nowhere, in any source, rabbinic or otherwise, do they appear together. In the stories about Hillel and in his sayings, it is almost as if Herod did not exist.[17] Although Hillel and Herod were, respectively, the greatest religious and political figures of their time, these two giants, one of light, the other of darkness, glide by each other untouched, each in his own realm. Josephus, who concentrates his massive historical work, *The Antiquities of the Jews*, on political matters, occasionally brings in religious actors (mentioning, for example, Hillel's masters – Shemaya and Avtalyon).[18] But although Josephus devotes many pages to Herod, he does not even mention Hillel! – a peculiar fact that underscores Hillel's apolitical stance. The rabbinic traditions, on the other hand, contain a few stories about Herod, but the only slender thread that connects him with Hillel is the story (given earlier) that has Menahem stalking out of Hillel's presence and entering "the king's service" (Herod's name is not even mentioned explicitly). In a sense this is the exception that proves the rule, for the single connection between them not only has no meeting between the two, but shows that association with one involves a break with the other. Menahem and his followers "went into the service of the king," but that was hardly the case with Hillel. There was an almost complete separation. Possibly, as we suggested earlier, the split between Hillel and Menahem grew out of their positions vis-à-vis Herod. Hillel, a man of peace, was ready to live with Herod (whose tyranny he certainly hated), but at arm's length. For Menahem and his followers, however, that was not enough. He was prepared for more than an accommodation: He wanted to enlist the religious community in Herod's plans.[19] And that was something Hillel could not tolerate.

15

Hillel and Herod:
Religion and Politics – Continued

THE SKULL

Knowing how much Hillel emphasized the love of peace in his teaching, it is unlikely he would have supported any violent opposition to Herod. A story that contains a saying of his may provide a further clue to his attitude to politics and violence.

> Once Hillel saw a skull floating on the surface of the water, and said to it: "Because you drowned someone, you have been drowned by others; and in the end those who drowned you shall themselves be drowned" (*Avot* 2:7; *Sukkah* 53a).

This saying teaches that there is divine judgment and, at least sometimes, punishment at the hands of heaven even in this world. According to the rabbinic conception, such punishment, in its "pure" form, is "measure for measure": Thus, he who murders by drowning will himself be murdered by being drowned.

A question immediately arises, though, about this story and Hillel's saying: How did Hillel know that this man had been a murderer or that he had drowned others? Quite obviously, all murdered people are not murderers. Nor are all murderers in the end murdered. Some traditional commentators think that Hillel knew that this particular man was a highwayman who had committed murder – possibly; others suggest that he knew the circumstances of his life and death through the holy spirit – that is strained. However,

if either of these explanations was intended, one would have expected the story to be more explicit about it and, as it is, it gives no
hint to support either one.

The point of Hillel's saying–which reflects the rabbinic outlook–is that sometimes it *does* happen that murderers are murdered.
It is not unheard of today, for example, that violent gangsters are
themselves executed–and there is a lesson to be learned from just
those instances, for divine justice is not always or even often
revealed in this world. Many killers die peacefully in their beds. But
when a murderer meets a violent end, people feel it to be especially
fitting and a pious person sees it as a sign, a revelation of God's
judgment, which, on faith he believes to be working in many other
situations where it is not evident. And if accounts are not settled in
this world, they will be in the next.

A rare instance of measure-for-measure heavenly intervention
in this world is a "miracle of divine justice." Most often a miracle is
thought of as a supernatural event, in the literal sense, that breaks
through and "violates" the laws of nature. But, traditionally, the
religious significance of such a supernatural miracle is not its unique-
ness. Quite the opposite: It is the exception that proves the rule–that
God controls everything in nature, only in this exceptional instance
He has permitted people to see it. A believer responds with faith that
He is behind all natural events, even when that is not revealed. In the
same way, an example of exact measure-for-measure divine retribution is the exception that proves the rule: an instance where the
pious see divine justice and draw from it a lesson–that God's justice
is always at work, even when it is concealed.

But how did Hillel know that this man was a murderer? The
gruesome and chilling sight of the skull floating on the water must
have stopped him on the spot as he walked along and must have
seemed to him like a sign, a message requiring an interpretation.
Although there is no reason to think that he knew the man and that
he was a murderer, as some speculate, it is likely that there was some
sort of unstable social or political situation at the time that provided
a context for this grisly execution. Perhaps there were violent
highwaymen active then or rebel bands fighting the government.[1]
In the same way, urban gang wars or guerilla wars are the cause and
backdrop for horrendous and unusually violent slayings in our time.
That kind of setting of recurring violence led Hillel to use this skull,
which was *likely* the result of that situation, as an object lesson, to

"speak to it"–as he thought aloud to himself–so his disciples or others present would hear and learn. And as we know from our own time also, it is just those situations that produce chronic violence, where the "cycle of violence" becomes more apparent, and those who "drown others" are most likely to "be drowned." Hillel did not know that this man had "drowned" others, only that a violent person had become a victim of violence.

Visualizing the scene as Hillel passed by a lake or river with others and saw this skull floating on the water, one is easily reminded of the Torah's graphic picture of the Egyptian persecutors of the Jewish people, drowned in the Red Sea. "And the Lord overthrew the Egyptians in the midst of the sea. The waters returned and covered . . . all the hosts of Pharaoh . . . And Israel saw the Egyptians dead upon the sea shore. And Israel saw the great hand which the Lord did against the Egyptians . . ." (Exodus 14:27–31).

Here also there was a revelation of the hand of God–not always revealed–and of His divine justice. When Moses's father-in-law Jethro came from Midian to visit the Jewish people in the Sinai Desert, Moses told him how God had saved the Jewish people from the Egyptians. Jethro then exulted and praised God, saying he now understood God's true greatness; and referring to the Egyptians, his words end: "because the very thing wherein they dealt arrogantly with Israel has come upon them."[2] The rabbis saw the drowning of the Egyptians in the Red Sea as punishment specifically measure for measure for their having drowned the Jewish babies by casting them into the river Nile. Expounding Jethro's words in the verse, by means of a popular proverb, they taught: "Because the very thing wherein they dealt arrogantly with Israel has come upon them–in the very pot which they cooked with, were they cooked."[3] Perhaps the measure-for-measure punishment of the Egyptians by drowning was in the back of Hillel's mind when he made his comment about the floating skull.

The repetitive form of Hillel's saying emphasizes the cyclical nature of violence: "Because you drowned someone, you have been drowned by others; and in the end those who drowned you shall themselves be drowned." It suggests that a spiritual law is involved, the conception being something like the Hindu idea of Karma.

The essential lesson of Hillel's saying is pacifistic, that he who lives by violence, dies by violence.[4] Its political relevance is that it indicates Hillel's visceral dislike of the use of force and suggests he might have disapproved of its use even in a struggle against unjust authority. According to Josephus,[5] it was their negative attitude to political violence that in later years separated the Pharisees, with whom Hillel was identified, from the Zealots, who rebelled against Rome. Otherwise, their religious views were largely the same. We can be certain that even in Hillel's time the oppressive authority of Herod and his Roman allies provoked violent opposition and rebellion among parts of the Jewish population. But this was not Hillel's way. On one side were those like Menahem, who joined with Herod; on the other side were the militants who joined battle with him; in the center were Hillel and most of the people.

HILLEL'S MASTERS—SHEMAYA AND AVTALYON—WITH HEROD

While our sources reveal little about Hillel's political views, they provide more information about the views and deeds of his masters, Shemaya and Avtalyon. Attention to the history they were involved in will help us understand Hillel's attitude and his relation to Herod and to politics.

When Herod was yet a small despot ruling over Galilee, it was Hillel's masters, Shemaya and Avtalyon, who stood up to his tyrannical ways and tried to stop him. In an extraordinary incident where Herod was called to the Sanhedrin in Jerusalem on a charge of political murder,[6] he came before that august assembly in an unprecedented and outrageous way, surrounded by a menacing bodyguard. Only Shemaya and Avtalyon, who feared no one but God, were not intimidated. They then prophesied to the other members of the Sanhedrin that because of their shameful and cowardly fear in allowing Herod to escape from punishment, he would one day return and destroy them.

Years later, when Herod attempted to seize control of the whole country from the Hasmoneans, and with Roman support besieged Jerusalem, Shemaya and Avtalyon realized that the time for opposing him had passed; he had grown too powerful and could not be stopped. To prevent useless death and destruction they advised, unsuccessfully, that resistance be ended and that the city's gates be opened to him.[7] Their position, which probably reflected not only their recognition of power realities but their disinclination to violence, should give us some insight into Hillel's attitude to politics and to the use of violence. Afterward, when Herod captured the city, he ruthlessly executed his Hasmonean rivals and most of the Sanhedrin – almost all of whom were Sadducean supporters of the Hasmoneans – except for the Pharisee leaders Shemaya and Avtalyon, whose prophecy was fulfilled. Although he remembered their words against him at the trial ten years earlier, he appreciated their more recent attempt to counsel surrender.[8] After this, Herod stripped the Sanhedrin of its political power and left it just its religious functions.[9]

The two sages' relation to Herod can be gauged from another incident years later. When Herod attempted to suppress sedition by demanding that all his subjects take a religious oath of loyalty to himself and to the Roman Caesar, Shemaya and Avtalyon and the other Pharisee sages refused (as did the Essenes) on religious grounds; but because of his respect for them Herod excused them, although he dealt with others severely. Their refusal to take the oath could have been considered seditious, but Herod, again, understood that their motive was purely religious and that they were not a threat to his power.

Thus, although Hillel's masters, Shemaya and Avtalyon, accommodated themselves to Herod's rule and acquiesced in political matters, they managed to retain a sphere of freedom for their religious activity. Fearless in opposing Herod on religious grounds, as at his trial and with the oath, they were also ready to concede elsewhere. This whole history, for which Josephus[10] is the source, and particularly his description of the execution of the members of the Sanhedrin, should be compared with the talmudic story[11] cited earlier about how Herod, after having slaughtered many of the rabbis, came to an accommodation with them as a result of his conversation with Baba ben Buta. Baba, who was already an old man when Hillel was *Nasi*, was part of the generation of Shemaya and Avtalyon.

Hillel's relations with Herod were probably similar to those that his masters had with the king and would have been conditioned by two factors: a clear perception of power realities and a disinclination to violence. But Hillel's position against violence, which is reflected in his saying "spoken" to the floating skull, should not be confused with a modern sort of programmatic pacifism that would be impossible for a traditional Jew. However, in a larger sense, his antiviolence attitude was based on a dislike of all politics – the realm of conflict, hatred, and death – and on a love of peace in all its paths.

II

Mission and Message

16

Disciples of Aaron

A KEY TEACHING

The first of Hillel's teachings found in *Pirke Avot* (*The Ethics of the Fathers*, at 1:12) is of special importance, expressing the theme that underlies almost all his teachings and actions. It is the key to his greatness and to his mission as a leader in Israel.

> Be of the disciples of Aaron,
> Loving peace and pursuing peace,
> Loving people and bringing them close to the Torah.

We will look at this saying phrase by phrase and make an analysis of its parts an overarching framework for our discussion through a number of chapters in this book.

The first of the three lines tells us to follow the example of Aaron, the high priest. The next two lines explain what that implies. What is strange to see is the "disciples" of Aaron. Throughout the Torah we hear again and again of the "sons" of Aaron, the lineage of the priesthood; but nowhere in the Torah and nowhere else in rabbinic literature do we hear of "disciples" of Aaron. Much about this minor enigma and about Hillel's teaching can clarified by a story about his masters, Shemaya and Avtalyon, who were (note this) the descendants of gentile converts.

SHEMAYA, AVTALYON, AND THE HIGH PRIEST

First, a little background: The *Mishnah* says that after the Yom Kippur service at the Temple in Jerusalem, the high priest was relieved that he had successfully completed his arduous responsibilities on that awesome day. He left the Temple with an honorary escort and went home, where, traditionally, he made a party to celebrate with friends and other guests. The text[1] says: "They accompanied him to his house and he made a feast for his friends, because he had come forth safely from the Holy of Holies."[2] Here is the story from the Talmud:

"A certain high priest once left the Temple with a large crowd accompanying him to his house, but when they saw Shemaya and Avtalyon, they left him to himself and followed after them. But then Shemaya and Avtalyon approached the high priest to take their leave from him, as is customary, and to receive the customary blessing. He said to them condescendingly: 'May the sons of the gentiles go in peace.' They answered: 'May the sons of the gentiles who do the deeds of Aaron the priest have peace; but as for the sons of Aaron who do not do the deeds of Aaron, they shall be without peace.' "[3]

Could it have been Hillel himself who passed on this story? Was he one of those who followed behind his beloved masters, Shemaya and Avtalyon? The two great rabbis were very popular with the people, it seems, because of their pleasant ways, the ways of peace. They were men of the people and did not lord it over others. Shemaya taught "hate lordship."[4] This was considered a secret of being beloved, as can be learned from a talmudic story that tells how Alexander the Great interviewed the Elders of the Negev (the Jewish sages of the south of the Land of Israel), and tested their wisdom by a number of questions. When he asked them "What should a man do to be beloved by men?" they answered: "Let him hate kingship and rule."[5] But the powerful king rejected their advice and gave his own answer: "Let him love kingship and rule and seek to do good to men."

Perhaps the rabbis who handed down this tradition, with Alexander's retort, considered both ways worthy. Perhaps Shemaya himself accepted a role as leader, as *Nasi*, and sought to do good to men—but with that, hated lordship. Hillel, whose humility also won the hearts of the people, learned that lesson about how to be a leader in Israel from his master Shemaya. This was the way of the best of the rabbis, to be gentle to the people and not lord it over them, for they were from the people and for the people.

The priestly leadership, on the other hand, came to be known for their roughness and arrogance.[6] The high priesthood had, during this time, become debased, with the high priest a mere sycophant, arbitrarily appointed by Herod and held in low esteem by the people. The high priest's sharp words to the two rabbis, Shemaya and Avtalyon, reveal his aristocratic arrogance full blown. Resenting a perceived slight to his honor and envious of their popularity, he insulted them in front of the crowd when they came to take leave of him and rudely brought up to them their gentile origins: "May the sons of the gentiles go in peace."

The priests, whose status was inherited, kept thorough genealogical records and were often proud of their lineage. A good example of this is found in the very beginning of the memoir of Josephus, the great Jewish historian of the first century C.E., wherein he shows his pride in his high priestly family and gives part of his genealogy. But such pride can easily lead to a disdainful prejudice against those of "lesser" descent. And the gap between the few high priestly families of the most noble lineage and the descendants of gentiles such as Shemaya and Avtalyon could hardly be greater.

Of special interest is the fact that Shemaya and Avtalyon's words seem to be the direct source of Hillel's saying about being "disciples of Aaron": "May the sons of the gentiles who do the deeds of Aaron the priest have peace; but as for the sons of Aaron who do not do the deeds of Aaron, they shall be without peace." The rabbis answered the high priest's insult by saying that peace from God and from men will be the portion even of those sons of converted gentiles who do the deeds of Aaron, and are his true "disciples"; but that will not be so for those who, though sons of Aaron, that is, priests, are not his "disciples." The deeds of Aaron, which were "loving peace and pursuing peace" in Hillel's words, bring a leader in Israel the blessing of peace from God and from men.[7] While the high priest's crude insult showed that peace was not his way, the sons of the gentiles – the great rabbis, Shemaya and Avtalyon – did the deeds of Aaron, of loving peace and loving people; and they, in turn, were beloved by the people, who saw in them their true leaders, leaders who hated lordship. It seems likely that when formulating his saying about the qualities of leadership in Israel, about being "disciples of Aaron," Hillel had before his eyes the ways and teachings of his own revered masters.

WELCOMING GENTILES AND REVERSING STATUS

The concept of "disciples of Aaron" implies a fluidity in the statuses of individual Jews and gentiles (although not in the groups as a whole) and the potential for a reversal. Thus, whereas the high priestly son of Aaron is not Aaron's disciple, the sons of converted gentiles, Shemaya and Avtalyon, are his disciples and are leaders in Israel. This open and liberal attitude characterized Hillel and his wing of the tradition.

The Talmud mentions the gentile ancestry of Shemaya and Avtalyon in a context that discusses the conversion to Judaism of Israel's oppressors or their descendants:

"Our rabbis taught: Naaman was a *ger toshav* [a gentile residing in the Land of Israel, who renounces idolatry and adheres to the seven commandments given to gentiles, the children of Noah]. Nebuzaradan, however, was a *ger tzedek* [a gentile who becomes a full convert to Judaism]. Some of the descendants of Haman taught Torah in B'nei Brak [a city in Israel]. Some of the descendants of Sisera taught Torah to little children in Jerusalem. Some of the descendants of Sennaherib taught Torah before multitudes. Who were they?—Shemaya and Avtalyon."[8] [Naaman was an enemy Assyrian general healed of leprosy by the prophet Elisha. Nebuzaradan, the Babylonian commander of Nebuchadnezzar's army, destroyed the Temple and much of Jerusalem and deported the people of Judea. Haman is the Book of Esther villain who tried to destroy the Jews. Sisera was leader of the coalition opposing Israel in the time of the prophetess Deborah. See the next paragraph in the text about Sennaherib.]

According to this tradition, Shemaya and Avtalyon were, surprisingly, related, both being descended from the same Assyrian king Sennaherib who had brought great destruction on Judea in the time of Isaiah. The rabbis took pride in the fact that the oppressors of Israel (such as Naaman and Nebuzaradan) or their descendants (the descendants of Haman, Sisera, and Sennaherib) saw the truth, converted, and joined the Jewish people. If ancestry was a religious barrier, sincere repentance overcomes all barriers.

The Talmud context of this teaching tells how Nebuzaradan, the military commander for the Babylonian ruler Nebuchadnezzar, conquered Jerusalem and killed many thousands of Jews – and claims that this was divine punishment for the murder of the prophet Zechariah by the Jewish people. But later, this Nebuzaradan himself repented and converted to Judaism. Thus, in the very place where the tradition criticizes the Jewish people for persecuting their own prophets, such as Zechariah (and explains that their persecution by the gentiles comes as divine retribution), it praises their gentile oppressors or their descendants who had converted.

This implies a potential reversal – that good gentiles will be accepted and bad Jews rejected. The source of this idea is the Torah's story of the reversal of Naaman, the Assyrian general, and Gehazi, the disciple of the prophet Elisha, for when Naaman showed faith in Elisha, Gehazi did not. Elisha healed the gentile Naaman of leprosy and accepted his repentance but rejected his greedy and lying Jewish disciple Gehazi, transferring Naaman's leprosy to him (2 Kings 5). Naaman is the first of the oppressors of Israel mentioned in the rabbinic teaching; the last people mentioned are Hillel's masters, Shemaya and Avtalyon, who were the most striking examples of how descendants of gentile persecutors could become leaders of Israel, teaching Torah before multitudes.[9] Shemaya and Avtalyon themselves suggested, in their words to the high priest, the possibility of a reversal between the sons of Jews (particularly sons of Aaron) and the sons of gentiles. All this background to Hillel's "disciples of Aaron" shows that this simple phrase contains within it a weighty and important conceptual schema.

SONS AND DISCIPLES OF ABRAHAM

We will gain perspective on Hillel's emphasis on being disciples of Aaron from the closely related rabbinic concept of being "disciples of Abraham." Just as the priests, the sons of Aaron, must not be arrogant and should emulate Aaron, so all Jews, who are "sons and daughters of Abraham," must not be overly proud of their honored ancestry, relying on it to win them favor in God's eyes; instead, they must emulate the qualities of Abraham and be not only his children but his disciples.[10] The rabbis teach: "Whoever has these three attributes is a disciple of our father Abraham . . . a good eye [judging others favorably], a humble mind, and a lowly spirit. . . ."[11] Elsewhere, they say in a similar vein: "Three traits characterize the Jewish nation: They are merciful, have a sense of shame, and do acts of loving-kindness . . . and a gentile who has these three traits is worthy of joining them and being a part of this nation; he who has them not is not worthy of joining them."[12] Again in the Talmud: "When someone [a Jew] has mercy on God's creatures, we can be certain that he is descended from our father Abraham."[13] What the first saying expresses by speaking about being a "disciple" of "our father" Abraham, the third conveys by the notion of certainty of Jewish descent. Kindness and modesty are part of the Jewish national character and cultural heritage. As the rabbis often say, Jews are merciful children of merciful parents. But, again, there is an implied "reversal": The ancestry of a Jew without these qualities is suspect; a gentile who has them is worthy of becoming a Jew.

Jews should not lack pride in being "children of Abraham, Isaac, and Jacob." But pride in their holy ancestors should inspire them to emulate their deeds. As one ancient rabbinic text puts it: "A Jew should always say to himself: 'When will my deeds match the deeds of my fathers Abraham, Isaac, and Jacob!' "[14] A similar perspective is found in a second saying in this text, in which the prophet Elijah exclaims: "I call heaven and earth to witness, that whether a Jew or gentile, man or woman, manservant or maidservant, everything is only according to a person's deeds, and according to his deeds, so does the holy spirit rest on him."[15] There are no fixed and uncrossable boundaries to spiritual attainment; the more worthy a person's deeds are, the more the holy spirit rests on him.

The related concepts of "disciples of Aaron" and "disciples of Abraham" both emanated from the same movement among the rabbis—a movement of which Hillel was a leader. However, this stream of tradition—that spoke about "disciples" of Aaron and Abraham—not only demanded true spirituality from Jews and encouraged them to actually fulfill their mission as children of Abraham, but also demonstrated receptivity and openness to gentiles who sought to join them (something that we will discuss more fully later).

According to the Hillelite view, the value for Jews of their "lineage," of being "children of Abraham," is that it helps them become "disciples of Abraham." Deeds are important, not mere birth. Jews with no claim to Abraham's traits of compassion and humility can have only a false pride in their ancestry, and gentiles who seek righteousness are praised and welcomed with open arms. The concept of "disciples of Abraham" implies a receptive attitude to gentiles and to conversion and the situation with "disciples of Aaron" is similar. Thus, Shemaya and Avtalyon compared the "sons of Aaron," the priests, those with special lineage among the Jewish people, with the "sons of gentiles," converts, those with little natural social status, and on the basis of their deeds reversed the normal priority. This was the view of the more open rabbis. Actually, one would not imagine that converts or their descendants would create such teaching, which would appear self-interested; instead, it would more likely come from those Jews engaged in converting gentiles. So the teachings about the "sons of Abraham" or the "sons of Aaron" and the "disciples" of each most likely preceded not only Hillel, but also Shemaya and Avtalyon, his masters.

BIRTH AND DEEDS

Hillel's innocent phrase "disciples of Aaron" contains important information concerning his views about birth versus deeds, and it will repay our effort to investigate another rabbinic tradition that reverses the natural social standing of birth in favor of deeds. In this teaching, the high priest himself is compared with a *mamzer*, someone of illegitimate birth (again, one of the least in natural social status): "Between a *mamzer* who is a Torah sage and a high priest who is unlearned, the *mamzer* who is a sage has precedence."[16] Two statuses compete here: that which derives from birth and that which derives from Torah knowledge. The high priest is the most high-born, and the *mamzer* one of the most low-born; the sage is the most knowledgeable in Torah, and the religiously ignorant person the least. The saying sets these two sources of rank and standing against each other and teaches that the determining power of Torah, knowing the word of God and doing it, is greater than the status accorded by birth and can reverse it. The notion of an unlearned high priest was not merely idle: Herod appointed and dismissed high priests arbitrarily,[17] and some of them were relatively ignorant of the Torah, a fact that certainly troubled many religious people.

Another rabbinic teaching compares the high priest to a gentile convert: "Even an idolater who converts and occupies himself with the Torah is equal to the high priest himself, for it is said about the Torah's teachings that 'a person shall do them and live by them.' It does not say 'priests,' 'Levites' or 'Israelites' [the three hereditary divisions of the Jewish people], but 'a person.' Thus, even a foreigner who accepts the Torah and occupies himself with it is equal to the high priest himself."[18]

RABBINIC VERSUS PRIESTLY LEADERSHIP

Regarding the matter of leadership, the significance of the teachings that compare the high priest with gentiles or Jewish *mamzers* was that they asserted the primacy of the rabbis, whose authority rested on their knowledge of the Torah, as against the priests, whose authority derived from their lineage. The leadership of the priesthood had declined disastrously. The priests were no longer the teachers of the nation, and with Herod appointing high priests arbitrarily, even an unlearned high priest was not unusual. The confrontation between Shemaya and Avtalyon and the high priest was just one minor incident in a long process, involving much tension, as the rabbis, from the people and for the people, took over the religious leadership of the nation from the priests who, as a class, had lost it. The story where the people escorting the high priest abandon him to follow the two rabbis is an almost graphic illustration of the historical movement and direction.

The restoration of the ideal qualities once represented by the priests became the goal of the rabbis. They countered the priests' claim to leadership, which was based on their being "sons of Aaron" by emphasizing that leaders must be "disciples of Aaron" with his qualities. In itself it is somewhat surprising to see Hillel offer Aaron as a model, where we might have expected his more famous brother Moses! But his attention to Aaron was partly due to the "problem" at the time with the "sons of Aaron," the priests, and the competition, as it were, between them and the rabbis. However, the Torah does praise Aaron for qualities that were especially attractive to Hillel and that were worthy of emulation.

One of the main Torah verses that Hillel looked to for his picture of Aaron was Malachi 2:6, which was understood to refer to Aaron the priest[19] – "The Torah of truth was in his mouth, and iniquity was not found on his lips; he walked with Me in peace and uprightness and turned many away from sin." The same elements mentioned in the verse – Torah, peace, and bringing back sinners – are found in Hillel's saying, about the disciples of Aaron loving peace and bringing people to Torah. As we will see later, this verse is cited in the ancient rabbinic literature as the Torah source for Hillel's saying.[20]

17

Loving Peace

So far we have explained the first line of Hillel's theme-saying, to "be of the disciples of Aaron." The second line begins to teach what that implies: "Loving peace and pursuing peace."

PEACE LOVER AND PEACEMAKER

Hillel took his lesson about peaceableness from Malachi 2:6 (quoted at the end of the previous chapter), a verse that was associated with Aaron. It is said there: "he [Aaron] walked with Me in peace." But Hillel's language was also influenced by Psalm 34:15, which says: "Seek peace and pursue it." Hillel taught that a person must "love" and "pursue" peace. Someone might think that he can love peace passively, sit at home and be at peace with the world. But when a person has a passionate love for peace, he will actively pursue peace. Commenting on Hillel's saying, the rabbis taught about the words of the Psalm: " 'Seek' peace in your own place and ' pursue' it in another place."[1] They also said: "If a person remains at home and does not venture into the world, how will he make peace between people? But when he goes out into the marketplace and sees people quarreling, he can come between them and reconcile them."[2] Hillel understood that the relations between people are dynamic; a person cannot have peace simply by avoiding harming others or by not arguing or by being passive. Peace requires active pursuit and love for one's fellowmen. A person must not only seek peace in his own life and sphere, but must be a peace*maker* and bring others together: husband and wife, neighbors, families, cities, nations. This was an ideal of the sages, who considered it a sign of a true sage, and taught: "Sages increase peace throughout the world."[3] This saying reflects Hillel's own conception and his teaching, for he uses these very words elsewhere, speaking of the goal to "increase peace" (*Avot* 2:8).[4]

CHARACTERISTIC RABBINIC PHRASES

To understand and appreciate the importance Hillel gave to loving and pursuing peace, one has to know as background the rabbis' view of peace. Peace was for them a value on the first level, and the word conveyed more to them than it does to a Western ear.[5] We can begin our investigation of this essential background by considering two characteristic phrases frequently used by the rabbis.

One such phrase, in its most typical and basic form, is: "To make peace between a man and his fellow, between a husband and his wife." Hillel's disciple, Yohanan ben Zakkai, for example, speaks of the person "who makes peace between one person and another, between husband and wife, between families, cities, nations, and kingdoms."[6] Peace should spread until it encompasses the whole world, for the kingdom of God is a kingdom of peace.

Another characteristic rabbinic phrase speaks of following "the ways of peace." Peaceableness and gentleness should pervade all of a person's doings. Thus, the rabbis held that: "All the Torah was given 'because of the ways of peace' and to establish peace, as it is written, 'Her ways are ways of pleasantness and all her paths are peace' (Proverbs 3:17)."[7] Peace was valued so highly that it was sometimes even preferred to truth. The Hillelite rabbis occasionally even conceded to a false view so as to avoid serious dissension and discord, their motive being "because of the ways of peace."[8]

Peace was central to the outlook of Hillel and the mainstream rabbinic tradition in a way not the case in Western culture. The West praises peace between nations, but it is not the all-pervasive concept it is with the rabbis, who cherished peace between a person and his fellow, between husband and wife, between one family and another, and in all social relations. As a result, the many teachings of Hillel and the rabbis about peace are often not properly understood, because the basic concept underlying them is unfamiliar.

LEGENDS OF AARON

Hillel made Aaron the priest his model for the ideal leader. The rabbis' legendary picture of Aaron will provide us with insight into Hillel's ideal and personality. We noted earlier the relation between Hillel's teaching about Aaron's ways and Malachi 2:6. A rabbinic comment on the phrase in Hillel's theme-saying about "loving peace" states: "One should love peace in Israel between one person and another as Aaron did, as it is said: 'The Torah of truth was in his mouth and iniquity was not found on his lips; he walked with Me in peace and uprightness and turned many away from sin' (Malachi 2:6)."[9]

Every phrase of this verse was interpreted about Aaron's character and spiritual personality: Aaron's "walking in peace" referred to his greeting people with the blessing of peace as he walked about on the streets and to his deeds as a peacemaker; "iniquity was not found on his lips" meant that his speech was gentle, that he did not judge sinners or mention their sins; that he "turned many away from sin" referred to the success of his peaceable ways in bringing many sinners to repentance.

Three Stories about Aaron

Rabbi Meir (second century C.E.) explained Hillel's teaching about being disciples of Aaron by telling three stories of how Aaron made peace between neighbors and between husbands and wives, and also how he brought sinners back to God. The first story is about peacemaking between neighbors.

Peace between a Man and His Fellow

"When two men had quarreled, Aaron would go and sit down with one of them and say to him, 'My son, do you know that your neighbor is heartbroken? He's ripping his clothes in anguish and crying out, "Woe is me! How can I look my friend in the face anymore after what I did to him? I'll die of shame – I know I'm in the wrong!" ' Aaron stayed with him until he had completely removed any bad feeling from the man's heart. Then Aaron went to the other one and sat with him, saying the same thing: 'My son, do you know that your neighbor is ripping his clothes in his anguish and crying out, "Woe is me! How can I lift up my eyes anymore? If I see my friend now I'll die of shame after what I did to him!" ' Aaron would stay with him until he had removed every trace of anger and hatred for his friend from his heart. Later, when the two met at Aaron's arrangement, they would fall all over each other, embracing and kissing each other."[10]

Peace between Husband and Wife

The second of the three stories illustrating Hillel's theme-saying tells how Aaron made peace between husbands and wives and prevented divorces.

"If a man angry at his wife had sent her from his house, Aaron would go to him and say, 'My son, why are you so mad at your wife?' 'I can't stand it anymore!' he would answer. 'Do you know what she's done?' And he told Aaron his side of the story. Then Aaron said to him, 'I'm her guarantor – I promise you that from now on she'll never do that again!' Then he went to the wife and said to her, 'My daughter, why are you so angry at your husband?' She would say, 'He cursed me and hit me!' Aaron calmed her and said, 'I promise you that from now on he'll never again curse or hit you!' So did Aaron do all his days with each separated couple until the husband took her back into his house. When the wife became pregnant and gave birth to a son, she would say, 'God gave me this son only because of the goodness and merit of Aaron!' And she named the baby boy 'Aaron.' Some say that as a result there were more than three thousand young men in Israel named 'Aaron.' "

Aaron told both husband and wife that he "guaranteed" the other's better behavior; if either spouse reverted to his or her former ways, the other one could come and complain to him; he would be responsible for seeing that he or she acted properly. This audacious pledge is equivalent to his bold use of lies – in the other story – to reconcile alienated neighbors. But, of course, Aaron could not actually ensure anything about the other spouse's behavior, and what this really shows is a dedicated religious leader so committed to restoring love and peace that he will go to any lengths to accomplish his goal – even throwing himself into the midst of a marital quarrel with his "guarantee" and staking his own reputation on the outcome.

Bringing Sinners back to God

The first two stories explain Hillel's saying about disciples of Aaron loving and pursuing peace and follow the pattern of the characteristic phrase about making peace "between a man and his fellow and between a husband and his wife." The third and final story explains Hillel's words about disciples of Aaron "loving people and bringing them close to the Torah" and shows how Aaron – as in Malachi 2:6 – turned many away from sin and brought sinners back to God.

"Why does the verse say 'and [he] turned many away from sin'? – Because when Aaron walked along the road and met someone very sinful, although others would have looked the other way and avoided that person, Aaron honored him by kindly greeting him with the blessing of peace. On the following day, when that man was about to commit some sin, he said to himself, 'How can I do this? How will I be able afterward to look Aaron in the face if I see him on the street? He was so kind and respectful to me, giving me the greeting of peace – I'll be terribly ashamed if I see him!' As a result, he held back from sinning."

This story portrays Aaron bringing sinners back to God through love and respect, expressed by his giving them the greeting of peace. How Aaron's method "worked" is well explained by the hasidic *rebbe* (leader), Rabbi Rafael of Bershad:

"Aaron is described [by Hillel] as loving and pursuing peace, loving people and drawing them to the Torah. *Because* he loved them they were drawn to the Torah and repented. When I love someone he will love *me* in return, like a reflection in water, as it says in Proverbs (27:19): 'As water reflects a face, so does a person's heart reflect that of his fellow.' Then, since *I* hate his bad deeds, he *also* will begin to hate them and will return to God in repentance."[11]

Rabbi Meir's three stories truly show what Hillel meant in his theme-saying about being disciples of Aaron, and they give us a vivid picture of an "Aaron-type" of rabbi – like Hillel himself.

LOVE AND PEACE IN SPEECH

Hillel sought to bring "sinners" back to God and the Torah. But no one quick to judge and criticize can hope to succeed in this task. Together with the stories about Aaron, it is taught:

"In his whole life Aaron never said to a single man or woman, 'You've sinned!' "[12]

This relates to a well-known teaching of Hillel about not judging others (which we will discuss later on). That Aaron never spoke of another person's sins was derived from the phrase in Malachi 2:6, that "iniquity was not found upon his lips."

The Greeting of Peace

Another legendary aspect of Aaron's gentle speech was his liberal use of the greeting of peace. In the society of Hillel's time the traditional blessing of peace in greeting – how and to whom it was given – signaled a person's attitude to others.

In the third story about Aaron, he is portrayed as greeting even sinners with the blessing of peace ("Peace be upon you!"), and he certainly gave it first, as the story makes clear that the "sinner," out of shame, would not have dared to be familiar with the great leader of Israel.

Another rabbinic text links a teaching about the greeting of peace to Hillel's theme-saying:

He who loves peace and pursues peace,
Who [humbles himself and] offers the greeting of peace
   to others first,
And always returns it when given,
To him will the Holy One, blessed be He, give as
   an inheritance the life of this world and the life of
   the World-to-Come, as it is said:
"The meek shall inherit the earth,
and shall delight in the abundance of peace" (Psalms 37:11).[13]

The same text has a similar saying in the name of Rabban Simon ben Gamaliel, Hillel's great-grandson: "How great is peace! For though Aaron the priest had many wonderful qualities, he was praised for that alone: because he loved peace and pursued peace, gave the greeting of peace first and returned it when given to him, as it is said: "In peace and uprightness did he walk with Me . . .' "[14]

Giving and returning the greeting of peace was considered the most basic expression of a peaceable attitude to one's fellows and was typically used to illustrate that desirable trait. The stereotypical expression – "to give the greeting of peace first and to always return it when given" – might go back to Hillel and even to his masters, as we will see. On the one hand, it was joined with Hillel's saying about peace by his great-grandson, Rabban Simon ben Gamaliel; and, on the other hand, it was (as we will see in the following) illustrated in practice by a talmudic story about Yohanan ben Zakkai, Hillel's disciple (who was a co-leader with Hillel's great-grandson). Also note how in the first of the two quotes just cited, peace ("the abundance of peace" of the Psalm verse) is the reward for following the way of peace. A person who cherished peace with others will himself have peace in this world and the next. This same thought was expressed in the story where Shemaya and Avtalyon said that the sons of the gentiles who acted like Aaron would be blessed with peace. At that time, remember, they were criticizing the condescending and rude *greeting* given to them by the high priest. This suggests that not only do the ideas about "disciples" of Aaron and loving peace go back to Hillel's masters, but so also does the related attention to greetings of peace. Whether or not the expression itself – about giving and returning the greeting of peace – originated with Hillel or those before him, certainly the concept behind it is integrally related to his teaching.

Giving the greeting first was a sign of honor, for the rule was that the lesser greeted the greater first. However, due to their humility and their affection for their fellowmen, some of the rabbis habitually offered the blessing of peace first; this was the way of those who actively sought to pursue peace. In the saying quoted earlier (from Simon ben Gamaliel, Hillel's great-grandson) it was said that Aaron, being a lover of peace, "gave the greeting of peace first and always returned it when given to him." As we said, Hillel might have originated that teaching, or perhaps he only received and transmitted it. Regardless, not only his descendant, but his disciple –

Yohanan ben Zakkai–followed the practice: "It was said of Rabban Yohanan ben Zakkai that no one had ever greeted him with the blessing of peace before he had himself greeted the other first–not even a gentile in the marketplace."[15] Elsewhere, the rabbis taught: "Always be first in greeting all men with the blessing of peace" (*Avot* 4:20).

Returning a greeting of peace was good manners, although occasionally good manners were waived. Blessings, even of greeting, were taken seriously and not considered merely matters of formality and politeness. We can understand, then, that some people excluded others whom they held in low esteem, gentiles and Jews, from their blessings of peace. But Yohanan ben Zakkai included even gentiles. And he was careful to extend such greetings even in the public marketplace, for some people who were gracious to casual acquaintances in a more intimate environment might neglect them in a bustling marketplace. In this he was following the way of Hillel, his master, to love peace and to love *all* people, even Jewish sinners and gentiles, bringing them close to the Torah.

Lying for the Sake of Peace

Returning to the first of the three stories about Aaron, it can be asked if his lying in order to make peace between the two estranged neighbors is not a questionable practice. However, the rabbis taught:

"All lying is forbidden – except to make peace between a man and his fellow."[16]

When Hillel was once accosted in the Temple by Shammaite extremists who sought to prevent him from offering a sacrifice proscribed by their religious ruling, he lied to them for the sake of peace, to avoid strife (*Betzah* 20a,b). Being a peace-loving person, Hillel was willing to lie and engage in an innocent deception, in order to avoid a possibly violent confrontation with these fanatics. Later we will quote this whole story and discuss it more fully.

Another tradition shows that lying for the sake of peace was an issue between Hillel and Shammai and their Houses. It was a Jewish wedding custom to dance before the bride and sing her praises.

Our rabbis taught: How should we sing the bride's praises when we dance before her? The House of Shammai says: You should praise the bride as she really is. The House of Hillel says: You sing "Beautiful and gracious bride!" The House of Shammai said to the House of Hillel: If she is lame or blind, do you still sing "Beautiful and gracious bride," when the Torah says "Keep far from lying words" (Exodus 23:7)! The House of Hillel replied: If your friend shows you a bad piece of merchandise he purchased in the marketplace, do you praise or criticize it? According to your view one would think it's fine to criticize it, but everyone knows that you praise what he bought! For the sages taught: "A person's mind should always be at one with other people" [*me'urav*, translated as "at one with," is literally "mixed in"] (*Ketubot* 16b).

MOSES AND AARON AS TYPES

Shammai and his House championed truthtelling, while Hillel and his House preferred peace. The rabbis held that this dispute, these two different religious paths, went all the way back to Moses and Aaron. They taught:

"Moses used to say: 'Let judgment pierce the mountain!' But the way of Aaron was 'Love peace and pursue peace and make peace between a man and his fellow,' as it is said: 'The Torah of truth was in his mouth and iniquity was not to be found upon his lips; he walked with Me in peace and uprightness and turned many away from sin' (Malachi 2:6)."[17]

Moses stands for Justice, Judgment, and Truth, Aaron for Peace and Mercy (*Hesed*).[18] The two brothers reflect and represent the two paired and contrasting attributes of God's nature – so often spoken of by the rabbis – the Attribute of Judgment and the Attribute of Mercy. Moses, who sought truth, was willing to judge others. Aaron's way was: Do not judge others; never say to them, "You've sinned!" So also with the bride: Hillel and his comrades were interested in love and peace and disapproved of what they perceived as Shammai's inflexible insistence on truth. This teaching comparing Moses and Aaron uses the very language of Hillel's theme-saying about being disciples of Aaron and certainly helps explain the fullness of its meaning. It may also help to explain why Hillel was so tolerant (as he was) of his abrasive colleague Shammai, for he saw that the argument between them was ancient and he knew that his opponent also was acting for the sake of heaven.

Another image employed to represent two different ways in Judaism, and where Moses and Aaron again are used as types for different kinds of rabbis, is that Moses was the best man (*shoshbin*) of the bridegroom – God – and Aaron was the best man of the bride – Israel. Each best man defended the interest of his side: Moses was looking out primarily for God's interest, Aaron for Israel's. Moses brought the King to the wedding and wanted to beautify Him before Israel. Aaron brought the souls of Israel and wanted to beautify them before God with praise. Since Aaron's single desire was to arouse the King's affection for the bride – Israel – he always sought to praise her.[19]

Earlier we saw that the Aaron-type rabbis, such as Hillel, generously praised the bride at a Jewish wedding; here we see that they wanted only to praise the bride of God – the Jewish people and all individual Jews – before the King, the Holy One, blessed be He. Thus, the Aaron-type, the best man of the bride, does not judge people, but tries to influence God to make peace with them and overlook their sins. He seeks to justify their ways before God so He will have compassion on them. The Moses-type, on the other hand, tries to do all he can to praise the bridegroom, God, and to justify His ways to the people: God's laws and judgments are just – it is they who are sinful. Behind these legendary types of Aaron and Moses stand rabbis such as Hillel and Shammai.

This difference in the ways of Moses and Aaron goes back to the story of the Golden Calf. At that time Aaron, who loved peace too much, yielded to the people and joined them in making the Golden Calf (Exodus 32:1ff.). But Moses acted as a zealot and called out: "Who is on the Lord's side? Let him come to me. . . ! Thus says the Lord God of Israel: 'Put every man his sword at his side . . . and slay every man his brother and every man his neighbor [who sinned through idolatry].' " Moses divided the people into righteous and sinners and took judgment on the worst sinners with the sword.

This Torah story illustrates the occasionally excessive harshness of the prophet-type such as Moses, who slays the sinners, and the excessive accommodation of the priest-type such as Aaron, who participates in building an idol. There are dangers in Aaron's way of seeking peace and being willing to change the truth for the sake of peace – but there are also dangers in the way of Moses. Hillel basically chose the way of Aaron, thinking that the "still small voice" had a better chance of bringing sinners back to God than did the fire and storm of judgment and rebuke. Judaism as always teaches a balance between the two ways (after all, Moses and Aaron were brothers), but only by wisdom can a person know how to balance them, and know when the time comes for each.

18

Being "Mixed in" with Others

SOLIDARITY AND SYMPATHY

Peace – according to the Jewish tradition and Hillel – is not merely a cessation of hostility, but the expression of a mystic solidarity between people.

In a talmudic teaching quoted in the previous chapter the House of Hillel cited a saying of the sages to support their practice of generously praising the bride at a wedding: "A person's mind should always be at one with other people," more literally, "mixed in" with others (me'urav). This saying is hard to translate, but is easy to understand once explained. The point is simply that a person should not hold himself aloof; he should be together with people and act in concert with them. In its fullest expression, it teaches that he should even be in sympathy with their thoughts and feelings on an inner level. It encourages the very important quality that today we call being sensitive to others.

DO NOT BE SEEN

This attitude to people was Hillel's own, as we learn from another, somewhat enigmatic, almost Taoist-sounding, teaching.

Hillel the Elder said:
Do not be seen naked, do not be seen dressed.

Do not be seen standing, do not be seen sitting.
Do not be seen laughing, do not be seen weeping –
As it is said: "A time to laugh and a time to weep,
a time to embrace and a time to refrain from embracing"
(Ecclesiastes 3:4) (*Tosefta Berachot* 2:24).

The mysterious goal of "not being seen" could be expressed idiomatically (if more prosaically) in English by saying that a person should
"blend in" with other people. The meaning is clarified by a more
easily understandable version of this teaching: "A person should not
rejoice when among those who are crying and he should not cry
when among those who are rejoicing," and so on.[1] This version and
another one end with a generalizing rule, variously expressed as: "A
person should not diverge, in behavior or attitude, from his
fellowmen;"[2] or: "A person should not differ from the custom of
people."[3] Although it is not as apparent in the English, this general
principle (in either form) is closely related to the one cited earlier – in
the final line of teaching about dancing before the bride – that a person's mind should be "at one" or "mixed in" with other people.

Elsewhere, Hillel taught that a person should not be aloof:
"Separate not yourself from the community" (*Avot* 2:5). But beyond
the negative aspect of not standing apart, he should be "mixed-in"
with others in a positive way. The examples used together with the
teaching about dancing before the bride are helpful for understanding the point, first, that one should praise the bride not according to a stingy truth, but generously and according to the need of
the hour and the meaning of the custom, sensitive to others' feelings.
Second, in the exchange with the Shammaites, the Hillelites used an
example they considered incontrovertible – that when someone
shows you a poor piece of merchandise he bought, do you criticize
it? Of course not – only an insensitive person does that! Rather, his
mind should be "mixed in" with that of his friend and in tune with
his feelings. He should see that his friend is happy with his purchase
and, sharing his happiness, praise it. That is the attitude of a person
sympathetic and sensitive to others.

SPIRITUAL ETIQUETTE

The Hillelites used this example of common etiquette –
praising another's purchase – to explain their position about praising

the bride. Hillel himself also seems to have used a proverbial saying – about not being out of step with others, not laughing when they are crying, and so on – in a similar way and for a similar purpose. It seems likely that something like these words about "Do not be seen naked, do not be seen dressed," and so on, was a traditional expression, in enigmatic form, of conventional social wisdom and etiquette. But that is not the meaning Hillel gave it. He adapted the saying to a more spiritual use. He was not concerned with social embarrassment or conventional correctness, but with love of one's fellowman, with peace between people on an inner level. When he said "Do not be seen laughing among those who are crying," and so on, he was not promoting social conformity,[4] but was teaching the inner sympathy that leads a person to share other people's concerns and also their joys and sorrows. Such inner sympathy will usually produce socially oriented ways so that when people join together in communal prayer or to study Torah or to do deeds of kindness, a "spiritually social" person will join with them and participate.[5]

After this traditional saying of social etiquette – that he adapted to spiritual purposes – about "Do not be seen laughing, do not be seen weeping," and so on, Hillel appends, as scriptural support, a verse from the Torah, about "A time to laugh and a time to weep" (Ecclesiastes 3:4), which is itself a wisdom saying not very different from the one it follows. The use of matters of etiquette and social custom as parables to explain spiritual truths was a particular characteristic of Hillel's teaching, as we will see later on also.[6] But beyond style, the essence of Hillel's teaching that a person's mind should be "mixed-in" with that of others is his lesson about the need for the kind of spiritual sympathy and sensitivity that will lead to a profound peace between people.

19

Charity and Peace

In another saying about peace, Hillel taught:

He who increases *tzedakah* [charity], increases peace (*Avot* 2:8).

This teaching, that charity fosters peace, may be based on Isaiah 32:17: "and the doing of *tzedakah* shall bring peace" – with *tzedakah*, righteousness, understood by Hillel in its later meaning of "charity."[1]

Hillel's saying has a number of dimensions. The peace referred to can be the peace between the rich and the poor, the peace between the poor and God, or the peace within the person giving charity.

Most of his sayings about peace that we have already discussed are about peace between people. Here, too, Hillel meant that charity increases communal peace and softens the harsh separation between rich and poor.

But charity also increases the peace between the poor and God. When poor people feel their deprivation unjust, they may develop resentment not only against the rich, but against God, and may become religiously alienated. The injustice of their poverty becomes a complaint against God. So the rabbis taught that giving charity not only fosters peace between rich and poor, but also makes peace between the poor person and God.

"God says to the one giving charity: 'This poor man was sitting and complaining to himself: "How am I worse than this other person? Yet he sleeps on a nice bed and I'm here on this worthless mat; he's sleeping in a big, comfortable house and I'm here in this miserable hut!" 'And you,' God says to the charitable man, 'stood up and gave him *tzedakah*; you soothed his hurt. By your life! I consider it as if you've made peace between him and Me!' "[2]

Finally, the peace that Hillel says is increased by charity may also be that of the individual who gives. The one-line saying of Hillel—that "He who increases charity, increases peace"—is a semi-independent part of a larger saying of his (*Avot* 2:8), which has another line seemingly in parallelism with this one:

He who increases possessions, increases anxiety.[3]

Accumulating possessions increases a person's anxiety; conversely, giving some of them away as charity increases his peace of soul. That Hillel intended this parallelism is supported by a related saying of his or what is perhaps simply a variant of this one.

He who increases good deeds is establishing peace within his own body (*Avot d'Rabbi Natan*, chap. 28).

Here the internal dimension of the increased peace is evident.[4]

An interesting perspective on this saying comes from a word by the great hasidic *rebbe*, Rabbi Simha Bunim of Pshis'ha, who commented on the rabbinic saying we mentioned earlier: " 'Seek' peace in your own place and 'pursue' it elsewhere." Rabbi Bunim taught: "Our sages say: 'Seek peace in your own place'—You cannot find peace anywhere but in your own self. In the Psalm (38:3) we read: 'There is no peace in my bones because of my sin.' When a person has made peace within himself, he will be able to make peace in the whole world."[5]

Was Hillel also thinking of this verse from Psalms when he spoke about good deeds establishing "peace within the body," just as he seems to have used Isaiah 32:17 ("and the doing of charity shall bring peace") for the similar saying, that charity increases peace? Compare how he used Psalm 34:17—"Seek peace and pursue it"—for his saying about being disciples of Aaron: "loving and pursuing peace."

Hillel certainly fulfilled his own teaching about loving and pursuing peace. That he made peace such a central part of his teaching should also give us a clue to his personality and character. It seems that he had himself achieved, through love for God and people, through his charity and good deeds, that great personal peace "within his own body" (as he put it). Hillel became famous, even in his own time, for his transcendent serenity and calm. But there were other sides to him as well, as we will see.

20

Loving People

The first half of the third line of Hillel's theme-saying about being disciples of Aaron is "Loving people"–literally, "Loving the creatures."

Simply on the formal level, this phrase is in parallelism with the first half of the second line, that is: "Loving peace . . . Loving people." There is, of course, an obvious connection between loving one's fellowmen and seeking to be at peace with them.

THE GOLDEN RULE

Hillel's teaching about "loving people" is his expression of the commandment "you shall love your neighbor as yourself" (Leviticus 19:18). Everyone knows the famous story of the gentile who came to Hillel and asked to be taught the entire Torah while he was standing on one foot. Hillel's answer was the Golden Rule.[1]

A certain gentile once came to Hillel and said, "I'm ready to become a Jew, but only if you can teach me the whole Torah while I stand here on one foot." Hillel answered him, "What is hateful to you, don't do to your fellowman; that is the whole Torah, and the rest . . . is just a commentary. Go then and learn it!" (*Shabbat* 31a).

The *Targum* of Hillel's disciple, Yonatan ben Uzziel, on Leviticus 19:18, indicates that the Golden Rule was understood as the practical rule of thumb for the fulfillment of the commandment to love your neighbor. The *Targum*, which translated the Hebrew Torah into the spoken language of the people, Aramaic, paraphrases "you shall love your neighbor as yourself": "you shall love your neighbor – what you hate, do not do to him." "As yourself" in Leviticus 19:18 is replaced by the Golden Rule. According to the Torah, the love of your neighbor is to be "as yourself" – in the same manner as you love yourself. But how do you know in practice the way to love another? Hillel's answer is that "as yourself" means that your own feelings are your guide: What you love is a clue to what the other person loves, what you hate is a clue to what he hates.[2] Of course, the application of this rule is not mechanical

We can see an example of its application in an ancient rabbinic commentary on Leviticus 19:34:

" '[As to] the stranger who dwells with you: you shall love him as yourself, because you were strangers in the land of Egypt' [Leviticus 19:34]. Just as it is said concerning Jews: 'you shall love him as yourself' [Leviticus 19:18], so is it said concerning strangers: 'you shall love him as yourself, because you were strangers in the land of Egypt.' Understand a stranger's feelings (literally, "Know what the soul of a stranger is") [and how to act lovingly to him], because you also were strangers in the land of Egypt."[3]

"Understand a stranger's feelings," for as a Jew you should know his sensitivities as a stranger from the inside, because you were once strangers in Egypt; and he feels as you felt. This is a good example of the way Hillel's Golden Rule works: not to do to others what you would hate having done to you, because the other person is "like yourself" and feels just as you would, or did, in that situation.

ALL PEOPLE

Hillel certainly believed that Leviticus 19:18 intended love for all people, Jews and gentiles alike.[4] It was a gentile, after all, whom he taught that the whole Torah is summed up in the Golden Rule. He did not mean that the Golden Rule first applied to him when and if he became a Jew, for the Golden Rule – by its very nature and logic – has no such limitation, but applies to all people.[5] Therefore, a Jew should not treat anyone, including a gentile, in a way that would be hateful to him if he were so treated.

The exact words in Hillel's theme-saying are, we noted, "loving the creatures (*briyot*)." (The word "creatures"—meaning created by God—has a nicer sound in Hebrew than does the English with its slightly peculiar connotation.) The theme-saying continues "and bringing them near to the Torah," indicating that "the creatures" includes even the nonreligious and the sinners. Hillel and his disciples often spoke of their fellowmen using the broad term "creatures," which includes all people, Jews and gentiles. Earlier we saw that the Hillelites taught that a person should extend the greeting of peace to "all men" (*kol adam*),[6] where this included "even the gentile in the marketplace." Later we will see that the House of Hillel believed that the Torah should be taught to "all men"—to Jewish sinners and even to gentiles who are drawn to it (like the one who asked Hillel to teach him while on one foot). The typical and inclusive use of "all men" in the Hillelite tradition parallels the thought behind Hillel's (and his followers') use of "the creatures"—for all people are God's creatures, created by Him and deserving the love of their fellow humans.

Sefer Haredim,[7] one of the great books produced by the kabbalists of the Land of Israel (sixteenth century), explains Hillel's words this way: "Loving the creatures and drawing them to the Torah—it does not say 'Loving Jews,' but 'Loving the creatures,' and this expression contains a hint of how Hillel, with his illuminated intelligence and sweet speech, drew near those gentiles who wanted to convert and brought them under the wings of the *Shechinah* (Divine Presence), as we see in *Shabbat* 31 [where the story of Hillel and the gentile on one foot and other similar stories of Hillel converting gentiles are found]."

POSITIVE AND NEGATIVE

The Golden Rule, which Hillel said is "the whole Torah," can be expressed positively—"Whatever you wish that men would do to you, do so to them"—or negatively—"What is hateful to you, do not do to others." The positive Golden Rule teaches what a person should do, the negative Golden Rule what he should not do. Clearly, in a person's relations with others, the latter precept, although less exalted, is more fundamental and basic. Hillel used the negative Golden Rule because avoiding harm to the honor and property of one's fellowman must precede love in the more positive sense. The first lesson is: If you would be unhappy when someone else treated you disrespectfully or caused you a loss in money or property, you must not treat others that way. Someone who does not have elementary respect for others and their rights cannot attain the higher level of love for them.

Therefore, the negative Golden Rule precedes, particularly in a case like that of Hillel in the story, where a rabbi is teaching a gentile or a simple Jew who is just beginning in Torah. When instructing a committed religious person who had progressed spiritually, the ideal would more likely be expressed as the higher, positive Golden Rule.[8]

GO AND LEARN

In the Golden Rule story, Hillel complied readily with the man's desire to know the whole picture at the beginning, but he was just as quick to leave him with encouragement that he "go and learn" the rest. Hillel believed that learning the Torah in its breadth and depth is an absolute necessity to truly knowing and fulfilling the will of God.[9] How can one love God or one's fellowman without knowing what that implies?

ON ONE FOOT

The gentile asked Hillel to teach him the whole Torah in the time he could remain standing on one foot. Edward Gershfield has explained this peculiarity well: "The Roman poet Horace, who was roughly a contemporary of Hillel, describes in one of his satires (Book 1, Sat. 4) the life and accomplishments of his great literary predecessor, Lucilius, who lived about a century earlier. He states that Lucilius was a prodigious writer, and could produce great quantities of poetry in a hurry; in fact, it was said of him that he could dictate two hundred verses *stans pedo in uno*, while standing on one foot! (*ibid.*, lines 9–10). Hillel probably never read Horace, but it is not unreasonable to think that Horace's expression was a current one, easily understood in those days by anyone with some education."[10] It is not clear from this phrase in Horace whether or not we should imagine the gentile questioning Hillel as actually standing on one foot; most likely, his use of the expression was merely metaphorical.

THE WHOLE TORAH

The gentile was anxious to know the essence of Judaism all at once, "on one foot" as he put it. Hillel answered by telling him that love of neighbor, the Golden Rule, was "the whole Torah." That Hillel was not afraid to get to the point is the mark of a certain kind of personality – a radical personality – that seeks to probe to the root of things and is willing to take a stand about priorities.

To some degree Hillel's project of discriminating between what is primary and secondary was motivated by a natural desire for clarity in understanding. Understanding the Torah's central principle would allow him and other sages to interpret its teachings correctly and to know the will of God in new situations and circumstances. Hillel's formulation and use of the seven rules of Torah interpretation had a similar motive.

But his desire and willingness to identify the central principle of the Torah has a still deeper significance. Religious conservatives and ritualists tend to put all beliefs and practices on an equal level, making what is unimportant important and what is important unimportant. Reformers and radicals, on the other hand, who seek to restore religion to its true, original form, strive – like Hillel – to say clearly what is central and what is not.

Still another incentive for him to reduce the Torah to a single principle was Hillel's attempt to bring Judaism to people far removed from it – to Jews who were "far away," and even to gentiles. When presenting the tremendous expanse of the Torah to those who knew little about it, who had not grown up with it, it was helpful to be able to put its meaning most simply, to pare it down to its vital essence. And this Hillel did.

Hillel was radical not only in his willingness to express the Torah's core teaching, but in his actual understanding of what that was, for he taught that love of man, the Golden Rule, is "the whole Torah." People today are so familiar with this story and teaching that they fail to see how radical it is. What happened to love of God? The answer is that Hillel focused on love of man because he so much

identified love of God *with* love of man, and believed that the basic
way to express love of God is *by* loving people. That is how the
Golden Rule is able to be "the whole Torah." The rabbis teach that
there are two types of commandments: those between God and
man and those between man and man. Hillel certainly appreciated
the importance of the first category, but knowing how easily people
concentrate their religiosity on ritual at the expense of love, peace,
and charity, he boldly taught that "the whole Torah's" essence was
fulfilled by loving people.

TWO DIRECTIONS

Hillel's teaching had two directions. In one direction his theme-
saying encouraged the most religious people – particularly the sages
and leaders – to emulate Aaron, who was a leader of the Jewish
people. We can understand that this saying was spoken primarily to
them because it called on them to bring *others* to the Torah.[11] The
second direction of Hillel's teaching was to the common people
among the religious and, perhaps particularly, to the nonreligious –
Jews and even gentiles – and is summed up in the Golden Rule, as in
the story of Hillel with the gentile "on one foot." In a sense, then,
we could say that Hillel's two central teachings are his saying about
being disciples of Aaron and the Golden Rule. To the sages and the
most religious people, Hillel taught that their particular fulfillment
of love of neighbor was to work to bring others close to God:
"Loving all people and bringing them close to the Torah" – and in
the Golden Rule story he himself is shown doing this. To the
common people among the religious and to the nonreligious, Hillel's
teaching was also to love their neighbor, and the Golden Rule was
the rule of thumb for how to go about it.

AKIBA AND THE DONKEY DRIVER

A story about Rabbi Akiba parallels the Hillel Golden Rule
story, and provides an interesting comparison.

"One day a donkey driver came to Rabbi Akiba and said to
him, 'Rabbi, teach me the whole Torah all at once.' Akiba answered, 'My son, if Moses our teacher, peace be upon him, required

forty days and forty nights on the mountain before he was able to learn the whole Torah, how can you expect me to teach it to you in one session? But know, my son, that the principle behind the whole Torah is this: What you yourself hate, don't do to your fellow man. That means that if you don't want anyone to harm what is yours, then you shouldn't harm anything of another person; if you don't want anyone to take what is yours, then you shouldn't take what belongs to someone else.'

"The man left Akiba and joined some of his friends. When walking together they came across a field full of vegetables. Each of his friends took two bunches and began to eat them; but he didn't take anything. They went on and came to another field full of cabbages. Each of his friends took two cabbages; but he didn't take anything. Finally, they asked him, 'How come you're not taking anything?' He answered, 'This is what Rabbi Akiba taught me: What you yourself hate, don't do to someone else. If you don't want anyone to harm you, then harm no one yourself. If you don't want anyone to take what is yours, then you don't take what belongs to another. That's why I didn't take anything.' "[12]

It is not accidental that in the Hillel story the questioner is a gentile, and in the Akiba story he is a simple Jew, a donkey driver. As said, the Golden Rule, particularly in its negative form – not to harm others, just as you would not want them to harm you – was the "short lesson" for those starting on the path of Torah. Part of the charm of the Akiba story, in fact, is due to the almost primitive simplicity of the lesson that the humble donkey driver learned.[13]

LOVE AND THE IMAGE OF GOD

Although Hillel and Akiba after him taught that love of man is a central pillar of the Torah's teaching, behind it is something even more basic. Love of neighbor is itself derived from an even greater principle: that man is made in the image of God; and a religiously inspired love of man flows from the more fundamental love of God.[14] We have already noted how Hillel identified love of humanity so closely with love of God that, in calling the Golden Rule the "whole Torah," he could concentrate on the former without even mentioning the latter. The love of man that the Torah teaches is, then, intimately bound up with the love of God. This most central teaching is, of course, right from the Book of Genesis, which says that humans are made in the image of God; it is the very heart of the Torah and was not invented by Hillel or the rabbis.

That Hillel considered the commandment to love people as based on their being made in God's image can be seen in two ways: first, by his use, in his theme-saying, of "loving *the creatures*" (*briyot*), rather than other possibilities, to refer to people in general. This Hebrew word *briyot* directly suggests that man is created in the image of God. Second, in another story (which we will discuss later) Hillel teaches that a person should treat his *own* body with loving care, because he also is made in the image of God. If he taught about the image of God in connection with this somewhat unusual duty of love, it seems certain that he based the more straightforward obligation to love one's neighbor on his being made in God's image.

The realization that one's fellowmen are made in God's image and are His creatures, the work of His hands, should inspire a person to relate to them with love and respect and care. As we saw earlier, the Hebrew term the "creatures" is very broad, including not only Jews but gentiles also. So when Hillel taught about "loving all people" (the "creatures") his use of that term has two significant connotations: (1) that people are created in the image of God and deserving of love; and (2) that this includes all people, gentiles as well as Jews.

Because people are God's creatures a religious person should pity them, particularly when they become separated from Him, and do everything possible to return them to their Creator (as in the continuation of the third line of Hillel's theme-saying: "loving people and bringing them back to the Torah"). But how can a person pity others and seek their welfare if he judges them harshly? Hillel's teaching about that aspect of love – not judging others – is the subject of the next chapter.

Love and Judging Others

JUDGE NOT

Hillel expressed an important aspect of love of neighbor in a well-known saying of his:

Judge not your fellowman until you come into his place (*Avot* 2:5).

This directly follows the logic of the Golden Rule that a person must put himself in the other person's place.[1] We saw earlier that a Jew was expected to love the stranger and understand his feelings and sensitivities, because the Jewish people themselves had been strangers in the land of Egypt, and "in that place." This lesson, of not judging until you have been in the other person's place, is in essence a counsel of sympathy. The implications of Hillel's saying are brought out in a story (which certainly seems legendary) about Rabbi Akiba, where the same lesson is taught.

"Rabbi Akiba was in the habit of mocking the weakness of those who committed sexual transgressions. One day the Satan appeared to him as a very beautiful woman sitting on a branch high in a palm tree. He immediately began to climb the tree! But when he got halfway up, the apparition disappeared and the Satan said to him roughly, 'If it had not been announced in heaven: "Take heed of Rabbi Akiba and his Torah!" I would not have valued your blood at more than two cents.' "[2]

Akiba was protected only by the merit of his Torah knowledge. Being put in the "place" of those he had mocked, and succumbing (in intent if not in deed), taught him a lesson about judging and about underestimating the power of Satan and the evil inclination. A similar point is made in a story about Rav Ashi, who was lecturing on the wicked kings of Israel. The day before he was to speak about King Menashe, the latter appeared to him in a dream and proved he knew more Torah than the rabbi himself. Rav Ashi asked him, "If you are so wise, why did you worship idols?" "If you had been living at that time," replied Menashe, "you would have lifted up the skirts of your robe to run after them to worship them!"[3] These stories about Akiba and Ashi teach the same lesson as Hillel's saying—that a person should not judge others until he has put himself in their place.

IN THE SCALE OF MERIT

One aspect of Hillel's teaching on judging is that a person should be reluctant to judge at all. Another aspect (as we will see shortly in a story) is that, when possible, he should judge others favorably, or, in the traditional idiom, "in the scale of merit"—so that the "scale" of judgment, which has two pans or scales, one of merit (innocence) and the other of guilt, is inclined toward the side of merit. It is taught: "Judge your fellowman to the side of the scale of merit, and do not weigh down his judgment on the side of the scale of guilt."[4] A person should search until he finds a way to justify and excuse someone who has done something that seems wrong. The rabbis advise: "Keep turning the matter around, over and over," until you find some merit, some justification, for the other person.[5]

HILLEL AS A RELIGIOUS JUDGE

When Hillel sat as a religious judge in the Sanhedrin and considered the case of the Alexandrian Jews whose mother had married their father after being engaged to another man, he searched for a way to justify their parents' actions. His compassion was so intense, he could not rest until he was able to spare the children from being declared illegitimate.

WHEN YOU LOVE SOMEONE YOU ALWAYS JUDGE IN HIS FAVOR

Finding justifications for another person's behavior is a sign of love, for if someone loves his neighbor as himself he will excuse and overlook his faults, just as he does his own. The Talmud records that one rabbi said: "I disqualify myself from being a judge in any case involving a Torah scholar. Why? Because I love him like my own self, and a person can never see faults and guilt in himself."[6] It was also taught: "A man should never be a judge to decide a case in which a friend is involved . . . because he will never see faults and guilt in someone whom he loves. . . ."[7] These teachings are about judging as a religious judge in a court setting. But–although there are differences–the basic logic applies also to judging other people in general. And then, the more a person loves his fellowmen, the more will he judge them favorably and for good.

HILLEL AND HIS WIFE

Hillel's attitude to judging others favorably–in the scale of merit–is illustrated by the following story:

Hillel the Elder once made a dinner for a certain man. But while he was entertaining his guest in the other room, a poor man came and stood at the door of the kitchen, where Hillel's wife was busy preparing the meal. He said to her, "I'm getting married today and bringing my new bride into my house–and I don't even have food there for a single meal!" Hearing this, Hillel's wife took all of the dinner she had just prepared and gave it to him. Then, starting over, she kneaded more dough and cooked another potful of food, took it in and placed it before her husband and his guest.

Hillel asked her, "My daughter, why didn't you bring the food in earlier?" When she told him what had happened, he said to her, "My daughter, don't think for a moment that I judged you badly; I judged you in the scale of merit, that all your deeds were only for the sake of heaven" (*Derech Eretz Rabbah* 6).

This story shows us the character and goodness of Hillel's wife—her generosity and open heart. She did not give half the food; she gave all of it, when her husband and his guest were waiting. Her act was not a small thing under the circumstances. Unfortunately, the tradition did not value women enough to bother to preserve her name (although admittedly the story's concern is with Hillel's judging her in the scale of merit and therefore focuses on him). We can imagine that she knew her husband well enough not to be afraid to act immediately, without asking his permission, even though a guest was in the house and would be discomforted. Certainly Hillel told her he had judged her in the scale of merit so she would not think that his question about the delay implied any criticism. In fact, once Hillel learned what had happened, he must have been deeply gratified at his wife's beautiful act of charity. This story tells us then that he had a partner worthy of him.

This incident also provides a concrete example of Hillel's peaceable nature. The attitude he expressed in his gentle and reassuring words to his wife was a formula for a good marriage, and for what the rabbis call *shalom bayit*, peace in the home.[8]

It is an interesting peculiarity that Hillel addresses his wife as "my daughter."[9] It was common for a rabbi to address a grown man or woman as "my son" or "my daughter," indicating a kindly attitude. The stories about Aaron made him address the men and women this way. It is unclear if this was a common form of address to a wife at that time or if it represents something more unusual. Perhaps it meant nothing more than "my dear." But in the context of the story it seems as if Hillel used this address to be especially gentle because of the delicacy of what he wanted to say.

Hillel judged his wife not only favorably, but according to the very highest motive, that "all her deeds were for the sake of heaven." We do not know if he judged everyone quite so generously, for he already knew her character and piety. But we can be sure that he judged all people favorably—in the scale of merit. The motive that Hillel ascribed to his wife was also his own. We are told elsewhere, in these exact words, about Hillel, that "all his deeds were for the sake of heaven" (*Betzah* 16a).

JUDGING SHAMMAI FAVORABLY

Hillel's deep-seated tolerance enabled him to see that even his religious opponents could be inspired by the highest motives. The tradition's famous saying about the controversy between Hillel and Shammai is: "These and those are the words of the living God." This statement probably reflects Hillel's own attitude to his religious adversary. Another formulation of the same perspective is:

Every controversy for the sake of heaven
   will never cease,
And one not for the sake of heaven
   will not last.
Which controversy was for the sake of heaven?
The one between Hillel and Shammai . . . (*Avot* 5:20).

In a controversy like that between Hillel and Shammai, each of the parties has pure motives, holding his position for the sake of heaven. Hillel was able to see, through the obscuring clouds of his dispute with Shammai, that all the deeds of his holy opponent, like his own, were for the sake of heaven. There are many other instances of this high-minded attitude in the Talmud. The ability to appreciate (even if only grudgingly) a religious opponent, was and is a settled part of the Jewish tradition and based on the perception that "all his deeds are for the sake of heaven." For this reason it seems likely that the sayings in the tradition that give Shammai an equivalent, if not always equal, status with Hillel have their ultimate origin in Hillel's own favorable judgment of his adversary. There is a special merit in being able to judge *religious* opponents favorably, and the tradition tells us (as we will see later) that this noble attitude, and the humility it implies, was the very thing that won for Hillel and his followers their ascendancy over the camp of Shammai.

COMING TO HIS PLACE AND JUDGING FAVORABLY

Hillel taught that a person should not judge his fellowman until he has come to his place, and also that he should judge others

favorably, in the scale of merit. The book *Seder HaYom*[10] has an
excellent explanation of how these two teachings fit together:

"You should not allow your heart to be poisoned against a
person when you hear something bad about him, but should weigh
what he has done according to *his* understanding, not your own –
because people see things differently. Although according to your
understanding there may be no basis for judging him favorably,
when you consider the way *he* sees it and according to *his* level of
understanding, you may find that he did not do anything wrong and
that he acted without any bad intentions at all. Grasping this is very
important . . . and it is the meaning of 'Don't judge your fellowman
until you come into his place.' 'His place' means his level of intelligence and understanding, for everyone is different, and on a different level also. When you look at things in this manner you will be
able to judge him favorably – according to his way of seeing things –
not unfavorably according to your way. And you will find favor in
heaven when you do this, for as you measure, so will it be measured
to you."

BRINGING OTHERS TO GOD–AARON AND SOFT SPEECH

Not being judgmental and critical of others, not being scandal-
ized by their sins and misdeeds, is absolutely required if someone
wants, like Hillel, to lead people ("sinners") back to God. Thus, the
legend that claimed that Aaron had never in his whole life said to
anyone, "You've sinned!" obviously considered this a key to his
success in bringing sinners to repentance. He always judged people
compassionately and favorably and did not use their sins as a reason
to despise them. A rabbinic tradition contrasting Moses and Aaron
explains why the people loved Aaron more than they loved his
brother:

"Because Moses always rebuked them about each and every
thing . . . but Aaron never judged them, inclining the scale to guilt,
and he never said to any man or woman, 'You've sinned!' "[11]

Aaron never spoke of the sins of others and he did not judge or
rebuke them. Because of this, because his way was the way of love,
he was more beloved by the people than was his holy brother, who
almost always took God's side, who was God's "best man" and

strictly adhered to the way of justice. The people revered Moses, who dealt with them according to the principle of "revealed rebuke, concealed love." But earlier we noted that being a "disciple of Aaron," which was Hillel's way, made a man beloved.

The nonjudgmental attitude and gentleness in speech that Hillel and his followers ascribed to the legendary Aaron, their model, undoubtedly reflect their own traits. They were slow to rebuke others or to speak of their sins and always gave a greeting of peace to all people. We can also learn about their speech from their teaching to praise the bride generously and from the legend about Aaron praising Israel, the Bride of God.[12]

MERCY ON THE DAY OF JUDGMENT

Further insight into Hillel's leniency in judgment and Shammai's severity can be gathered from a report in the Talmud about the different positions taken by their followers concerning the Day of Judgment. Although the views of the schools ("Houses") cannot always be attributed to their founders, it seems likely that here they can, and I will consider that the case.[13]

The House of Shammai says: There will be three classes of people on the Day of Judgment – the completely righteous, the completely wicked, and those in between. The judgment of the completely righteous is immediately written and sealed for the life of the World-to-Come and that of the completely wicked is immediately written and sealed for *Gehinnom* (hell), as it is said (Daniel 12:2): "And many of them that sleep in the dust shall awake, some to everlasting life and some to shame and everlasting disgrace." But those in between shall go down to *Gehinnom*, and when they tearfully pray they shall come up again, as it is said (Zechariah 13:9): "I will bring the third part through the fire, and I will refine them as silver is refined, and will try them as gold is tried, and he shall call on My name, and I will answer him." It was concerning this last class of men that Hannah said (1 Samuel 2:6): "The Lord kills and gives life. He brings down to the grave and brings up again."

But the House of Hillel says: When God revealed Himself to Moses and proclaimed before him His glory, He said [He is] "abundant in mercy (*hesed*)" (Exodus 34: 7) – for He inclines the scale of judgment toward the side of mercy. And it was about this third class of men, who are neither completely righteous nor completely wicked, but in between, that David said (Psalm 116:1): "I love the Lord because he hears my voice in prayer"; and regarding them was the whole Psalm written, including (116:6): "I was brought low [through my sins] and He saved me [nonetheless]" (*Rosh HaShanah* 16b).

Hillel and Shammai did not differ concerning the eternal destinations of the completely righteous and the completely wicked: These would go to heaven and the others to hell. But they did differ about those in between, the great majority: Shammai said they would go to hell, be purified, pray, and then enter heaven; Hillel said they would pray and go directly to heaven. What was the basis for Hillel's position? He interpreted "abundant in mercy," in the Torah's description of God's attributes, as meaning "inclining to the side of mercy." He taught that God always inclines the scale of judgment to the side of mercy, and so will He do on the Day of Judgment. The expression used here, "inclining (the scale of judgment) to the side of mercy" is equivalent to what is meant by "judging in (with an inclination to) the scale of merit."

One of the Torah's most important teachings is found in the powerful scene of Exodus 33:12–34:8, where Moses asked God to reveal to him His "personality," who He is – and God "passed by him" and proclaimed: "The Lord, the Lord, a God merciful and giving, patient, and abundant in mercy and truth; keeping faith with thousands, forgiving iniquity, transgression, and sin." The tradition calls this list The Thirteen Attributes of God's Mercy. One of the central teachings of the Torah and of the rabbis is that a person must strive to be like God and imitate His Thirteen Attributes of Mercy. The famous saying is: "Be like Him: as He is merciful and giving, so should you be merciful and giving."[14] (The first two attributes stand as shorthand for the whole list.)

Hillel understood "abundant in mercy," one of the Thirteen Attributes, as meaning that God judges with mercy, and he taught that people also should judge others mercifully and "in the scale of merit." It is certainly interesting to see that Hillel had particularly reflected on the Thirteen Attributes of Mercy, which the rabbis considered the basis for teaching how people should imitate God.

And it is appropriate that Hillel should be especially attuned to the Thirteen Attributes, for God then revealed to Moses His merciful and forgiving "face." There is another side to God's "personality" too: He is a "merciful and gracious (giving) God"[15] but also "a jealous God"[16] who demands justice, who judges and has wrath on His enemies. Hillel leaned toward the side of the face of mercy, Shammai toward the side of the face of judgment. But – according to the Hillelite rabbis – the Torah teaches that the face of mercy is the "inside," God's more inner will and personality; at times He judges and is angry, but the inside is always love. The tradition places Hillel above Shammai, but Shammai's way of judgment is also a side of God and must not be discarded. What is required is a balance of justice and mercy, with an inclination to mercy.

SUPPRESSING OR FORGIVING SINS?

There is more to be learned from the Talmud discussion in *Rosh HaShanah* 16b–17a (quoted above); let us consider part of the continuation:

> The House of Hillel says: "abundant in mercy" (Exodus 34:6) means that God inclines always to the side of mercy in judgment. How does He do this? Rabbi Eliezer [who had Shammaite sympathies][17] says: "He suppresses [the sins], as it is said (Micah 7:19): 'He will again have compassion upon us; He will suppress our iniquities. And You will cast all their sins into the depths of the sea. . . .' " Rabbi Yosi the son of Rabbi Hanina says: "He bears [forgives], as it says: 'He bears [forgives] sin and passes over transgression . . .' " [Micah 7:18, 19 says that God (v. 18) "bears (forgives) sin and overlooks transgression. . . . (v. 19) He will suppress our iniquities." One rabbi focused on 7:18, the other on 7:19].

The two suggested methods for how God exercises His mercy in judgment are that He suppresses the sins or that He forgives them. The former represents the Shammaite view and the latter the Hillelite view. "Suppressing" sins means that they are not actually forgiven, but merely "set aside." Of particular interest is that the way the Hillelites (and Hillel) understood "abundant in mercy" and "inclining the scale of judgement to the side of mercy" to work was by forgiveness of sins. This explains their attitude to human as well as to divine forgiveness. Only when a person is merciful and forgives others their sins is he able to judge them favorably and in the scale of merit.

The Shammaites also believed that God was "abundant in mercy" and lenient with sinners, but their conception differed from the Hillelites, who preached forgiveness, for the Shammaites could not bring themselves to accept more than a "suppression" of sins.

Another ancient tradition about this difference, essentially parallel to the other, casts further light on the dispute between the two Houses. Each House fancifully interpreted the word for lamb (*keves*) differently, according to their different conceptions of the nature of the atonement effected by the daily burnt offering of a lamb in the Temple:

> "Lambs of the first year" (Numbers 28:3)–The House of Shammai says: Lambs [*kevasim*] because they suppress [*kovshim*] the sins of Israel, as it is said: "He will again have compassion upon us. He will suppress our iniquities. And You will cast all their sins into the depths of the sea" (Micah 7:19). But the House of Hillel says: Everything suppressed will in the end come up again. Lambs [*kevasim*] alludes to the fact that they wash away [*mekabsim*] the sins of Israel, as it is said: "Though your sins are like scarlet, they shall be as white as snow; though they are red like crimson, they shall become like wool" (Isaiah 1:18). Ben Azzai said: "Lambs *of the first year*"–because they wash away the sins of Israel and make them like a little child in its first year, pure and sinless.[18]

Again, the Shammaites say that sins are only suppressed or submerged, no more; the Hillelites prefer to think of God as "washing away" people's sins, so they are fully cleansed and forgiven. Ben Azzai further relates this to a well-known traditional image that when a person repents all his sins are forgiven and he becomes like a newborn child.

The outstanding quality of Shammai and those like him was their great fear of sin; therefore, they did not readily accept the idea that God simply "forgives" and forgets. For them sins were only suppressed; if a person's behavior did not change, these earlier sins would be counted in the judgment along with the later ones. And it might be expected that their conception of God's ways influenced, or reflected, the way they treated others: They too were likely to be short on forgiveness. Hillel and his followers, on the other hand, tended to judge people in the scale of merit and to forgive them completely, as they believed God to do.

HOW TO FULFILL THE COMMANDMENT TO LOVE

So far we have discussed Hillel's teaching about fulfilling the commandment to love one's neighbor, which he considered "the whole Torah." Aside from being kind and giving, a person should express his love by being slow to criticize or condemn others, by judging them favorably and forgiving their faults and sins. But the main way a leader such as Hillel could love others and serve his flock – particularly those who had strayed – was by leading them back to God. That is what Hillel did, as we will see in the next chapter.

22

Under the Wings of the Divine Presence

The final part of Hillel's theme-saying, the second half of its third line of teaching, is: "Loving all people and *bringing them close to the Torah*."

AARON AS THE MODEL

We have already discussed this to some extent; the third story about Aaron showed how he brought many sinners to repentance by his love and respect for them. "Loving all people" was the means for "bringing them close to the Torah."

AT THE GATE

A little-known Hillel story of great significance clarifies his teaching to "bring people close to the Torah."

Hillel the Elder would stand at the gate of Jerusalem through which men would leave the city to go to their work, and ask them, "How much will you earn today?"

Someone would answer, "One *dinar*."

Another would say, "Two *dinars*."

Then Hillel asked, "And what will you do with the money?"

"It's just enough to keep us alive from day to day," they replied.

Then Hillel said to them, "Why not come and inherit Torah and inherit life in this world and the World-to-Come?"

And so did Hillel do all his days, until he brought them under the wings of the Divine Presence (*ARN-B*, chap. 26).

This story shows Hillel fulfilling his own teaching of loving people and bringing them to the Torah and under the wings of the *Shechinah*. But it has been preserved in only one somewhat obscure place in the tradition (*ARN-B*) and, as a consequence, it has almost been "lost"; it is very rarely discussed or spoken of. Along with many other related stories and sayings we will consider, it lets us see how radical Hillel was. He was a street-corner missionary who went out to the streets of Jerusalem to persuade people to return to God.

Life

The argument found in Hillel's mouth in this story of him at the gate of Jerusalem is that the working people earned by their hard labors only enough for a meager day-to-day existence, literally "life of the hour"; why do they not also devote themselves with equal energy to seeking God, to pursuit of the Torah, and earn themselves eternal life? In a sense, Hillel told them that they had little to lose by seeking the rewards of spiritual life. He compared the two kinds of "wages" for the different types of "work" (material versus spiritual), and contrasted the "life of the hour" (that they mentioned) with the life of this world and the World-to-Come. If these laborers would turn to the Torah they would not only win the life of the World-to-Come, they would gain in this world also: In place of the "life of the hour," they will have the "life of this world," for even living in poverty, when one is with God, is sweet, is having "this world."[1] Hillel himself had been a day laborer and had lived in poverty—earning less than they, only a half *dinar* a day—in order to seek the "words of the living God" (the phrase used in the story of his almost expiring under the snow on the roof of the House of Study). For it is these words of Torah that give true life to a person. The argument by which Hillel attempted to persuade the laborers is reflected in two of his sayings in *Avot* 2:8:

> He who has acquired the words of Torah,
>   has acquired the life of the World-to-Come.

and

> He who increases Torah, increases life.[2]

Hillel was not asking the laborers he spoke to at Jerusalem's gate to cease working; they had to work to support themselves and their families, just as Hillel had done in earning his *tarpik*-coin. But at the end of the day Hillel would offer teaching directed to the common working people in the House of Study; it was that to which he was calling them. And perhaps there would even be some who would be inspired enough to seek to become fully learned in the Torah and, like Hillel himself once, do what was necessary to that end.

What did Hillel teach the laborers he drew to the Torah? An ordinary man who attended his lectures only in the evening would not hear complex halachic interpretation of the legal portions of the Torah, nor memorize the rules deduced, but would learn only practical instruction of the kind evident in Hillel's maxims that guided him gradually to an improvement of his moral and religious conduct. Hillel's teaching was probably based on a full exposition of selected chapters of the Torah, applied to the requirements of daily life and illustrated by the sayings and lives of the biblical heroes and the sages of Israel. By that method he taught a person to avoid everything wrong and sinful and to perform the positive duties of a Jew toward his fellowmen.[3]

BRINGING CLOSE THE FAR–THROUGH PEACE

At the center of Hillel's teaching was love of neighbor and the Golden Rule. Such love always involves charity to the poor and deeds of kindness, but for the religious leader it also means working to return to God those who are "far away," which is why Hillel spoke to the leaders, disciples of Aaron the high priest, about "loving all people and bringing them close to the Torah." The traditional idiom refers to people being nearer or farther away, and bringing people back in repentance to God or to the Torah is called "bringing near, or close, those who are far away."

Hillel and the rabbis saw peace as intimately connected with their approach to those "far away," for peace bridged the gap between the religious and nonreligious. Offering the blessing of peace in greeting to all people, to sinners, to gentiles, was part of this attitude, as in the story of Aaron bringing sinners back to God. Therefore, Hillel's theme-saying speaks of loving and pursuing peace first, as the preparation for bringing people back to the Torah.

Two other rabbinic teachings help us understand how Hillel saw the significance of peace in his work of bringing close those who are far away.

"How important is peace! For it was peace that the Holy One, blessed be He, gave as the means to bring close both proselytes and repentant sinners, as it is said, 'Peace, Peace – to him that is far away and to him that is near' (Isaiah 57:19)."[4]

The Isaiah verse shows God Himself offering the greeting of peace to those far away as well as to those near. The same rabbinic text also states:

"How important is peace! For it precedes even the praise given to God. And so do we find in the Torah (Exodus 18:1–8) that when Jethro visited Moses in the desert, Moses' first words to him were not to give praise to God and tell him about the Exodus from Egypt, or the Ten Commandments, or the splitting of the Red Sea, nor about the manna or the quail; his first words to Jethro were of peace, as it says, 'And they inquired, each of the other, about his peace [this would ordinarily be translated: his welfare]' (Exodus 18:7). Only afterward did Moses speak in praise of God: 'And Moses told his father-in-law about all the great events and the miracles' (Exodus 18:8). Why does peace come before the praise of God? Because peace settles a person's mind and makes him receptive and ready to hear everything else."[5]

The rabbis considered Jethro, Moses' gentile father-in-law, who came to the Jewish People in the desert, the paradigm or "type" of the gentile who came to convert. In the ancient rabbinic writings, almost every detail of the story about him in the Torah is interpreted in this light, and from these interpretations we can learn the rabbis' thoughts about converts and conversion.[6] Telling the potential proselyte of God's miracles for the Jewish people was considered standard practice. But first came peace, in attitude and speech, for it was that which opened the channel of communication, which opened the other person's heart, and began the process of drawing him close. That is why Hillel began with loving and pursuing peace, in order to draw people to the Torah.

CLOSE TO THE TORAH AND UNDER THE WINGS OF THE SHECHINAH

Hillel's theme-saying in *Avot* speaks of bringing people close to the Torah, for the Torah is the means of bringing them close to God. Another, parallel formulation is found in the story of Hillel at the gate of Jerusalem: bringing people close to, or under the wings of, the Divine Presence (the *Shechinah*). This phrase goes back to the biblical story of Ruth's conversion to Judaism. In Ruth 2:12 Boaz praises Ruth for her courage in joining the Jewish people and for her good deeds, and he blesses her, saying: "May a full reward be given you by the Lord God of Israel, *under whose wings you have taken refuge*" (italics added). The rabbis considered Ruth the paradigm of the woman convert, just as Jethro was the paradigm of the man convert. As with the Jethro story, many of the rabbinic interpretations and comments about her story in the Torah express their attitudes and practices with relation to converts and conversion.

The phrase "bringing people under the wings of the Divine Presence" was used for gentiles who converted, but also for alienated Jews who were brought back to Judaism. To bring close those who were far away, to bring them close to the Torah and under the sheltering wings of the *Shechinah*, was Hillel's dream and his work, his labor of love. That the characteristic, traditional rabbinic phrase, "to bring people close to the Torah" or "under the wings of the *Shechinah*," is associated with Hillel is noteworthy. It is found in Hillel's theme-saying, where he expressed his idea of the mission of a leader in Israel, his own mission, and also in the story that shows him doing just that, "all his days," at the gate of Jerusalem.[7]

Since the tradition compared Hillel to Ezra in having reestablished the Torah when it was being forgotten, it is possible that Hillel and his followers popularized this important phrase—of bringing people close to the Torah or under the wings of the

Shechinah–with all that it implies. Similarly, many other typical phrases and characteristic images associated with the missionary movement to return sinners in repentance may have emanated from Hillel and his House, for example, the characteristic phrase warning religious people not to "close the door" in the face of returning and repentant sinners, or the image of God "extending His hand" to reach out to sinners, and so on. Shammai and his House were against Hillel's reaching out to "sinners." One reason that Hillel's teaching has been "lost" in the tradition is that his activity in pursuing alienated Jews and even gentiles has not been seen in its full scope, partly because of historical factors that impeded a Jewish interest in converting gentiles. Consequently, the teachings– Hillel's and others'–that encouraged this outgoing way were largely forgotten.

GATHERING AND SCATTERING

Another saying of Hillel's counsels other teachers (as in his theme-saying) about spreading knowledge of the Torah:

Hillel the Elder said:
When others are gathering, scatter;
And when others are scattering, gather.
When you see that the Torah
  is beloved of Israel and all rejoice in it,
You should scatter it abroad, as it is said,
"There is he who scatters and yet has more" (Proverbs 11:24).
But when you see that no one gives heed to the Torah,
You gather it in, as it is said,
"It is a time to act for the Lord–
  they have made void Your Torah!" (Psalms 119:126)
(*Tosefta Berachot* 7:23, 24).

When people are anxious to learn the Torah, a sage should go out and spread its teachings abroad; but when they are uninterested and unreceptive, he should keep it to himself, for it cannot be forced on people. Moreover, since they do not care to learn the Torah and it is in danger of being forgotten, he should devote himself even more to study and should store up its wisdom until a later time, when once again the people will rejoice in it.

This advice sounds as if it were the product of experience. Perhaps when Hillel was a young man few gave themselves fully to Torah study and the religious life. Hillel later criticized the sages of the Land of Israel for having failed to attend on Shemaya and Avtalyon. But when others of that generation did not receive all that they should have from those great teachers, Hillel did. He fulfilled his own saying: "When others are scattering, gather. When you see that no one heeds the Torah, you gather it in." The verse from Psalms ("It is a time to act for the Lord – they have made void Your Torah!") is a cry of the zealot for love of God. It teaches that although others may ignore or violate the Torah, a pious person should not follow them, but should rededicate himself even more. Hillel himself was willing and ready to "act for the Lord" when others were lax and the Torah was being neglected; later, when his greatness was recognized, he became *Nasi* and restored the Torah to Israel, teaching multitudes.

But more than the sages' tradition of learning needed to be revived and rescued. Many of the common people had fallen away. Some of the sages were not interested; they were willing to let the "sinners" go their own way and be punished. Others were deeply concerned but did not know what to do. Hillel saw the urgency of the situation and his love for Israel would not let him rest. He then fulfilled the other part of his saying: "When others are gathering, scatter!" The common people were now ready to receive, and Hillel knew how to satisfy their thirst for the word of God. The rabbis expressed the mark of true teachers of Torah, such as Hillel, by saying that "More than the calf wants to suck, the cow wants to suckle."

He also encouraged other sages to follow his lead. To those who were reluctant to take time from their own Torah study in order to teach others, fearing that doing so would hamper their own religious development, Hillel quoted Proverbs 11:24 – "There is he who scatters and yet has more." He meant that teaching Torah to others will not decrease a person, but bring a blessing to his Torah knowledge and spiritual life.

In this teaching of his, Hillel used and interpreted a popular proverbial expression that contrasts gathering and scattering and counsels acting contrary to the majority of people. Just on the formal and stylistic level, we can note how Hillel linked the proverb about scattering (when others gather) with the Torah verse about scattering (and having more).

TRY TO BE A MAN

Hillel often encouraged people to differ from the majority, and to act when others were passive. Both as a student and as a teacher Hillel fulfilled the words of another saying of his:

In a place where there are no men, try to be a man!" (*Avot* 2:6).

This heroic saying seems even more special because not only did Hillel act, but he called others to take the lead and be heroes. He brought people back to God and encouraged others to do the same. This sort of attitude and call on the part of a leader produces a movement. Perhaps these words also cast light on why Hillel, who may at first have been reluctant, was willing to replace the Sons of Bathyra as *Nasi*.

Another version of the gather/scatter saying links it to the one just quoted:

Hillel said:
When others are scattering, go indoors!
If no one is buying, buy!
In a place where there are no men, try to be a man! (*Sifre Zutta*
Pinhas 27:1).

This version of the gather/scatter proverb differs somewhat from the other. What has been translated "scattering" and "go indoors" are idioms that literally mean "scatter the foot" and "gather the foot." So the saying, literally, is: "When others are scattering the foot, gather the foot!" The meaning is that when others are fleeing, you should seek safety in your house.[8] Hillel's teaching uses two proverbial phrases – about going indoors when others are scattering[9] and buying when others hold back – that have the same meaning as the English expression "going against the stream," namely, to do the opposite of what others do. The actual teaching, and the application of these proverbs, is Hillel's saying about being "a man" and being ready to do what needs to be done, regardless of others' hesistance.

In the first-quoted teaching (*Tosefta Berachot*), Hillel interprets "gathering" and "scattering" as being about Torah. Here the gathering/ scattering proverb (like the "buying" proverb) requires no specific interpretation of its terms, as it is used merely as a metaphor for acting boldly and differently from others. Its only purpose is to make the saying about being "a man" more pointed. Neither is there any specific application of this teaching to Torah study, although that application would be natural enough, along with a good many others. Hillel used the gather/scatter expression in two quite different ways. Perhaps it was a favorite of his.

ONKELOS

The proverb "If no one is buying, buy!" was originally a counsel of clever trading, but the use to which the Jewish tradition put it can be seen not only in Hillel's teaching but in the following story about the famous gentile convert Onkelos (second century C.E.).

"Onkelos, the nephew of the Roman emperor Hadrian, wanted to convert to Judaism, but was afraid of his [anti-Jewish] uncle's reaction. He went to him and said, 'I want to get involved in commerce.' 'There's nothing to stand in your way,' answered Hadrian. 'Are you lacking gold or silver? My treasuries are open to you.' 'What I want to do,' continued Onkelos, 'is to engage in commerce abroad and become familiar with the ways of different peoples and nations. So I would like your advice, uncle, as to how to accomplish this and become a successful trader.' 'The trick is this,' replied Hadrian. 'When you see any merchandise whose price has gone way down, buy it, for it's sure to go up again later and you'll be able to sell it at a big profit.'

"So Onkelos went to the Land of Israel and began to study Torah. After some time, Rabbi Eliezer and Rabbi Joshua became aware of him. They also saw that his countenance was being transformed and they said to each other, 'Onkelos is truly learning Torah.' When he came to them he asked them many Torah questions and they answered each one.

"After some time, he returned home and his uncle Hadrian,

noticing the change in him, inquired, 'Why do you look so different? What's happened? Have you taken a big loss on your merchandise, or is someone causing you trouble?' 'No, uncle,' replied Onkelos, 'it's not that. And you're my relative; who would dare give me trouble?' Hadrian again asked him, 'Why then does your face look so different?' 'It's because I've learned Torah,' said Onkelos, 'and I've also had myself circumcised.' Hadrian looked at him closely and asked, 'And who told you to do this?' 'It was you who advised me,' said Onkelos. 'When?' demanded Hadrian. 'When I told you I wanted to get involved in commerce,' said Onkelos, 'and you said to me: "When you see any merchandise whose price has gone very low, buy it, because it's certain to go up again." So I searched among all the nations, and I didn't see any nation that had descended more than Israel. And I know that it's certain to rise again, for so says the prophet Isaiah: "Thus says the Lord, the Redeemer of Israel and its Holy One: To the deeply despised, abhorred by the nations, the servant of rulers: Kings shall see you and stand up; princes, and they shall prostrate themselves before you; because of the Lord, who is faithful, the Holy One of Israel, who has chosen you." ' "[10]

The Roman emperor Hadrian viciously persecuted the Jewish people and Judaism. One motif of this story is God's promise that persecuted Israel, brought low by Hadrian, will rise again. Isaiah's words of consolation are spoken to Hadrian himself by his nephew, Onkelos. Onkelos not only converted, but became famous for translating the Five Books of Moses into Greek under the direction of Rabbi Eliezer and Rabbi Joshua. As we noted in connection with the tradition of Shemaya and Avtalyon's descent from Sennaherib, the rabbis took pride in descendants of Israel's oppressors who joined the Jewish people; here, with Onkelos, it is a relative, a nephew of Hadrian. Ironically, Hadrian himself is presented as having "advised" Onkelos to convert.

But our particular interest is seeing that the "advice" to buy the merchandise whose price has fallen the lowest is similar to the proverb used by Hillel: "If no one is buying, buy!" We can imagine that Hillel could have directed his saying, "When others are scattering, go indoors! if no one is buying, buy; where there are no men, try to be a man!" not only to Jews but to gentiles as well. Are the Jewish people held in low esteem? Are only a few gentiles converting and joining them? Don't worry about what others do. Where there are

no men, you be a man. Join the People of God, for if only a few have
the courage, your deed is that more precious in His eyes. Hillel's
movement inspired gentiles also, and he was receptive to those who
came to convert, about which we will see more later. The story
about Onkelos gives us a helpful clue to the context of Hillel's saying
and how he might have used it.

23

A Mission to All Men

We will better understand Hillel's missionary activity by considering some of the aggadic stories the rabbis told about biblical heroes, for those stories express their own values and reflect their own deeds. We earlier discussed how they used Jethro and Ruth as models of converts. In a similar way they used Abraham, Jacob, and Aaron as models for "missionaries" who bring Jews back to the fold and draw converts to Judaism.

ABRAHAM, AARON, AND JACOB

The model in the aggadic tradition for Hillel's mission of "bringing people under the wings of the *Shechinah*" is Abraham. He was held to be the first to have blazed this path. Aaron, the high priest of the Jewish people, was used in legendary stories as a model for bringing back Jews who have strayed. But Abraham, the father of all Jews, was also, as the tradition calls him, the "father" of proselytes[1] and is portrayed bringing gentiles under the wings of the *Shechinah*. Bringing close straying Jews and bringing close gentiles are often (although not always) related: Those who are inclined to be open to one group are often open to the other; and so too with those who are closed. Hillel was open. And behind the many and varied stories in the tradition of how legendary Torah heroes—Abraham, Aaron, and others—brought people under the wings of the *Shechinah*,

125

stand Hillel and his House and his followers in later generations, who poured their own beliefs and ways into these legends.

An ancient rabbinic text explains the phrase of Hillel's theme-saying that we are considering: " 'And bringing them close to the Torah'–How is this to be done? This teaches that a person should urge his fellowmen until he wins them over[2] and causes them to enter under the wings of the *Shechinah*, similar to the way our father Abraham won people over and made them enter under the wings of the *Shechinah*. And not Abraham alone, but Sarah also."[3] Another version explains: "For our father Abraham would proselytize the men, and Sarah would proselytize the women."[4]

Note the teaching that *everyone* should follow Abraham's practice. The rabbis, who used Abraham to represent their own ideals and ways, said that Sarah took the lead among the women, as an equal partner with her husband. The lesson would certainly seem to be that Jewish women should follow Sarah's practice. Were there women in the time of the rabbis who missionized among their sisters? It would seem so, but unfortunately we know nothing about them.

Another important aggadic saying about Jacob clarifies the instruction to "urge" and "win people over":

"Jacob used to 'hunt' men, and bring them under the wings of the *Shechinah*."[5]

This sentence is almost identical in meaning to what is said about Abraham, and "urging people, to win them over," or "hunting" them to bring them under the wings of the *Shechinah* should both be seen as traditional missionary expressions. According to the aggadic tradition, Abraham was the first to have gone out and brought men under the wings of the Divine Presence. What Jacob added, to refine the path blazed by his grandfather, was that he was not only vigorous in pursuit, but especially skillful and clever in his approach to men; he "hunted" them, so to speak.

Hillel himself fits the picture these legends draw of the Torah heroes Abraham and Jacob, for he was determined in his pursuit of his strayed fellow Jews. He would "urge" them, he would "hunt" them, doing everything possible to attract them to the Torah and bring them back under the wings of the *Shechinah*. We can see this "hunting" of men both in the way Hillel went out, in pursuit, into the streets of Jerusalem to draw people in with his persuasive words, and also (as we will discuss farther on) in the clever and subtle way he dealt with those he hoped to lead under the wings of the *Shechinah.*

That Hillel "hunted" or "pursued" the nonreligious can be seen also from what is suggested by the parallelism of the verses in his theme-saying. Line two has *"Loving* peace and *pursuing* peace," line three *"Loving* men" and also *pursuing* them: by going out to those who are *far away* and *"bringing them close* to the Torah." The rabbinic teaching on the second line, about peace, was to go out to the marketplace, where people congregated, to make peace between them; so too the teaching of the third line is also that you are to go to the marketplace or gate of the city, to persuade them to return to God and the Torah. This was Hillel – at the gate of Jerusalem.

TEACH ALL MEN

Hillel and Shammai differed sharply about bringing back strayed Jews and in evaluating the potential of Jews from poor or nonreligious backgrounds. An ancient teaching of the Men of the Great Assembly urges: "Raise up many disciples."[6] The Houses of Hillel and Shammai interpreted this directive of their predecessors very differently regarding the standards for who was eligible to be a disciple:

"Raise up many disciples" – The House of Shammai held: Only teach respectable people – sons of good, religious families and the descendants of such families. The House of Hillel said: Teach all men (*ARN-B*, chap. 4, beg.).

A second, fuller version adds to our understanding:

"Raise up many disciples" – The House of Shammai held: A man should only teach someone who is intelligent and cultured,[7] from a good religious family, and wealthy. The House of Hillel said: Teach all men[8] because many transgressors in Israel were attracted to Torah study and became good people; and some even came to be counted among the perfectly righteous and the *hasidim* (pious) (*ARN-A*, chap. 3, beg.).

Hillel, Shammai, and their followers believed in teaching Torah to the masses of people, although undoubtedly Hillel was more determined to pursue those who did not come on their own to learn. Hillel and Shammai also differed about who was eligible to be a disciple. A person who intended to study Torah intensively[9] had to commit himself to spending most of the day with his teacher or teachers. If he had no wealthy family to support him, how could he hope to learn? The Shammaites did not want to waste time and effort recruiting disciples from among the poor, who would later often be forced to "drop out." They preferred restricting Torah study to the wealthy. Hillel's attitude was different. He had himself been poor, even if it was by choice. He had worked as a day laborer for a meager wage and, probably more than the one time we know about, had been kept out of the House of Study by the doorkeeper, when he could not afford the fee for entrance. It is understandable, then, that he had sympathy for young people from humble backgrounds and appreciated their potential as disciples.

The Shammaites had a similar negative view about youth from "questionable" nonreligious family backgrounds. They did not consider them "good material." They wanted, essentially, to restrict the teaching of Torah not only to the wealthy, but to the children of religious parents. While the Shammaites were only interested in teaching people who were *already* "good" and "respectable" according to their views, the Hillelites were prepared to teach all, with the hope and belief that they would *end up* with good people. The Shammaites had a distinct and noticeable upper-class orientation; Hillel and his House, on the other hand, were with the common people. Hillel was for the many, Shammai for the few.

Hillel was anxious to teach all people, whether rich or poor, Jew or gentile, even "sinners." How could he deny the life-giving Torah to anyone? We saw earlier that Hillel taught the Golden Rule to a gentile, and Akiba, a Hillelite (who had himself once been unlearned and illiterate), taught it to a simple Jew, a donkey driver. These stories are *typical* in nature, not unique. They are not merely single incidents that happened one time and no more. Rather, the single story represents many incidents of the same sort.

Hillel had faith in people and hoped to expand the borders of the religious community. He was inspired by the fact that "many transgressors in Israel were attracted to Torah study and became good people," some even perfectly righteous and *hasidim*. Hillel's goal was to teach Torah to the poor, to the unlearned, and he went out to the streets to draw them into the House of Study. They needed to study Torah with application; a few words from the rabbi about the Golden Rule were not enough. So too did he tell the gentile: "Go and learn!"

24

Three Proselytes

CONTRASTING ATTITUDES

The Talmud in *Shabbat* 31a has three stories that contrast the very different ways Hillel and Shammai received gentiles who were considering conversion. Earlier we quoted only the Hillel part of the Golden Rule story, which is one of the three; in the full text, Shammai appears too.

Our rabbis taught: A person should always be patient and humble like Hillel, and not impatient and irritable like Shammai . . .

A gentile once came to Shammai and asked, "Rabbi, how many Torahs are there?" "We have two," replied Shammai, "the Written Torah and the Oral Torah, which is handed down by word of mouth from generation to generation." The gentile then said, "I can believe in a Written Torah, but I can't accept an Oral Torah. Make me a proselyte, then, but on condition that you teach me only the Written Torah." Shammai spoke to him sharply and told him to leave.

The same man then went to Hillel, who converted him according to his "condition." On the first day of instruction, Hillel began to teach him the Hebrew alphabet, saying, in order, "*Aleph, bet, gimmel, dalet*" and so on. But the next day, when repeating the lesson, he reversed the order of the letters, saying, "*Dalet, gimmel, bet, aleph*." His new student asked in

130

surprise, "Didn't you tell me the opposite order yesterday?" "You're right," answered Hillel, "but if you see that you need to rely on me [and my knowledge of the oral tradition] even for this simple matter [about the Written Torah – the order of the letters of its alphabet], why not also rely on me when I tell you that there is an Oral Torah [in addition to the Written one]?" This gently delivered lesson made its point and the new convert decided to accept the whole Torah, both written and oral.

On another occasion a gentile came to Shammai and said, "I'm ready to convert, but only if you can teach me the whole Torah while I'm standing on one foot." Shammai, hearing this outlandish condition, chased him out the door with the builder's measuring stick he had in his hand. The man then went to Hillel, who converted him and, fulfilling his "condition," taught him: "What is hateful to you, don't do to your fellow-man. That is the whole Torah; the rest is just the commentary. But go now and learn it."

Another time a certain gentile was passing behind a House of Torah Study and overheard a scribe reading to the congregation a verse from the Torah: "And these are the garments that they shall make: a breastplate, an ephod and a robe" (Exodus 28:4). Impressed by the glorious clothes described in the verse, he came into the House of Study as the scribe was finishing, went up to him and asked, "Who are these clothes for?" "For the high priest," replied the scribe. The gentile thought, "I'll go and become a proselyte on condition that they make me the high priest." He went to Shammai and said, "I want to convert, but only on condition that you appoint me high priest." Shammai chased him out of the house with the builder's cubit he was holding.

The man then went to Hillel, who agreed to convert him. But when Hillel began to instruct him, he said, "Is it possible for someone to stand and serve[1] a king if he does not know the court ceremonials? Go then and learn what the duties of the high priest are." The convert went home, began to study the Torah, and reached the verse that says that none but the sons of Aaron may perform the priestly duties: "And anyone else who approaches, in order to perform this service, shall be put to death" (Numbers 3:10). Perplexed, he went and asked his teacher Hillel, "Who is this talking about?" "This applies even to David, the king of Israel," answered Hillel. The convert then went home again and drew the conclusion about himself:[2] "The Israelites are called sons of God, and on account of His love for them He called them 'My son, My first-born, Israel' (Exodus 4:22). If for them such a warning was written: 'And anyone other than the sons of Aaron who approaches shall be put to death,' how much more does this apply to a mere convert like myself, who comes with just his staff and traveling bag?" He went back to Shammai and complained, "Why didn't you explain things to me, instead of just chasing me out? Am I eligible to be a high priest? Isn't it written in the Torah: 'And anyone else who approaches shall be put to death'?!" He then went to Hillel and said, "O patient and gentle Hillel, may blessings come upon you for having brought me under the wings of the Divine Presence!"

Later on, all three proselytes happened to meet in one place and they said, "Shammai's impatience and irritability would have driven us out of this world and the World-to-Come, but Hillel's patience and gentleness brought us under the wings of the Divine Presence!"[3]

"HILLEL'S CONVERTS"

The unifying conclusion at the end, with the proselytes meeting, is almost certainly editorial, added when the three originally independent stories were collected together. A second version of this material (in *Avot d'Rabbi Natan*, chap. 15)[4] has another addition after the story about the gentile's admiration for the high priest's clothes.

It is said that two sons were born to this proselyte. He named one Hillel and the other Gamaliel; and people used to call them "Hillel's converts."

Hillel's grandson was (Rabban) Gamaliel, and that name remained in his family later. Perhaps this convert named one of his sons Gamaliel after Hillel's grandson. It may be, however, that the man named his son after Hillel's father—if Gamaliel was his name, a possibility suggested earlier—honoring Hillel through him.

The proselyte's naming of his two sons relates to the story about Aaron, where the women whose marriages he saved named their baby boys after him. It again shows the connection between the "real life" Hillel and those Aaron stories.

OBSTACLES AND OBJECTIONS

One of the themes that unites the stories of Hillel, Shammai, and the three converts is that attempts to receive gentiles into the fold often encountered obstacles. Some gentiles considering conversion objected to various teachings or practices and occasionally tried to set "conditions" of one sort or another – such as a refusal to accept the authority of the Oral Torah tradition (as in the first story) or a demand to be told the whole Torah in a nutshell without going through the rigor of study (as in the second story). Some teachers, such as Shammai, became impatient with these various objections and conditions; the gentiles' objections became obstacles and objections to converting them. In other cases, rabbis were concerned with the gentiles' motives, which were sometimes less than pure, such as a desire for position and honor (as in the third story).

The gentile's question in the Two Torahs story was perhaps influenced by what he had heard from Sadducean critics of the Pharisees. Whereas the Pharisees assigned the Oral Torah a place side by side with the Written Torah and interpreted the latter accordingly, the Sadducees refused to accept any precept not expressly commanded in the Written Torah.[5] When he asked "Rabbi, how many Torahs are there?" he already had in mind his later objection: "I can believe in a Written Torah, but I can't accept an Oral Torah." Although Shammai gave him the standard Pharisaic answer, that there are two Torahs, one Written and one Oral, the man would not accept it. Josephus reports that as a youth he made trial of the three different sects of his time – Pharisees, Sadducees, and Essenes – to see which he preferred, until he finally settled on the Pharisees.[6] Just as this potential proselyte went to Hillel only after first going to Shammai – both famous Pharisee teachers – he had probably had earlier contact with Sadducees, who prejudiced him against the idea of an Oral Torah. Hillel's calmness in responding to the "Sadducean" objection of this gentile perhaps gives evidence of how he dealt with the Sadducees themselves, not attempting to force his ideas on them, but trying to convert them to the Pharisaic view by gentle persuasion.

Hillel was always patient with potential converts and skill-fully led them forward to greater understanding and a deeper com-mitment. His wise and clever manner of dealing with them was the way he "hunted" people to bring them under the wings of the *Shechinah*. In the Two Torahs story he cleverly reversed the order of the letters of the alphabet from one day to the next to make his point that the student of Torah must rely on his teacher. In the story of The High Priest's Clothes he did not correct the man, nor reject him because of his misguided ambition; he merely suggested a course of study—so the man would discover his own mistake. Hillel always started where the person was and used that to encourage him to further study. He told one man to learn the "commentary" to the Golden Rule, another to learn the duties of the high priest, because "Is it possible for someone to stand and serve a king if he does not know the court ceremonials?"

It might seem perplexing that Hillel said to the gentile who stood on one foot: "Go and learn," rather than "Come and learn with me" (in the story of his proselytizing at the gate of Jerusalem, he said: "Why not come and inherit Torah . . .?"). But actually both are meant, and correct, as we see from the related story of the gentile who wanted to be high priest. Hillel converted him and said: "Go then and learn . . ."—and after studying at his own home, he later returned to his teacher Hillel for further instruction.

Note also, in the story of The High Priest's Clothes, the comparison of the gentile and the high priest, similar to what we saw in the story about Shemaya, Avtalyon, and the high priest, or in the rabbinic saying that a gentile who converts is equal to the high priest himself. Here the potential convert actually wants to be the high priest! According to the rabbis, a gentile who comes to convert should be properly humble. A potential convert's motives were tested, among other things, by telling him of the low state of the Jewish people (in that time). If this deterred him, so be it; but if he said, "I know it, and I'm not worthy of sharing their lot," they received him immediately and converted him.[7] Hillel's potential convert was not interested in humility, but in the full honor of the high priest; that was his condition! Hillel gently deflated him. In fact, once the man realized that not even King David was eligible for the priesthood, he learned humility and applied the lesson to "a mere convert like myself, who comes with his staff and traveling bag." But we have to see a little dose of rabbinic humor in this: the poor gentile coming to convert with just his staff and bag, a pauper with dreams of the rich clothes of the high priest no less! The portrayal of the inquiring gentile – although representing a real tendency in some gentiles who hoped to gain, in status or materially, from their conversion or who were less than humble in recognizing their position as newcomers – is, then, somewhat tongue-in-cheek.

Hillel's sympathetic attitude to these men was perhaps affected by the fact that his own teachers were descendants of gentile converts; that alone would have motivated his kindness to gentiles who were knocking – if only tentatively – on the door and would have made him appreciate that such converts could rise to the greatest heights. His own upbringing in an exile community within a gentile country (Babylonia) might also have made him less ethnocentric and inward-looking.

It is important to understand that these stories collected together in the Talmud are *typical*; there were undoubtedly many more cases like this where Hillel received gentiles and converted them. In fact, that *three* similar stories have been preserved is remarkable. It is a very strong current that casts up three stories of the same kind.

LESSONS

Although, as said before, these stories were certainly originally independent, it is worthwhile looking at the editorial "frame" when considering the lesson or lessons to be derived from them as a group. That frame, provided by the editor who collected the three stories, is made up of the first and last sentences that are, respectively, the introduction and the conclusion. The introductory sentence says to be patient like Hillel and not irritable like Shammai. The conclusion, which is put into the mouths of the three proselytes met together, is the statement that Hillel's patience and gentleness brought them under the wings of the *Shechinah*, while Shammai's opposite personality would have deprived them of that blessing. Two things, then, are highlighted: the contrast between the personal qualities of the two rabbis, Hillel and Shammai, and the effects of their different conduct on potential converts. Although Hillel's admirable personal traits have their own merit, these stories, and their frame, indicate that the *particular* attention given to them, and to Shammai's contrary traits – why these should be imitated and those avoided – is that Hillel's manner draws in gentile converts and Shammai's chases them away. This is another indication of the strong interest that Hillel and his followers (who passed down these stories) had in the conversion of gentiles.

In all three stories the gentiles came to Hillel; he did not seek them out. Contrarily, in the story of his appeal to the Jewish laborers at the gate of Jerusalem and his attempt to draw them to Torah study, he went after them and pursued them. Thus, although we cannot say that Hillel had a mission to proselytize gentiles (as he did to alienated Jews), it is nevertheless likely that he was open to accepting gentile converts and was not shy about appealing to interested gentiles when he came into contact with them.

The Aramaic translated as Hillel's being "patient" and "humble" is only one word, not two. Hillel was an *anvatan*. The basic meaning is a "humble" person, although the specific usage often refers to a humility expressed in patience and gentleness. Similarly, only one word is behind what has been translated as Shammai's being "impatient" or "irritable." Shammai was a *kapdan*, the opposite type to the *anvatan*, not in being prideful, but in being strict, irritable, and impatient with others. Hillel was praised, then, for his humility, and people were told to be like him – because that attitude won converts to Judaism.

The value of humility in attracting converts was also one of the lessons the rabbis drew from the Jethro story, which, as we mentioned earlier, was a focal point for their reflections on converts and conversion. This, for example, is the lesson they learned from Numbers 10:29, which describes how Moses dealt with Jethro:

"God instructed the Israelites to act and speak kindly to those gentiles who came to convert, and to act humbly toward them."[8]

There would be a natural tendency for some Jews to condescend to gentiles who came to convert. But just like the rabbis held that a convert must be humble and consider himself unworthy of joining the Chosen People (like the man who had wanted to be high priest, but finally realized that he had just arrived with only his staff and bag), so must Jews be humble before the person who had the courage, like Abraham the first proselyte, to leave his family and people to join them in their divine mission.

ON CONDITION

In the three proselyte stories in the Talmud (*Shabbat* 31a), Hillel first converts the gentiles, presumably agreeing to their "conditions," and only afterward corrects their views by gentle persuasion. By current standards this procedure is extraordinary. The *Avot d'Rabbi Natan* version has a more expected sequence: Hillel does not seem to accept any condition. He does not first convert the person; he tells him to sit down and brings him around to the correct view; only then (we understand) is the gentile eligible to be converted. This latter scenario follows what came to be the accepted procedure among the rabbis: "A gentile who has committed himself to adhere to all the teachings of the Torah except one–is not received."[9]

We know that at one point, after Hillel and Shammai had passed from the scene, a Shammaite revolt in the decision-making body of the religious community led to the enactment of eighteen measures that, to a great extent, were directed against intermingling with gentiles. Perhaps this ruling was part of that movement, while at an earlier, more open, time, Hillel had indeed been willing, as these stories in the Talmud show, to accept gentiles who came with certain reservations, trusting that over time and through his influence as a teacher, they would fully embrace the generally accepted views and practices of the Jewish people.[10] Shammai and his followers, on the other hand, refused to accept a gentile who had a reservation or "condition." When the stories show Shammai chasing away gentiles who suggested such conditions for their conversion, his response was not simply due to his cantankerous personality, but expressed his position about conversion as reflected in the halachic ruling previously quoted. So too with Hillel. It was not just his gentle nature that led him to accept the converts in the stories, but his position on the requirements for conversion. Since the more restrictive position became the conventional one, it is easy to see how the tradition might have toned down the sort of boldness Hillel exhibited in the stories, first converting the gentile and then persuading him to accept traditional views and practices. This would indicate that the Talmud (*Shabbat* 31a) version is the earlier and more original one. By the minor shift of a detail, removing the "conversion first," the *ARN* version effectively muted a radical aspect of Hillel's approach.

The opening line for the three proselyte stories condemns Shammai for being irritable, a *kapdan*. Hillel himself taught elsewhere:

An irritable person (a *kapdan*) cannot teach (*Avot* 2:6).

Shammai had no patience for the misconceptions of the three gentiles who came to him, and so he was not able to teach them, as could Hillel.

DO NOT SAY WHAT CANNOT BE ACCEPTED

Another saying of Hillel, also directed to teachers of Torah, follows a line of thought similar to the previous quote.

Say not something that cannot be understood, because you think that in the end it will be understood (*Avot* 2:5).

This sentence could also be translated:

Say not something that cannot be *accepted* now, because you think that in the end it will be *accepted.*

This obscure saying has resisted the efforts of commentators, who have offered mostly strained interpretations. But the *ARN* chapter 15 version of the story, where the man sets a condition for his conversion that he be made the high priest, shows that the very thing that Shammai failed to teach with his rebuke, Hillel was able to teach with his patience. These are the relevant parts. First, Shammai's response to the man is:

"Have we no priests or chief priests in Israel, to serve in the high priesthood, that we need to install a mere proselyte like yourself, who just arrived with his staff in hand and his traveling bag slung over his shoulder?!" After rebuking the man for his impudence, Shammai angrily chased him out of the house.

The man rejected Shammai's words, although in fact they were correct. He could not "understand" the point or "accept" the lesson because of his own contrary idea and because of the way it was delivered—as a rebuke. Hillel, on the other hand, went along with the man's false notion of becoming high priest and even began his "training" for the position! But by this means the proselyte arrived at the exact same conclusion – even if by a different argument[11] – as the words of Shammai that did not enter his ears. Compare what is said about him to Shammai's words:

> The proselyte drew a lesson on his own and said to himself: "If ordinary Israelites cannot be priests, how much more does this apply to a mere proselyte like myself, who came to convert with just my traveling bag slung over my shoulder!"

What the man would not accept from Shammai, and probably could not accept at all at that time, he came to see on his own, later, with Hillel's quiet guidance. In a similar way, the story about Aaron said that because Aaron befriended the sinner and did not rebuke him, the man later rebuked himself.[12] Thus, Hillel cautioned Torah teachers against saying things that a person could or would not accept because of where he was at that time: "Say not something that cannot be understood [accepted] now, because you think that in the end it will be understood [accepted]." A teacher was not to justify himself with the claim that "in the end" he'll see that I'm right!

In reflecting on Hillel's thoughtful way of dealing with converts and with students in general, it is evident that he had a holy knack for putting himself in another's place. He taught that the Golden Rule was the essential teaching of the Torah, that you should consider how the other person feels and treat him or her accordingly. As part of loving your neighbor, he taught: "Judge not your fellowman until you put yourself in his place," and view the matter from his perspective. So too as a teacher, and also as a rabbi receiving gentiles who were interested in conversion, he was patient and measured out his teaching according to the abilities and comprehension of his students. He counseled other teachers also to follow that guideline, of saying and teaching only what could be absorbed at the time and not judging students harshly because they are not ready to receive or accept more.

In his saying about "gathering" and "scattering," Hillel advised that when people are attracted to Torah learning, a sage should spread its teaching, but when he sees that they are disinterested, he should not try to force it on them, but should concentrate on his own studies – again, Hillel's sensitivity to what the other person can accept at a particular time.

Hillel's word about not saying what cannot be accepted now has something of a parallel in another teaching of the rabbis that uses similar language:

"Just as it is a *mitzvah* for a person to say a word of instruction or rebuke that *will* be accepted and heeded, so is it a *mitzvah not* to say something that will *not* be accepted."[13]

The final words—"not to say something that will not be accepted"—are very close to the language of Hillel's saying: "Say not something that cannot be accepted now, etc."[14]

SLOW TO REBUKE

The Shammai-type is always quick to judge and quick to "teach" and rebuke others. The Hillel-type is more patient. The rabbinic comparison of Moses and Aaron[15] said that Moses always rebuked the people while Aaron judged them favorably and never said to anyone: "You've sinned!" The Torah ordained the *mitzvah* to correct others when they transgress (Leviticus 19:17), but a sensitive person refrains when he sees his words will be rejected and will serve no purpose; he rarely admonishes others because he sees how frequently it is useless or even counterproductive.[16] A gentle and insightful teacher, such as Hillel, who is aware of how resistant people are to criticism, tends to consider this the usual case and chooses a more patient and indirect approach.

QUICK TO REBUKE

Shammai's alacrity to fulfill the *mitzvah* of rebuke appears in a story that tells how (sometime after Hillel's death?) he once rushed to rebuke Hillel's greatest disciple, Yonatan ben Uzziel.

"*Mishnah*: If someone bequeathed his estate to a stranger, leaving nothing to his children, what he did is done and valid, but the sages are not pleased by it. . . . Our rabbis taught: A certain man, whose children were going in bad ways, bequeathed his whole estate to Yonatan ben Uzziel, who sold a third (to use the money for his own benefit), dedicated a third to the Temple, and returned the remaining third to the dead man's children. When Shammai the Elder was informed of this, he immediately picked up his staff and traveling bag and went to rebuke Yonatan ben Uzziel, for Shammai held that if the deceased willed that his children be cut off, then Ben Uzziel had no right to give them the money. But Yonatan ben Uzziel said to him, 'Shammai! If you think you have the right to nullify what I've sold or what I've dedicated to the Temple, only then can you nullify what I've given to the children; but if I'm the real owner of the estate now, and this is my money, then you can't say a thing about anything I've done!' Hearing these bold words and realizing that he was beaten by the strength of the argument, Shammai exclaimed, 'Ben Uzziel has conquered me with his chutzpah (audacity)! Ben Uzziel has conquered me with his chutzpah!' "[17]

Shammai grabbed his walking stick and traveling bag the moment he heard what had happened and raced to give a rebuke. He wasted no time but quickly "descended" on Yonatan. We can understand from the story that Shammai took the strict position in the matter of the estate money; Hillel and his followers, on the other hand, were more displeased with dissension within a family and were always peacemakers, even after the death of the father. The issue is not important to us in itself, but the story does show Shammai's quickness to rebuke. In passing, we can note that Shammai, when outargued, did, as we can gather from his mock protest, have a sense of humor, and appreciated that the younger sage could stand up to him and match his own fire.

Shammai's rebukes were certainly for the sake of heaven. But Hillel and those like him, being humble, judged others favorably and tried to overlook their sins. They were slow to rebuke and realized that rebuke usually fails to accomplish its goal of improvement. Between Shammai's rebukes, which were for the sake of heaven, and Hillel's way not to rebuke, which was also for the sake of heaven, the tradition decided that Hillel's way was superior.[18]

BRINGING CLOSE VERSUS PUSHING AWAY

There is another valuable lens through which we can view the three proselyte stories contrasting Hillel and Shammai. To use characteristic rabbinic metaphors, they are about "bringing people close" or "pushing them away." Two stories say that Shammai "pushed" (or "chased") the man out of the house with the builder's cubit he had in his hand.[19] To use another rabbinic idiom, Shammai, and those like him, "pushed people away with two hands." Elsewhere the rabbis used the prophet Elisha as the negative example for what *not* to do, for he harshly rejected his erring disciple Gehazi (on whom he inflicted Naaman's leprosy, as a punishment for his greed and lies – 2 Kings 5:27).

"Our rabbis taught: Always let the left hand push away and the right hand draw close, not like Elisha, who pushed away Gehazi with two hands. . . ."[20]

Shammai also is used as a negative example in the stories that compare him with Hillel; he chased the gentiles away with a stick! Actually, it was a builder's measuring stick, from which some commentators have concluded that Shammai's occupation was that of a builder or carpenter. The teaching about Elisha pushing away with two hands says that the proper way is to push someone away with one hand and draw him close with the other. One can indeed understand this method in dealing with disciples or potential converts[21]; but in actuality, just as Elisha (and Shammai) pushed away with two hands, *Hillel drew people in with two hands.*[22]

GOD THE KING VERSUS HIS ANGELIC COURTIERS

The clue to understanding the attitude of Hillel and his camp, who wanted to bring Jews back in repentance and draw in gentiles, is found in the little aggadic stories they told about *God's* attitude to their missionary work. (Remember how the beliefs of the Hillelites and their successors were reflected in the legends they told of the "missionary work" of Abraham, Jacob, and Aaron.) Typically, in these stories, God's "hand is outstretched" to receive in open welcome those who seek to return to Him. He always wants the "door open," as another proverbial expression puts it, and objects to those who "close the door" in the face of repentant sinners who seek to approach Him. The angels, however, are portrayed as cantankerously protesting God's leniency. They are unhappy at any deviation from strict justice: Sinners must be punished; no repentance or forgiveness! Somewhat comically (this is part of the rabbis' sense of humor) they "close the windows" of the Heavenly Palace, so God will not hear the prayers of repentant sinners. To provide a way for repentance, God has to dig a hole below the Throne of Glory(!), creating a hidden passage out of sight of His own obstructionist "courtiers" – so sinners, like thieves stealing into the Palace, can reach him.

We cannot fully analyze this marvelous legendary scene, but the angels represent God's Attribute of Judgment (some stories have the Attribute of Judgment, rather than the angels, complaining), while God Himself represents the Attribute of Mercy. *Both* the king (called God) and the courtiers (called angels) represent different aspects of God. The rabbis made Mercy the "king" or God, and Judgment the "courtiers" or angels, *because* they believed that Mercy *overrules* Judgment, like a king who considers the opinion of his courtiers, but decrees according to his own view. From another perspective, the protestations of the angels represent the complaints of the strictly righteous, such as Shammai, who objected to what they perceived as the overly lenient attitudes of rabbis such as Hillel to those not "adequately" religious. The Hillelites, who told these stories, believed that the Shammaite opinion, which was unsympathetic to returning sinners and gentiles, *had* some weight in heaven, but that ultimately God's inner will accorded with their way of mercy and compassion. The angels' negativity – closing doors, shutting windows – reflects Elisha's pushing away with two hands and Shammai's pushing away with the builder's cubit. God's opening doors, digging secret tunnels, stretching out His hand to receive repentant sinners and gentiles reflects how Hillel and his camp drew people in with two hands. Compare this rabbinic teaching:

"The sages taught in the *Mishnah*: When a gentile comes to convert, a hand is stretched out to him, to bring him in under the wings of the *Shechinah*."[23]

The outstretched hand of God in the legendary stories was in "real life" the hand of the rabbis like Hillel, who taught: Love all people, and bring them under the wings of the *Shechinah*. Hillel himself pulled people in, off the streets, with "two hands." Why then did the tradition quoted earlier say that the proper way was "one hand pushes away, the other draws in"? There is no question that this is a wise teaching with many applications to disciples and potential converts, and it is not contradictory to "pulling in with two hands," as may seem on the surface. Similar proverbs should not be naively compared. But it seems that whereas Shammai "pushed away with two hands" and Hillel "brought close with two hands," the middle way became the traditional position for two reasons: first, historical conditions caused Hillel's openness and welcome to gentiles to be almost entirely discontinued; second, in an almost graphic sense, "one hand pushing away/one hand drawing in" (itself certainly an independent and ancient proverbial image) struck a compromise between the contrary positions of Hillel and Shammai. This is an example of the merging of the ways of Hillel and Shammai – mentioned at the beginning of this book – that tends to obscure the picture we have of Hillel's own practice, of loving people and drawing them, not with one hand but with two hands, to the Torah.[24]

25

Receive All Men

The three stories of Hillel's and Shammai's encounters with the gentiles who came to convert show the contrasting ways they *received* people. "Receive" (קבל) is a key traditional term in teachings about a person's relations with others. It applies to everything from the way a person reacts in a chance meeting on the street, to receiving a guest into his home, or to a rabbi's receiving someone who comes to ask him a question or a gentile who comes to convert – as with Hillel and Shammai. All these behaviors are included in this broad term. Investigating the rabbinic teachings about receiving others will give us a fuller understanding of the meaning of the stories of Hillel and the gentiles.

What is remarkable is that the tradition's most basic saying about this subject is in the name of Shammai: "Shammai used to say: . . . Receive all men with a cheerful countenance."[1]

Clearly, this is the exact opposite of the way Shammai is portrayed in the trio of stories about the potential converts! One could argue that the Hillelites have exaggerated in their stories the roughness of their adversary Shammai,[2] or that Shammai was teaching about a quality he valued, but that eluded him in practice. Or perhaps he started off rough and "learned his lesson" later.[3] But although any of these suggestions might be correct, another explanation of the anomaly, that the saying about "receiving all men" is in Shammai's name, is that this attribution is simply a (somewhat shocking) mistaken attribution of a Hillel saying to his opposite number.[4] "Receiving people cheerfully" is, after all, the way *Hillel* is portrayed in the three stories with the gentiles (and elsewhere[5]), which teach how to *receive* gentiles who are interested in converting, so as to bring them to God. And in fact a *midrash* promotes receiving people warmly and cheerfully as the proper missionary attitude, speaking of the person "who receives people with a cheerful countenance and brings them under the wings of the *Shechinah.*"[6]

This indeed was Hillel's ideal and goal, what he is shown doing in the three stories with the gentiles. If we insisted on maintaining that the saying about "receiving all men with a cheerful countenance" was from Shammai and that he learned his lesson later in life, we might have to say that he learned it from Hillel! Being open and warm in receiving others would seem to be a trait that belongs with Hillel and his camp; it is just another side of the emphasis the Hillelite rabbis put on the greeting of peace.

Much can be learned about Hillel's warm reception of gentiles from the aggadic stories and teachings on this subject. We noted earlier how Jethro, the gentile father-in-law of Moses, was, in the rabbinic literature, the paradigm of the gentile who comes to convert. A *midrash* describes how Jethro was received when he came to the Jewish people in the Sinai desert and a feast was given to honor him: " 'And Aaron came with all the Elders of Israel to feast with Moses' father-in-law before God' (Exodus 18:12). But was it 'before God' that they ate? It was before Jethro! From this we learn that he who receives his fellowman is as if receiving the Divine Presence."[7] Thus, although Jethro was "only" a gentile who came to convert, that is, someone "small," all the great men of Israel went to give him honor; and receiving him was like receiving the Divine Presence.

Thus far about Aaron and the Elders; the other relevant *midrash* on this verse (Exodus 18:12) is about Moses: "And Aaron came with all the Elders of Israel to feast with Moses' father-in-law before God" (Exodus 18:12). But where did Moses go? Why is he not mentioned? Didn't he go out to meet Jethro at first, as it is said: 'And Moses went out to meet his father-in-law' (Exodus 18:7)? Now where did he go? This teaches that he was standing and serving at table while the others sat and feasted; that is why he is not mentioned as feasting with the others.

"And from whom did he learn this behavior? From our father Abraham . . . [who is an example of the greater man serving lesser men, for it was taught]: 'Our father Abraham was the greatest in the world, yet he served the angels [who came to visit], even though he thought they were just ordinary men, and idol-worshiping Arabs at that!' "[8]

Aaron, Moses, and all the great men of Israel went out to *receive* Jethro, the gentile who came to convert. And the greatest of the great, Moses himself, who was "very humble, more so than anyone on the face of the whole earth," did even more, he stood, as a servant, and served the others, while they sat at table, Jethro at the head. Moses is said to have learned that from Abraham, who received the three angels warmly and also served them a meal. The rabbis taught that these angels had appeared to him in the guise of the lowliest of men – idol-worshiping Arab nomads. Abraham, the rabbis tell us, made it his regular practice to receive gentiles and serve them at table, in order to win them to belief in the One God and convert them to Judaism (of course he did not convert the angels!). The story of Jethro and Moses has the same point: to receive even gentiles, like Jethro, treating them with kindness and humility, so as to lead them under the wings of the Divine Presence.

This is the background to understand Hillel's warm reception of the gentiles, whom he later converted. And, as they often do, these aggadic stories about Aaron, Moses, and Abraham represent the rabbis' depiction of their own ideals. There is no question, however, that much about Hillel's way of dealing with potential converts and the true significance of these aggadic stories has been lost in the tradition.

This concludes our discussion of Hillel's "theme-saying." I hope the reader agrees that there was more to it than might have appeared at first sight.

III

The Hasidic Personality

26

Hillel's Personality

The introductory line to the three proselyte stories contrasts Hillel and Shammai, one being a stern, irritable person (a *kapdan*) and the other a gentle, patient, and humble person (an *anvatan*). That the tradition so clearly holds up a great rabbi as a bad example, that "a person should . . . never be an irritable type, a *kapdan*, like Shammai" is somewhat surprising in itself. And the stories do put him in a poor light. But the critical attitude probably has its roots in Hillel's own view of his comrade. Hillel said that "an irritable person cannot teach" (*Avot* 2:6). Whom was he talking about if not Shammai and those like him?[1]

Hillel, who wanted to bring close those who were far away, had to train himself to be gentle and patient and to receive people with warmth. He could not allow himself to be irritable, the kind of person from whom people fled if they were not chased away beforehand. He could not be easy to anger as Shammai so obviously was (that is one meaning of being a *kapdan*); although, of course, Hillel did not conquer anger only to advance his missionary purposes, as, by itself, it is an extremely bad trait and poison to spirituality.

THE 400 ZUZ BET

The rabbis taught: "Do not be easy to anger" (*Avot* 2:15) and, to illustrate their teaching, cited the following story that presents Hillel as the model of the calm person who is hard to anger.[2]

151

Our rabbis taught: "A person should always be patient and humble like Hillel. . . ."[3]

Two men once made a bet of four hundred *zuz* (a large sum of money) about whether one of them could make Hillel lose his temper. The one who said he could do it then went off to try. He worked out his plan and went to Hillel's house in the late afternoon on Friday before the Sabbath, when everyone was busiest in preparation for the holy day of rest. When he arrived at the door, Hillel was washing his hair, as people customarily bathe and clean themselves thoroughly in honor of the Sabbath.[4] The man banged on the door[5] and called out, "Is Hillel here? Is Hillel here?"

Hillel wrapped himself in his cloak and came out to him. "My son," he said, "how can I help you?'

"I have a question to ask," was the man's reply.

"Ask, my son, ask," said Hillel.

"I want to know," he said, "why are the heads of the Babylonians so round?"

"My son, that is a very important question. The reason is that they don't have well-trained midwives there."

The man went away and waited for a while until Hillel had returned to his hairwashing, then he came back and called out again loudly, "Is Hillel here? Is Hillel here?"

Hillel again wrapped his cloak around him and came out to speak with him. "My son, how can I help you?"

"I have a question to ask," the man replied.

"Ask, my son, ask," said Hillel.

"Why are the people of Tadmor (a Syrian desert city)[6] so weak-eyed?"

"You've asked a very important question, my son," said Hillel. "The reason is that they live in such a sandy country and the sand gets in their eyes."

The man went away and waited for a while until Hillel had returned to his interrupted hairwashing, then he came back and banged on the door once more, shouting, "Is Hillel here? Is Hillel here?"

Hillel once again wrapped his cloak around him and came out to speak with him. "My son, how can I help you?"

"I have a question to ask," the man replied, "but I'm afraid you might become angry with me."

Hillel drew his cloak around him, sat down before him, and said, "All the questions that you want to ask, please ask."

Seeing his plans frustrated, the man cried out, "Are you the Hillel that everyone calls the '*Nasi*' the 'Prince' of Israel?"

"Yes," answered Hillel.

"If so," the other blurted out in exasperation, "then may there not be many like you in Israel!"

"Why is that, my son?" asked Hillel.

"Because of you," said the man, "I've just lost a bet—of four hundred *zuz*—that I could get you angry!"

"Calm yourself," said Hillel. "It's better that you lose four hundred *zuz* and still another four hundred *zuz* than that Hillel should lose his temper" (*Shabbat* 31a).

Since the men actually *bet* on being able to upset Hillel, it seems that even during his lifetime his calmness and humility were already legendary. People believed that *nothing* could anger him. There must have been numerous instances where his patience had been tested and found unshakable. This story is only the most extreme example, and unique, because in this case the test was planned.

Rabbis were ideally at all times at the disposal of those who had questions to ask them. A story tells how when Rabbi Simon ben Gamaliel (Hillel's great-grandson) and Rabbi Ishmael were about to be martyred by a Roman executioner, they were searching their deeds to see if any sin of theirs could have brought this punishment on them by heavenly decree. They certainly had not committed any major sins, but they were willing to accept the judgment of God for what others would consider very slight transgressions. One rabbi asked his friend: "Did a woman ever come to ask you a question about her purification, or a man, to ask about his vow—and you didn't receive them because you were sleeping, or in the middle of a meal, or occupied with something else, or perhaps the servant would not permit them to enter?" The other answered: "Whether I was asleep or having a meal, the servant had an order never to stop anyone from coming in to see me."[7] When the man in the 400 *Zuz* Bet story came to Hillel's house, the situation was similar to what is described here, with the same meaning.

These two men had made a high wager. An average day laborer earned only one or two *dinars* a day, and Hillel himself, in his poverty, had earned half a *dinar*. These fellows were casually betting four hundred *dinars* (a *dinar* was equal to a *zuz*[8]) – about a year's wage for a working man – although the loser was upset enough about his loss. The two were obviously members of the wealthy upper class. Their attitude was, to begin with, one of aristocratic disrespect for this great religious leader.[9] Probably Hillel's famous humility and patience "inspired" these two wealthy idlers to devise a novel way of amusing themselves.

In his plan to annoy Hillel, the man chose the time when Hillel would be most preoccupied, when he was making his religious preparations for the Sabbath. And being interrupted in the middle of washing your hair is certainly calculated to upset a person. In another version (*ARN-B*, chap. 29) he disturbs Hillel not before the Sabbath, but at night, when he is sleeping, and wakes him a number of times. This parallels a detail of what one rabbi asked the other in the text previously quoted – whether anyone had ever been kept from asking him a question of religious law because he was sleeping.

The man who came to provoke Hillel shouts loudly and rudely from the street in a way hardly befitting a request to see someone of Hillel's stature; and instead of going in, he forces the great man to come out to him. Rather than asking an urgent religious[10] or even practical question, he asks Hillel about matters of little consequence, questions of mere curiosity; and considering the circumstances in which they are asked, his questions are stupid and foolish altogether.

In his first attempt he pokes fun at Hillel's own origin as a Babylonian Jew. Presumably, his question about the round heads of Babylonian Jews (it would seem that the reference to "Babylonians" means as elsewhere "Babylonian Jews") was intended to provoke Hillel's anger by insulting his background and also by indirectly calling attention to how his shampoo had been interrupted. Perhaps the man had improvised this question when he saw that Hillel's head was wet or had been wrapped unusually, as he had just been washing his hair. In the story of Hillel's ascent to the office of *Nasi*, we saw that Hillel had been uncharacteristically aroused to anger by prejudice against Babylonian Jews.

When the man's first attempt fails to make Hillel angry he does not continue asking questions, but leaves and returns, and thereafter does so a number of times, waiting each time until Hillel has gone back to his shampoo! This still does not work, so he informs Hillel that he has "many more questions," hoping that this open-ended request at such an inopportune time will strain even

Hillel's patience; and he tries to nudge things in that direction (while also revealing what is on his own mind) by "innocently" mentioning his fear that all this might cause Hillel to become angry.[11]

But just as the man outdoes himself in provocation, Hillel excels in patience and humility. Each time Hillel interrupts what he is doing and goes out to speak with him. Although he is the "Prince" (*Nasi*) of Israel, he disregards his own honor; his thought is only to serve. Hillel was certainly aware (one would think) of the man's lack of consideration, but he judged him in the scale of merit. If to him these were "important questions," so were they to Hillel. He speaks to him gently, always calling him "my son," and is very solicitous of his needs, encouraging him to ask his questions. He responds to each question by first praising its "importance." And when the man says at the end that he has "many questions," Hillel shows respect for the religious exchange between rabbi and questioner – and that he is not at all rushing away – by adjusting his cloak and sitting down patiently to make himself comfortable.

A Talmud[12] story tells that Rabban Gamaliel II (a descendant of Hillel and himself *Nasi*), when traveling in Israel from Akko to K'zibh, was asked by a man to dissolve a vow that he had taken. "Rabban Gamaliel then dismounted from his donkey, wrapped himself in his cloak, sat down, and dissolved the vow." Elsewhere, the Talmud[13] similarly describes the actions of Rabban Yohanan ben Zakkai, Hillel's disciple, when he was about to hear a disciple of his discourse on the most profound religious subject. He "dismounted his donkey, wrapped himself in his cloak and sat down," explaining his action by saying that the *Shechinah* itself would be present when such things are spoke of. Thus, Hillel treated the man's questions with the utmost respect.

But when Hillel, with supreme patience, invites him to ask whatever he would like and as many questions as he would like, the man finally bursts out with the "question": "Are you the one whom they call the *Nasi* of Israel?" – and with his wish that there not be more like him! A rabbinic story tells of an arrogant rabbi who rudely insulted an ugly man about his looks. The man did not know that the person abusing him was a rabbi, but when he later heard others calling him that, he said to them: "If that is a rabbi, may there not be more like him in Israel!"[14] Ironically, Hillel got the same rebuke, not for proving unworthy, but because he was so *very* worthy! The man's final "question," asking if Hillel was the one everyone called the *Nasi*, shows that his shouting out "Is Hillel here?" without any title had been a calculated insult.

Not only was Hillel himself calm, but he calmed the man, who became upset at seeing the money of his large bet drifting away. He came to make Hillel lose his temper, but before that happened, he lost his own. There is a touch of humor in this reversal, where the one who came to provoke Hillel's anger becomes angry, and "prays" that there not be more saints like him! Finally, after being told about the bet, Hillel concludes by explaining to him that it is preferable that he lose even twice what he had bet than that Hillel lose his temper.

The conjunction of four hundred *zuz* and the possibility of Hillel losing his temper is not fortuitous. In fact, the sum of four hundred *zuz* was a typical legal fine for losing your temper and physically humiliating another person.[15] "Calm, calm is worth four hundred *zuz*" became a proverb.[16] Hillel's telling the man that it is better that he lose even double his four hundred *zuz* than that Hillel lose his temper is probably an allusion to this proverb, although in a roundabout way, for Hillel's calmness was not saving him from an expensive fine, but was losing the rash bettor his large sum of money.

We see in this story how Hillel responded to "foolish" questions – not foolish in themselves, but in their contexts. The three proselyte stories similarly showed his patient response to foolish requests. Hillel taught: "An irritable person cannot teach," together with its paired saying:

A shy person [afraid to ask questions] cannot learn (*Avot* 2: 6).

These related teachings complement each other, and a talmudic version combines them in its lesson to a rabbi or a teacher: "Don't be irritable, so that someone will not be able to ask you a question" (*Kallah* 3). Hillel obviously believed that no question was to be rejected out-of-hand as stupid or foolish, and no simple person was to be embarrassed or discouraged from feeling he could approach and ask whatever he pleased. It was not only a pedagogical matter, however, for certainly Hillel was loath to embarrass and humiliate anyone by showing contempt for his question.

As to the actual questions and answers in this story, we saw earlier[17] that the tradition claimed for Hillel the very broadest knowledge, with no area of learning uncovered. That the questioner in this story would presume (even with his peculiar motives) to ask Hillel questions of natural history shows that such topics were considered to be within the range of his learning. In fact, Hillel answered the questions, demonstrating a scientific appreciation of the adaptation of a creature to its environment. The text of *Soferim* 16:9 said that Hillel had learned "even the speech of mountains, hills, and valleys, the speech of trees and grasses, the speech of wild and domestic animals." Y. L. Katznelson[18] made the interesting suggestion that this means (or originally meant?) that Hillel gave *talks on* mountains, hills, and valleys, that is, on natural geography, and also on botany and zoology ("the speech of plants and animals"). The questions and answers of the 400 *Zuz* Bet story indeed support this view. Note that Hillel's answers show his detailed knowledge of natural geography, the conditions of different habitats, and so on. In a second version[19] he exhibits expertise in biology, the first question he answers being why cows have long tails and donkeys have short ones. Hillel's answers about localized human physical traits (the round heads of Babylonians, the weak eyes of Tarmodians, the wide feet of Africans) and their adaptive value similarly demonstrate his biological expertise. His wide-ranging interest in scientific matters and in the diversity of nature certainly says something about the type of person Hillel was and about his open-minded intelligence.

HUMILITY

Rabbi Yitzhak of Vorki, a great hasidic *rebbe*, made a beautiful comment on this story about Hillel. He said:

"We have learned: 'Our rabbis taught: A person should always be humble like Hillel . . .' [He then went on to recount the story of The 400 *Zuz* Bet that illustrates these words and posed a question to his listeners:] The story shows that Hillel did not become angry and was not annoyed at the man. But where is the humility of which the teaching speaks?

"The rabbi asked the question, and also answered it: 'A proud man, who thinks he is greater than his fellow, sees his own doings as more important than the other man's. Therefore, when the other person comes to him, or speaks to him, he says arrogantly: "I have

no time; I'm completely engrossed with matters much more important than your concerns." On the other hand, the humble man, the
lowly man, looks on his fellow as someone greater than himself;
consequently, he sees the other's doings as more important than his
own. Therefore, how can he refuse him when he comes to see him?
Is it conceivable that the hewer of wood will tell the king, who has
just come and interrupted him in the middle of his work: "I have no
time to talk to you"? So Hillel, who put aside everything else in
order to listen attentively to the man who came to bother him, did
indeed prove his great humility. . . . He did not even think of putting
him off by saying nicely: "Please come after the Sabbath." Why?
Because of his great humility.' "[20]

Hillel was indeed renowned as a humble man, and we can get
further insight into what that actually meant from two other related
teachings, one early rabbinic and one hasidic. The first, a rabbinic
teaching, is about Rabbi Judah the Prince (Nasi), a sixth-generation
descendant of Hillel, who was simply called "our Rabbi":

Our Rabbi was very, very humble. He used to say: "Anything
that anyone tells me to do, I do – except for what the Sons of
Bathyra did for my ancestor Hillel, removing themselves from
their high position and elevating him to be Nasi" (Genesis
Rabbah 33:3).

This descendant of Hillel excelled in just that trait for which his
illustrious ancestor was famed: He was a very humble man. That
Rabbi Judah put his words in direct connection with his ancestor
Hillel indicates that we can rely on his understanding of what is
implied by designating someone a "humble man" (the word anvatan
is used both with Hillel and with Rabbi Judah). The traditions about
Hillel were surely passed down in his family. The most humble
attitude he expresses, of doing what others want and negating one's
own will, is just what is meant by the rabbinic saying: "Nullify your
own will before the will of your fellowmen."[21] This saying belongs
with and is followed[22] by: "Nullify your will before the will of
God."

Elsewhere,[23] a version of this latter teaching is found in the
name of Rabbi Judah the Prince. It is likely then that the former
teaching is his also and that what he held to for himself, as seen in
his remark about doing what others want, is what he taught to
others: to be humble and to nullify your will before that of your

fellowmen. Is that not exactly what Hillel is shown doing in the story of The 400 *Zuz* Bet? Doesn't he do what the other man wants, negating his own will? Doesn't he even consider the other man's foolishness, which Hillel calls "an important question," greater than his own preparation for the holy Sabbath?

Further help in understanding the significance of Hillel's designation as a "humble man" comes from a teaching of the hasidic *rebbe*, Rabbi Rafael of Bershad, who took Hillel's saying about Aaron as his own personal ideal.[24] A hasidic book reports:

"Rabbi Rafael once spoke for a long while on . . . how after a man's death, when he comes before the Heavenly Court for judgment, he will be asked: 'Did you study the Torah and do kind deeds? Did you proclaim your Creator as your king, morning and evening, by reciting the *Shema* (the "Hear O Israel")? And did you proclaim your fellowman as your king, by treating him with the utmost gentleness and by always trying to please him?' If a person has these qualities his judgment will be favorable. And Rabbi Rafael spent some time emphasizing this, that you should treat your fellowman as if he were your king, always treating him with gentleness and making every effort not to act contrary to his will."[25]

Rabbi Rafael expresses the same thought as in the previously quoted teachings: that a person should do the will of God and the will of his fellowmen; and he uses the same metaphor of the king as did the Vorker Rebbe in his parable of how a hewer of wood would not dare tell the king, "I have no time to talk to you." These various related traditions from Hillel's descendant, Rabbi Judah the Prince, and from the two hasidic *rebbes*, the Vorker and the Bershader, help us understand an aspect of what it meant that Hillel was praised as a "humble man." We will have more to say about Hillel's humility in later chapters.

27

Hillel the Hasid

O HASID!

An essential clue to understanding Hillel is to realize that *he was a hasid.*[1] The tradition has preserved a single line from the eulogy delivered at his funeral – obviously its theme – that contains three characterizations of him:

O *hasid*! O humble man! – disciple of Ezra! (*Sanhedrin* 11a).

Hillel, then, was identified by his contemporaries as a *hasid*. That was also his own ideal, as can be gathered from this teaching of his:

An *am-haaretz* (ignorant person) cannot be a *hasid* (*Avot* 2:6).

We will discuss this teaching later in the chapter.

Just as Hillel's theme-saying served as a framework for an extended discussion in the first section of this book, the eulogy describing him as a *hasid*, humble man, and disciple of Ezra will in a loose way serve as a framework for the next section, with each of its three parts considered in turn. First, for a number of chapters, we will consider the designation "*hasid*."

MEANINGS OF HASID

What is a *hasid*? Most simply it means "a pious person." Although the term has come to be associated with the adherents of

the Baal Shem Tov's hasidic movement that began in the eighteenth
century, it still retains its original and broader meaning of a particular
Jewish religious type, namely, someone deeply religious who goes
beyond the ordinary or conventional standards and does "more." But
matters are complicated by the fact that even the generic term *hasid*
is used in two somewhat different ways. On the one hand, a *hasid* is
a person of extreme piety. But piety can be of two kinds: motivated
primarily by love or by fear. (Although "fear" of God actually denotes
awe and reverence, we will use the conventional translation.) So
another usage of the word *hasid*, actually the more common one,
refers exclusively to the hasid whose piety is from love. This kind of
hasid loves not only God but people; he includes humanity in his
devotion to God. Hillel was a *hasid* in both senses of the term: he was
not only extremely pious, but kind and loving to people.

By emphasizing Hillel's hasidism, our point is not to claim
that that characterization alone adequately describes him or that he
fit every detail of the type, but that his being a *hasid* goes a long way
in explaining his religious personality. We should also note that in
our discussion we will not always be able to indicate which of the
two generic usages of the term *"hasid"* is intended; although usually
we will use it in the second sense, of the *hasid* from love, the reader
will have to determine this from the context.

HASID *VERSUS* PARUSH

But what about the other kind of piety motivated by fear of
God? The pious person whose main motive is fear can be called a
"hasid" by the first definition – since he does "more" – but not by the
second. As suggested, the difference appears in his relation to other
people, for he often concentrates on devotion to God and ritual and
neglects his fellowmen, particularly those outside his religious circle.
Such a *"hasid"* is usually called by another term, more specific to
this particular Jewish religious type: He is a *parush* (pl. *parushim*).
While Hillel was a *hasid* in the full sense, Shammai, his comrade-
adversary, was a *parush*. Although from one point of view the
extremely pious *parush*, such as Shammai, is a *"hasid,"* from another
point of view he is the exact opposite of the *hasid* from love, because
whereas the latter is distinguished by his love for people, the *parush*
is distinguished by his separation from those he considers sinful or

irreligious, according to his strict standards. A *parush*, a "separatist" literally, is someone who separates not only from worldliness and from sin, but also from sinners and gentiles.

In the common English transliteration, a *parush* is a "Pharisee," but that word has been given an unfortunately negative connotation by Christian anti-Semitism. Moreover, the "Pharisees" was the name of an influential religious faction – to which both Hillel and Shammai belonged – during the time of the Second Temple; but the religious type, which gave its name to the party, not the reverse, is not restricted to members of that faction (or to that particular time period).

It is important to understand these opposed types of *hasid* and *parush*, and especially the *hasid*, to fully understand Hillel's personality and character and what he represents in the tradition. To that end, as we proceed, we will consider a number of general teachings that deal with this matter.

LOVE AND FEAR; HESED AND GEVURAH

Hillel, then, was a *hasid* and Shammai a *parush*. These are both essential types in the fabric of Judaism; both are fully part of the tradition and of its self-understanding also. The tradition, in fact, often expresses itself in such dualities. For example, the rabbis distinguish between the two main religious motives and teach that a person should act from both love and fear of God.[2] But while the mainstream tradition typically demands a balance of the two motives, it firmly asserts the superiority and preeminence of love.[3] Since the *hasid* acts from love, he is usually recognized as representing a higher spiritual level than the *parush*, who acts from fear. (These characterizations of the motives of *hasid* and *parush*, and other such generalizations, are intended as broad strokes. There are no "pure" types and a religious Jew will always have a necessary mix of the two motives.) However, different levels of both these motives and the interactions between them complicate matters. For example, fear of God can be a lower fear of punishment or a higher devotional fear. The fear of the *parush*, for example, is based in love. The *parush* is a *hasid* in being extremely pious; but his love for God is expressed mainly through fear, in reverence and awe.

The dual motives of love (*ahavah*) and fear (*yirah*) parallel the dual cosmic spiritual principles of *Hesed* and *Gevurah* – Love and

Strength. *Hesed* is love or kindness (the words *hesed* and *hasid* are cognates); *gevurah*, more difficult to translate, is strength, rigor, severity, strictness. The *hasid* inclines to *hesed*, the *parush* to *gevurah*. Hillel, who emphasized divine service from love, was a *hasid* and leaned to the side of *hesed*.

DOING "MORE"

We have spoken about the two usages of *"hasid"* – for someone extremely pious or, more specifically, for someone whose piety is motivated by love. Let us consider some texts that relate to Hillel's hasidism in the first sense, of going beyond conventional religiosity and doing "more."

One Extra Time

Bar He He[4] said to Hillel[5]: "What is the meaning of the verse 'Then you shall look again and see the difference between a righteous man and a wicked man, between one who serves God and one who serves Him not' (Malachi 3:18)? Why the repetition? Is not the righteous man the same as one who serves God, and the wicked man the same as one who serves Him not?"

Hillel answered [interpreting the verse differently from its simple meaning]: "The one who serves God and the one who 'does not' serve Him are really both completely righteous people. But you cannot compare someone who repeats his Torah lesson one hundred times to someone who repeats it one hundred and one times."

"Is it just because of that one time that a person is called one who does not serve God?" exclaimed Bar He He.

"Go and learn from the station of the donkey drivers," replied Hillel. "It costs one *zuz* to hire an animal for ten miles, but to hire it for eleven miles – just one extra mile – you pay two *zuzim*" (*Hagigah* 9b).

Hillel's point was that true service of God always seeks to go further, to give that extra effort "with all your might" – which is how the Torah says to love God (Deuteronomy 6:5). When a person reaches his limit, that one extra time may require as much effort of strength and will as all that went before. That was how Hillel overcame the obstacle he once faced, of having no money to gain entrance to the House of Study. The "extra" is the whole thing; it is the sign of the *hasid*. Both persons described in the Malachi verse are righteous, but one is more: he is a *hasid*, and compared to his service of God, the other "serves not."

Two other rabbinic teachings, which use very similar language to that of Hillel here, provide the context to understand his words. They show that Hillel's teaching is just one specific example of a larger concept. First, Hillel says that the two people referred to in the verse are completely righteous. The Talmud teaches that "Greater is he who serves God from love than he who serves from fear,"[6] and tells how Rabba compared two of his disciples, saying to them: "The two of you are completely righteous, but you from love and you from fear." This closely parallels Hillel's thought and language and helps clarify his meaning.

Hillel continued his explanation, saying: "You cannot compare someone who repeats his lesson one hundred times to someone who repeats it one hundred and one times." Another rabbinic text states, in words that parallel Hillel's: "You cannot compare someone who serves from love with someone who serves from fear."[7] Thus, Hillel's answer to Bar He He means that the extra effort in study is the sign of a *hasid* who serves from love, and that his service is incomparably greater than that of someone who serves from fear.[8] Hillel's remark also provides us with insight into his evaluation of those religious people who served from love versus those who served from fear. Although the latter were indeed righteous and servants of God, compared to the *hasidim* they were hardly servants at all; it was as if they "served not."

Hillel's lesson was not limited to his example about Torah study; it applied to all service of God, and the one hundred versus the one hundred and one times was largely figurative. But not entirely so. As we have discussed previously, Torah study in those days was mostly oral, and memorizing traditions by verbal repetition was as important as the original hearing from the master. This repetition was itself a service of devotion, and a student expressed his love of God by repeating his lessons even more than the usual large number of times, until he was absolutely certain they were committed to memory.

Up or Down – No Standing Still

Another saying of Hillel is similar to his teaching to Bar He He about doing "more." He said:

He who does not increase, will decrease (*Avot* 1:13).

This typically hasidic saying reflects a spiritual master's perception of the inherent dynamism in the life of the soul, that one cannot stand still spiritually: one either rises or falls.[9] The person who seeks to rise higher and higher and increase more and more is the *hasid*. The great hasidic teacher, of the movement of the Baal Shem Tov, the Yehudi, said: "If a person sees that today he is on the same level in his service of God as on the previous day, with no advance or improvement, he should know for certain that not only is *that* the case, but he has indeed *fallen* from his rung, and that his level of service today is lower than the day before. Because spiritually . . . a person cannot stand still; he moves, and it is either one way or the other."[10] Essentially, these words just explain the significance of Hillel's saying, that he who does not increase, will decrease.

Great Lengths

Hillel explained the significance of one extra repetition of a person's Torah lesson by telling Bar He He to learn from the donkey drivers: After ten miles they doubled the price for a single extra mile. Another story reports a bantering conversation between Hillel and a donkey driver, who tongue-in-cheek told the renowned teacher, "I am better than you."

A donkey driver once came up to Hillel and jokingly said to him, "Rabbi, look how I'm superior to you! You had to trouble yourself to travel the long distance from Babylonia to Jerusalem. But as for me, I just walk out the door of my house and I'm here; I almost sleep at the very gate of Jerusalem!"

Hillel was silent and paused for a moment before answering the man.[11] Then he asked, "How much will you charge me to hire your donkey to travel from here to Emmaus?"

"A *dinar*," said the donkey driver.

"And until Lud?"

"For that, two *dinars*."

"And until Caesarea? How much?"

"Three."

"I see," said Hillel, "that as I increase the distance, you increase the price."[12]

"Yes, that's right," the man agreed, "the payment is according to the length of the trip."

"If that is the case," said Hillel, "is not the payment and reward for *my* leg-work – all the way from Babylonia! – equal to that of your donkey?" And that is how Hillel fulfilled the saying: "According to the painstaking is the reward"[13] (*ARN-B*, chap. 27; a *dinar* was equal to a *zuz*).

In this story the donkey driver teases Hillel about his "superiority" over the great man in being a home-grown Jerusalemite, whereas Hillel is just a Babylonian. Hillel appreciated the donkey driver's amusing chutzpah and returned the joke, but he humbly avoided answering in a way that would humiliate the donkey driver, a lowly workingman, by asserting his own status as a great rabbi. So he made his point in a self-disparaging manner. We can imagine him answering with a smile, as if to say, "Yes, but I'm at least as good as your donkey, aren't I?" The man jokingly claimed to be superior to Hillel, but Hillel's answer did not assert – even humorously – his superiority, only that he would be rewarded for his efforts. By comparing his "legwork" to that of the donkey's, it is clear that Hillel had not traveled the long distance from Babylonia to Israel by riding in a coach or on an animal, but by walking.

Using his wit and humor, Hillel defeated his friend with a winning answer; but there is a real lesson in that answer also. The editor of the story notes at the end how Hillel fulfilled the proverb "According to the painstaking is the reward." Elsewhere, this proverb is attributed to Hillel.[14] The rabbis taught that even the seemingly insignificant conversation of Torah sages should be studied, for everything they say is informed by holy wisdom. That, indeed, is why this story about Hillel's casual conversation with the donkey driver, and his quip, was preserved. Hillel's point was that in divine service the easiest way is not always best. It is often the hard way that should be chosen. In the example he gave to Bar He He, the effort that goes beyond conventional limits is the sign of love and of the *hasid;* here, in his conversation with the donkey driver, his example of, literally, going to "great lengths" is the sign of the *hasid.* One reason the young Hillel rejected his brother's offer of monetary assistance was that those who love God should not seek to avoid hardship in their divine service, for overcoming difficulties has a corresponding spiritual reward. That same lesson, taught here, is also why he was willing to travel all the way to Jerusalem to study Torah, for according to the painstaking is the reward.

MORE TORAH

As noted at the beginning of this chapter, Hillel's hasidic ideal can be seen from his teaching:

An *am-haaretz* cannot be a *hasid* (*Avot* 2:6).

An *am-haaretz* is deficient in Torah knowledge, and a *hasid* most perfectly fulfills God's will. Hillel says that these two qualities – one a deficiency, the other a perfection – cannot go together. A person cannot be pious, doing "more" of God's will, if he has not learned "more" Torah, for the Torah explains what His will is. Hillel certainly valued not only love, but also fear of God; this saying is found together with its companion, and the full teaching is:

An unlearned man cannot be a sin-fearing man,
And an *am-haaretz* cannot be a *hasid.*

The *hasid* represents the side of love, and the sin-fearing person the side of fear. Torah brings one to both love and fear of God. Hillel, who emphasized love more than fear, was a *hasid.* But although a *hasid* fears sin and separates from sin, he differs from the *parush* in not separating from sinners. Hillel, like his model Aaron, wanted to befriend sinners and bring them to God; he went toward, not away from them. As we saw, the Hillelite position was to "teach all men," because through Torah many transgressors had become not only perfectly righteous, but even *hasidim.* That was the goal for Hillel and his followers: to become *hasidim.* But an unlearned *am-haaretz,* even if he was piously inclined, could not rise to the high level of being a *hasid*; for that, total immersion in the Torah life was required. How far can a person advance in doing the will of God in its fullness, if he does not know what that involves?

Bor *and* Am-haaretz

The rabbinic literature contains various opinions about the definitions of the *bor* (translated here as "an unlearned man") and the *am-haaretz* in Hillel's saying. We cannot be exactly sure of Hillel's meaning, or if he intended to differentiate between the two terms at all; perhaps he was using them only as approximate synonyms for a person lacking Torah knowledge. "*Am-haaretz*" is a term broad enough to be used sometimes for religious people of limited Torah education and other times for antireligious people of the worst and lowest sort (in Hillel's saying the former is clearly intended).[15] Yet the term "*bor*" generally describes a lower level than an *am-haaretz*, someone not only ignorant, but crude and uncouth.[16] Since the sin-fearing person is inferior to the *hasid* (serving God from fear being a lower level than serving from love), it may be that the *bor* is intended to be inferior to the *am-haaretz*.

Errors of an Am-haaretz

A parable in an ancient rabbinic text explains Hillel's saying that "An unlearned man cannot be a sin-fearing man." Since both the saying and the parable are anonymous there, it is not impossible that the latter, like the former, is from Hillel.

"An unlearned man cannot be a sin-fearing man. A parable is told about this. To what can it be compared? To a king who tells his servant – who has never cooked in his life – to cook him a meal. The end result is that the servant ruins the food and angers his master. Or the king tells his servant – who has never folded a cloak in his life – to make the proper fold. The end result is that the cloak becomes dirty because the servant folded it wrong and he angers his master."[17]

Although the servant has all the good intentions to fulfill the command of his master, the king, he hasn't the slightest idea how to go about it. That is also the case with someone who wants to serve the King of the Universe. Therefore, an unlearned man cannot be truly sin fearing. Even if he is pious and has all the good intentions in the world, he will inevitably make regrettable and unfortunate mistakes, since he lacks the guidance of the Torah's wisdom.

This parable about the servant being unable to properly serve the king because he does not know how to cook or to fold a cloak is remarkably similar to a parable Hillel used to encourage one of the three proselytes to study Torah, saying: "Is it possible for someone to stand and serve a king if he does not know the court ceremonials?" The similarity between the two parables and their applications – that to be sin fearing and truly serve God, a person must study and know the Torah – suggests the possibility that Hillel was the author not only of the one parable but of the other also.

Hillel's claim then is that Torah knowledge is indispensable to achieving higher attainments in the true service of God, to be sin fearing, or even more, a *hasid*. A rabbinic story tells of Rabban Yohanan ben Zakkai's encounter with a priest who was attempting to be a *hasid* by fulfilling his priestly obligations to the fullest degree. He failed, however, because he lacked Torah knowledge. Not having attended on the sages, he made serious errors in his ritual conduct.[18] The story, which is cited in connection with Hillel's saying: "He who does not attend upon the sages deserves death," illustrates the kind of mistake an *am-haaretz* can make and why he cannot be a *hasid*.

Another story that illustrates the same saying of Hillel tells of a mistake Rabbi Akiba made before he was a rabbi, when he had just become religious and had not yet attended on the sages and learned Torah as a full disciple; he was still an *am-haaretz*. His mistake was in dealing with a *meit mitzvah*, the obligation a person has to bury a dead body he finds, for which no one else is responsible. Rabbi Akiba tells the story in his own words, and at the end states Hillel's saying without attribution:

"Rabbi Akiba said: 'This is how I began to attend on the sages: I was once on my way somewhere, and came across a dead body on the road. I lifted it up and carried it for four miles, until I reached a cemetery and buried the man. When I came to the House of Study and told Rabbi Eliezer and Rabbi Joshua what had happened to me, they said, "Each and every step you took carrying that body is as bad as if you had spilled innocent blood. You should have buried him on the spot." I said to myself then, "If I'm guilty of wrongdoing when I intended to do a good deed, how much more so when I don't have good intentions!" From then on I didn't budge from attendance on the sages.' And so Rabbi Akiba used to say: 'He who does not attend upon the sages deserves death.' "[19]

At that time, Akiba was still an unlearned am-haaretz; and certainly in carrying the corpse for four miles he was trying to be a hasid! Yet–he was mistaken. Why? Presumably because one honored a dead person by burying him where he lay, not by "dragging" him to a cemetery.[20]

Hillel's teaching that an am-haaretz cannot be a hasid means that piety and good intentions are not enough, for an am-haaretz inevitably makes mistakes that contradict the will of God. But these mistakes that prevent him from being a hasid are not all simply mistakes in ritual (as with the priest) or even in nuances of ethical conduct (as with Akiba). An important teaching in Avot 5:13 gives an illustration of a more serious kind of mistake an am-haaretz can commit:

There are four characters among people:
He who says "What is mine is mine and what is your is yours"
    is an average character. Some say, though, that this is
    a character like that of the people of Sodom;
He who says "What is mine is yours and what is yours is
    mine" is an am-haaretz;
He who says "What is mine is yours and what is
    yours is yours" is a hasid;
He who says "What is mine is mine and what is yours is mine"
    is a wicked person.

The am-haaretz in this saying believes that "what is mine is yours and what is yours is mine." This is the kind of person who uses the property and possessions of others without permission, and thinks himself justified because he would not mind if they used his possessions. Such a person may even imagine himself a hasid, because he gives freely of his own. The real hasid, however, says "What is mine is yours and what is yours is yours." He gives but does not take; nor does he expect anything in return. This is another, more serious "mistake" that an am-haaretz can make, and another example of why, according to Hillel, "An am-haaretz cannot be a hasid."

28

A Hasid *from Love*

In the previous chapter we saw that Hillel was a *hasid* in being extremely pious, and doing "more." He was also a *hasid* in the fuller sense of extending his love not only to God, but to people. We have learned much about this already, for everything concerning Hillel has been peace, love, humility, gentleness, and patience.

ANCIENT DEFINITIONS

Two connected sayings in *Pirke Avot* (5:13, 5:14) contain what are perhaps the most important rabbinic teachings on the nature of a *hasid* from love.[1] They are: (1) that a *hasid* is hard to anger and easy to appease; and (2) that he gives freely, without expecting anything in return. Hillel fits both these definitions. As for the first, here is the full teaching:

There are four kinds of temperament:
He whom it is easy to anger and easy to appease,
    his loss disappears in his gain;
He whom it is hard to anger and hard to appease,
    his gain disappears in his loss;
He whom it is hard to anger and easy to appease
    is a *hasid*;
He whom it is easy to anger and hard to appease
    is a wicked person.[2]

171

The ideal character, the person hard to anger and easy to appease, is called a *hasid*. As we saw earlier, the rabbis considered Hillel the model of patience, and used the 400 *Zuz* Bet story to illustrate their teaching, "Do not be easy to anger."[3] The stories of how he received the gentiles who came to convert also demonstrated Hillel's legendary patience. Perhaps he was so hard to anger that his being "easy to appease" was rarely tested.

MINE AND YOURS

The second teaching in *Avot* 5 about the nature of the *hasid* was discussed briefly at the end of the previous chapter, but there we focused on its reference to a "mistake" of an *am-haaretz*:

There are four characters among people:
He who says "What is mine is mine and what is yours is yours"
  is an average character. Some say, though, that this is a
  character like that of the people of Sodom;
He who says "What is mine is yours and what is yours is
  mine" is an *am-haaretz*;
He who says "What is mine is yours and what is
  yours is yours" is a *hasid*;
He who says "What is mine is mine and what is yours is mine"
  is a wicked person.[4]

We can associate Hillel with this hasidic attitude, that "what is mine is yours and what is yours is yours," for he taught[5]:

What is mine is not mine. What need have I of what belongs to others?[6] (*ARN-B*, chap. 27).

This is very close, in thought and language, to the "saying" of the *hasid* in the other teaching.

To understand Hillel's words fully, let us consider the general significance of the teaching in *Avot* 5:13 about "mine" and "yours." First, note that it has the same form as *Avot* 5:14 (about whether a person is easy or difficult to anger or appease). The ideal character in this teaching about different attitudes to possessions is, like in the other about temperaments, the *hasid*. Both sayings are certainly ancient traditions – handed down from the *hasidim* of early times. In fact, that the *hasid* is slow to anger and quickly appeased and that his attitude is "what is mine is yours and what is yours is yours" are probably the two most important teachings in the older tradition about the character of the *hasid*. And both provide excellent insight into the character and beliefs of Hillel.

The *hasid* has, through love of God and man, dissolved the barriers of the ego, of "me and mine": thus, Hillel's famous humility, which was the source of his mild temperament and the reason he could not easily be angered or offended.[7] In place of a "me and mine" attitude, pious people see everything as belonging to God, all "possessions" are His. The rabbis taught:

"Give Him what is His, for you and what is yours are His."[8]

Once a person has this hasidic attitude he does not fasten onto his possessions; giving to others is easy. His view is expressed in the rabbinic teaching:

"Say: 'Not with what is mine have I given to others and helped them, but with what God has given to me.' "[9]

The *hasid* gives freely of his own and does not covet what belongs to others.[10] As Hillel taught, his thought is: "What is mine is not mine. What need have I of what belongs to others?"[11] As *Avot* 5:13 explained, the *hasid*, unlike the *am-haaretz*, gives but does not take; he not only maintains that "what is mine is yours," but also that "what is yours is yours." Undoubtedly, Hillel fulfilled his own teaching, which describes the *hasid's* attitude to possessions. Although it is easy to intellectually analyze such concepts, let the reader pause to consider what kind of person Hillel was, to be able to say, mean, and fulfill: "what is mine is not mine."

The *hasid's* nonpossessive personality comes from his love for God and people. What *Avot* 5:13 expresses in "static" form, about attitudes to property, "mine and yours," is taught elsewhere, in "dynamic" form, in terms of the *hasid's* active and overflowing love and kindness. The *hasid*, like God, is "merciful and giving," he gives freely to all, expecting no return.[12]

The significance of the paired teachings in *Avot* 5:13 and 5:14, which define the *hasid's* mild temperament and nonpossessive attitude, is that both can be connected to Hillel – one through the 400 *Zuz* Bet story and the other through a similar teaching of his – to support our evaluation of him not only as a *hasid*, but as a *hasid* from love.

29

The Hasid *and* Hesed

KIND EVEN TO ONESELF

Hillel, as a *hasid*, had a vision of holiness different from that of his *parush* comrades, such as Shammai. He sought a holiness that infused everyday life rather than separated from it, and that was expressed in kindness – to others and even to oneself – rather than in self-denial. A story about Hillel instructing his disciples illustrates his hasidic view.

"Let all your deeds be for the sake of heaven" – like Hillel. Once when Hillel left to go somewhere, his disciples asked him, "Where are you going?"

"I'm going to do a *mitzvah*," he answered.

"What *mitzvah*, Hillel?"

"I'm going to the bathroom."

"Is *that* a *mitzvah*?" came the astonished reply.

"Yes, it is," he said, "for it's a *mitzvah* to see that the body is not brought to harm."

Another time, they asked him, "Where are you going, Hillel?"

"I'm going to do a *mitzvah*."

"What *mitzvah*, Hillel?"

"I'm going to the bathhouse."

"But is that a *mitzvah*?" they asked.

174

"Yes," he said, "for it's a *mitzvah* to keep one's body clean. And I'll tell you why this is so. Consider the statues of famous men that stand in the palaces of [gentile] kings: The person put in charge of cleaning and polishing them is well paid by the government; not only is he given a good yearly salary, but his work is prestigious enough that he is considered fit to mix with the great and powerful in society. How much more then will we be rewarded for cleaning and caring for our bodies, for we have been created in the image and likeness of God Himself, as it is said: 'for in the image of God did He make the man' " (Genesis 9:6) (*ARN-B*, chap. 30).

Hillel and other *hasidim* were particularly interested in Torah verses that spoke of *hesed*. We discussed earlier the Hillelites' interpretation of "abundant in *hesed*" in Exodus 34:6–that God, in judgment, inclines to the side of mercy. A second version of the Hillel story quoted here is linked with a Torah verse about *hesed*, kindness, Proverbs 11:17: "The man who acts for the good of his soul is a man of *hesed*" (*gomeil nafsho ish hesed*). This verse, which is not used in the other version, speaks of the character of a "man of *hesed*," that is, a *hasid*, and Hillel stories are cited for illustration. Note in what follows that the verse has been variously translated in different instances according to how it is understood in the accompanying teaching. It has been translated here as: "A kind man is. . . ."

"A kind man is kind even to himself and his own body" (Proverbs 11:17)–like Hillel.

[This is followed by the story of Hillel saying that going to the bathhouse is a *mitzvah* (without the parallel about the bathroom) and his parable of the statues. Here they are statues of kings and compared to humans made in the image of the King of the Universe. The text continues:]

Another interpretation of "A kind man is kind to his soul" (Proverbs 11:17)–this refers to someone like Hillel, for once when he was walking with his disciples and took leave of them, they asked him, "Rabbi, where are you going?"
"To show some kindness to my house guest," he replied.

"After this was repeated for a number of days in succession and he gave this same answer each time, they were perplexed and asked, "Do you have a guest in your house *every* day?"

"Is not this poor soul of mine a guest within my body," he replied, "for it is here today, and gone tomorrow" (*Leviticus Rabbah* 34:3).

In the other, *ARN-B*, version, the stories of Hillel going to the bathhouse to wash or to the bathroom to relieve himself illustrate and explain the introductory saying–"Let all your deeds be for the sake of heaven." Both parts are about Hillel going to do a *mitzvah*– a deed for the sake of heaven–and both are about the body. (We can remark in passing that the rabbis held that delaying going to the bathroom, when necessary, is harmful to the body and to a person's health.) Elsewhere it is said about Hillel in just these words, that "all his deeds were for sake of heaven."[1] This was also exactly how he praised his wife when she delayed bringing in the meal for the guest (having given it to a poor man), telling her he did not judge her, because he knew that all her deeds were for the sake of heaven.[2]

The disciples were surprised, but their master taught them that a person must know God in *all* his ways, not only during Torah study and prayer, when doing "religious" things, but even when eating, taking a bath, or relieving himself: Every act is to be a *mitzvah*, a deed for the sake of heaven, a fulfillment of the will of God. The examples in the two stories are about the body, because the point is that doing the will of God is even connected with care of the body and bodily necessities, even those–as in the examples–that were not generally held in the highest esteem.

In the stories of Hillel going to the bathroom and bathhouse, we can note first the simple fact of his concern with care of the body and with cleanliness. In the 400 *Zuz* Bet story he was shampooing his hair at home in honor of the oncoming Sabbath. To bathe, he went to the public bathhouse. Otherwise, Hillel considered attention to bodily cleanliness as being a part of one's service of God and as showing honor to the image of God. An anonymous rabbinic teaching states: "A person should wash his face, hands, and feet every day for the honor due to his Creator, as it says: 'For His own sake did the Lord create every thing' (Proverbs 6:14)."[3] Cleanliness has many spiritual aspects (since physical cleanliness conduces to spiritual "cleanliness"), and Hillel's motives were probably complex. But his expressed motive – about caring for the body for God's honor and because it is in His image – as well as the parable of the statues, suggests that his attitude was that – like all else – his body did not belong to him, but to God. To encourage proper regard for the body as a religious value, Hillel noted the unusually large salary and prestige of the superintendent of statues and suggested that a person's care for his body is favored by God and carries with it a great spiritual reward – meaning that when such activity is done with the appropriate intention and consciousness, it leads to spiritual advancement.

Hillel might have seen such "non-Jewish" statues in one of the theaters, circuses (for chariot races), or public bathhouses built by Herod.[4] Reflecting on the meticulous care they were given and the prestige of their caretaker, he created a parable to teach about caring for the human body, which is in the image of God.

Hillel's parable about the statues and its lesson show his appreciation for the teaching that humans are made in the image of God. The Torah says: "you shall love your neighbor *as yourself*" – a person must love himself, since he too is made in the image of God. Hillel's point was not that the body itself is in the image of God (who is incorporeal), but that a person's soul is in God's image, and the body must be honored because it is the "seat" of the soul. Essentially, the concepts of the image of God and the human soul are referring to the same thing.

Hillel's humanism, his view that other people and even a person's own self are made in the image of God, is the sign of a *hasid*, so too is his emphasis on *all* a person's deeds – even bodily ones – being performed for the sake of God. The *parush*, less sympathetic to the divinity of man, also finds worldly and bodily activities distracting necessities.

The Hillel stories in this text show what was meant by attending on a sage. Since Hillel's every action was for the sake of heaven, his disciples tried to observe everything he did and how he did it, so they too could learn. Here, by accompanying Hillel as he left the House of Study and questioning him about his actions, they learned their teacher's religious motives – even when he went to the bathhouse or bathroom.

The *ARN-B* version of this text has the double story about Hillel going to the bathroom and bathhouse and his parable about the statues. The *Leviticus Rabbah* version has only about the bath-house and the parable, and then a second story (not found in the other version) of a similar kind. Buchler remarks about this other story, where time after time Hillel says to his disciples that he is leaving to do a kindness for his house guest, that it gives us "very interesting information about Hillel's method of teaching."[5] What undoubtedly impressed him was that Hillel intentionally persisted in making this statement to them, until he had succeeded in arousing their curiosity, so that they would question him about it.

When Hillel said each time that he was "going to do a kindness (*hesed*) for the house guest," his soul, what that was in any particular instance is not stated,[6] but his intention was exactly the same as when he said at other times: "I'm going to do a *mitzvah*." Every deed should be a *mitzvah*, and every *mitzvah* is a kindness to the soul and benefits the soul (and sometimes also the body).

Hillel took human mortality seriously, in a way that moti-vated him to do deeds that had eternal value. He was always aware of the purpose for which his soul had come down to earth, as a "guest," and what he must accomplish before it returned to its true home. Since he did this *hesed* to the soul day after day, we can imagine that he was referring to the many kinds of *mitzvot* and good deeds he did continually.

Hillel's remark to his disciples, about doing *hesed* to his "house guest," the soul, links to the verse that the editor connected with these stories – Proverbs 11:17 – that speaks of a "man of *hesed*" who is kind to his soul. The original meaning of the Proverbs verse was probably: "A man kind to others is, by that, caring for his own soul." But the teaching associated with the Hillel stories understands it differently, and in more than one way, and it has been translated above according to how it was understood in the various contexts.

In the *Leviticus Rabbah* version of the text, where the verse introduces each of the pair of stories, it seems that the two stories represent two different interpretations of the Proverbs verse, with each understanding the Hebrew word *nafsho* according to one of its two meanings: as "himself" or "his soul." The first story is about caring for the body, and the verse is understood as "one who is kind (even) *to himself* (*nafsho*)," the thought being primarily of the body, and the teaching, that a person should care for his own body (by bathing and so on). The second story is about doing a kindness for the "house guest," the soul, and the verse is understood as "one who is kind *to his soul* (*nafsho*)," the thought being primarily of the soul, and the teaching, that a person should do good to his soul by serving God.[7] The editor who joined these two related stories – about Hillel going to the bathhouse and about the "poor guest" – and connected them with the Proverbs verse about the "man of *hesed*," correctly saw that Hillel's kindness to both body and soul was typically hasidic.

THE SOUL AS A GUEST

The simile of the soul as a guest in the body was popular in Hillel's time, not only among Jews, but among the Romans.[8] In one variation on this theme, the soul was conceived not as a guest in a house or inn, but as imprisoned within the body. According to Josephus, the Essenes held that people's souls "are united to their bodies as to prisons . . . but when they are set free from the bonds of the flesh (by death), they then, as released from a long bondage, rejoice, and mount upward."[9]

The ascetic Essenes saw the body as a prison, an uncongenial habitation for the soul. The more moderate and life-affirming Pharisee Hillel saw it as a "temporary home," where the soul is a somewhat uncomfortable "guest." When Hillel spoke of the "poor" soul, he probably meant that although the body provided poor "lodging," the heavenly soul is still able to receive "good hospitality" if a person is righteous and cares for it properly.

BETTER TO HAVE BEEN CREATED?

A tradition relates that the Schools of Hillel and Shammai argued for two and a half years whether or not it was good for a person to have been created. The Hillelites said it is better for a person to have been created, the Shammaites that it is better not to have been created.[10] The sin-fearing Shammaites were pessimistic. Acutely aware of the countless temptations people face in this world, they believed that the great majority of them were destined to sin and would be severely punished for it in *Gehinnom* (hell). Therefore, it was better for them not to have been created at all. The Hillelites, on the other hand, having a more benign and charitable attitude to the world and to people, said it was better to have been created.

Although Hillel had an optimistic view of life, he was perhaps influenced somewhat by the contrary perspective, in speaking of the "poor" soul dwelling as a guest in the body. But when we consider his positive attitude to the body in the related story (with its parable about the statues), it would seem incorrect to take his words about the "poor" soul as reflecting particularly and negatively on the body. His intention was probably more general: that being sent down to this world from its heavenly abode was not an unmitigated benefit for the soul, and its immersion in materiality involved dangers.

TWO KINDS OF HOLINESS

Leviticus Rabbah introduced each of its pair of Hillel stories with Proverbs 11:17 – "A kind man [a man of *hesed*, a *hasid*] is. . . ." A talmudic discussion that uses this same Proverbs verse clarifies the hasidic relevance of the Hillel stories. In a dispute about asceticism and fasting, one side argues that a person who fasts and denies himself (beyond what the Torah enjoins) "is called holy," the other side that he "is called a sinner." Resh Lakish, taking the latter position, adds that a person who not only refrains from fasting, but treats his body with care, "is called a *hasid*" – and he bases his claim on the same verse as that found with the Hillel stories – Proverbs 11:17.[11]

"Resh Lakish said: He is called a *hasid*, as it is said: 'A kind man is kind even to himself and his own body' (Proverbs 11:17)."

This verse is understood and used in the same way as in the Hillel stories. But it is important to see that this argument in the Talmud is part of the larger one between the *hasid* and *parush*. The *parushim* held that the person who fasts, who denies himself and separates from worldly enjoyment "is called holy." One of the main rabbinic interpretations of the Torah's exhortation to "be holy," is "be a *parush*." The theme of the Torah portion *Kedoshim* in the Book of Leviticus is holiness: It begins (19:1, 2) and ends (20:26) with a command to be holy and has another in the middle (20:7). (The Torah is divided into weekly, named portions, read in a yearly cycle on successive Sabbaths in the synagogue.) An ancient rabbinic commentary on Leviticus has these words on the first and last of the three commands:

> On 19:2 – "Be holy" – be *parushim*.
> On 20:26 – "And you shall be holy unto Me, for I the Lord am holy" –
>   As I am holy, so must you be holy;
>   as I am *parush* (separated), so must you be *parushim*.[12]

The Torah's command – to be holy because God is holy – is the source of the concept of the imitation of God. Shammai and other *parushim* believed that just as God is separated from this world's materiality, so should the holy man be separated. This attempt to imitate God's exalted spirituality inspired their asceticism and fasting.

But while the *parushim* interpreted the essence of holiness as: "Be a *parush*," Hillel and other *hasidim* understood it differently, as: "Be a *hasid*."[13] The same rabbinic commentary that has the *parush* interpretation has another that reflects the hasidic side of the argument:

"Abba Shaul said: How should a king's retinue behave? – They should imitate the king."[14]

As the King's "retinue," Israel must imitate God's ways. We know from the Talmud, more specifically what Abba Shaul (mid-second century) held to be the true fulfillment of this *mitzvah*. Interpreting Exodus 15:2, he taught:

"Be like Him: as He is giving and merciful, so must you be giving and merciful."[15]

This is ancient hasidic teaching, not something originated by Abba Shaul.[16] According to the *hasidim*, the command to imitate God's holiness means primarily that people should be merciful and giving (gracious), imitating His Thirteen Attributes of Mercy[17] and following the ways of *hesed*.

The *parushim*, in awe and reverence, saw God as separated, high above this world, and imitated Him by separating from worldliness. The *hasidim*, however, felt His presence close to men. According to their view, the Divine Presence infuses the world and is the source of all goodness. All their religious activity was directed to becoming aware of that presence.[18] And just as God's holiness infused the world, so did they attempt to imitate Him by engagement in the world, not by separating from it.

While one side in the rabbinic dispute saw the goal of being holy fulfilled by being a *parush*, by fasting[19] and by depriving oneself, the other side opposed asceticism. Their conception of the ideal holy man was the *hasid*, who is giving and merciful and who imitates God in acts of *hesed*. They not only disapproved of excessive fasting and self-deprivation, but taught that a person should be kind even to himself and should care for his body. Thus, in the talmudic argument about fasting, where one side claimed that a person who fasts "is called holy," their ideal being the holiness of a *parush*; the other side, represented by Resh Lakish, was not only against fasting – calling the person who fasts a sinner – but said that the person who cares well for his body is "called a *hasid*." Their ideal was the holiness of a *hasid*. The latter ideal was that of Hillel, who cared for his body by bathing and so on. Proverbs 11:17, appearing in both places, helped us see the link between Resh Lakish's[20] words in the talmudic argument about fasting[21] and the stories about Hillel. Therefore, Hillel's teaching to be kind to the body is not only hasidic in itself, but reflects a broader hasidic view of holiness as compassion and kindness.

HILLEL VERSUS SHAMMAI ABOUT THE BODY

In one version of the Hillel stories (where Hillel says that going to the bathroom and bathhouse are *mitzvot*) the teaching ends with a line (that we left out earlier) about Shammai's attitude to caring for one's body:

> Shammai taught differently from Hillel. He used to say: "Let's just do our obligations to this body" (*ARN-B*, chap. 30).

The talmudic argument about asceticism[22] is the same as the argument between Hillel and Shammai and goes back to them. Shammai's ascetic attitude, to give only grudging respect to the body, was the way of the *parushim*; the nonascetic, happier attitude of Hillel, to have mercy even on one's own self and body, was the way of the *hasidim.* While remaining within the bounds of the Torah's essential moderation, the *parushim* separated themselves from this world's pleasures[23]: fasting and self-denial were a major part of their path to holiness. We will see later that, contrary to the prevailing view, Shammai wanted even his little boy to fast on Yom Kippur.[24] The religious debate over how to treat the body is certainly ancient. For the sake of God and His service, should a person merely give the body its due–as Shammai taught–and otherwise neglect it, despise it, and wear it out roughly? Or should he regard it as belonging to God, the "house" of his soul, which is made in the image of God– as Hillel taught–and treat it with honor, care, and kindness? This argument between Hillel and Shammai, being for the sake of heaven, has not ceased over the centuries; it still continues. The Baal Shem Tov, the founder of the hasidic movement of more modern times, was, in the same way as Hillel, opposed to the fasting and other ascetic excesses of the *parushim* of his day.[25]

Although asceticism has a rightful place in Judaism, the settled judgment of the tradition is with Hillel's hasidic view, that kindness extends even to oneself and that the body is not to be despised, but to be honored.

A Different Way

CONTRASTS IN HOLINESS

Hillel and Shammai had markedly different attitudes to the body. In the teaching about Hillel going to the bathhouse and bathroom, he was concerned to care for his body, while Shammai was satisfied just to do his "obligation" to it. Hillel was pious from love of God and was kind even to his own body. Shammai was pious from fear of God and his excessive fear of sin made him wary of the body's attraction to sense-pleasures. Another teaching contrasts the distinctive and divergent ways of Hillel and Shammai.

Our rabbis taught:
Shammai the Elder always ate in honor of the Sabbath. If he found a nice animal to be slaughtered for the Sabbath meals, he put it aside, saying, "This one is for the Sabbath." If he later found another one even nicer, he put the second one aside for the Sabbath and had the first slaughtered to be eaten [during the week].
But Hillel the Elder had a different way, for all his deeds were for the sake of heaven, as it is said: "Blessed is the Lord day by day" (Psalm 68:20).
This is also taught in a *baraita*, that the House of Shammai used to say: "From the first day of the week after the Sabbath (Sunday), look ahead and prepare for the next Sabbath." But the House of Hillel said: "Blessed is the Lord day by day" (*Betzah* 16a).

It is said that Hillel had a "different way" (literally: a different "measure"), because Shammai's practice was also recognized as a "way in holiness." Regardless, another version of this tradition says explicitly what is only implied here–that Hillel's way was superior.[1]

SHAMMAI

Shammai's custom is easy enough to understand. According to the Torah, Jews are to honor the Sabbath with fine food and drink, with nice clothes and everything good. Shammai believed they should also express their love for the Sabbath by remembering it throughout the week, by looking forward expectantly to its coming and by preparing the best food possible.[2] Thus, Shammai and his followers began to think about the next Sabbath as soon as this one concluded. Presumably, Shammai had at his Sabbath meals his own household, as well as disciples and guests. His wife, together with the servants that such an important man must have had, took care of the food. But the rabbis taught that to honor the Sabbath even a wealthy man or a great sage should do some part of the actual preparation, such as buying the fish or chopping the wood for the oven.[3] Shammai chose the animal that would be slaughtered to feed the large company at the festive Sabbath meals.[4] One can imagine his pious efforts throughout the week, as he tried to outdo whatever animal he had previously managed to acquire for the Sabbath meals, and how he would deliberate his choice of the best among the animals available. Shammai's practice allowed him to look forward to the Sabbath and prepare for its coming. It also connected even ordinary, weekday meals with the Sabbath, so that he "always ate in honor of the Sabbath," aware he was eating this rather than that because he was leaving the better food for the holy Sabbath.

HILLEL

Hillel's way–of all his deeds being for the sake of heaven and "Blessed is the Lord day by day"–is less easy to comprehend. It is not so clearly described or explained, and it requires a little more effort to understand. Hillel did not prepare for the Sabbath from the first day of the week. The Torah teaches to prepare on the day before the Sabbath—*erev Shabbat*—on Friday during the day, for the Sabbath begins with the setting of the sun on Friday evening (Exodus 16:4, 5, 22). A rabbinic proverb says: "He who has troubled to prepare food on *erev Shabbat* will have something to eat on the Sabbath. But when someone has not prepared food on *erev Shabbat*, what will he eat on the Sabbath?"[5] Hillel trusted that God would provide, on *erev Shabbat*, something worthy for the Sabbath meals. He did not deprive himself during the week of some good food (or other good thing), leaving it for the Sabbath, but enjoyed it and blessed God for what He gave each day. The Sabbath, of course, was special and holy, but at least in this regard was like other days, for Hillel had full trust that just as God provided for each day, so would He provide for *Shabbat* on *erev Shabbat*. And whether for weekdays or the Sabbath, he gave full thanks for whatever he received. That is the meaning of his use of Psalm 68:20: "Blessed is the Lord day by day."

Hillel applied the Psalm verse to all the days of the week, not just to the Sabbath.[6] "Blessed is the Lord day by day" meant to him that a person should trust that God will provide for his needs each day, not worrying about the next, and should thank God each day, satisfied with whatever he received.[7] When he was younger, Hillel had himself worked as a day laborer; usually he found work and had money for his family and for the doorkeeper of the House of Study, but some days he did not. Certainly it was then that he learned to "bless the Lord day by day."

Blumenthal[8] remarks that "Shammai, of course, acted like a rich man (picking the best food, etc.) . . . Hillel, remembering his early poverty, was grateful for each day's food."

To express his gratitude for the goodness he received and to reinforce his trust in God, Hillel often called to mind, and perhaps uttered aloud, Psalm 68:20—"Blessed is the Lord day by day." Another story shows how he went to the Book of Psalms for another verse to express his attitude of complete trust in God in a different kind of situation. In the face of any threatening news Hillel firmly trusted in God's protection and recited the words of Psalm 112:7 about the pious man: "He will not fear threatening news, his heart is firm, trusting in the Lord." We will consider that story and its teaching in the next chapter.

SERVING GOD NOW

But there was more to Hillel's "way" than his great trust in God as expressed by Psalm 68:20. Along with the quote from the Psalm, we are told that all his actions were for the sake of heaven[9] (we discussed this earlier in other contexts[10]). Surely, though, all Shammai's actions were also for the sake of heaven. Hillel himself appreciated that,[11] and this teaching also recognizes that Shammai too had a "way" in the service of God. Something more particular, then, is meant by saying here that all Hillel's deeds were for the sake of heaven.

In the previous chapter we discussed the paired stories where Hillel said that taking a bath or going to the bathroom, and generally caring for one's body, was a *mitzvah*. One version of that text *was used to illustrate the saying: "Let all your deeds be for the sake of heaven."* That is the clue to understanding the place of that same saying in the comparison of Hillel's practice to Shammai's always eating in honor of the Sabbath.

In the light of that other text's teaching, we can understand that Hillel not only bathed and relieved himself, but also ate as a *mitzvah*, with the intention of caring for his body and himself, because he was made in the image of God. When Shammai ate he was serving God, but his weekday eating was only a preparation, as it were, for the festive Sabbath meals, which are *mitzvot*. Hillel's weekday eating was itself a service of God now, and not just a preparation for something later; that made his way superior to Shammai's because it was more direct divine service.[12] His actions were "for the sake of heaven" in a way that Shammai's were not. Shammai deprived himself on weekdays (even if only in a relative sense) and served God by setting aside food to prepare for the Sabbath meals; Hillel served God each day by caring for himself, by eating with an intention of keeping his body healthy, and by thanking and praising God for what He had provided. Again, the *parush* serving God through asceticism, the *hasid* serving through *hesed* (kindness), even to himself. Hillel the *hasid* was also serving "through *hesed*" by his daily gratitude for God's *hesed* in providing him with food.

However, this text also shows the limitations on asceticism in Judaism. Shammai and other *parushim* may have found occasional fasting conductive to spirituality – as suggested in the previous chapter – but Shammai also served God by eating; and he seems to have eaten adequately on weekdays and abundantly on Sabbaths and festivals.

HOLY AND PROFANE

The Sabbath is one of the pillars of Jewish belief and practice relating to holy and profane. The *parush* always leans toward divine service that concentrates on the holy; he minimizes and ignores what is profane and entirely subordinates it to the holy. For example, the *parush* considers Torah study and prayer holy, working and eating, profane; the Sabbath is holy, weekdays, profane. He concentrates as much as possible on the holy at the expense of the profane. It is characteristic then that Shammai emphasized the holy Sabbath in his religious practice. The way of the *hasid*, however, is not "separation" of holy and profane, but infusing the profane *with* the holy. It is equally characteristic then that Hillel saw the blessing in *every* day (although of course he also kept the Sabbath holy!).

For Shammai the weekdays and weekday eating were profane. Only the Sabbath and Sabbath meals were holy; then he felt he truly served God. For him, eating on weekdays was, in itself, a bothersome necessity forced on him by the body's requirements. The only thing about it that gave him joy was to direct this profane eating toward the coming Sabbath by his custom of always selecting the better food for the Sabbath meals. He thus served God in his weekday eating, but only "indirectly." Hillel, on the other hand, ate all his meals as a service of God. Eating was for him a *mitzvah*, as were bathing and all other bodily functions. The Sabbath meals were especially holy, but the hasidic way was to serve God in the act of eating at all meals.

MITZVAH

Shammai's concept of a *mitzvah* was narrower than Hillel's. For Shammai a *mitzvah* was only what was explicitly and specifically commanded in the Torah (Written or Oral). Thus, for him, the Sabbath meals were *mitzvot*, when he could truly serve God by eating. For a *hasid* such as Hillel, however, every act could and should be a *mitzvah*, even everyday bodily affairs, such as eating. When we see the surprise (in the story) of his own disciples at the concept that going to the bathhouse or bathroom is a *mitzvah*, we can imagine Shammai's lack of appreciation for Hillel's less literal, but more spiritual, approach.

In the previous chapter we considered the teaching-story that contrasted the ways of Hillel and Shammai, and that showed us Hillel's hasidic attitude to bodily functions, to going to the bathhouse and bathroom. The teaching-story of this chapter also contrasts the two great rabbis and (among other things) shows Hillel's hasidic attitude to eating.

ACTIVE AND PASSIVE

Hillel's hasidic piety had two sides—active and passive. The text said about Hillel's "different way" that "All his deeds were for the sake of heaven, as it is said, 'Blessed is the Lord day by day' (Psalm 68:20)." The active side, represented by "All his deeds were for the sake of heaven," was Hillel's intention in eating. He ate, just as he performed all other bodily functions, as a *mitzvah*, for the sake of heaven, showing *hesed* to his own body and person created in the image of God. The more passive side of his way, represented by Psalm 68:20, "Blessed is the Lord day by day," was that he refused to deprive himself, as did Shammai, but received the good that God gave each day, offering appropriate thanks and blessings.[13] The active side was his doing everything for the sake of God; the passive side was his recognition that everything that happened to him and that he received was from God—and was therefore good.

Both sides—active and passive, doing and receiving—are part of the happy and joyful way of the *hasid*. The *hasid* enjoys life; he eats and drinks, like a normal person, showing *hesed* to his own self. He also recognizes the Source of the *hesed* he receives. Sanctifying all actions, even those that fulfill bodily needs, is typically hasidic. So is the pious attitude that emphasizes uttering blessings and recognizing God's goodness.[14] For Hillel, all of life was encompassed in a relation of love with God. All his deeds were for the sake of heaven and were motivated by love of God; and he considered everything that happened to him as good, since it came from God, who also acts toward His creatures only from love. This unity of experience—acting, and receiving everything that happens—in love, gave Hillel a supernal peace of soul that allowed him to transcend all the troubles and tribulations, all the commotion and tumult of this world.

His Heart Is Firm, Trusting in the Lord

THE HASID TRUSTS

As a true *hasid,* Hillel trusted God to provide him with all his needs and referred to Psalms 68:20–"Blessed is the Lord day by day." Another story tells of a different aspect of his fervent faith and trust in God.

> Our rabbis taught: When Hillel the Elder was once on the road approaching the city and heard a loud outcry, he said to those with him: "I am certain that this is not coming from my house." About him, and such as him, does the verse say: "He will not be afraid of threatening news, his heart is firm, trusting in the Lord" (Psalm 112:7) (*Berachot* 60a).

Glatzer says: "Here, Hillel's *hasidut* [hasidism, piety] was tested. Under the circumstances, anxiety would have been a normal reaction. Not that evil cannot befall a man; but the *hasid* does not anticipate evil. Anxiety is conquered by trust."[1]

EMPTY PRAYER VERSUS TRUST

The context of the Babylonian Talmud version of this story and the somewhat different text of the story itself in the Jerusalem

Talmud version clarify its meaning. As for the former, the *mishnah* in *Berachot* 54a says:

> Someone who cries out over what has already happened is praying an empty prayer. Someone whose wife is already pregnant and prays: "Let it be your will, O God, that my wife have a boy!" – is praying an empty prayer. Someone who is on the road approaching the city and hearing a loud outcry there prays: "Let it be Your will, O God, that this not be coming from my house!" – is praying an empty prayer.

In discussing the latter example, the *Gemara* (*Berachot* 60b) cites the story about Hillel hearing the cries while on the road and not being afraid. The Jerusalem Talmud version has an important variation.

> *Mishnah:* . . . Someone who cries out to God over what has already occurred is praying an empty prayer. . . . If a person is on the road approaching the city and hearing a loud outcry prays: "Let it be Your will, O God, that this not be from my house!" – that is an empty prayer. . . . *Gemara:* . . . If a person is on the road approaching the city and this happens, what *should* he say? – "I am certain that these cries are not from my house." Hillel the Elder said: "[He should say:] 'He will not be afraid of threatening news [his heart is firm, trusting in the Lord] (Psalms 112: 7)' " (*Y. Berachot* 9:30).

The Babylonian Talmud has a teaching about improper prayer, and it has a story of Hillel saying "I am certain, etc.," at the end of which a Psalm verse is applied to him. The Jerusalem Talmud, which has no Hillel story, only a generalized teaching about what any person should say in a situation of threatening news, clarifies the connection to improper prayer. It makes clear that although a person should not improperly pray, he should verbally express his trust in God, by uttering either "I am certain, etc." or, as Hillel suggested, the Psalm verse, "He will not be afraid . . . his heart is firm, etc."

The teaching about the "time-limit" on prayer is that praying "after the fact" is futile. Two examples are given: about the pregnant wife and about hearing cries when approaching the city. In the former case, the male or female fetus is already formed in her womb, and God will not change nature to answer such a prayer. In the latter case, whatever disaster or problem that caused the outcry has already occurred, and the time for prayer has passed.

Before the fact a person may pray. And *after* the fact, if he actually suffers from troubles, for example, a religious person justifies God's way, believing that all He does is for good, and so on. The teaching here in the Talmud, however – taught or illustrated by Hillel – relates to the question of what to do in the "gray area," when, although a person might expect or fear troubles, he does not know if a bad event that has occurred has affected him. And it is too late for him to pray. It is the gray area of "threatening news," to use the words of the Psalm. This is the situation described in the Talmud when someone is on the road approaching town and hears cries. The natural response is fear, to think, "What if it is coming from my house!"

What should a person do then? What is the correct religious attitude at such a time? The teaching is that prayer is *not* appropriate. Instead, a person should firmly trust that God will keep him from any harm and that the cries are not from his house. By unshakable trust he will ward off anxiety and fear, for the only fear a religious person should have is fear of God.

The story about Hillel hearing the cries while on the road is cited in the Talmud in the context of teaching about empty prayer, about the time for prayer and the time for trust. But the Hillel story itself just illustrates the proper pious attitude of trust and has no reference to empty prayer. It stands on its own in showing Hillel's great trust in God; the issue of empty prayer is not directly relevant.

But what if Hillel had found out upon reaching home that the cries *were* from his house? Can a person jump so quickly from trusting God to justifying and accepting affliction? The truth is that this problem exists in any situation where a person trusts strongly that God will protect, help, or answer prayer. A pious person's faith must be strong enough to trust that God will keep him from harm, and also to believe that when "harm" comes, it is for his own good.[2]

That was Hillel's own exalted spiritual level, and Glatzer correctly connected this story to Hillel's hasidism, for great faith and trust in God are especially characteristic of the *hasid*. Of Hillel himself, we can say, using the words of the Psalm verse in the story: His heart was firm, trusting in the Lord.[3]

32

Hasid *and* Parush

DO NOT SEPARATE FROM THE COMMUNITY

We have discussed the contrary types of *hasid* and *parush* and seen that Hillel was a *hasid*. He taught:

Do not separate from the community (*Avot* 2:5).

The word for "separate" has the same root as *parush* (the "separatist") and this saying of Hillel's reflects his general attitude about *parushim* and separatism. The *hasid* moves toward people, the *parush* separates. The *hasid* draws people near, the *parush* pushes them away. The *hasid* seeks peace, the unity of men, he wants to be "mixed in" with others; the *parush* is more ready to dispute, to make divisions, to shun and oppose those of whom he disapproves.

When Hillel counseled "do not separate," he was not only speaking about Pharisee *parushim* such as Shammai, but the even more extreme separatists of his time, the Essenes, who left settled towns to pursue their religious goals in the isolation of the Judean wilderness. In the following they speak of their mission and their separation from "sinners":

"[Members of the sect] shall separate from the habitations of men of iniquity and shall go into the wilderness to prepare the way of the Lord, as it is written: 'Prepare in the wilderness the way of the Lord, make straight in the desert a highway for our God' (Isaiah 40:3)."[1]

193

The Essenes almost gave up on the community that they left and abandoned – an attitude contrary to all that inspired Hillel.[2]

We discussed earlier[3] Hillel's teaching about not standing among those sitting or sitting among those standing, and so on, and related it to the Hillelite maxim about being "mixed-in" with people. Hillel's saying about "not separating" from the community conveys the same thought. No reason is given to explain that saying, and the reasons would surely be multiple. One might be found in a saying of Hillel's that follows the other in *Avot* 2:5:

Trust not in yourself until the day of your death.[4]

The pious have always recognized the company of other religious people as the best security against a person's going astray. Also relevant is a teaching of Hillel's in which he responded to a question about the meaning of a Torah verse:

"That which is crooked cannot be made straight, and that which is lacking cannot be numbered" (Ecclesiastes 1:15).

Bar He He said to Hillel: "Why does it say cannot be 'numbered'? Should it not say: 'that which is lacking cannot be "supplied" [parallel to: that which is crooked cannot be "made straight"]'?"

Hillel answered: "The reason for this wording is that 'that which is lacking cannot be *numbered*' refers to someone whose comrades wanted to *number* him in a group forming to do a *mitzvah* – and he declined to join them" (*Hagigah* 9b).

Hillel's main teaching is that a person should be alert to do *mitzvot* and good deeds that come to his hand, for an opportunity that has passed will not return and cannot be retrieved. But he specifically mentions the way comrades join for the performance of a *mitzvah*. Such groups, either permanent or *ad hoc* (as here, since the opportunity passes) are part of the community's positive influence on an individual. A talmudic maxim states: "Members of a group [*havurah*] are quick to act."[5] The custom of forming groups for doing deeds of loving-kindness, of *hesed* – such as helping the poor, visiting the sick, burying the dead, comforting the mourner, and so on – was and is a vital part of the Jewish tradition. Hillel's teaching suggests that a pious person should eagerly join groups forming for worthy purposes, and if he fails to do so – and "separates" from others – his loss cannot be made up. Probably Hillel himself had frequently not only participated in but initiated such groups.

The *parush* worries about the negative influence of sinners and the nonreligious on the religious and advocates separation. But the *hasid* thinks differently: He wants the religious to influence the nonreligious. He actually runs after nonreligious people, as Hillel did. A *hasid* is, then, motivated to stay closely united with the community by his desire to influence others for good.[6]

However, the meaning of Hillel's saying "Do not separate" goes even deeper than the benefits of community and religious comrades. Certainly many interpretations of his words could be suggested from the hasidic viewpoint. But ultimately the *hasid*'s solidarity with others and his abhorrence of separation is based on his awareness of the mystic unity of people – for the Divine Presence dwells in the community – and his desire that this mystic unity become revealed in the reign of Peace.[7]

SHAMMAI THE PARUSH

Understanding someone like Shammai, who exemplifies the type of the sin-fearing *parush*, will help us appreciate the contrary type exemplified by the *hasid* Hillel. The extent of Shammai's fear of sin can be seen from two similar stories told about him. The first is about fasting on Yom Kippur, where the generally accepted view was that children are exempt:

"Shammai the Elder did not want to feed his little boy on Yom Kippur with one hand, but the sages ordered him to feed him with two hands."[8]

The second story is about the Festival of Sukkot, when the main *mitzvah* is to dwell in a *sukkah*-booth. Women and girls, however, are exempt,[9] and so are boys until the age of thirteen according to the generally accepted view.[10]

"When Shammai the Elder's daughter-in-law gave birth [right before or during Sukkot], he removed part of the ceiling and placed *sukkah*-covering over the bed in which she lay with the infant, for the sake of the baby boy."[11]

Shammai was strict in matters of *halachah*, with himself and with others. (Although it was not all strictness: Shammai so loved the *mitzvot,* and his new grandson, that he wanted to acquire this holiness even for the baby.) In almost all the many halachic cases where the House of Shammai differed with the House of Hillel, the ruling of the Shammaites was strict, that of the Hillelites lenient (although there were exceptions). These two stories show Shammai's piety in fearing sin. There is no question that piety inspired by fear, even sometimes to peculiar excess, can be a beautiful religious service of God. However, when it involves denying food to a little boy or troubling a mother and her newborn baby with construction over their heads, it loses a little of its charm – though it still has charm! But Hillel's hasidic piety inspired by love would be unlikely to lead him to serve God by so troubling children and just-delivered mothers.

33

The Way of Hesed

TWO WAYS

The path of *hesed* was recognized by the rabbis as a distinct one in Judaism. There are two ways a person can take in this world, as God said to Israel: "See, I have set before you this day life and good, and death and evil" (Deuteronomy 30:15). To choose life is to choose the "way of the Tree of Life" (Genesis 3:24), which is the Torah.[1] But the rabbis taught there are also two separate paths within the good way of the Torah.

The Prophet Samuel

"The Holy One, blessed be He, said: 'Behold, these two ways have I set before Israel, one is good, the other evil. The good one is of life, the evil one of death. The good way itself is made up of two ways, one of righteousness and the other of love (*hesed*). . . .' The prophet Samuel stood between them and said: 'On which shall I go? If I go on the way of love, the way of righteousness seems better; and if I go on the way of righteousness, that of love seems better! So I call heaven and earth as my witnesses, that I will not give up either, but will hold on to both!' "[2]

Hillel and the *hasidim* followed the way of *hesed*, Shammai and the *parushim* the way of righteousness (meaning the righteousness of fulfilling the Torah). Of course, Hillel too was righteous and fulfilled the Torah, and Shammai also valued *hesed*. The issue was one of emphasis and balance. *Hasidim* focus on the relation between man and man and express their love for God by love for their fellowmen. *Parushim* are more concerned about the relation between man and God and primarily focus on the fulfillment of God's law, the *halachah*. Because of his humane hasidic perspective, Hillel could say that the Golden Rule is the "whole Torah." Even today this perplexes some rabbis, who wonder how the Golden Rule includes the commandments between man and God. But Hillel did not mean the "whole Torah" in the literal sense, only that love for humanity is the essence of true religiosity. Viewing the relation between man and God largely from the human side, sympathetic to human weakness and fallibility, Hillel interpreted the *halachah* leniently. Shammai, viewing that same relation from the perspective of the obligation owed to God, emphasized religious demands and was strict.

The aforementioned teaching of the Two Ways advocates holding on to both ways, of love and righteousness, although they sometimes seem contradictory. The prophet Samuel was associated with that resolve because of 1 Samuel 2:26, which says that as a boy Samuel grew and was in favor with both God and man. The favor of God, it was said, comes from "righteousness," while the favor of man comes from the "love" a person has for his fellowmen.[3]

The teaching of the Two Ways of love and righteousness, of the divergent ways of the *hasidim* and the *parushim*, is the appropriate background against which to understand the conflicting ideals of Hillel and Shammai. But while that teaching makes clear that the tradition recognized two separate paths, it also reflects the decision of the mainstream to merge them and follow both at once. That decision inevitably resulted in a dilution of Hillel's hasidic ideal with the contrary ideal of Shammai.

While the preceding teaching presents the two ways as of equal value, other texts contrast the ways of Hillel and Shammai and prefer Hillel's. In one instance that judgment is explicit, saying that Hillel's way was not only "different" but "superior."[4] Undoubtedly those texts emanated from the School of Hillel.

ABRAHAM'S – AND HILLEL'S – FEAR OF SIN

The mainstream of the tradition considered the way of love (*hesed*) superior to that of righteousness, but counseled pursuing both. Similarly, although service from love was placed above service from fear, a person was taught to seek a balance of the two motives. Hillel also certainly balanced *hesed* and righteousness, love and fear. Righteousness and adherence to Torah law was his very life. Fear of sin was an integral part of his religious ideal. He taught that "an unlearned man cannot be a sin-fearing man"[5] and that no matter how far a person has progressed spiritually, he should never trust himself or abandon his fear of sin until the day of his death.[6]

Hillel expressed his attitude to fear of sin in a *midrash* about Abraham. The Torah says that Abraham led a few hundred of his retainers against the invading army of a coalition of eastern kings who had captured his nephew Lot while plundering Sodom and Gomorrah. Abraham rescued Lot and restored the booty (Genesis 14).

Hillel the Elder said[7]:

"Abraham recaptured all the plundered wealth of Sodom and Gomorrah and returned safely; and not even one person was lost,[8] as it is said: 'And he brought back *all* the goods' (Genesis 14:16).[9] But Abraham was troubled and afraid, saying, 'Can it be that among all those I've slain, there was not one righteous person?' The Holy One, blessed be He, said to him: 'Fear not, Abram' (Genesis 15:1). (With reference to this it was said: '[He pursued them and passed on safely;] dust of the road shall not come on his feet' [Isaiah 41:3].) 'You have not soiled your feet [with the dust of sin] in this matter' "[10] [In the traditional idiom, the "dust" of a sin are acts on the very borderline of sinning.] (*Pirke d'Rabbi Eliezer*, chap. 27).

With his small band of retainers, Abraham rescued his nephew Lot from a much larger military force, without losing a single person. Yet, although engaged in a justified attack, he was so sin-fearing he trembled at the thought that perhaps there were one or more righteous people among the many soldiers he had slain from the invading army. From one point of view, we can admire Hillel's *midrash* for what it says about Abraham's humane concern for even one righteous person among the slain. It reminds us of Abraham's later worry, that among the many wicked people in the cities of Sodom and Gomorrah, which God intended to destroy, there were at least a few who were righteous—and his prayer that their lives be spared (Genesis 18–19). From another point of view, we can appreciate Hillel's description of Abraham's pious fear of sin. Both aspects of the *midrash* about Abraham give us insight into Hillel's own religious perspective.

After the story of Lot's capture and rescue by Abraham, the Torah says: *"After these things* the word of the Lord came to Abram in a vision, saying: *'Fear not, Abram,* I am thy shield, thy reward shall be exceedingly great'* "* (Genesis 15:1 – italics added). Noting the connection between the events that preceded and the somewhat unexpected "Fear not," Hillel asked: What was Abraham afraid of? His midrashic answer was that he was afraid lest he had unwittingly sinned by slaying a righteous person, even in a justified act of war against an invading army.

Hillel reflected on the story about Abraham in the light of two verses from Isaiah (41:2, 3) that he interpreted as referring to God's raising up Abraham from Ur of the Chaldees,[11] and Abraham's raid on the army of the kings: "(v. 2) Who raised up one from the east, whom righteousness met wherever he set his foot? He gave the nations before him and made him rule over kings; so that his sword made them as dust, his bow as driven stubble. (v. 3) He pursued them and passed on safely; even dust of the road shall not come on his feet."

Hillel used the first and second clauses of Isaiah 41:3 to interpret Abraham's battle with the army of the kings. He said that Abraham pursued them and returned *safely* – without losing one person. Then, although Abraham worried that he had sinned, the one "whom righteousness met wherever he set his foot" (41:2), "did not soil his feet with dust of the road"[12] (41:3) – He had not inadvertently sinned by slaying even one righteous person. Therefore, God reassured him, saying: "Fear not, Abram, I am thy shield," for He had protected him.

To understand the full import of Hillel's *midrash*, we can note that the rabbis state elsewhere: "This is the way of the *hasidim*: although the Holy One, blessed be He, gives them a sure promise [that they will not sin], they do not cast off the fear of God."[13]

We can easily see Hillel himself behind his sensitive description of Abraham. Hillel was a *hasid* from love, yet he clung to fear of sin. He was humble and aware of his own insufficiency; he did not trust himself, but God, and believed that: "He will protect the feet of His *hasidim*" (1 Samuel 2:9).[14] That is the attitude the rabbis taught in their saying about God's sure promise to the *hasidim*, and what Hillel

taught in his *midrash* about Abraham. Thus, Hillel's pious fear of sin
and refusal to trust himself was finely balanced and was sweetened
by his hasidic faith and trust in God's protection.

Although Hillel reflected on a military expedition by
Abraham–and one totally justified as a rescue mission–his *midrash*
has a clearly pacifistic tinge, for what was Abraham afraid of?–that
he had slain even one righteous person among the wicked multitude
of the invading army.[15]

The fear of God is traditionally understood as restraining a
person from sinning.[16] But some *hasidim*–such as Hillel certainly–
were so firmly established in the love of God, the higher service, that
it seemed they no longer needed the fear of God to keep them from
sin. Nevertheless, Hillel, who was humble and lowly in his own
eyes, taught that a person should not trust himself, for how can he
know when his lower nature might overwhelm him?[17] Even
Abraham, he taught, had clung to his fear of sin!

Although Hillel leaned to *hesed*, he also had his *gevurah*, his holy
rigor. In his midrashic teaching discussed earlier, he had no com-
punctions about Samuel rebuking King Saul for his excessive compassion in sparing the wicked Amalekite King Agag. But while
Hillel sought a balance between love and fear and between *hesed* and
gevurah, the whole question is where the line is drawn and what the
balance is–and in that Hillel and Shammai, the *hasidim* and the
parushim differed.

HILLEL THE HASID: A SUMMARY

We have now completed our discussion of the first term in
Hillel's eulogy, that he was a *"hasid."* Obviously, many teachings
and stories have shown his hasidic leanings. We had previously
seen, for example, that he expressed his love for God primarily in his
love for people. To summarize this section, let us recall that Hillel
was identified by his generation as a *hasid* (in the eulogy) and that
that was his own ideal ("An *am-haaretz* cannot be a *hasid*"). He was a
hasid in the sense of doing more ("one hundred and one times"; "he
who does not increase, will decrease") and also a *hasid* from love
(being hard to anger, as in the 400 *Zuz* Bet story, and giving without
expecting a return: "What is mine is not mine. What need have I of
what belongs to others?"). In the typical hasidic way, all his deeds,

even those for the body–such as eating or going to the bathroom and bathhouse–were for the sake of heaven and motivated by love for God and compassion, *hesed*, for his soul (the "guest" in the body). And just as he acted with love, he also received–in a hasidic way–whatever came to him from God with love, saying, "Blessed is the Lord day by day." His hasidic trust in God was so strong that he was unfazed by threatening news and, although he feared sin, fully trusted that God would protect him from unwitting transgressions.

Although a few scholars[18] have recognized Hillel's hasidism, this prominent aspect of his personality has hardly penetrated the popular conception of the great rabbi. More than anything else, this side of him has been "lost." Much of what we have learned about Hillel from the very beginning of this book has demonstrated his hasidic nature. And as we continue our discussion, with the next term in Hillel's eulogy, that he was a "humble man," we will touch on additional aspects of his hasidic piety. That is only natural, since hasidism and humility are like close and inseparable friends, as his eulogy itself makes clear by pairing them in praise: "O *hasid*, O humble man!"

34

The Humble Man

In their eulogy the sages characterized Hillel as a "humble man." Elsewhere they taught: "A person should always be patient and humble like Hillel. . . ."[1] Their description exactly fits what we know of Hillel from the stories about him.

HUMILIATION AND EXALTATION

A famous saying of Hillel explains his attitude to humility and pride.

My humiliation is my exaltation;
my exaltation is my humiliation (*Leviticus Rabbah* 1:5).

(More literally, "My being lowered is my being raised up; my being raised up is my being lowered.")

This saying is in the form of a paradox, because there is a paradox about "greatness" in the heart of religion, as the *Zohar*[2] says: "He who is little is great; he who is great is little." When a person is elevated by his own pride, or by the honor other people give him, his fullness of self removes him from God; when he is lowered by his own honest reflection, or insulted or humiliated by others, his pride is destroyed and his humility brings him closer to God. This is the underlying logic of Hillel's teaching about pride and humility.

Hillel spoke these words concerning humiliation and exaltation about himself and testified to his own state of mind. But there is no doubt that for us to actually understand this extraordinary level in spiritual consciousness is very difficult. Can we actually conceive what it means to experience honor as humiliation and humiliation as exaltation?

THE PARABLE OF SEATING AT A FEAST

Hillel's saying is illustrated in the rabbinic tradition by a parable:

"At a feast, seat yourself two or three places lower than what your honor might demand, and wait until they say to you 'Come further up!' Do not move up on your own, lest they say to you 'Go down!' It is better that they say to you 'Come up, come up!' and not 'Go down, go back down!' That is what Hillel taught, saying: ' My humiliation is my exaltation; my exaltation is my humiliation.' "[3]

This parable describes a custom of the feasts of the time, where seating was according to status, but the guests sat themselves as they arrived. Therefore, the seating was sometimes readjusted by the host, who entered later. A person who seated himself too high up and too prominently would be terribly embarrassed if asked to go farther away from the head of the table. Contrarily, someone who was called to move closer would feel pleased and honored before all. Although the parable's advice to sit lower than one's status was originally simply a counsel of secular wisdom to prevent social embarrassment, the Hillelites instead used it as a counsel of religious wisdom to encourage humility and to teach people how to act vis-à-vis God. The lesson was that just like the host at a feast, God will lower those who exalt themselves and exalt those who are humble. As we saw in the story of his ascension to become *Nasi*, Hillel, who himself sat low, was called up to greatness.

HILLEL AT THE REJOICING OF THE WATER-DRAWING

A story about Hillel teaching in the Temple provides further insight into his saying about exaltation and humiliation.

Hillel used to say: "If we are here, who is here?" and "If we are not here, who is here?"[4] [These two lines were not spoken at the same time, but "sequentially" as the following story explains.[5]]

Hillel the Elder was once sitting in the Temple court at the ceremony of the Rejoicing of the Water-drawing [during Sukkot], when people were standing and praying. Seeing that their hearts were uplifted with pride, he said to them, "If we are here, who is here? Don't you know that we and our praises of God are accounted as nothing? For aren't there thousands and tens of thousands of ministering angels who continually worship him and are always ready to serve Him?[6] as it says: 'Is there a limit to His legions?' " (Job 25:3).

But when Hillel saw that his words had had their effect and their hearts were broken, he said to them, "If we are not here, who is here? Although thousands and tens of thousands of ministering angels always stand before God singing His praises . . . only the praises sung by Israel please Him and are sweet to Him, as it says [about King David]: 'The anointed one of the God of Jacob and the sweet singer of Israel' (2 Samuel 23:1); and it says [about God]: 'You are holy, who sit listening to the praises of Israel' " (Psalm 22:4) (*ARN-B*, chap. 27).

When the people became too high-spirited and proud (literally: their hearts rose) through the exaltation of their intense praying and joyful singing of praise, Hillel lowered them, saying: "If we are here, who is here?" Against the worship offered by the myriads of holy angels, ours is nothing. Why are you so proud? But when they were humbled by having this cold water thrown on them, he praised them effusively, because their now-humble divine service lifted them to great spiritual heights, above the angels. "If we are not here, who is here?" If we were not in the Temple, would God be present? For our songs and praises are dearer to Him than those of the angels and draw Him – away from them in heaven – down to this world. When their hearts were lifted up, he lowered them; when their hearts were broken, he lifted them up. He did this in the manner of a true spiritual master. This story reveals the exact same "process" as in Hillel's saying, "My humiliation is my exaltation; my exaltation is my humiliation,"[7] and that is the religious perspective he was trying to communicate to the people.

Hillel's statement that when humans serve God sincerely they are spiritually superior to the angels and that God prefers them to the angels reflects his humanistic perspective.[8]

GOD DETERMINES

Another aspect of Hillel's words that "my humiliation is my exaltation; my exaltation is my humiliation" appears more clearly in an anonymous variant of the saying that has a less paradoxical form but employs the same terms and expresses essentially the same meaning. This other version is very common in the rabbinic literature and is also associated with Hillel.[9]

Everyone who humbles himself,
   the Holy One, blessed be He, exalts;
and everyone who exalts himself,
   the Holy One, blessed be He, humbles.

(The Hebrew verbs are the same as in Hillel's saying.)

In his version, Hillel spoke in the first person to reveal his internal spiritual perception, his own state of mind. Perhaps this version in the third person emphasizes the external reality, namely, how God will determine a person's position and status, according to his humility or pride. Thus, this version is used as the lesson of a story we will study in a later chapter that teaches that God raised up the House of Hillel to preeminence over the House of Shammai because they, like Hillel, their master, were humble.

35

Hillel and the Once-Rich Poor Man

SENSITIVE CHARITY

Another story about Hillel's humility appears in a talmudic context where the rabbis are discussing charity. The focus is on a teaching in Deuteronomy 15:7, 8 that people should not harden their hearts or close their hands when their poor brother needs help, but "You shall open your hand wide to him, and shall surely lend him sufficient for his need, in that which he needs."

> Our rabbis taught: [Why does the verse end with what seems to be a superfluous phrase:] "in that which he needs" [?]–[This teaches that you shall supply him with his needs] even if they are a horse to ride on and a servant to run before him. It was related of Hillel the Elder that he bought for a man of a wealthy family who had become poor[1] [not only his basic necessities, but] a horse to ride upon. And he would see to it that the man had a servant to run before him. One day Hillel was not able to find a servant to hire, and he himself ran before him for three miles (*Ketubot* 67b).

At that time having the use of a horse, rather than a donkey, was the mark of someone from the upper classes. It was also customary for a rich man on horseback to have a servant run before him to clear the way and announce his coming.[2] Having a horse and servant was a matter of prestige and honor.[3] Thus, the rabbis said that if that is the need of someone who was wealthy and has become poor, a charitable person should get him even that.[4]

Although it is reasonable to ask if religious people should be concerned with protecting the delicate honor of the upper classes, this teaching actually reflects Judaism's great sensitivity. In Deuteronomy 15:7, 8 the Torah instructs people to open their hands to the poor and help them according to their need. The exact wording, literally translated, is that they should help their poor brother "sufficient for his *need*, in that which he *needs*." Why, the rabbis asked, is there this seemingly redundant reference to their need? They answered that this teaches that not all *needy* people have the same *needs*. And while some people's needs may seem excessive, they must still be helped. One cannot treat all poor people alike, disregarding their individuality. A once-rich poor man, for example, cannot be treated exactly like other poor people; his needs are different, and great. He will be destroyed if he is suddenly reduced to a minimal charity and deprived of all the accustomed supports to his feeling of self-worth. Although the rabbis insisted on an equal dignity for rich and poor – for their dignity came from God, in whose image they were created, and not from wealth – yet, this did not forbid all attention to the sometimes contrary realities of class. Judaism has a sensitivity beyond the first level, which would be to help all the poor in the same way, ignoring the special needs of such as the once-rich poor. Possibly, a common and over-simple prejudice against the rich and the upper classes would obscure the fact that they too are people who need mercy and that those among them who have become impoverished have needs of a particular sort. And, of course, the teaching here is not limited only to the once-rich; its application is to all the poor – that they be treated with sensitivity and respect, as individuals.

By buying the man a horse and hiring him a servant, Hillel fulfilled the rabbinic teaching on Deuteronomy 15:8, about helping the poor man "sufficient for his need in that which he needs." But in fact either the teaching was later derived from the story, or the teaching and interpretation of the verse were Hillel's own. Evidence for the latter is that as *Nasi* Hillel instituted the *prosbul* based on his reflection on the very next verse, Deuteronomy 15:9, which reads: "Beware that there not be an unworthy thought in your heart, thinking, 'The seventh year, the year of the release of debts is at hand,' and you act selfishly with regard to your poor brother and you give him nothing. . . ."[5]

This story about Hillel providing a horse and servant and then himself running for three miles has been preserved by the tradition in a context that instructs people to attend to the needs of the poor in their individuality. But though it exemplifies that teaching, it is even more remarkable in what it tells us about Hillel and his character. On the one hand, in giving freely of his money, buying a horse and hiring a servant, it shows Hillel's goodness and his concern for his fellowman. It also shows his sensitivity to the individual needs of the poor people to whom he gave charity, for he was aware of what each particular person needed.

HUMILITY

However, there is something beyond that. The Talmud teaching about charity, which the story illustrates, parallels the story only insofar as Hillel supplied the man with the horse and a servant to run before him. What about Hillel himself running for three miles? In a display of astonishing humility, the greatest rabbi of the Jewish tradition took the place of a servant, to show his love for a fellowman. To protect the dignity of another human, he was completely willing to abandon his own. Such a deed goes way beyond the bounds of conventional religiosity. So much is this the case that a more than momentary consideration of his action can easily leave us amazed.

But this is often true with stories about the greatest of the rabbis. The reason is that their view of reality is so different from our own that some of their actions, though they fascinate us, seem strange, and even sometimes comical. The different worldview of Hillel, expressed in this story, is one that in truth puts God at the center. In the previous chapter we discussed Hillel's famous saying: "My humiliation is my exaltation; my exaltation is my humiliation." What Hillel believed, and indeed experienced, was the exact reverse of most people's perceptions: To an ordinary person humiliation is not exaltation. It is that peculiar reversal of perspective, manifested in his running before the horse, that astounds us. Certainly his saying about "my humiliation is my exaltation" casts a direct light on this story, in which Hillel lowers himself in a way that most people, even the most pious, could hardly contemplate.

It could be asked, however, if the impoverished "rich" man would not have been embarrassed by what Hillel did. Perhaps so, but more important, he would have had the most emphatic lesson about false honor, to which he was attached, and true honor, which he saw in Hillel. Certainly Hillel was not thinking about such matters, or calculating too finely, when he did this fiery deed. All he saw was the distress of his fellowman. Neither did he think, in his holy humility, that he was too good to perform the task of a hired servant. So, blind to the possible embarrassment he might cause, and to the bizarre incongruity of what he was about to do, he himself ran before the horse.

CONTEXT AND FRAME

Sometimes a story can appear in a context that directs our attention to one aspect of the action while overlooking another aspect that is subtly lost. The tradition has preserved this story in one place – in a charity context about helping the poor according to their individual needs, and as much as required, even if their needs seem exaggerated. In the lesson of the rabbis no link is made to the matter of Hillel's extraordinary humility. Even if the teaching on the verse about charity was Hillel's, it was the rabbis who editorially attached it to the story. They could also have attached this story to his saying, "my humiliation is my exaltation." Then the second part of the story about Hillel running before the horse would have been given greater prominence and its lesson about humility in service would have been brought out. About that aspect of the story nothing is said and no teaching is given telling us what to learn from it. Yet, an important lesson could be learned from Hillel's deed: that a person should be ready to humble himself to serve his fellowman. But the fact that the story has been preserved *only* in a charity context and not in a context that teaches about humility in service to others means that this latter aspect has been obscured. This side of the story has been neglected and effectively lost. The tradition does not speak about it or develop it.

Hillel's running before the horse has been cast into the

shadows because the editorial "frame" in which the story was preserved emphasizes one aspect and turns our attention away from another, and even more remarkable, aspect. And perhaps because of this one-sided frame, this wonderful story about Hillel has never come to prominence in the tradition, and it is rare that we are asked to reflect on the extraordinary religious character of Hillel that it highlights.

Indeed, the relative paucity of references to this story is still another way that it has, for all intents and purposes, been lost. For certain stories and sayings are picked up in the tradition; they are quoted again and again, being found in numerous versions and contexts even in the ancient rabbinic texts. They are cited so often throughout the ages that everyone knows them. Others, however, lie quietly, untouched, maybe in only one place in the vast rabbinic literature, sometimes in a less frequented part of that literature. They are not quoted or developed, and few people know about them. The story about Hillel running before the horse fits into this latter category.

This story has, in a subtle way, been lost. And the same is true of many other things about Hillel. Indeed, it was this striking and remarkable story that first made me realize how much about him has become obscure. It showed me a fiery, hasidic side to his personality of which I had not previously been aware. On the one hand, it has a distinctly biblical flavor, reminiscent of the fiery prophet Elijah running before the chariot of King Ahaz – to give him honor, as Rashi explains.[6] On the other hand, it is equally reminiscent of the radical piety found in stories of the hasidic *rebbes* of the movement of the Baal Shem Tov. It might seem unexpected to find the calm sage Hillel as a link in a chain of three, between Elijah and the Baal Shem Tov. But we have already seen many other examples of Hillel's passionate hasidism.

This story of Hillel running before the horse portrays what is perhaps the most radical act of hasidic piety that is found in a story of any rabbi of earlier or later times. It is certainly the most amazing story about Hillel. Yet, it is almost unknown. If we ponder it carefully, we are obliged to abandon any misconception we might have about Hillel's mildness. He had another side.

36

Gentle and Bearing Insult

HEAVENLY DECISION

A tradition tells that long after their founder's death, the House of Hillel finally attained lasting supremacy over their adversaries, the House of Shammai.[1] Appropriately, the controversy for the sake of heaven between Hillel and Shammai was decided by a heavenly voice.

> For three years the House of Shammai and the House of Hillel were engaged in a dispute: these claimed "The *halachah* is according to our ruling" and the others answered "The *halachah* is according to our ruling." But then they heard a heavenly voice saying: "These and those are the words of the living God–but the *halachah* is according to the House of Hillel."
>
> Since these and those are the words of the living God, why did the House of Hillel merit to establish the *halachah* according to their ruling? Because they were gentle and bore insult (*nohin ve'aluvin*) and because they studied not only their own views, but those of the House of Shammai. More than that, they would even give precedence to the opinions of the House of Shammai and review them first. . . . This teaches us that whoever lowers himself, the Holy One, blessed be He, exalts, and whoever exalts himself, the Holy One, blessed be He, lowers (*Erubin* 13b).

The striking judgment of the tradition about the opposed teachings of Hillel and Shammai is that both "these and those are the words of the living God," although Hillel's rulings are followed in practice because of the Hillelites' humility. That the Hillelites "were gentle and bore insult," whereas the Shammaites were not, merely follows from the contrast between their leaders personally, as the rabbis said: "A person should always be patient and humble like Hillel, and not impatient and irritable like Shammai."[2] Elsewhere they contrasted these different personality types using similes: "A person should always be soft and flexible like a reed, and not hard and rigid like a cedar."[3]

The Hillelites were exceptionally humble. Considering the specific terms used to characterize them will give us insight also into Hillel's humility. The Hebrew words *noah* and *aluv* (plurals: *nohin*, *aluvin*)–given here as "gentle" and "bearing insult"–are difficult to translate, but they are fairly distinctive and it will be worthwhile paying attention to their meanings.

NOAH

That someone is *noah* means he is gentle and easily complies with others' wishes. Remember the words of Hillel's descendant, who was characterized as very humble: "Anything that anyone asks me to do, I do."[4] Being "soft and flexible like a reed" is an apt simile to illustrate this saintly quality. Another aspect of being *noah* is being patient under oppression and abuse.[5]

ALUV

The other word used to characterize the Hillelites, *aluv*– "bearing insult" or "being submissive"–was a very important one in the time of Hillel; note the word in his own mouth when he referred to the "poor soul" (*nafsha aluvta*) that is a guest in the body. This word has since gone into disuse and is almost lost from the religious vocabulary. To some degree this may represent a waning of interest in some aspects of what it stands for. *Aluv* is an especially difficult word to translate into English. It comes from a root that ordinarily means "insulted" or "humiliated," yet it represents an esteemed religious quality. Perhaps we could say that it is the humiliated side of humility, characterized by the acceptance of abuse and insult without complaint. (Compare Hillel's teaching, with a different verb: "My humiliation is my exaltation.") Sometimes *aluv* is translated as "lowly." Ben Zoma used it to describe Moses:

"Who is the lowliest of the lowly (*aluv shebe'aluvim*)? He who is as lowly as our teacher Moses, as it is said: 'Now the man Moses was very humble (*anav*) [more so than anyone who was on the face of the earth (Numbers 12:3)].' "[6]

The context of this Torah verse, as understood by the rabbis, was that Moses had overheard Miriam and Aaron complaining about him, and kept silent (Numbers 12:1–3). The *Midrash* says:

"Now the man Moses was very humble" – for he heard their words and was silent . . . He was humble of mind and when he heard someone insulting him, he would not answer back."[7]

This kind of humility was considered characteristic of the *hasid*. It was taught: "He who hears himself cursed and is silent is called a *hasid*."[8]

The rabbis considered such humility a necessary quality in someone who sought peace. Elsewhere, they joined Hillel's saying about disciples of Aaron loving and pursuing peace with the following teaching:

"There is no one as lowly of spirit as he who would pursue peace. How could it be otherwise? For how could a person pursue peace without lowliness of spirit? Thus, if someone curses him he answers with the blessing, 'Peace be upon you'; if someone argues with him, he remains quiet and does not respond. . . ."[9]

The atmosphere of the word *aluv* comes through in a well-known talmudic teaching about saintly people who do not seek to humiliate those who humiliate them.

> Those who are humiliated by others,
>   and do not respond in kind;
> Who hear themselves abused,
>   and do not answer with abuse;
> Who act from love of God, and rejoice in affliction:
> Of them does scripture say:
> "Those who love Him shall be as the sun
>   when it comes out in full strength" (Judges 5:31).[10]

The first line uses the root of *aluv* twice (*ha'ne'elavim ve'einam olvim*): those who are humiliated by others and (literally) do not humiliate (their abusers). Hillel and those who followed him were *hasidim* who served God from love, and an important aspect of their ideal – being *aluv* – is expressed in this teaching. The Hillelites were "gentle" and "bearing insult" (*noah* and *aluv*). Like Moses and like their master Hillel, the best among them could hear themselves abused and insulted without answering, could be provoked without being aroused to anger.

The text about the dispute between Hillelites and Shammaites over whose rulings would be enforced said that the House of Hillel studied the House of Shammai's opinions first. Certainly the House of Hillel gave honor to the contrary views of their opponents because that was their master's habit (as we will shortly see). The House of Shammai, on the other hand, had a less generous attitude to their adversaries' views. They would not study the Hillelite view, let alone give it precedence. The pronouncement of the heavenly voice – "Both these and those are the words of the living God" – probably reflects the broad-minded outlook of the House of Hillel, since it reflects their practice, referred to in the story. Although this three-year dispute took place long after Hillel's death, it seems likely that the heavenly voice was echoing the sentiments of Hillel himself.

EARTHLY STRUGGLE

How sweet are the words of the tradition explaining why the *halachah* is like Hillel and his House: "because they were gentle and bore insult." But this characterization contrasts sharply with the impression we get of the Shammaites. The relations between the two Houses were sometimes tense, and most of the tension seems to have emanated from the Shammaite hard-liners. Although we are told how the dispute about the *halachah* was finally settled by means of a heavenly voice after Hillel's death, there are stories that depict a more earthly struggle, during his lifetime.

Hillel Harassed in the Temple

One of the halachic issues in dispute between Hillel and Shammai was whether it was permissible to sacrifice a burnt offering in the Temple on a festival day. Shammai said no; Hillel yes.[11] According to both teachers, however, peace offerings *were* permitted on a festival, although they differed on whether or not a person could lay on hands Shammai saying no, Hillel yes. Hillel once went to the Temple on a festival and took an animal for a burnt offering into the Temple court to lay his hands on it. This was a double offense in the eyes of the Shammaites, who held that it was forbidden to sacrifice a burnt offering or to lay hands on a sacrificial animal on a festival day.[12] Hillel was immediately surrounded by zealous disciples of Shammai who were ready to forcibly prevent anyone from acting contrary to their position. Now while burnt offerings *had* to be male animals, peace offerings – that the Shammaites also approved of – could be either male or female. Hillel extricated himself from this threatening and possibly violent confrontation by deceiving those who had accosted him into thinking that the male animal he had brought with him was a female and therefore not a burnt offering, but a peace offering acceptable to them too.

Here is the story:

> Our rabbis taught: Once, on a festival, Hillel the Elder brought a burnt offering into the Temple court to lay his hands on it there. A group of disciples of the House of Shammai, seeing him, immediately gathered and surrounded him. "What is that animal for?" they asked. "It's a female," he said, "and I've brought it as a peace offering sacrifice. Here, look," and he swung its tail aside a little as if to show them that it was a female. He thus distracted them, so that they left and went on their way.
>
> On that day the House of Shammai tried to dominate the House of Hillel and to establish the *halachah* about these matters according to their opinion. But an elderly disciple of Shammai, named Baba ben Buta, who knew that in truth the *halachah* was according to the view of the House of Hillel, arranged for a tremendous number of the best sheep, all the flock of Kedar that were in Jerusalem, to be brought to the Temple court. He then proclaimed, "Whoever wants to lay on hands, let him come and lay on hands; and whoever needs to bring a burnt offering, let him take one of these animals and offer it!" Many people came forward to take animals, laid their

hands on them, and offered them up as burnt offerings, all according to the ruling of the House of Hillel. That very day the House of Hillel got the upper hand; the *halachah* was established according to their view and no one dared say anything about it (composite of *Betzah* 20a–b and *Tosefta Hagigah* 2:11, p. 236; cf. also *Y. Betzah* 2:4, 61c).

Hillel went to the Temple to offer a sacrifice to expiate some felt sin, fearing sin being part of his religious ideal (*Avot* 2:6). Baba ben Buta, the elderly rabbi who advised Herod to rebuild the Temple, is elsewhere said to have been one of a number of pious men whose fear of sin was so great that each brought a special guilt-offering for a doubtful sin every day.[13] In this story he decisively supports Hillel.

Hillel loved the Temple, which was the center of Jewish religious life. We previously discussed a saying of his, taught to the assembled multitudes in the Temple on a festival, that a person should express his love for God by frequent visits to His House. We can be sure that Hillel was often there. One of the great benefits of the Temple, much valued by the people, was that the sacrifices performed there, when accompanied by sincere repentance, provided a way for sins to be forgiven. The ancient Passover hymn *Dayenu* recounts in succession a list of God's many blessings in bringing the Jewish people out of Egypt and leading them to the Promised Land of Israel. The song culminates in a line telling of the last and greatest of His kindnesses, that "He built for us the Chosen Dwelling, the Temple, to atone for all our sins." When Hillel brought his burnt offering to the Temple, he went seeking this purification that the Temple provided.

But our main interest in this story is to see that Hillel suffered an indignity at the hands of Shammaite zealots without protesting, and that he finally won the day with the help of another elderly and influential Shammaite, Baba ben Buta.

A sidelight of the story is that it shows Hillel willing to use an innocent deception to avoid a confrontation with the extremists who surrounded him. We discussed this earlier in the context of the rabbinic permission to lie for the sake of peace.[14] The talmudic commentator Rashi says: "Out of his great humility, Hillel altered the truth, for the sake of peace."[15] Rashi's point about Hillel's humility is well-taken: Rather than standing on his honor and confronting the fanatics who accost him – the *Nasi* – the great man abases himself by using deception, all for the sake of peace.

An air of persecution pervades the story just recounted, although it concludes with the House of Hillel finally winning the upper hand, and with the *halachah* being established according to their view.[16] The same feeling comes from another story of this sort that tells of the day when the Shammaites succeeded in overcoming Hillel. This time the dispute began over a matter of ritual purity connected with agriculture.

A Sword in the House of Study

When one vintages grapes for the vat, to produce wine, Shammai maintains they are liable to uncleanness, while Hillel holds they cannot become unclean. Hillel said to Shammai, "You say that grapes can become defiled and therefore must be vintaged into ritually clean baskets. Why then do you not insist upon that when olives are gathered too, for surely the same reasoning applies?!" "If you provoke me," Shammai retorted, "I *will* rule that uncleanness applies to the olive gathering too!" The followers of Shammai then planted a sword in the House of Study and proclaimed: "Let anyone who wants to, enter; but no one leaves!"[17] That day Hillel was bent over and humbled and sat before Shammai like one of the disciples; and it was as grievous a day for Israel as the day on which they made the Golden Calf (*Shabbat* 17a).

It seems that the Shammaites somehow arranged to take a vote at a moment when they were in a majority and before the Hillelites could muster their forces. Hillel was made to give up his seat as the *Nasi* to Shammai, and had to sit with the disciples.[18] The bitterness of the Hillelites faced with the bullying tactics of their opponents is evident in this tradition. The dominance attained by Shammai and his followers in the religious councils, even if only temporary, and the decrees they instituted during that period, were seen to have had fateful and disastrous consequences for the Jewish people: It "was as grievous a day for Israel as the day on which they made the Golden Calf."[19] This latter phrase is proverbial for an error of catastrophic proportions.[20] There may also be a suggestion that the disloyalty and faithlessness to Hillel's leadership was as great a misfortune as when the people made the Golden Calf, forsaking God and abandoning the leadership of Moses, His servant.[21] Although Hillel and Shammai are wedded in the tradition—as opponents—this dramatic story is the only one where they appear in the same scene and interact. It displays both Hillel's humility and Shammai's belligerence.

The two stories of Hillel being threatened and humiliated in the Temple and in the House of Study give us vivid pictures of the sometimes tense relations between the two Houses, the struggle between them, and the occasional note of persecution involved. However, this element should not be exaggerated. The two camps, although often at odds, and occasionally sharply so, did work together to discuss the Torah and develop the *halachah*.[22] The tradition states that in the time of Hillel and Shammai the number of irreconcilable differences was in fact kept limited to a few issues. Later, however, when they had passed from the scene and their disciples were in charge, the disagreements and arguments multiplied.[23]

PURE SPEECH

Shammai's ascendancy over Hillel, as recorded in the previous story, was, it seems, for a relatively brief period. In the longer run, the House of Hillel finally attained a supremacy decreed by a heavenly voice, and the *halachah* was established according to Hillel's rulings. The tradition explained that the Hillelites' victory was because they were "gentle and bearing insult," the particular example being that they not only studied their opponents' views along with their own, but gave them precedence. A story in the Talmud not only shows two of Hillel's disciples reviewing their halachic studies before their master, but reciting the very ruling in the story just discussed—about gathering grapes into ritually clean baskets. The focus of the story, however, is about Hillel discerning signs of future greatness in his young disciple Yohanan ben Zakkai.

Two of Hillel's disciples were sitting before him [reciting *mishnah*-teaching they had learned]. One of them was Yohanan ben Zakkai.[24] Stating the question of the *mishnah*, the other disciple said: "Why must grapes be gathered into ritually clean baskets, while olives can be gathered into unclean baskets?" When Yohanan's turn came to repeat the same *mishnah*, he said: "Why must grapes be gathered into ritually clean baskets, while olives do not have to be gathered into clean baskets?" Hillel, noting that, unlike his fellow disciple, he had avoided using the word "unclean," said of him, "I am certain this one will become a teacher of Torah in Israel." And it was not long before that happened (*Pesahim* 3b).

In this story Yohanan ben Zakkai repeats word for word the question Hillel himself had once asked Shammai, about a ruling of Shammai's with which he disagreed: "Why must grapes be gathered into ritually clean baskets, while olives do not have to be gathered into clean baskets?"[25] This was at the session in the House of Torah study when Hillel was defeated and sat bent over and humbled before Shammai, like one of the disciples. When Hillel had challenged Shammai's ruling, however, the issue was yet undecided; Yohanan ben Zakkai merely recited the question while reviewing his lesson – to prepare for its (Shammai's) answer. Originally, Hillel had opposed requiring ritual purity for the grapes, but Shammai's stricter view prevailed. This story, in which Hillel reviews with his disciples the practical *halachah* according to Shammai's ruling, provides some evidence not only for the statement that the *halachah* eventually came to be like the House of Hillel because they studied the opinions of their opponents, but for their practice being based on Hillel's own custom.

The point of the story itself, however, is to teach: one, the virtue of purity of speech; and, two, that the character of great men, such as Yohanan ben Zakkai, can be seen early on, especially by those who are themselves great, such as Hillel. Hillel's own masters first saw something special (and more dramatic) in him when they rescued him from beneath the snow on the roof of the House of Torah study. What Hillel saw in the young Yohanan ben Zakkai, as opposed to the other disciple, was a purity of speech that reflected his purity of soul. Whereas the other student had used the word "unclean," Yohanan ben Zakkai avoided even having that word on his lips and, instead of saying that the olives could be gathered into unclean baskets, preferred to say that they did not have to be gathered into clean ones. He used the same pure speech Hillel had himself once used in speaking to Shammai.

According to the rabbis, it is a matter of spiritual cleanliness to avoid using language that even suggests impurity, for impure words on the tongue subtly affect a person's soul. In the context of this Hillel story, the Talmud teaches that a person should always keep his speech entirely pure and never let an impure word pass his lips. Perhaps Hillel was not as strict as Shammai in rulings about ritual purity – such as those connected with gathering produce in the fields – but he was very sensitive and strict when it came to purity of speech. We discussed earlier some other aspects of the speech of Hillel and his disciples and House – how they were gentle and careful not to hurt others, preferring peace over unvarnished truth, and how they avoided speaking of others' sins and faults. The story of Hillel with his two disciples reciting the *mishnah* provides further insight into the care he gave to matters of speech and how highly he valued pure speech. Since the language a person uses is a sign of his spiritual level and of the purity or impurity of his soul, when Hillel noticed the delicacy in his young disciple's choice of words he realized, with the prescience of a spiritual master, that his disciple had attained a level that made it certain he would one day be a great teacher in Israel.

In the early mystic tradition it was taught: "Cleanliness leads to purity and purity to holiness."[26] Hillel valued bodily cleanliness (inside and out) as giving honor to the image of God in which humans are created, even to the extent of considering visits to the bathroom or bathhouse *mitzvot*; his praise of Yohanan ben Zakkai in this story shows how much he valued spiritual purity in matters of speech.

The way this interesting story fit into the context of our discussion was that it showed Hillel listening to his disciples reviewing Shammai's ruling, like the statement in the tradition that the House of Hillel studied their opponents' opinions along with their own, even giving them precedence, because they were "gentle and bearing insult." In these qualities – of being *noah* and *aluv* – they were certainly following the example of their humble master.

HILLEL AS NOAH AND ALUV

The story of Hillel's patience in receiving the rich man trying to anger him to win a bet illustrates particularly well that he was *noah* and *aluv*, humbly doing what others want and accepting abuse without complaint. He readily complied with the man's frivolous wishes, forgetting his own urgent needs, and when insulted (although indirectly) as a "round-headed Babylonian," or with "May there not be many more like you in Israel!" he did not answer back rudely or with insults. And what could be more *noah* and *aluv* than serving the needs of the once-rich poor man, abasing himself to run before his horse? We have seen other striking examples of Hillel's humility and lowliness in this chapter. When he was accosted in the Temple by the Shammaites, he did not respond with anger; when they placed a sword in the House of Study, he did not answer their zeal with his own. Hillel's fervor and zeal were not directed against others, but only for—for God, for people, and for the Torah. We have now completed our discussion of the second term of Hillel's eulogy, that he was a humble man. We will have more to say about his zeal for Torah learning and the third term of the eulogy, his being a "disciple of Ezra," in the next chapter.

37

Disciple of Ezra

EZRA AND AARON

In the final words of Hillel's eulogy, which praises him as a *hasid* and a humble man, he is called a "disciple of Ezra." He was also, as we can understand from his own theme-saying, a "disciple of Aaron." "Ezra the Scribe," as he is known in the tradition, was the spiritual father of the scribes and sages, and it is said that when the Torah was "forgotten" in Israel, he came up from Babylonia and restored it. The rabbis considered Hillel a worthy disciple of Ezra in a similar period of crisis and decline.

RESTORING THE TORAH

At first when the Torah was forgotten in Israel, Ezra came up from Babylonia and reestablished it. When once again it was forgotten, Hillel the Babylonian also came up to the Land of Israel and reestablished it (*Sukkah* 20a).

Hillel restored the Torah to its former glory in two ways. On the one hand, he influenced the sages and the manner in which they studied and interpreted the Torah: His views and methods were reflected throughout the *halachah*. On the other hand, Hillel also powerfully influenced the common people and spread the Torah to many who had become separated from it.

Hillel certainly achieved greatness in the Torah. He had two excellences in *halachah*, as a master of traditions and as an expert interpreter. Perhaps in this latter field he was also an innovator and involved in the formulation of the seven rules of Torah-interpretation; he certainly had a part in their popularization. However, we have in Hillel's name only a very limited number of midrashic teachings (that interpret scriptural verses), some halachic *midrash* (interpretations of a legal nature) and some aggadic *midrash* (legendary and nonlegal).

Hillel's lasting influence derives not only from his scholarship, but from his stature as a man of God and a religious leader. These sides of his personality are well portrayed in the stories about him and are evident in his own sayings. Most of his teachings are forceful and well-crafted proverbs and maxims about the religious life and morals. It is through these sayings that Hillel reached his broadest audience, among the sages and the common people.

EXPANSIVE KNOWLEDGE

In considering Hillel's great Torah knowledge, as a "disciple of Ezra," it is worth taking another look at a tradition briefly discussed earlier.

There was nothing of the words of the sages that Hillel had not learned; he had even learned the languages of all the peoples of the world; as well as the speech of mountains, hills, and valleys; the speech of trees and grasses, the speech of wild and domestic animals, the speech of demons – he was expert in parables too. Why was all this necessary? Because it is said, "God desired to make Israel worthy, so He expanded the borders of the Torah and made it glorious" (Isaiah 42:21) (*Soferim* 16:9).[1]

This text does not specifically mention the usual categories of the "words of the sages" – such as *Targum, Midrash, Halachah, Aggadah* – which are taken for granted, and lists only the exceptional areas of Hillel's knowledge.

All Human Languages

Hillel is said to have known all human languages, which were traditionally held to be the seventy languages of the seventy legendary nations of the world.[2] A later talmudic report[3] states that such incredible linguistic virtuosity was actually a qualification for appointment to the Sanhedrin. Hillel, who was believed to have been the head of the Sanhedrin, would of course have been expected to fulfill that requirement, but the tradition is obviously fanciful and fantastic.

We discussed earlier Katznelson's suggestion that Hillel's knowledge of the speech of mountains, hills, and valleys and of animals and plants originally meant that he had extensive knowledge of natural geography and natural history (biology), and possibly even lectured on those subjects. Katznelson also asked whether Hillel's knowledge of "all human languages" did not really allude to his familiarity with Greek language and science. He undoubtedly meant that Hillel's acquaintance with science was largely *through* his knowledge of Greek. Hillel seems to have known Greek, if he chose the Greek name *prosbul* for his famous ordinance. There is further support for his familiarity with Greek language and Greek wisdom from the fact that those subjects were studied in the house of the *Nasi*, Hillel's grandson, Rabban Gamaliel.[4] Did Rabban Gamaliel himself then learn and even teach Greek wisdom? And did Hillel, his grandfather?

Aramaic, the language of both Israel and Babylonia in Hillel's time, was his native tongue. As a scholar he of course also knew Hebrew. Unquestionably, an ability in other languages – such as Greek and Latin – would have been useful for a Jewish religious leader serving in a high position such as *Nasi* and dealing with resident or visiting foreigners who spoke those languages. Nor would it have been beyond the capability of a genius like Hillel to learn a number of languages. "All human languages" might then be an exaggeration of the folk mind, which goes easily from "many" to "all."

The Languages of Mountains, Hills, and Valleys

All the languages referred to in *Soferim* 16:9 – other than the human ones – relate to secret mystical knowledge, whether or not they are considered legendary and fictitious. The peculiar "speech of valleys," for example, appears in a story where the great mystic, Rabbi Simon bar Yohai, speaks to a valley and commands it to miraculously fill up with golden *dinars*.[5] In other legends, Eleazar ben Durdaya asks two mountains to pray for him, but they refuse,[6] and – in a story about Moses' death – the angel of death speaks to the mountains and the hills.[7] It seems reasonable to assume that Hillel's knowledge of the language of mountains, hills, and valleys was really the kind of knowledge of natural geography he demonstrates in the story of The 400 *Zuz* Bet, where he speaks about the sandy environment of Tarmod that affects the eyes of the people of that place or the marshy terrain of areas in Africa that affects the feet of the inhabitants.

The Languages of Animals and Plants

As for the languages of animals and plants, we have already noted how that same 400 *Zuz* Bet story shows Hillel's scientific knowledge of natural history (for example, comparing the long tails of cows with the short tails of donkeys). Legend turned this into something mystical, or so it seems. King Solomon was praised in the Torah as the wisest of men: "And he spoke about trees, from the cedar that is in Lebanon to the hyssop that comes out of the wall; he spoke about the beasts and birds, and about creeping things and fishes" (1 Kings 5:13). Thus, Solomon's tremendous learning included natural history. But the folk mind, far from science itself and thinking the reality all too prosaic, transformed this report into legends – scattered throughout rabbinic literature – about Solomon's secret knowledge of the "languages" of the beasts and birds, and so on.[8] The same sort of transformation may have occurred with Hillel, changing his biological knowledge into something more religious, mystical, and exotic.

Although Hillel's knowledge of the "languages" of animals and plants was most probably scientific, the face-value sense is clearly that it was mystic. Typically, the language of the animals means what it does in folktales – that animals communicate as do humans, but in their own languages. Thus, the mystic adept who understands their language can receive important information from them. There is a story, for example, that the mystic, Rabbi Pinhas ben Yair (Rabbi Simon bar Yohai's son-in-law), interpreted the chattering of mice to a group of farmers and told them that the mice were damaging their stored grain because it had not been properly tithed.[9]

It is hard to know where to draw the line between fictitious legends produced by the folk imagination, and true stories of mystic knowledge, but probably most or all of these traditions about the knowledge of the languages of mountains, hills, and valleys, or animals and plants, fall into the former category.

The Baal Shem Tov and other hasidic *rebbes* of his movement were said to have possessed a mystic knowledge of animal language. If we would seek to put this into a framework where it becomes more believable, the following hasidic story is helpful.

"The Yehudi [a hasidic *rebbe*, Rabbi Yaakov Yitzhak of Pshis'ha] and Peretz his disciple were crossing a meadow. Cattle put out to pasture there were lowing, and where it was watered by a stream a flock of geese rose from the water with a great cackling and beating of wings. 'If only one could understand what all of them are saying!' cried Peretz. 'When you get to the point of understanding the very core of what you yourself are saying,' said the rabbi, 'you will understand the language of all creatures.' "[10]

Although this tale is of course many centuries later than Hillel, something of the same thought is expressed in a Talmud story of mystical significance, about Hillel's disciple, Yohanan ben Zakkai, and one of that teacher's disciples. In the story, Eleazar ben Arach, sitting with Yohanan ben Zakkai in a field, expounds before his master what he has learned about mysticism on his own. "Then Rabbi Eleazar ben Arach began to speak about the Account of the Divine Chariot [esoteric mystic teachings], and a fire descended from heaven, surrounding all the trees in the field. And all the trees began to sing a song of praise to God. . . ."[11]

If this is what is meant by the mystic languages of plants and animals, perhaps Hillel knew it also.

The Language of Demons

We might be inclined to quickly dismiss the claim that Hillel knew the language of demons, but there are reasons to pause and consider a rationalistic explanation. It may be that this legend contains a kernel of truth, namely, that Hillel had a particular interest and concern with magic, in order to oppose it. In legend, King Solomon was famous not only for his knowledge of the language of animals, but also for knowing the language of demons and having power over them.[12] One talmudic legend, for example, tells how Solomon conjured some demons into his presence and forced them to reveal secret knowledge.[13] It should be mentioned that in Jewish tradition demons are not quite as malevolent as in Christianity, where they are agents of Satan. In the traditional Judaism of those times they still retained more of a folk character and were less theologically charged. Regardless of the fantastic nature of such legends about Solomon and the demons, they do show us what Hillel's knowledge of the language of the demons was supposed to entail.

However, even these legends about Solomon are likely to reflect the beliefs and practices of the times when they were created or were current. After mentioning King Solomon's expert knowledge of plants and animals and his ability to exorcize demons, Josephus reports having seen a Jewish exorcist cast out demons, using techniques passed down from Solomon and, in the name of Solomon, adjuring the demons, once cast out, not to return.[14] Elsewhere, Josephus says that the Essenes were expert healers and had secret books with the names of angels[15] (presumably, such knowledge enabled the mystic healer to make the angels reveal secrets or otherwise do his will, as in the legends of Solomon and the demons[16]).

A halachic ruling in the name of a descendant of Hillel, Rabban Simon ben Gamaliel, states: "On the Sabbath we do not put questions to demons."[17] The meaning is not clear, although it certainly relates to Hillel's supposed knowledge of the language of demons. It also relates to the legend where Solomon forces the demons to reveal secrets. If some occult technique used in the time of Rabban Simon ben Gamaliel was supposed to accomplish this, we do not know what it was. That questioning the demons was forbidden on the Sabbath indicates it was permitted on weekdays. The legend showing Solomon involved in this activity certainly implies approval, at least by those who passed on the legend. Whether Rabban Simon ben Gamaliel approved or was trying to limit a negative phenomenon (at least on the Sabbath) is unclear.

It is inconceivable that Hillel was involved in magic! – even if some occult practices had made inroads into certain religious circles. If there is something real behind the statement that he knew the language of demons, it might be that he knew *about* magic, "what magicians were up to," and could deal with them when necessary. The late talmudic statement mentioned earlier about qualifications for appointment to the Sanhedrin states that members of the Sanhedrin must *"know about magic, and speak all seventy human languages . . .* [italics added]."[18] Hillel was said to have known all human languages and also the language of demons – the same pair as here – except that the language of demons is replaced by a knowledge of magic.

Hillel's *midrash* about Samuel and Saul[19] made the point that Saul not only failed to do the word of God, but also asked a necromancer to call up the spirits of the dead. Was Hillel concerned about those *in his own time* who were involved in magic and "asking demons"? In *Avot* 2:8 he commented disapprovingly: "the more women (wives), the more magic." (This saying, which might trouble some people, will be discussed in a later chapter.) Thus, the claim that Hillel knew the language of demons might not be purely legendary and might be based on his knowing about magic and demonology in order to oppose them.

Parables

The last area of Hillel's Torah expertise mentioned in *Soferim* 16:9 is parables. We have many proverbs from Hillel, but only a small number of mostly sketchy parables.

Parables were especially useful in teaching the common people, and that is why Hillel would have known many. Some scholars, however, considered them less important, like the icing on the cake. Consequently, as the huge oral tradition handed down from generation to generation was condensed, parables – particularly lengthy ones – might have been most likely to drop out over time. Who knows how many of Hillel's parables were lost? We will have more to say about Hillel's parables in the next chapter.

Expanding the Torah's Borders

Soferim 16:9 concludes by asking why Hillel troubled himself to learn all these esoteric subjects, and answering with a quote from

Isaiah that "God desired to make Israel worthy, so He expanded the borders of the Torah and made it glorious." Hillel loved wisdom and knowledge and did not exclude any form of them from his active interest. Intelligent and liberal, he studied many subjects that others might have considered "secular," since for his open-minded piety all of Nature expressed God's glory and even science became Torah. In a curious way, legend took what might seem to be his most "secular" side and transformed it into the most mystical, claiming he knew the languages of plants and animals and so on. Yet, although some of his contemporaries probably disagreed with his undogmatic attitude and some in later generations might have misinterpreted the character of his wide-ranging studies, Hillel certainly brought honor on the sages and Israel by his own way of freely "expanding the borders of the Torah."

Hillel's Teaching Style

A COLLABORATION

Hillel saw the process of teaching and learning as an intimate collaboration between teacher and student. He taught: "A shy person cannot learn and an irritable person cannot teach."[1] A shy person cannot learn because he hesitates to ask questions about what he does not understand, and an irritable person cannot teach because he is bothered by questions and discourages them. As we saw in the stories of The 400 *Zuz* Bet and The Three Proselytes, Hillel himself was the most patient of teachers, who never considered any questioner or question foolish. He wanted to know where a student was now, even if his ideas were misguided, so he could effectively lead him onward. In The 400 *Zuz* Bet he gently addressed his questioner as "my son" and praised every question he asked, as "important." Perhaps with a teacher like Hillel even a shy person *could* learn.

A MASTER TEACHER

A number of times already we have noted Hillel's skill as a teacher. He always started where each person was, and then encouraged him to study more. Thus, after first teaching the gentile the Golden Rule, he told him to learn its "commentary." And he did not rebuke the confused convert who wanted to he high priest, but, starting where the man was, directed his self-study to the high priest's duties so he would learn for himself that his goal was inappropriate. Hillel even formulated a pedagogical principle for teachers: "Say not something that cannot be understood, because you think that in the end it will be understood."[2] A teacher must instruct each student according to his level at the moment.

Hillel also knew how to stimulate his students' minds. Once when he left his disciples a number of times on successive days, he said each time that he was going to care for his "houseguest," until their curiosity led them to question him about it and to discover he was talking about his soul. Another time, when he was teaching a new convert the alphabet, he reversed the order of the letters from one day to the next, to elicit his student's question, and then made his point, that if the student had to rely on the oral instruction of his teacher to understand such a simple written matter, he must surely rely on the Oral Torah tradition to explain the Written Torah. On another occasion, Hillel dramatically spoke to a skull floating in the water, in his disciples' presence, in order to teach *them*. Hillel was certainly a master teacher.

PROVERBS AND POPULAR WISDOM

Hillel, who was fascinated by proverbs and created many of them, often used folk proverbs to address the people in the language of their own popular wisdom. He constructed a "bridge" between the people and the Torah by combining in his teaching their folk proverbs with Torah verses. Again, it was a case of his starting where they were. Thus, he combines: (1) "Do not be seen naked, do not be seen dressed; do not be seen standing, do not be seen sitting; do not be seen *laughing*, do not be seen *weeping*" with "A time to *laugh* and a time to *weep*, a time to embrace and a time to refrain from embracing" (Ecclesiastes 3:4). (2) "*When* others are gathering, *scatter*; when others are scattering, gather" with "There is he who *scatters* and yet has more" (Proverbs 11:24) and "*It is a time* to act for the Lord – they have made void Your Torah!" (Psalms 119:126). (3) "To the *place* that my heart loves, there do my feet lead me" with "In every *place* where I cause My name to be mentioned, I will come to you there and bless you" (Exodus 20:21). This practice of Hillel's suggests his respect for popular wisdom and his recognition that many of the sayings in the Wisdom books of the Torah were the "divine popular" wisdom of earlier generations.

SOURCES FOR PARABLES

A skillful teacher of religion will often use parables and similes to explain subtle spiritual concepts by means of more tangible physical images. We had seen earlier[3] that Hillel was renowned for his knowledge of parables.

Custom and Etiquette

It seems to have been characteristic of Hillel's teaching style to use social customs and etiquette as sources for parables and parabolic images. In a teaching of his – one we discussed earlier, in the context of his encouraging pilgrimage – he taught the people that God would respond to their frequent visits to His House, the Temple, by visiting their houses and blessing them. He spoke in the name of God, saying: "If you will come to My House, I will come to your house; and if you will not come to My House, I will not come to your house." Hillel obtained this image from the etiquette of return visits.

Using another parabolic image from the etiquette of hospitality, Hillel spoke of the soul as an unfortunate traveler, a visitor in another's house, and he said that the "host" (the person himself) should act kindly to his guest. Again, Hillel told the convert who wanted to be high priest to study the Torah's teaching about the duties of that office and used the parabolic image of a courtier needing expertise in court etiquette: "Is it possible for someone to stand and serve a king if he does not know the court ceremonials?" In teaching that a person should be "mixed-in" with other people, Hillel used a traditional saying of conventional social wisdom and etiquette, about not being out of step with others, not laughing when they are crying, not standing when they are sitting, and so on, to convey a spiritual truth. It seems, then, that Hillel particularly used social customs and etiquette as a basis for some of his parables and teachings.

Rates for Hiring Donkeys

Other parables of Hillel were drawn from a different source. Hillel frequented the Temple in Jerusalem, but he also frequented another focal point, the gate of the city, where people gathered, where they went in and out, to and from their work. The story of Hillel at the gate of Jerusalem showed him speaking to the laborers who were leaving on their way to work. Another group he would have met at the gate of the city was the donkey drivers.

When Hillel explained to Bar He He why a person who repeats his Torah lesson a hundred times cannot be compared to someone who repeats it a hundred and one times, he said: "Go and learn from the station of the donkey drivers. Hiring an animal for ten miles costs one *zuz*, but for eleven miles – one extra mile – you pay two *zuzim*."[4] Obviously, Hillel himself visited the donkey driver station, where he picked up the information for this parable. The donkey drivers probably had their base at the gate of the city, where they hired out their donkeys for trips near and far. Every day Hillel talked to the laborers at the city gate, to draw them to the Torah, and he talked with the donkey drivers too. Perhaps he occasionally made use of their services and knew their rates from personal experience.

In another story discussed earlier,[5] a donkey driver teased Hillel about his origins, saying that whereas Hillel had to come from Babylonia, his own house was almost "at the gate of Jerusalem" – which was probably where they were standing as they talked, near the donkey drivers' station. Hillel returned his good-humored jest by explaining that just as the man's rates for his donkey were according to the length of the trip, so would he, Hillel, be rewarded for coming all the way from Babylonia. With Bar He He, he formulated his parable from a peculiarity of the price scale in hiring donkeys, namely, that there was a set fee up to a certain distance, and then a sudden jump in the price. With the donkey driver, Hillel drew his parable from the fact that when donkeys were hired, payment was according to the distance: The longer the distance, the higher the price. In each case he used a simple parable to explain spiritual realities.

We can also compare Hillel's question to the donkey driver, about the rates for hiring his donkey, to his question to the laborers going out to work – both were asked at the gate of Jerusalem. To the latter, he said: "How much will you earn today?" When told a *dinar* or two—just enough to survive—he told them to seek the greater reward of the Torah life. It was a regular feature of rabbinic teaching then to compare the "wages" God paid, to those that men received in this world for their work. Hillel must have used that comparison often in his conversations with workingmen. A comment of Glatzer on Hillel's question to the laborers at the gate of Jerusalem applies as well to his question to the donkey driver.

"Hillel's method of starting a conversation reminds us of the Stoics and the Cynics, and, of course, Socrates. He refers to the occupation of the one spoken to; it is this person's terminology and mode of thinking which Hillel uses to answer in order to let him discover for himself what the right thing is."[6]

Once again we see Hillel as the master teacher, starting where people are and patiently leading them to the truth, and to the Torah.

Hillel and the Rich

STUDY VERSUS BUSINESS

Hillel had much to do with the common people, with the day laborers and the donkey drivers, but he also had contact with and taught the rich. The story of The 400 *Zuz* Bet showed the haughty attitude he sometimes faced in dealing with men of the upper class. The tone of Hillel's teaching to the rich, or the would-be rich, can be gathered from some of his sayings. We can hear a ring of sarcasm in this word:

Not everyone who is much engaged in business becomes wise (*Avot* 2:6).

Hillel here deflates the pride of the men of commerce who consider their success in accumulating riches a sure sign of their wisdom. The unstated point of the sarcasm is that a person who seeks wisdom should not spend his time engaged in business, but more appropriately in studying Torah. As Hillel says elsewhere:

The more one sits and studies Torah, the more wisdom (*Avot* 2:8; this saying is translated slightly differently below).

Compare: "The men of Alexandria asked Rabbi Joshua ben Hananyah: 'What should a man do to become wise?' He said to them: 'Let him engage much in sitting learning Torah, and engage little in business.' "[1] Rabbi Joshua was one of the five close disciples of Rabbi Yohanan ben Zakkai, Hillel's disciple, and was essentially repeating the words of his master's master.

FALSE VERSUS TRUE GOALS

The last quoted saying of Hillel is part of a larger teaching of his in *Avot* 2:8 that is directed to the false opinions of the rich:

The more flesh, the more worms;
the more possessions, the more anxiety;
the more wives, the more witchcraft;
the more maid-servants, the more lewdness;
the more men-servants, the more thievery;

But the more Torah, the more life;
the more sitting in study, the more wisdom;
the more counsel, the more understanding;
the more charity, the more peace.

In the first half of this teaching, Hillel deprecates the crude ambition to be rich and "fat," and the false goals of increasing possessions, wives, and servants. According to Hillel, such strivings are worthless and lead only to trouble and disappointment. The tone is harsh and purposely seeks to arouse disgust by exposing and exaggerating the dark side of the drive for materialistic success. The increase that has value is that of Torah and good deeds. A person should be ambitious to grow and improve, but spiritually. While wealth leads only to anxiety now and worms at the time of death, Torah leads to peace, and life in this world and in the World-to-Come. Earlier we discussed Hillel's hasidic teaching about always doing "more," always "increasing."[2] In a sense, he considered ambitious people "worldly *hasidim*," ever striving to increase their wealth; they too wanted "more," but the wrong more.

Most if not all of the sentences that make up this teaching in *Avot* 2:8 should be seen as essentially separate and independent sayings.[3] Hillel liked the form: Increasing this, increases that.[4] This form had a history in the Wisdom tradition, such as in Ecclesiastes 1:18 and many other places. Hillel took these sayings that he had probably created and used over a period of time and shaped them into a whole; but when they are looked at separately, the meaning of some is better appreciated.

"The more flesh, the more worms [in the grave]." The word "flesh" (basar) is a crude reference to bodily weight, but since the same word means "meat" that is eaten, there might also be a passing allusion condemning a lust for meat characteristic of the rich.[5] Besides eating well, wealthy men wanted to accumulate possessions, wives, and servants. But increasing possessions increases the anxiety of caring for and protecting them. We see from Hillel's words that at that time a man could have "more wives" than one; perhaps polygamy was still common in certain circles of the wealthy.[6] Because his intent was to disparage the urge to accumulate (and only indirectly to discourage polygamy) Hillel states that more wives lead to more witchcraft. The Talmud says: "In general, it is women who practice magic"[7] (because they were excluded from fully participating in Judaism?). Perhaps wives of one man engaged in magic to win their husband's affection or harm their rivals.[8] Many female servants in a household were an ever-present temptation for the men, whether family members or male servants. As is well known, some masters sexually exploit female servants,[9] and some servants pilfer their master's property. Hillel's purpose to expose the sordidness of greed and reveal the results of misused wealth should be understood, and he should not be accused of having a low opinion of servants, or, for that matter, of showing prejudice against women by his condemnation of witchcraft.[10] He was simply describing reality and might as well be accused of having a low opinion of masters and men. The saying mentions three sinful activities: witchcraft, lewdness, and thievery. Hillel not only opposed all three, but perhaps had a special concern as Nasi to condemn and discourage magic and witchcraft. Simon ben Shetah, one of the pair that preceded Hillel's masters, Shemaya and Avtalyon, in the religious leadership, vigorously opposed witchcraft among the women of Israel.[11]

With Avot 2:8 Hillel tried to dispel the materialistic delusions of the rich and teach them to direct their ambition to spiritual goals. Fittingly, in a teaching for the rich, he concludes with praise of charity ("the more charity, the more peace"). If we consider its second half and focus on the spiritual rewards that Hillel said flow from the Torah path, they are, in order: life (increased vitality in this world and eternal life in the next); wisdom; understanding; and, as the seal, the final blessing that is the receptacle to contain all other blessings – peace.

"The more Torah, the more life" in *Avot* 2:8 is a key saying and tells us much about Hillel. What kind of person makes "more life" a goal? Clearly, someone full of life and vitality. For Hillel, Torah was not an end in itself in the narrow sense. When he deprecrated empty striving after material pleasures and comforts, he was not seeking to encourage bookishness; he did not replace the ideal of the merchant with that of the reclusive scholar, who never leaves the House of Study and lives his life exclusively through books and ideas – even those of Torah. That is why the energetic and vigorous Hillel left the study hall to go to the marketplace to make peace, and to the city gates to offer "more life" to burdened laborers. How? through Torah. He called them back to the study hall, but the goals were increased life and increased peace. In the second half of *Avot* 2:8, life and peace, mentioned at beginning and end, are the spiritual goals; the inner pair of Torah wisdom and understanding are essentially means to lead a person to attain those blessings in this world.

The More Counsel, the More Understanding

We have already dealt separately – in this and other chapters – with three of the four sayings in the second half of *Avot* 2:8.[12] The remaining saying is: "The more counsel, the more understanding." "Counsel" (particularly about practical matters and "life-decisions") was typically sought from family, friends, and sages. A sage who studied Torah for pure motives, for the sake of God alone, was considered to be specially blessed with an ability to help people by his counsel.[13] The Torah's Wisdom books frequently commend the value of *much* advice, for example: "In a multitude of counselors there is victory" (Proverbs 24:6). Thus, Hillel's words – that "the *more* counsel, the more understanding" – mean taking advice from a number of religious people – Torah sages, if possible – before acting. Through the ages rabbis have always helped people who came to them for advice about their affairs, both worldly and spiritual. Probably Hillel, who took a deep interest in the welfare of the people, was himself a much sought-after adviser.

Hillel's saying about increasing understanding through counsel must also be looked at as part of the larger saying of *Avot* 2:8, and particularly its second half. In that context, note that Torah is followed by "sitting in study," which would ordinarily mean in the setting of an academy, and that after Torah is mentioned generally, the pair of wisdom and understanding are specified. Hillel's intention seems to have been that by associating with Torah teachers and comrades in study, a person will attain not only scholarly wisdom, but the practical understanding to make correct decisions in pursuing a religious life. Thus: "The more sitting [with others] in study, the more wisdom; the more counsel [from others], the more understanding."

NO EXCUSES

Hillel tried to persuade the rich and the poor to seek Torah. Both were preoccupied: the rich with their riches and the poor with their poverty. Hillel told the laborers on their way to work that their efforts would win them only their mere necessities, while devotion to Torah offered much greater rewards. He told the rich that they would not find happiness by increasing their possessions – but only in Torah and charity.

Hillel knew that both the rich and the poor alike claim they are overwhelmed by their daily concerns and troubles. But his response was: "If not now, when?" (Avot 1:14). In the same vein, he warned:

Say not, "When I have time, I'll study";
   perhaps you will never have any time (Avot 2:5).

Shammai's saying: "Set fixed times for your Torah study"[14] sounds like a companion to Hillel's. Both teach that the demands of a person's spiritual life must come first, other things second; not the reverse. His religious practices should be fixed, his main concern and occupation; worldly matters should be "fit in." Although the two sayings of Hillel and Shammai are indeed complementary, it confirms our expectation that the strict Shammai emphasized the fixing of times for study, while Hillel turned his attention to the inside, to the psychology of the situation and the need to correct a common delusion, and from that perspective he offered his sage instruction.

IV

Holy Spirit,
Holy Legacy

40

A Good Name versus a Great Name

A GOOD NAME

The ringing praise of Hillel in the mouths of his contemporaries is the good name he won for himself – as a *hasid*, a humble man, and a disciple of Ezra. He himself attached importance to a good name among one's fellowmen, as we see from a saying of his.

> He who has acquired a good name,
>   has acquired it for himself;
> and he who has acquired words of Torah,
>   has acquired life in the World-to-Come (*Avot* 2:8).

Hillel paired a good name with the acquisition of Torah, for the Torah teaches a person to show the love and concern for others – by charity, good deeds, and acts of kindness – that win him a good name with his fellowmen.[1]

In the previous chapter we discussed Hillel's related saying: "The more Torah, the more life." Torah gives life in both this world and – as emphasized in the saying we are considering – the World-to-Come. The parallelism in Hillel's saying – of "for himself" and "in the World-to-Come" – indicates that a good name is "for oneself" because it not only benefits a person in this world, but accompanies him into the next. A rabbinic teachings says: "A good name is forever, it never fails."[2] The rabbis similarly taught that charity is "for oneself." Contrary to the common view, they claimed that money stored up is "for others," because while it may benefit a person in this world, it will not help him in the next. When he dies others will inherit it, and even in this world it can be lost or stolen. However, what he donates as charity is not – as it may seem – for others but for himself, because good deeds of eternal worth accompany him to the next world.[3] Claiming that a good name and charity are "for oneself," while accumulation of wealth is "for others," is of course an exact reversal of the secular perspective, and that is the very point. Since worldly people insist on doing what is "for oneself," Hillel and the religious cleverly turned that argument around to their own use by looking at what is "for oneself," and in one's interest, from the aspect of eternity.

Since the respect and affection of one's fellowmen is often acquired by charity, the pursuit of a good name conflicts with a person's avarice. In fact, in *Avot* 2:8 Hillel's saying about the good name and Torah follows his stark contrast of the false value of material gain with the true value of increased spirituality: the more flesh, wives, servants, and possessions versus the more Torah and charity. These are essentially two independent sayings, and have, therefore, been discussed separately; nevertheless, the editor who joined them in *Avot* 2:8 correctly perceived their close relation.[4] Perhaps Hillel himself was the "editor" and joined these two sayings as a basis for some of his sermons.

The Torah verse that attracted the most rabbinic commentary about the good name is Ecclesiastes 7:1: "A good name is better than precious ointment." Good oil for anointing was a sign of wealth. Proverbs 22:1 is more explicit: "Choose a good name over great riches." A rabbinic teaching explains: " 'Choose a good name over great riches, and good grace in men's eyes over silver and gold' – See how precious a good name is in this world, for even if a person has vast wealth, if he has not acquired a good name, he has not acquired a thing."[5] What does a person gain by wealth, if he is disliked by his fellowmen?

Hillel's saying joins the acquisition of a good name to the acquisition of Torah. In a sense, they stand respectively for a person's obligations to man and to God, with the good name being of particular interest to Hillel and the *hasidim. Parushim* are inclined to concentrate on Torah at the expense of all else. They can elevate Torah so much that they become intolerant of their less learned and less religious fellowmen, and they separate from them. But *hasidim* such as Hillel, whose goal is the kingdom of peace and the mystic unity of people, are more concerned with deeds of kindness (*hesed*) and cherish the good opinion of others. They cannot say: "I'll win God's favor; what do I care what people think." Thus, Hillel's teaching, that a person must win not only God's approval, but a good name – the approval of his fellowmen – should be seen in its larger context as expressing his basic humanism and as being part of his teachings about peace, about not separating from the community, being "mixed-in" with others, and so on. It is obvious too why a good name would be precious to *hasidim* such as Hillel, who love people and desire to be loved in return. How appropriate then that the founder of the modern hasidic movement, Rabbi Israel ben Eliezer, should have attained the popular epithet, the "Baal Shem Tov," whose Hebrew meaning is: "he who has acquired a good name."[6]

Although Hillel taught that Torah knowledge and a good name must go together, there is a sense in which a good name is superior even to Torah. A person can be an expert scholar and perform much of the Torah without truly caring for other people. But a sign that someone has grasped the Torah's essence – which, as Hillel taught, is loving one's neighbor as oneself – can be found in his possession of a good name.[7] That is one meaning of the rabbinic saying: "There are three crowns: the crown of Torah, the crown of priesthood, and the crown of kingship; but the crown of a good name is above them all."[8]

To some degree the teachings of Hillel and the rabbis about a good name are strange to people from the West, which has a different social concept. The situation is something like what we found with Hillel's and the rabbis' concept of peace. There is no real parallel in English to the Jewish *religious* concept of the good name. What we call a "good reputation" is superficial and has no religious connotation. But although there may be no word or phrase in English that captures what is meant by a good name, the lesson of Hillel's teaching about it still applies today.

A GREAT NAME

Being respected and having a good name is, of course, not quite the same as fame or a "great name." God promised Abraham a "great name,"[9] and Abraham was held in high esteem by the people of the land, who called him a "great prince" or *nasi.*[10] Hillel also became famous and won that same title (which became a title of office and leadership among the Jewish people) of *Nasi.* Hillel's fame was unsought. To those who sought honor, he taught:

A name made great is a name destroyed (*Avot* 1:13).[11]

This teaching that fame is empty befits Hillel's humility. However, the Hebrew of this saying can be translated and understood in more than one way. The preceding translation is the most likely one; another with a different nuance would be:

A name is made great; his name is destroyed.

This would teach the evanescence of fame, a "great name," which may be here today but gone tomorrow, if not during a person's lifetime, then after his death. This interpretation is found in a rabbinic comment on Hillel's saying:

" 'A name is made great; his name is destroyed' – Someone becomes famous in the city: 'So-and-so is handsome,' people say, or 'He's as strong as they come.' But tomorrow you try to find him and you did not even know that he had died and passed from the world."[12]

This interpretation follows a common motif of the Psalms, about the transitory nature of life, and fits with a saying of Hillel's elsewhere that uses similar language about the poor soul, which is "here today, but gone tomorrow."[13]

Hillel, who wanted to humbly serve others, wanted a good name – which came from good works – not fame or a great name. He was always aware that honor and glory belong to God and that a person should never "use" God's honor for himself. Another saying of his (collected with the one previously quoted, in *Avot* 1:13) states:

He who makes his own use of the crown shall perish.

The image is of a king's crown: Anyone else who dares even to handle it, let alone put it on, deserves a punishment of instant death. Using for oneself the honor of the King of the Universe is fraught with spiritual danger. Particularly the rabbis, who have the crown of the Torah, must not use the honor that others bestow on them – to honor the Torah and God – for themselves. The priests had lost their position as leaders by their misuse of the crown of the priesthood; Hillel wanted to ensure that the rabbis who took their place would not commit the error of misusing their crown of the Torah. And who could have been a better model for them than their revered *Nasi*, the modest and humble Hillel, who had won the crown of a good name?

The Holy Spirit

IN GURYA'S HOUSE

Hillel's eulogy is joined to two other traditions.

Our rabbis taught: Since the death of the last prophets—Haggai, Zechariah, and Malachi—the holy spirit was removed from Israel, but they would still hear a heavenly voice.

Once, while the sages were reclining at a meeting, in the upper room of the house of Gurya in Jericho, they heard a voice from heaven, saying: "There is one among you who is worthy that the Divine Presence rest upon him as it did on our teacher Moses, but his generation does not merit it." Hearing this, all the sages fixed their eyes on Hillel the Elder.

And when he died they said in his eulogy: "O *hasid*! O humble man! disciple of Ezra!" (*Sanhedrin* 11a).

The Bat Kol

The story about Hillel is introduced by a single line of independent tradition that says that although prophecy ceased in Israel "something was left"—the heavenly voice. Literally, this is a *bat kol*, a "daughter of a voice"—the idiom for an "echo"—meaning, in its religious usage, that this remained when the direct voice of prophecy was no longer heard. The editor placed this sentence before the

Hillel story not only because the latter has an example of a heavenly voice, but because it states that Hillel could have restored prophecy had the generation been worthy.

The parallel account in the Jerusalem Talmud (*Sotah* 9:13, 24b), says that Hillel was "worthy of the holy spirit." In the tradition, possession of the holy spirit is often used synonymously with the resting of the *Shechinah* (Divine Presence) on someone. In *Sanhedrin* 11a the same is intended: Note the mention of the holy spirit at the beginning. In other words, Hillel could have restored the holy spirit that had disappeared with the last prophets. Not only that, but he could have reached the level of Moses. It is high praise indeed for Hillel to be compared to Moses[1] and considered worthy of an equal revelation. I assume that the three paragraphs I have separated in my translation were originally three independent traditions. The one about Hillel and the sages in Gurya's house is attached to the eulogy because they both speak of Hillel's great stature – how he was praised from heaven by the heavenly voice and on earth at his eulogy.[2]

The story about Hillel and his brother Shebna also had a heavenly echo. There, it quoted a scriptural verse and testified to Hillel's great love of God ("If a man were to give all the wealth of his house for love, he would be utterly despised"). This scene in Jericho takes place later in Hillel's life and clearly has a larger significance. It also tells us to what degree Hillel's greatness was recognized during his lifetime, even if not by all.

But did the sages present actually hear a heavenly voice? I am not inclined to take this literally.[3] I imagine it to mean that a remarkable incident occurred – who knows what it was – that made evident to the assembled sages that Hillel was an awesomely holy person. They all sat silently in a supercharged atmosphere, at one in their realization that they were in the presence of someone utterly unique, and it was only the lowliness of the generation that prevented Hillel from achieving even greater things than he had already accomplished.

An Unworthy Generation

According to the rabbis, God gives the holy spirit of prophecy for the sake of the generation, for the people, not for the individual.

That Hillel's generation was unworthy could mean simply that the whole generation was not on a high enough spiritual level. Such a thing can indeed happen; one man can stand out from his generation, stand above it entirely, as if he were from another world. But many of Hillel's disciples were extraordinary. More likely, then, the fact that Hillel did not attain what he could have because his generation was unworthy refers mainly to his opponents. He could have gone higher and raised the whole people higher, if he and his teachings had been universally accepted.

Since Hillel was popular among the masses of people and among the wing of the rabbis whom he represented in the leadership, the primary candidates for making the generation unworthy are Shammai and his wing of the Pharisee movement. The tradition that reports Shammai's temporary success in humiliating Hillel and forcing his own views through on a number of issues, laments that "that day was as grievous for Israel as the day on which they made the Golden Calf." The rueful sentiment sounds similar to the "unworthiness of the generation." Shammai's constant opposition impeded Hillel at every step.

Nevertheless, there are other candidates for "unworthiness," such as the Sadducees and the high priestly families who (in the person of their foremost member, the high priest) set themselves against Hillel's masters, Shemaya and Avtalyon, and most probably against Hillel also. Herod and his cohorts also deserve mention, so too the rich, such as the two who thought nothing of toying with Hillel's dignity in their bet. In fact, even the poor man who teased Hillel about his Babylonian origins evinced a lack of respect. Certainly there were still others who looked down on Hillel as a Babylonian and resented his leadership.

We know nothing about the purpose of this meeting of the sages[4] in the story, nor why they met in Jericho and in Gurya's house.[5] What is somewhat remarkable is that this is the only place name we have for a story about Hillel outside of Jerusalem.[6]

EIGHTY DISCIPLES

The story of Hillel in Gurya's house in Jericho said that he was on the highest spiritual level and worthy that the Divine Presence rest on him as it did on Moses. Another tradition says the same about many of his disciples.

> Our rabbis taught:
> Hillel the Elder had eighty disciples:
> > thirty of them were worthy that the Divine Presence
> > rest on them as on Moses our teacher;[7]
> > thirty were worthy that the sun stand still in the
> > sky for them as it did for Joshua the son of Nun;
> and twenty of them were ordinary (*Sukkah* 28a).[8]

Moses and his disciple Joshua are used elsewhere by the rabbis to represent different spiritual levels, Moses being compared to the sun, Joshua to the moon, the lesser light who reflected his master's greatness with some diminution.[9] Hillel's disciples were recognized as an extraordinary group; certainly the "ordinary" ones were only ordinary compared with the others.

Thirty of his disciples were said to be equal to their illustrious master and on Hillel's own exalted level. The phraseology parallels what is said in the other story about Hillel himself. The second group of thirty is said to be worthy of rare miracles (such as the sun standing still). Since the lower-level disciples were said to be worthy of miracles, the same would certainly be understood for Hillel and the first group of his disciples. Of course, being worthy of miracles does not mean that they actually occurred, yet if no miracles were ascribed to Hillel's disciples, such a tradition would be somewhat anomalous. Both reception of the holy spirit and the power to do miracles through prayer were signs of divine favor and high spiritual levels. A story in the Talmud tells how in the generation after Hillel, while the Second Temple still stood, the sun turned back for a saintly Jew named Nakdimon ben Gurion, just as it had for Joshua.[10]

Generally, the report about Hillel's eighty disciples, many of whom were exceptional and extraordinary, is intended to glorify them and him. We can consider it the mark of the founder of a movement, such as Hillel was, to have many disciples on a very high spiritual level. Certainly he had hundreds and possibly thousands of disciples and followers; but these eighty were the core group, his full disciples, who followed his discipline and were under his personal direction. Presumably they were the foundation for what grew to be a strong movement in Judaism, in fact the central movement of its time, the House of Hillel.

The number eighty for Hillel's disciples may be conventional to some degree. The tradition that Menahem, Hillel's original partner in the leadership, before Shammai, left the office and went into the service of Herod, says he was followed by eighty pairs of disciples, all of them clothed in silk robes. A second version about Hillel's disciples also says that they were eighty *pairs*. Presumably the members of each pair studied together.

YONATAN BEN UZZIEL AND YOHANAN BEN ZAKKAI

What is remarkable, though, is that we know the names of only two, or possibly three, of this large group of Hillel's eighty disciples: Yonatan ben Uzziel, Yohanan ben Zakkai, and possibly Bar He He. Following the report of Hillel's eighty disciples and their levels of attainment, we are told that "the greatest of them was Yonatan ben Uzziel and the least (or youngest?[11]) was Yohanan ben Zakkai." Elsewhere, Hillel himself is recorded as having said that although Yohanan was the youngest of all his disciples, he too would be "a father to wisdom and a father of generations" of spiritual children (disciples) to follow.[12] Of course, years later, in the terrible crisis caused by the Roman destruction of the Temple and Jerusalem, it was Yohanan ben Zakkai who stood in the breach and ensured that Judaism survived and adapted to the new conditions. According to the tradition, the contribution of Yonatan ben Uzziel, Hillel's greatest disciple, was his translation (*targum*) of the books of the Prophets into the people's spoken language, Aramaic. By revealing the secrets of the prophecies in his explanatory translations, he was said to have prevented disruptive disputes over the meaning of the texts.[13] It is said that when Yonatan ben Uzziel sat and studied Torah any bird that overflew him was burned up as with fire.[14] Certainly the "burned birds" of Yonatan are figurative.[15] The meaning is that his devotional involvement in Torah study was so very holy–intense and fiery–that no foreign presence could intrude into his sphere without being obliterated; his holiness was impenetrable. The tradition about Hillel's eighty disciples, and the greatest and least among them, is followed by praise of Yohanan ben Zakkai, stating that there was no area of Torah he did not master, and listing all the many branches of the Torah in which he excelled.[16] Yohanan ben Zakkai, then, was praised especially for breadth of Torah knowledge and Yonatan ben Uzziel was praised for intensity. We can extrapolate back to the master from these two exceptional direct disciples and get some insight into the Torah level of Hillel himself, who was said to have restored the glory of the Torah when it was being forgotten. Indeed, one version of the tradition about Yonatan ben Uzziel and his fiery Torah study exclaims: "If this is the disciple, what was the master!"[17]

A LADDER TO HEAVEN

In the story about Hillel in the house of Gurya in Jericho the heavenly voice said that he was worthy of the holy spirit. What brought him to that exalted level? Some background is necessary. A famous sentence of ancient rabbinic teaching gives the sequence of rungs on the ladder of spiritual attainment. It is in the name of Rabbi Pinhas ben Yair (second century C.E.), the son-in-law of Simon bar Yohai, the great rabbi most closely associated with the mystical tradition.

"Rabbi Pinhas ben Yair used to say: 'Zeal leads to cleanliness, cleanliness to purity, purity to separation from worldliness, separation to holiness, holiness to humility, humility to the fear of sin, the fear of sin to hasidism (piety), hasidism leads to the holy spirit, the holy spirit leads to the revival of the dead, and the revival of the dead comes through Elijah, of blessed memory.' "[18]

Other versions of this sentence have mostly minor variations in the order of the stages. One, however, has an important addition after the full list: "And [said Rabbi Pinhas ben Yair] Hasidism is greater than all of them [other spiritual qualities], as it is said: 'Then You spoke in visions to your *hasidim*' (Psalm 89:20). Rabbi Joshua ben Levi, however, disagreed with Rabbi Pinhas ben Yair, and said that humility is greater than all of them, as it is said: 'The Spirit of the Lord God is upon me, because the Lord has anointed me to bring good tidings to the humble' (Isaiah 61:1). It does not say '*hasidim*,' but 'the humble.' From this you learn that humility is greater than all of them."[19]

Clearly, this teaching of the ladder of spiritual ascent is only for

the most serious aspirants. The sequence of steps seems to have been
in debate. Pinhas ben Yair held that the highest attribute was hasidism, Joshua ben Levi that it was humility. According to the Torah
verses they cited for support, it was this or that quality that led to God
speaking to a person in visions, or the Spirit of the Lord coming upon
him. Note that in Pinhas ben Yair's "ladder" saying, hasidism is the
last attribute directly dependent on a person's efforts, with the holy
spirit, revival of the dead, and "Elijah" being levels of attainment that
are gifts from God. "Elijah" here refers to the spiritual level that the
rabbis call "revelations of Elijah," where Elijah appears to a person to
teach him mystic wisdom. There is a close relation between such
visions and possession of the holy spirit. The "revival of the dead"
refers not to the eschatalogical event at the end of days, but to the
miracles wrought by holy men, such as Elijah, who raised the dead.[20]

The two rabbis differed as to whether hasidism or humility
was the greatest attribute that led to the holy spirit. In that light we
can consider again the associated traditions of: (1) the heavenly voice
about Hillel in the house of Gurya in Jericho and (2) Hillel's eulogy.
The former says that Hillel was worthy of the holy spirit and the
latter praises him as being a *hasid* and a humble man. Now we can
see that the possession of these two exalted attributes in their
fullness *made* him worthy of the holy spirit. The talmudic commentator, the Maharsha, says on this tradition about Hillel: "It was said
in Hillel's eulogy 'O *hasid*! O humble man! etc.' and for that reason
he was worthy that the *Shechinah* rest on him, for those two
attributes of hasidism and humility lead to the holy spirit, as it says
in *Avodah Zarah* 20b [the ladder of spiritual ascent], for one view
there is that Hasidism is the greatest of attributes and leads to the
holy spirit, and the other view is that humility is the greatest and
leads to the holy spirit."

PROPHECY AND WISDOM

The tradition said that "since the death of the last prophets . . .
the holy spirit was removed from Israel." It also said that Hillel was
worthy that the holy spirit descend on him as on Moses, but his
generation was not worthy. Are we, then, to understand that due to
the lowliness of his generation Hillel did *not* attain the holy spirit? It
would be strange indeed if a teaching like that of Pinhas ben Yair
existed for the spiritual advancement of the *hasidim*, and yet

someone such as Hillel, the greatest of the great, had not in fact succeeded in reaching the final goal. This is hardly possible and is not actually the case. Many great rabbis throughout the generations had the holy spirit, but not the holy spirit of *prophecy*. Hillel also had the holy spirit, but he did not hear the voice of God or see visions – his inspiration was of a different sort. He was not a prophet, because his generation was not able to hear the kind of words a prophet speaks, but a sage. Hillel guided his own life by the promptings of the holy spirit, and spoke to the people not with prophecy, but with the holy spirit of divine wisdom.[21]

The rabbis knew the difference between the two voices that communicate God's word to the people – prophecy and wisdom – and knew that wisdom is softer. Prophecy is more direct, but only the strong can take its direct blast of rebuke. Wisdom knows how to speak indirectly and can more easily win back sinners. Perhaps that is why Hillel's generation was "unworthy," because instead of appearing in glory, Hillel's holiness had to cover itself in humility and lowliness to win back, by soft words, so many who had become separated from God.

The rabbis perceived a decisive change in the spiritual economy caused by the disappearance of prophets. The story about Hillel (being worthy, etc.) is one example of their reflection on this matter. Another rabbinic teaching says: "From the day the Temple was destroyed, prophecy was taken from the prophets and given to the sages."[22] The rabbis recognized that while the torch had been passed, something had changed. Do not be misled by the language of the saying, for "prophecy" is not what passed to the sages – they were sages, not prophets. Rather, the holy spirit of divine wisdom was working through Hillel and the other sages to communicate the will of God to man.

But for all the excellence of wisdom[23] – the rabbis knew that something important had been lost with the disappearance of prophecy: the open revelation of "Thus says the Lord." In the teaching about the cessation of prophecy and the connected story about Hillel in the house of Gurya in Jericho, they communicated a profound sense of loss and regret and their belief that if not for the faults of his generation – too many of whom were far from God or opposed to his leadership – Hillel could have received a greater measure of heavenly inspiration, and raised the people of Israel to even greater heights. We will hear more about Hillel's holy spirit in the next chapter.

42

The Rejoicing of the Water-drawing

Some notable sayings of Hillel, and a story about him, have the Temple ceremony of *Simhat Beit HaSho'evah*, the Rejoicing of the Place of the Water-drawing, as their backdrop and context, and that fact is of great significance, particularly with regard to Hillel's possession of the holy spirit. But to appreciate that, it is necessary first to consider in some depth the nature of the Rejoicing (as we will sometimes abbreviate the full name).

TRADITIONS ABOUT THE CEREMONY

This event, which was part of the Temple services, took place on a number of days during the week of Sukkot, the Festival of Booths.[1] Today, Sukkot is associated with the primary *mitzvah* of the holiday, dwelling in booths, *sukkahs*, and also with the ceremonial waving of the four plant species: the *etrog* (citron), palm branch, myrtles, and willows. But in Hillel's time, the Rejoicing of the Place of the Water-drawing was also a highlight of the festival. With the Temple's destruction, however, most aspects of this observance disappeared. The basic part of the ritual service was a water-libation (pouring water on the altar), performed after the morning daily burnt offering. In ancient times this had been conceived as the "drink" offered to God with His "food"; the water was part of a symbolic "meal" reverently offered to the Lord in His House by His servants. Later, another meaning became more prominent, the belief that God sent the blessing of rain (water) in return for this water-offering, and that timely and plentiful rains depended on the performance of the ritual.[2] The water for the libation was taken from the Pool of Shiloah near Jerusalem, and a grand and ceremonious procession led there and back to the Temple, where the water was poured out on the altar. The joyous sounds of flutes and harps accompanied the procession as well as the water-drawing and at the libation in the Temple there was music provided by the Levites.

It was said that whoever had not seen the Rejoicing of the Water-drawing had never seen rejoicing in his life.[3] The main celebrations, however, were at night, during devotional vigils awaiting the morning water-libations. Before the holiday, four huge golden candlesticks were erected in the Temple court, and during the holiday their light, which shone down from the heights of the Temple Mount, could be seen all over the city.[4] At night, in the light of these candlesticks, the people gathered in the Court of the Women in the Temple, and the most pious danced and sang before them in holy joy, holding aloft – and some even juggling – torches. It must have been a remarkable sight.

"In the Court of the Women the *hasidim* and men of deeds danced before the people with torches in their hands and sang hymns and praises of God. Standing in order on the fifteen steps that led down from the Court of the Israelites to the Court of the Women, the Levites accompanied them with song and music on harps, psalteries, cymbals, and numberless instruments. . . .

"The *hasidim* and men of deeds sang 'Happy is our youth that did not shame our old age,' and the repentant sang 'Happy is our old age that has atoned for our youth.' And both these and those together would sing 'Happy are those who have not sinned; but he who has sinned, let him repent and he will be forgiven.' "[5]

A few names are associated with this wonderful scene. We are told: "Ben Yehotzedek was famous for delighting everyone with his spectacular acrobatic leaps during the dancing."[6] Those who danced, sang, and taught were great people. One of those named is Hillel's great-grandson. "When Rabban Simon ben Gamaliel rejoiced at the Rejoicing of the Water-drawing, he would juggle eight torches without one touching the other. And when he prostrated, he fell down, holding himself up with his fingers alone, kissed the pavement, and then threw himself upright again – an altogether impossible feat."[7] The figure most prominently associated with this event, however, is Hillel himself, as we will see shortly.

The scene at the Rejoicing is that of an outpouring of religious joy. This befits the leading part taken by the *hasidim*. Such exploits of ecstatic joy come from the deepest love and devotion. This celebration should, in fact, be understood as a full manifestation of what is meant by serving God from love. Hillel had said that when a Jew's heart was filled with love for God his feet carried him to the Temple; once there and at such a time of celebration, the love in his heart caused his feet to leap and dance. When Simon ben Gamaliel did his acrobatic prostrations he kissed the pavement out of his boundless love for the House of God.

One of the distinguishing aspects of this celebration in the Temple is its popular character. The rabbis, or those of them who were *hasidim* and men of deeds, took the leading part, not the priests. As far as the Temple ceremonies go, this is unique. It probably explains why the Sadducees, who represented the interests of the Temple establishment, objected to the water-libation ceremony, which was supported by the Pharisees.[8] The dispute about it was a long-standing one between the Temple authorities and the popular leaders of the people, such as Hillel.

"[It was asked:] Why is this celebration called the Rejoicing of the Place of the 'Drawing-up'? [Although the Hebrew word for "drawing-up" is used for water and other fluids, water is not mentioned in the name of the ceremony.] It was answered: Because from there they drew up the holy spirit, as it is said: 'And you shall draw up water with joy from the wells of salvation' (Isaiah 12:3)."[9]

Among the higher-minded of the people, this symbolic and spiritual meaning of the water-drawing superseded the more this-worldly interest in its effect on the blessing of rain.

The rabbis taught that the holy spirit would not descend on a person sad or dull, but only on someone joyful from doing a *mitzvah*.[10] The Torah story they often mentioned to illustrate this was the prophet Elisha asking a musician to play so the holy spirit would come upon him.[11] They also said that the prophet Jonah had come up to Jerusalem for the Festival of Sukkot and that the holy spirit came upon him at the Rejoicing of the Place of the Water-drawing.[12] These traditions clearly reflect the situation during the time of the rabbis also, when due to the exultation at the Rejoicing in the Temple – the exuberant communal prayer of praises and hymns, music, song, and dance, even juggling and acrobatics – some of the great *hasidim* present attained the holy spirit. It was said that they became "vessels" to receive the holy spirit and then poured it forth in inspired teaching to the masses of people.[13]

HILLEL AND THE REJOICING OF THE WATER-DRAWING

This amazing event is the spectacular backdrop for three sayings that Hillel spoke to the people. Probably the sayings that were preserved are actually only *themes* of discourses he gave. His prominence at this celebration where the *hasidim* took such a leading part is something very much worthy of note. We have already discussed one of the sayings, although without mentioning that it was spoken at the Rejoicing of the Water-drawing.[14] That was the teaching that a person's feet lead him to the place his heart loves, and God saying: "If you come to My House, I will go to yours."[15]

Clearly this teaching directly relates to the event at which it was spoken – the Rejoicing of the Water-drawing, the high point of the pilgrimage festival of Sukkot. Hillel taught the people that their attendance at the Temple, their feet "carrying" them there, was a sign of their devotion and would bring them God's blessing in return. Hillel used the proverb of a person's feet carrying him to the place his heart loves. In the *Midrash* the rabbis give a piquant illustration of the "magnetic" attraction houses of God have for the most pious: King David "complains" to God about his unavoidable religious distraction, saying: "Master of the World! Every day I make plans to go to this or that place. But when I start off, my feet inevitably carry me to synagogues and Houses of Torah study!"[16] David's prayerful complaint might seem to be just a rabbinic whimsy, but with some God-intoxicated people, such a thing can be literally true. Hillel himself was so attracted to the House of Study that he could not be kept away by the doorkeeper, and while on the roof was so entranced at hearing the words of the living God that he did not even notice being covered over with snow. If such was his devotion to the House of Study, how much more so to the Temple!

IN THE NAME OF GOD

In Hillel's teaching he spoke in the first person, in the name of God: "If you come to *My* House then *I* will come to your house, etc." Since there could be some confusion about this, the editor of a later version felt the need to add an explicit reference to God as the speaker: "So did the Holy One, blessed be He, say: 'If you come to My House, etc.' "[17] But it is noticeable that, in what is certainly the more original version, Hillel did *not* make this clarification. This is somewhat strange and suggests that there is something out of the ordinary here.

Another saying that Hillel spoke in the Temple during the Rejoicing of the Water-drawing:

If I am here, all are here; but if I am not here, who is here?[18]
(*Sukkah* 53a).[19]

Due to the absence of any explicit reference to God, some commentators have mistakenly thought that Hillel was speaking about himself. But this is another example – like Hillel's other teaching at the Rejoicing – of his using the "I" of God. This saying teaches that all the noise and pomp of public worship have meaning only if the people maintain the right spiritual attitude, if their hearts are directed to God. That is what draws His presence to them. If God is present in the Temple, then the presence of the people "registers" and means something; without His presence all the multitudes at the Rejoicing, all their music and dancing, ceremonies and celebrations, come to nothing and count for nothing.[20]

We have, then, two sayings where Hillel spoke in God's name, boldly using the "I" and "My" of God. When we put this together with the statement that at the Rejoicing the great *hasidim* "drew up" and were "vessels" for the holy spirit, which they poured forth in teaching to sate the people's thirst, it seems clear that Hillel was one of them, and that these sayings are examples of his teaching with the holy spirit in the name of God.[21] In the previous chapter we interpreted the story about Hillel being worthy of the holy spirit, but his generation preventing it, as meaning that he had the holy spirit of wisdom, not of prophecy. Although the words he spoke to the people at the Rejoicing were indeed inspired by the holy spirit, they were not prophecy.

THE DIVINE PRESENCE

The spectacle at the Rejoicing was so overwhelming that people could forget its purpose. It is not infrequent that no thought is given to the presence of God at religious gatherings. Judaism teaches that there is a special manifestation of the Divine Presence in numbers of people, as with a *minyan*, the minimum prayer quorum of ten; the larger the number, the greater the manifestation. Nevertheless, everything depends on the inner intention; without that the *Shechinah* departs. Without the right spiritual attitude, a gathering or celebration – such as the Rejoicing with its frenetic activity – becomes a mere expression of animal energy. Both of Hillel's sayings mentioned earlier show his concern with the presence of God. The Temple was God's House; the people came to the pilgrimage festivals to appear before God, but also to experience the Divine Presence. The saying went that "just as they came to be seen, so did they come to see."[22] This was true for all three festivals, but perhaps particularly so for the Rejoicing of the Water-drawing on Sukkot, when the holy spirit was present in abundance.[23] The jubilation at the Rejoicing produced a manifestation of the Divine Presence so powerful and palpable that the people could "see" it with their eyes. During the nighttime vigils the Court of the Women was flooded not only with the light of the giant candlesticks, but with the Divine Light.

We know from elsewhere that the *hasidim* – who took a dominant part in the Rejoicing – were especially concerned that their hearts and minds be totally focused on the *Shechinah* when they prayed; without a direct awareness of God's presence, they felt their prayer worthless.[24] Their attitude was similar to what is expressed in Hillel's teaching to the people celebrating in the Temple: "If I am here, all are here; but if I am not here, who is here?" Another teaching of Hillel's, spoken at the Rejoicing of the Water-drawing, is related to this latter saying. One version of the story in which it is found was quoted earlier;[25] a second version with a minor but interesting difference is worth considering here.

When Hillel the Elder was at the Rejoicing and saw the people celebrating wildly, he would say to them: "When we are here, who is here? Does He need our praise? It is written: 'Millions [of angels] ministered to Him and myriads stood ready before

Him' (Daniel 7:10)." But when Hillel saw that they were celebrating exuberantly, but remained spiritually attuned, he would say: "If we were not here, who would be here? Although many praises are offered before Him, Israel's please Him more than all the rest. How do we know? Because the Torah speaks of 'the sweet songs of Israel' (2 Samuel 23:1) and 'He [God] who sits enthroned upon the praises of Israel' (Psalms 22:4)" (*Y. Sukkah* 5:4).

Hillel's final citation means that Israel's praises cause the descent of the *Shechinah*. In this version of the story the contrast is between Hillel chastening or praising the people as they act wildly or evenly in their joy.[26] In the version quoted earlier, on the other hand, the contrast was between the people's pride or humility in worship. When the greatest rabbis in Israel danced before the crowds, juggling torches, they humbled themselves and ignored their dignity to serve God with fiery love. But while exulting in their worship, they kept their hearts and minds turned to God. Hillel saw to it that when the rest of the people rejoiced, they also remained spiritually attuned and humble and did not allow light-headedness or pride to distract them.

The pithy questions in both versions of this story – "When we are here, etc." and "If we were not here, etc." – are very close to the other saying, also connected with the Rejoicing, that "If I am here, all are here, etc." Hillel intended both sayings to caution the people against being carried away by their exuberance and losing hold on what is central. The two sayings make a similar point with similar language, but there is a difference in perspective.

- If I am here, all are here;
  but if I am not here, who is here?

- When we are here, who is here?
- If we were not here, who would be here?

Both these sayings[27] are about the presence of God and man in the face-to-face encounter; but while one is from God's side ("If I am here"), the other is from that of the people ("If we are here"). That is why they are "opposites." God can say: "If I am here, *all* are here," but the people must say: "If we are here, *who* is here?" Moreover,

God's presence validates that of the people; therefore, "If I [God] am here, all are here." The people, on the other hand, must nullify themselves before God; if they do not, but are prideful and full of themselves, then: "If we are here, who is here?" The answer is: "no one"; for God will not be present. There is a mutuality between God and man: If a person comes to the Temple experience or the encounter of prayer with mind and heart turned to God, with singleness of attention and humility, if he is truly "there," then God will also be present. This explains why Hillel has two similar-sounding sayings, one about the people's being authentically present and one about God's presence. These sayings mirror the perspective of the *hasidim*, who, on the one hand, attached special importance to the direct experience of God's presence in prayer; and, on the other hand, were oriented to mysticism and like all mystics talked about the relationship of God and man in terms of reciprocity and reflection.[28] So not only do we find Hillel the *hasid* among the *hasidim* at the Rejoicing, but his teachings there express traditional hasidic views.

During the Rejoicing of the Water-drawing, when the holy spirit was in abundance, Hillel taught in God's name by divine inspiration. He, along with other great *hasidim*, was a "vessel" and drew up the holy spirit in buckets, as it were. Much of what he taught at that time seems also to have been about the need for the kind of sincerity and inwardness in worship that would call forth an answering revelation of the Divine Presence. His lesson applied not only to the Temple, for whenever a person truly directs himself to God, God makes Himself present.[29] When all a person's deeds are acts of worship, performed with love and humility, the *Shechinah* is always with him.

We can be certain that Hillel who twice was praised by a heavenly voice – for his passionate love of God and as being worthy of prophecy – achieved this. He did not attain prophecy, but he received the holy spirit and the *Shechinah* rested on him, for his mind and heart were constantly directed to God and all his deeds were done for the sake of heaven.

43

Hillel's Death

MORTALITY AND MORALITY

Hillel's perception of the transitory nature of life – of the poor soul that is only a guest in the body, here on earth today and gone tomorrow – spurred him to be "kind" to his soul. Since death can come unexpectedly, a person must repent and turn to God today, not tomorrow. So every day Hillel performed *mitzvot* and good deeds, for his precious "guest" might leave at any moment. In a similar way Hillel interpreted for Bar He He Ecclesiastes 1:15 – "that which is lacking cannot be numbered" – that a person should always do *mitzvot* and good deeds when the opportunity arises, for once the time has passed it is gone forever, never to return.

Another saying of Hillel also called to mind the day of death, in speaking of the need for constant vigilance and unceasing religious efforts: "Trust not in yourself until the day of your death." If Hillel knew that a person's time in this world is brief, we should not be surprised. He himself had had an early brush with death, almost freezing under a blanket of snow on the roof of the House of Study. Perhaps that experience made him recognize the fleeting nature of this life. We had also seen him reflecting out loud about the short-ened life of one whose skull was floating on the water. Actually, however, Hillel himself lived to a ripe old age. The legendary tradition exaggerates, however, in stating that he lived one hundred and twenty years, like Moses, this being the number of years that in

Judaism is a symbol for the fullest life lived before God. He probably died about 10 C.E.[1]

ON HIS DEATHBED

A story of his deathbed scene directly follows the tradition about his eighty disciples, the greatest of whom was Yonatan ben Uzziel, and the least or youngest, Yohanan ben Zakkai.

At the hour of Hillel's passing all his disciples gathered in the room where he lay on his bed, but Yohanan ben Zakkai, who also came, did not go in. Noticing his absence, Hillel asked them, "Where is Yohanan?"

"He's just outside," they told him, "standing at the doorway."

"Let him come in," said Hillel, "he's worthy." When Yohanan came in, Hillel said to them, "The least among you is a father of wisdom and will be a father of generations; as to the greatest among you all, how much more so!" And he said to them further, "About you is it said in the Torah [by Divine Wisdom], 'I will cause those who love me to inherit richly, and I will fill their treasuries' " (Proverbs 8:21) (*ARN-B*, chap. 28).

Final Words

On his deathbed Hillel praised his disciples in a way they probably had not heard from him before – although we have seen how the tradition praised them: thirty as worthy of the holy spirit, thirty as worthy of the sun standing still. He told them that even Yohanan, the youngest among them – who had not considered himself fit to enter the awesome scene at the passing of his holy master, when certainly the Divine Presence filled the room – was full of wisdom, and for many generations after people would draw sustenance from his Torah.

At an earlier time, when Hillel had heard Yohanan's purity of speech in avoiding the use of even the word "unclean," he had predicted his future as a great teacher in Israel. Now he went beyond that. Calling him a "father" to wisdom and to generations, besides being an idiomatic usage meaning a "source," is an allusion to a traditional play on words. The Egyptian title *avreh*, called out before Joseph in Genesis 41:43, was fancifully interpreted by the rabbis (who split the word in two) as "a father (*av*) to wisdom – although young (*rah*) in years."[2] Although Yohanan was still very young, he was already an "elder" in Torah wisdom. Hillel's use of the word "father" also meant that even the youngest of his disciples would be a "father" to many generations of disciples of spiritual "children" following in his ways. As he lay on his deathbed, surrounded by these *his* spiritual children, we can imagine Hillel's inner satisfaction in realizing that his own "line" in Torah would continue, through them, for generations to come.

A spiritual master is a constant source of blessings for his disciples, but when death approaches he no longer holds anything back. As a spiritual father – similar to what an earthly father does – he bestows blessings on his children with an open hand, giving each of them a spiritual "inheritance."[3] Hillel attested that they were all lovers of God, Torah, and wisdom, and promised that the words of Proverbs 8:21 would be fulfilled in them. In that verse personified Wisdom says: "I will cause those that love me to inherit richly, and I will fill their treasuries"; their "inheritance" would be more wisdom, and their "filled treasuries" would be the many and varied fields of Torah knowledge in which they would attain mastery. In the text that follows these words, Hillel's promise is made concrete in a list of all the branches of Torah in which Yohanan ben Zakkai achieved expertise.[4]

In a time of distress for his disciples, when their beloved and revered master was leaving them, Hillel comforted them with the approval of a spiritual father proud in their attainments. In referring to Wisdom's inheritance to those who love her, he was indirectly speaking of his own spiritual inheritance to them. By applying the Proverbs verse to them he gave them *his* blessing and *his* assurance, that when he was gone Wisdom would not cease to bless them: He had taught them in a way that would cause their Torah knowledge to be fruitful and multiply, and he was confident of their future.

At the beginning of this book we quoted the Talmud's praise of Yohanan ben Zakkai's greatness in Torah and its similar praise for his rabbi, Hillel.[5] Yohanan said that although he had learned a tremendous amount from Hillel, it was still only like a fly dipping in the ocean to bathe and then flying off; how much does it take away?[6] He humbly compared himself to an insignificant insect and said that what he had absorbed was no more than a drop compared with the vast ocean of Hillel's wisdom. So when Hillel was on his deathbed, his youngest disciple, Yohanan, had such awe of his great and holy rabbi that he felt himself unworthy to enter his presence at that hour and stood humbly outside the door. But Hillel noticed the absence even of his youngest disciple, and particularly praised him when he was brought in. Just as the deathbed was a time for blessings,[7] it was not unusual then for a great rabbi to speak words of prophecy about a disciple – such were his words about Yohanan ben Zakkai.[8] Certainly, this story is as much about Yohanan as about Hillel. And Yohanan did become a "father to generations," for in the fateful period after the destruction of the Temple, he applied what he had learned from his master and established Judaism anew, giving it its form for many future generations. Hillel's prophecy about him came true.

44

If I Am Not for Myself

THREE QUESTIONS

The last saying of Hillel to be considered is probably his most famous one:

If I am not for myself, who will be for me?
And if I am for myself alone, what am I?
And if not now, when? (*Avot* 1:14).

The form of this saying, putting three questions one after the other, is striking. Moreover, each of the questions is in the first person, as if expressing the self-reflection of the listener himself. Altogether the effect produced is a powerful one.[1]

FOR MYSELF

Let us consider each line separately. "If I am not for myself, who will be for me?" This thought mirrors and affirms the average person's commonsense view about the need for self-interest. The *answer* to the question posed is: If *I* am not for myself, *no one else will be*. The necessary conclusion is that I must be for myself. Note the formal similarity of this line to another saying of Hillel: "If I am not here, who is here?"[2]

FOR MYSELF ALONE

"And if I am for myself alone, what am I?" This second line is about a person's relations to others and reverses the view of the first line about being for oneself. Although I must care for myself, limiting myself to that alone hardly makes me worthy of being called a person (as Hillel says: "What am I?").

INTERACTION

By stating the case for self-interest so strongly in the first line, Hillel not only expresses a truth, but draws in the listener, who is often suspicious and dismissive of dreamy and naive religious teachers.[3] Once the listener is thus drawn in, he is more open to the equally strong logic of the second line, about helping others – which *also* reflects the view of most people.

One of the distinctive aspects of this teaching of Hillel's is the way it, somewhat paradoxically, joins two contradictory perspectives. But don't most people share the seemingly contradictory views in the first two lines of Hillel's saying? They stubbornly refuse to abandon their self-interest; yet they also yearn to be good and fear sinking into a narrow and ugly selfishness. In these first two lines, Hillel establishes that he is not willing to give up either self or others and, by boldly placing the two values side by side, expresses a view of unusual depth and power. His perceptive recognition of the duality in people's motivation and, beyond that, his affirmation of its legitimacy, gives us an appreciation of how his psychological acuity aided his work as a religious teacher.

So the first two lines of the saying cogently express the two sides of "for oneself" and "for others." It is left to the wisdom of the listener to know the time for each and what the balance between them should be; that problem is not solved for him here.

But matters become even more complicated, for the second line interacts dialectically with the first. Once a person actually realizes that to be authentic he must be for others also, that too becomes "for himself." As Hillel said: "He who acquires a good name [primarily by helping others] has acquired it *for himself.*" Paradoxically, it is also true of selfless activity that "If I am not for myself [by doing good to others], who will be for me?" Thus, the dialectic between self and others of the first two lines can work on all the levels of self, wherever a person is found. Even when seeking spiritual salvation it is true that "If I am not for myself, who will be for me? And if I am for myself alone, what am I?" Spiritually, a person has to save himself, but if he seeks to save himself alone, what is he? Thus, Hillel used to encourage scholars obsessed with their own spiritual progress to teach others, by quoting Proverbs 11:24: "There is he who scatters and yet has more."

WHEN?

The first two lines repeat what every person knows: that he must act in his own behalf and must also help his fellowman. Each line poses a question that requires a response from the listener.

The final line asks a question that brings the teaching to a climax and presents an urgent demand: You know all this; when are you going to act? This question—"If not now, when?"—warns people against the all-too-human tendency to think they can delay their decision about spiritual matters. It also warns them against thinking they can "first" care only for themselves and worry about others "later on." Hillel says: If you do not act now, your vague and future "when," your hope and intention of turning to God later on, is simply a pious self-delusion. Only you can help yourself, and now is the time to act.

Hillel used to stand at the gate of Jerusalem, speaking to laborers going out to work and trying to persuade them to enter the world of Torah. There were probably many times he had to respond to the self-delusions of people delaying their commitment. Another maxim of his is: "Don't say 'When I have time I'll learn Torah'— perhaps you will never have any time!"[4] And what then? We saw in a previous chapter that Hillel taught that a person should not allow the opportunity for a *mitzvah* or good deed to pass by. In a broader sense, he should not allow his life as a whole to "pass by." Before his soul, the "guest" in the body, takes its leave, he must act, now and not later, and turn to God. That was Hillel's own way, and, with all his intensity and energy, he tried to communicate his inspired urgency to others.

In Favor of Shammai

THE PEOPLE CHOSE HILLEL

The tradition felt called upon to contrast Hillel's character and personality with Shammai's and made the unusual judgment on a great teacher, that "a person should never be irritable like Shammai." Hillel, the humble *hasid* and sage, was the ideal. Klausner makes the incisive comment that:

"Shammai was the symbol of Pharisaic Judaism only in the eyes of her enemies; but in the eyes of the people as a whole it was Hillel who was the symbol, Hillel and not Shammai. The popular stories about Hillel are many; those about Shammai are almost just a shadow which the ones about Hillel cast behind them. This itself is a clear indication that Shammai was not a beloved figure among the people; it was not his life which served as material for the workings of the popular imagination."[1]

There is certainly a good deal of truth in this remark of Klausner, but two points should be added, one about Hillel, the other about Shammai. First, although Klausner is right that Hillel became the ideal of the Jewish people, it has often been the case that this ideal has been allowed to fade; indeed, there in no question that in certain respects Hillel's teaching has even been "lost." The controversy between Hillel and Shammai, being a controversy for the sake of heaven, has never ended, but too often it seems as if Shammai's heirs, although not winning, are entirely too vigorous.

SHAMMAI'S SIDE

The second point necessary to qualify Klausner's comment is in favor of Shammai. It is true that Hillel represents an ideal superior to that represented by Shammai: Love of God is greater than fear of God, mercy overrules judgment. But a book could be written from the *other* side of this argument, for strict justice and righteousness *are* part of the beauty of Godliness, so is the unvarnished truth that is not afraid to offend people's feelings. If these qualities are lost and do not effectively temper and strengthen the softer and gentler side, the indiscriminate love, mercy, and forgiveness that remain become distorted and warped. Rigor is needed for authentic spirituality; renouncing worldliness to separate from what draws a person away from God is exalted and noble. Without the stern ascetic example of Shammai, Hillel's hasidic path of serving God by eating and bathing easily degenerates into mere indulgence. Hillel's way tends to universalism, Shammai's to nationalism—both are necessary. Israel's chosenness means that she must be a light to the nations, yet she must not be counted among them. Zeal for the honor of the God of Israel and the People of Israel has its rightful place among religious values. Righteous anger and indignation also have a place, for there is a time for holy strength. Love for Jews alone is ugly and repulsive, but having no special love for one's own people, the People of God, moreover, is equally shameful. Love for all—Jews and gentiles alike—is the correct path for good-hearted people, but to be overly concerned about what the gentile world thinks is demeaning and unworthy. In these few words I have tried to communicate, if only slightly, the truth of the opposite, Shammaite, view.

Shammai represents a face of God; he is not merely a foil for Hillel. As this book is about Hillel and his teaching it almost unavoidably caricatures Shammai. It presents one side of a controversy, but there is another. Hillel's way tends to faults of its own and needs to be corrected by the rigor of the opposite side. To glorify Hillel, we do not have to overly disparage Shammai; to show Hillel's light, we do not have to pretend that Shammai is utter darkness. The Talmud praises Hillel and condemns Shammai with regard to one important aspect of their behavior: Hillel's humble patience and Shammai's irritability. One should understand the limits of such a comparison, however, as the tradition did when it said about them and their different ways in holiness that, although Hillel's teachings were superior, "these and those are the words of the living God." So much for the defense of Shammai.

46

A Unique Balance

A SPECIAL MAN AND MESSAGE

What made Hillel special? What won him the reverence and devotion not only of his own generation but of Jewish generations through the ages? It goes without saying that he was an exceptional sage, scholar, and saint; he knew the Torah fully and lived it fully. He was also an inspiring, dedicated, and effective leader who had the courage to act decisively for his people's welfare and trained others to carry his religious message.

What was that message? One of Hillel's main personal characteristics, which makes him stand out as a religious figure, is that his love for people equaled his love for God – and that was the basis for his teaching. Hillel answered the gentile standing on one foot that the Golden Rule, love of one's neighbor, is the "whole Torah." We are so used to hearing this that we can fail to realize its significance and how radical it is in focusing on man. Too often intense religiosity goes astray by overly concentrating on ritual worship, and Hillel believed, and acted on his belief, that love of God must be expressed primarily through love of fellowmen. Moreover, he was not satisfied merely with teaching or with social action to alleviate the suffering of the masses; he was attentive to the requirements of each particular individual, helping him "in that which he needs."

A truly great man is always curiously unique and ordinary at once. A heroic religious figure is one of a kind, yet intensely typical and accessible in a way that enables him to be a model for masses of diverse people. How can certain leaders attract and appeal to so many different kinds of people? One mystical Jewish view says that they have "collective souls" that include within them the souls of all those who are drawn to them and whom they lead. The greater the leader, the more souls he contains within him, the more individuals for whom he is the spiritual root. Therefore, while a great leader is unusual and unique – for those capable of inspired leadership are few – at the same time he must have much in common with many people and many different kinds of people. How is that possible? Perhaps it is precisely his unique ability to blend seemingly contradictory religious values and attitudes that gives him his broad-based appeal.

RECONCILING DUALITIES

Therefore, another insight into the peculiar chemistry of Hillel's character and personality comes from recognizing his ability to combine in his own person a number of seemingly contradictory traits and to achieve a true balance of dualities that are not easily or often reconciled.

Hillel's famous saying begins "If I am not for myself, who will be for me? And if I am for myself alone, what am I?" One of the most striking things about this is its inherent balance between self and others. Hillel also sought to balance and unite the sometimes contradictory attitudes of the love and fear of God, for although his way was primarily that of love, of *hesed*, he also held firmly to the way of righteousness.

Love and Peace

A duality that goes far in helping to characterize Hillel is that of Love and Peace. Hillel has the *hasid* in him – the side of love. His love of Torah was to excess, he gave everything for it; he lived in poverty and would not accept help, even from his brother. He went up on the roof, oblivious to the snow as he listened to the words of the living God, and repeated his lesson one hundred and one times. He had in him the love that breaks conventions. He ran before the horse of the once-rich poor man, he ran after the laborers each day at the gate of Jerusalem, he ran to the Temple, his feet "carrying him." His worldview was not of *this* world, but, as the rabbis called it, the World of Truth. It was so God-centered that it was upside-down by normal standards, everything was reversed: what is mine is yours, humiliation and exaltation change places. Hillel is present and prominent at the Rejoicing of the Water-drawing, that special festival of the *hasidim*, where love broke forth in dancing and singing – but there too he knew that even the fullest outpourings of joy must not be wild, but in spiritual balance.

For along with the side of love, Hillel also had something else, a gentle side that sought peace within and without. His theme-saying has both: to love people – to run after them, pursue them, in order to bring them back to God – but also to love peace. So he sought to teach, but was not oppressive or overbearing; he avoided rebuke and often worked indirectly. He refrained from speaking of others' sins, but communicated the message of God's Torah through a loving greeting, by drawing people close with cords of peace. Although he was brilliant, he was never sharp with foolish questions and respectfully answered whatever he was asked.

This strong feeling about peace is not always present in *"hasidim,"* pious people. Often they become *parushim*; their own fiery love for God becomes so intense that it can burn up their fellowmen. Their devotion turns to jealousy for His sake, and zeal narrows their sympathies. With Hillel, however, a transcendent peace and tranquillity pervaded his personality. He was a passionate *hasid*, but also a lover of peace and a peacemaker, someone who was gentle and soft. He was the model of calmness and serenity who could not be angered, a teacher of unlimited patience who received everyone, at any time. The rabbis taught that a person totally immersed in the Torah, who follows its teachings from pure motives, is "raised up above all actions."[1] Does this enigmatic phrase describe the otherworldly serenity and peace that we perceive in Hillel's character?

The full combination of these two sides, of love and peace, poised in a perfect balance, produces a distinctive religious type, at once both vigorous and mild. The rabbis said that heaven is composed of the primal elements of fire and water, in a fusion where neither loses its original nature.[2] Hillel personifies that heavenly character.

The Sage and the Hasid

Another duality that illuminates Hillel's personality and character is that of the Sage and the *Hasid*. The ideal of the sage is Torah and wisdom, the head; the *hasid's* ideal is love and devotion, the heart. The sage primarily relates to God as He reveals Himself in the Torah and tends to separate from the unlearned; the *hasid* is more oriented to people: he seeks community and expresses his love for God in his love for his fellowmen.

Sages and *hasidim* are not separate, discrete groups – they overlap – but a number of stories in the rabbinic literature plainly describe a tension of sorts between the sages and the *hasidim*, between those who leaned to this or that end of the religious spectrum.[3] This is not to suggest that in Hillel's time the sages and *hasidim* were frequently at odds, for they generally held each other in mutual esteem. What made Hillel himself unusual, however, is that he was such a perfect blend of these two types and could appeal to both groups. As a disciple of Aaron, Hillel modeled himself after the father of the priests, those who are close to the people and mediate between them and God. The Kabbalah says that priests are from the side of *hesed*, meaning that the ideal priests are *hasidim*.[4] So, loving his fellowmen, Hillel sought to bring those who were far away back to God. But, as a sage, he did so through the Torah. In his eulogy, he was praised not only as a humble *hasid*, but as a disciple of Ezra, the father of the scribes and sages.

Hillel's saying that "An *am-haaretz* cannot be a *hasid*"[5] indicates, on the one hand, that his ideal was to be a *hasid*. On the other hand, his judgment was that no one could be a *hasid* without a full measure of Torah knowledge. If properly understood, this saying can be seen to contain some of the tension that existed between the ideals of the sage and the *hasid* – and to express an implied criticism of those *hasidim* who might be inclined to neglect the Torah. But if an *am-haaretz* cannot be a *hasid*, who can? The answer is: the sage, the Torah scholar, who is the opposite of the unlearned *am-haaretz*. Hillel had, then, a "dual ideal" of the *hasid*-sage. But although his saying suggests some implied criticism of a possible tendency among the *hasidim*, Hillel had his criticisms of the sages also. In the same *mishnah* as the saying just quoted, he states that "An irritable person cannot teach" – that, of course, being the task of the sage. Who can teach then? The answer is: the humble *hasid*, who is the opposite of the irritable person.

UNIQUE INTEGRITY

Hillel was equally unhappy with *hasidim* who neglected Torah and with sages who lacked humility and love for their fellowmen. But he was able to meld both ideals – the precious religious attributes of both *hasid* and sage – in his own person. He had the beautiful excess of the *hasid*, his love, humility, and gentleness, along with the greatness in Torah, the wisdom and balance, of the sage. Hillel, who sat at the head of the House of Torah study, who was the *Nasi* and leader of the sages, was also the one who sat at the Rejoicing of the Water-drawing in the Temple, and presided over the *hasidim* and men of deeds who took the lead in that joyous celebration.

Hillel's perfection was his ability to fuse into one graceful whole the two halves of the Jewish tradition, the way of the sage and the way of the *hasid*. And it was he who created the type and set the mold for generations to follow. As the rabbis said: "A person should always be . . . like Hillel."

*   *   *

The traditional tomb of Hillel is in a cave near Meron, in the mountains of the Upper Galilee, in the Land of Israel.[6]

Appendix 1

Editorial Collections of Sayings

Various sayings of Hillel are collected in *Pirke Avot* and its commentary, *Avot d'Rabbi Natan*. In the former, earlier text, some of the sayings are collected in blocks; thus, *Avot* 1:13 is a group of four, 2:5 a group of five, 2:6 a group of four (the first two "double sayings"); 2:8 can be analyzed in different ways. Generally, all the sayings are independent and the groupings are editorial. Therefore, I usually interpret each saying separately and only in exceptional cases consider its relation to others collected with it, when it seems possible Hillel himself may have occasionally used them together. The editors typically collected certain sayings together according to purely external similarities, perhaps because that helped people memorize the sayings.

Thus, *Avot* 1:13 collects four Aramaic sayings (most others are in Hebrew) that have a "bad end": "A name made great is a name *destroyed*; he who does not increase, *decreases*; he who does not study *deserves death*; he who uses the crown [for his own purposes] *wastes away*." *Avot d'Rabbi Natan*, chapter 12, which cites this group from *Avot*, notes: "He [Hillel] said four things in the Babylonian tongue [Aramaic]." I do not know if these sayings were collected because of their being in Aramaic, because of the "bad end," or both.

Avot 2:5 collects five sayings that begin: "do not" (Hebrew: *al*): "*Do not* separate from the community; *do not* trust in yourself until the day of your death; *do not* judge your fellowman until you come into his place; *do not* say something that cannot be accepted [now] because [you think] in the end it will be accepted; and *do not* say,

'When I have leisure I will study'; perhaps you will never have leisure."

Avot 2:6's four sayings all begin (in the Hebrew) with "not," "cannot," or "no" (Hebrew: *ain* or *lo*). The first two are double sayings. "An ignorant man is *not* sin fearing and an unlearned man is *not* a *hasid*; a shy person *cannot* learn and an irritable person *cannot* teach; *not* everyone who engages much in business becomes wise; in a place where there are *no* men, try to be a man." This latter saying has the "no" as the second word.

Avot 2:8 presents a more complicated situation. Let us quote the text before discussing it:

1a) The more flesh, the more worms;
   the more possessions, the more anxiety;
   the more wives, the more witchcraft;
   the more maid-servants, the more lewdness;
   the more men-servants, the more thievery;

1b) But the more Torah, the more life;
   the more sitting in study, the more wisdom;
   the more counsel, the more understanding;
   the more charity, the more peace.

2) He who has acquired a good name,
   has acquired it for himself;
   and he who has acquired words of Torah,
   has acquired life in the World-to-Come.

Parts 1a and 1b have many sayings of the form: the more this, the more that, meaning: increasing this, increases that. Hillel probably developed these sayings independently but used them both separately and together. The final saying, part 2, about a "good name" was appended because: (1) Part 1b begins by saying: "the more Torah, the more life," and part 2 has: "he who acquires Torah acquires the life of the World-to-Come"; (2) Part 1 disparages materialism and accumulation of possessions and ends with encouragement of charity; the "good name" of part 2 often came from charitable activities; (3) Part 1 compares the two kinds of "increase"—material and spiritual—and teaches which "acquisitions" are worthy, part 2 speaks of what to "acquire"; (4) Part 1b reverses the worldly view of 1a about what increase should be sought, and part 2 reverses the worldly view of what is "for oneself." Both sayings, that is, Part I and Part 2, are independent and able to stand on their own. Although it is most probable that the second was appended to the first by an editor because of the connections mentioned, it is also possible that Hillel himself occasionally used them together this way, and he was the "editor."

See also Appendix 2, "From Which Hillel Are the Sayings in *Avot* 2:5–8?" for a discussion of that issue.

Appendix 2

From Which Hillel Are the Sayings in Avot 2:5-8?

Some scholars[1] consider the sayings of "Hillel" in *Avot* 2:5-8 to be from one or the other of two later Hillels, both of whom were descendants of Hillel the Elder and lived generations after him. They identify the "Hillel" mentioned in *Avot* 2:5 as either a scholar Hillel (the son of Gamaliel III and the grandson of Judah the Prince), who lived in the third century c.e., or a *Nasi* Hillel (the son of Judah Nesiah and grandson of Gamaliel IV), who lived in the fourth century. Their arguments for this are as follows: After the sayings of Hillel (the Elder) in *Avot* 1:12-14, the text continues with sayings of various of his descendants (1:15-2:4), but then unexpectedly returns to Hillel in 2:5-8. They conclude that the first block of sayings is from Hillel the Elder and the second block from the later Hillel. Furthermore, the sayings in 2:2-4 preceding this second block of Hillel maxims are from Rabban Gamaliel III, which would suggest that the next group is either from the Hillel who was his son or from the Hillel who was his great-grandson. In one textual version, *Avot* 2:5 reads *"Rabbi* Hillel says"; "Rabbi" is never used for Hillel the Elder, and when it is used it refers to another Hillel.[2]

However, prominent scholars, such as Klausner, Weiss, Herford, and Glatzer, agree that the block of sayings in *Avot* 2:5-8 is from Hillel the Elder.[3] The arguments for this position are as follows: (1) The text does not distinguish the "Hillel" of the second block from that of the first. (2) The sayings following the second block are from Rabban Yohanan ben Zakkai, Hillel's disciple. (3) Many of the component sayings can be more or less convincingly linked to Hillel the Elder. Thus: [a] The idea of the first of the sayings in *Avot* 2:5, "Do not separate from the community," is found in Hillel the Elder's teaching in *Tosefta Berachot* 2:24 – "Do not be seen naked, do not be seen dressed, etc." (see pp. 88–89 in my text) and also relates to his teaching about joining groups forming to do good deeds (see p. 194). [b] The next saying in *Avot* 2:5, "Judge not, etc." is similar if not identical to a saying of Hillel the Elder about judging found in a story about him and his wife in *Derech Eretz Rabbah* 6 (see pp. 105–106). [c] The third saying in *Avot* 2:5, "Say not something that cannot be accepted now . . ." fits Hillel the Elder's teaching style as portrayed in a story about him in *Shabbat* 31a (see pp. 130–132). [d] The second saying in *Avot* 2:6, "A shy person . . ." fits the contrast made between Hillel the Elder and Shammai in *Shabbat* 31a. [e] The final saying in *Avot* 2:6, "In a place where there are no men, try to be a man," essentially expresses the same idea as the saying of Hillel the Elder in *Y. Berachot* 9:8, 14d, "When others are gathering, scatter; when others are scattering, gather." In fact, the two sayings are joined together in *Sifre Zutta* Pinhas 27:1 (see p. 121) and attributed to "Hillel." [f] The story and saying in *Avot* 2:7 about the floating skull is found also in *Sukkah* 53a in the name of Hillel the Elder. [g] The many sayings in *Avot* 2:8 about the more this, the more that, are in a favorite form of Hillel the Elder's, as can be seen from the story about him in *ARN-B* chap. 27 (see pp. 165–166). [h] The final saying in *Avot* 2:8, "He who has acquired words of Torah, etc." is found in a slightly different form in *Avot d'Rabbi Natan-B*, chap. 26, in a story about Hillel the Elder (see pp. 114–115 in my text). (4) All in all, then, the sayings of *Avot* 2:5-8 fit what we know of Hillel's character, personality, and religious activities.

Bosniak, "The Life of Hillel," pp. 90–91, suggests that the original editor of *Pirke Avot* divided Hillel's sayings into two blocks, using one to introduce a father–son line of traditions, of Hillel's descendants, and another to begin a teacher–disciple line of traditions, where Yohanan ben Zakkai follows Hillel. There are other ways to explain the situation.[4]

To conclude, we can be fairly confident that the sayings of this block of tradition are indeed from Hillel the Elder.

Appendix 3

Hillel and Shebna – Another Interpretation

The story of Hillel and his brother Shebna is found in an interpretative, editorial context that is not totally clear and that discusses the meaning of part of Song of Songs 8:7, which reads: "If a man were to give all the wealth of his house for love, he would be utterly despised." This is the full text in *Sotah* 21a:

> What is the meaning of the phrase "he would be utterly despised"? Said Ulla: "Neither like Simon the brother of Azariah, nor like Rabbi Yohanan of the Prince's family, but like Hillel and Shebna. For when Rav Dimi came to Babylonia from Israel, he said: 'Hillel and Shebna were brothers. Hillel devoted himself to Torah, while Shebna involved himself in business. Later on, Shebna said to his brother, "Come, let's be 'partners' and split everything evenly." But a heavenly voice was heard in answer, [echoing the words of the Song of Songs and] saying, "If a man were to give all the wealth of his house for love, he would be utterly despised" (Song of Songs 8:7).' "

The Hillel story should not be interpreted exclusively from the perspective of Ulla's later "frame." Rav Dimi's Hillel story stands on its own and may have a focus different from Ulla's. In explaining the end of Song of Songs 8:7 and exactly who or what would be despised and why, Ulla distinguishes two other cases of the Yissachar-Zebulun partnership from that of Hillel and Shebna. In the other two cases, the offers of partnership were accepted and fulfilled; the

285

offer of Hillel's brother was rejected. But what difference is Ulla concerned with? In interpreting Rav Dimi's Hillel story and Ulla's context there are two possibilities:

(1) My interpretation of the story (see the text of chapter 3) is that Shebna's offer was refused because Hillel's love of God was so intense that no one could "buy" a share in it (just as no one could "buy" a half-share in the Baal Shem Tov's love of God by supporting him!). A *midrash* in *Song of Songs Rabbah* 8:10 supports this view:

"Rabbi Hiyya, the son of Rabbi Abba of Yaffo, said: 'He who learns Torah while suffering hardship receives a reward of one thousand. He who learns without hardship receives only two hundred. From whom do we learn this? – from the tribes of Yissachar and Naftali. Since the tribe of Naftali studied the Torah in the midst of hardship, they received a reward of one thousand, as it is written, "And from Naftali, captains one thousand" (1 Chronicles 12:35). But since the tribe of Yissachar was supported by Zebulun and learned Torah without hardship, they received only two hundred, as it is written, "their chiefs two hundred; and all their brothers see to it that they are fed" (1 Chronicles 12:33).' "

The one thousand versus two hundred of the verses is fancifully interpreted to indicate a difference in rewards because Naftali was motivated solely by love for God and gave no thought to any suffering involved, while Yissachar, at least to some degree, avoided hardship that might come in the service of God.[1] While the rabbis supported the Yissachar-Zebulun partnership to foster Torah study, they did not consider it the highest ideal or appropriate for the highest people. Thus, Hillel and the heavenly voice refused Shebna's offer because Hillel's love for God was so strong he would not consider relying on anyone else but God, regardless of any hardship he might suffer.

This interpretation of Rav Dimi's story does not depend on any interpretation of Ulla's editorial context (which may or may not share its view), but if one interpreted that context from the perspective of this interpretation of the story, what makes Hillel's case different is that Simon *the brother of Azariah* and Rabbi Yohanan *of the Prince's family* studied while being supported by others and therefore had to share their spiritual reward and fame with their benefactors and were known by their names. According to Ulla, Hillel was different because he was spared this diminution of his greatness. How would it sound, after all, if he were known as "Hillel, Shebna's brother"! The Maharsha interprets Ulla this way, saying that Hillel rejected the offer of partnership so he would not be "despised" (as in the verse). This interpretation is also supported by a *midrash* that mentions Simon, Azariah's brother—also mentioned by Ulla—to illustrate that a scholar who accepts such a Yissachar-Zebulun partnership must share the credit for his Torah teaching. The *midrash* comments on a halachic teaching that is introduced in a peculiar way:

" 'Simon, Azariah's brother says in his [Azariah's] name.' But isn't Simon greater than Azariah? Why does he teach this in his brother's name? The reason is that Azariah would go out to engage in commerce, come back and provide for Simon, putting food in his mouth, so to speak, so that his brother could study Torah without interruption. Therefore, Simon's teaching is given in the name of his brother, without whose help he could not have studied. The case is similar to that of Zebulun, as the verse says: 'Rejoice O Zebulun in your going out' (Deuteronomy 33:18). But isn't Yissachar greater than Zebulun? Why all the rejoicing for Zebulun? The reason is that Zebulun would travel on the high seas to engage in commerce, come home, and put food in Yissachar's mouth. Therefore, he was given the reward for his labor" (*Yalkut Shimoni* Proverbs 3, p. 973).

So far, my interpretation.

(2) Another possible interpretation is that Shebna's offer was made too late, after Hillel had already studied some time in poverty. The Hebrew *lesof*, which I have translated "later on," could also mean "finally," with the suggestion of "too late." According to this interpretation (held by the *Iyun Yaakov* and *Eitz Yosef* commentaries in *Ein Yaakov*) the focus of the story is on Shebna and critical of his late offer, and Ulla's teaching differentiates this late offer, which was rejected, from the other two, which were timely and accepted. Although Shebna was "despised," Azariah who helped Simon, and the Prince's family who helped Rabbi Yohanan, were not despised.

This interpretation puts a lot of stress on the word *lesof*—as meaning "finally" and "too late." I translated it, according to my interpretation, as "later on," which could indicate almost any time period; it simply means the offer was made after the two had started somewhat along their separate paths. Shebna's offer was not rejected because of its tardiness or because of anything Shebna did or didn't do, but because *Hillel* and his love was exceptional. In my interpretation Hillel is the focus, not Shebna.

There are a number of reasons to reject the interpretation that the key to the story is that Shebna's offer was late. If that interpretation were correct, it would mean that if Shebna's offer had been timely Hillel would have accepted it. But we have seen that the Yissachar-Zebulun partnership was *not* the ideal. It is incorrect, in my view, to imagine that a person such as Hillel, who was willing to study in utter poverty (see chapter 4, this volume) did so only because he could not make a convenient "arrangement" for support. Also, let us say that Shebna made his offer "too late." Does that mean that Hillel was calculating: "Oh no, brother! I've already studied and achieved some measure of greatness; it's too late to buy me out! (although you could have done so earlier)."

According to this other interpretation, the story is basically about Shebna, not Hillel. Since Hillel would have accepted an earlier offer, the story could have been about any scholar. If so, why all the fuss for a heavenly voice! Does God speak just to reject a mistaken late offer of this sort? The heavenly voice makes sense, however, if the point of its quote of the Song of Songs verse is to praise Hillel's passionate and exceptional love of God. And actually, what did Shebna do that was so wrong? Perhaps his brother had studied in poverty for a year or two, and then Shebna decided to support him and to arrange a Yissachar-Zebulun partnership. Perhaps he was not financially able to support him earlier. Was his "lateness" so terrible? If this is the point of the story, I don't see its force. The story's interest is not in Shebna's "inferior" offer being "despised," because it was late, but in Hillel's love for God being so "superior" it could not be shared

The correct interpretation of the Hillel story is what is most important, however. Whether my interpretation of Ulla's remarks is correct is of purely secondary interest. Ulla's "frame" may or may not fit the original meaning of the story.

A final aspect of this story concerns when and where it occurred. The text says the story was brought back to Babylonia by Rav Dimi, but that fact would not in itself mean it happened in Israel, just that it had been preserved there, where Hillel spent the whole later part of his life. Hillel went to Israel as a young man to study with Shemaya and Avtalyon (see chapter 4, this volume), but there is no reason to think his brother ever moved to Israel. It seems probable, then, that the offer was made when the two were together in Babylonia. Hillel probably returned to live in Babylonia again after studying in Israel (see preceding, p. 22 and following, pp. 294-295), but by then he was a mature and accomplished scholar. Most likely, Shebna's offer preceded Hillel's first trip to Israel and his fame. The more famous he became, the less likely that he would need support. It is certainly farfetched to imagine Shebna making his offer of partnership when Hillel was already the *Nasi*, a leader of the Sanhedrin.

Why Hillel Went up to Jerusalem from Babylonia

A tradition says Hillel went to Jerusalem from Babylonia because of three matters of *halachah* (religious law).

The first concerned the role of the priests in dealing with diseases. The Book of Leviticus (13:29–37) says that a priest should examine the symptoms of a person afflicted with a scall, that is, a scaly eruption in the hair or beard, and when they disappear, should pronounce him ritually clean. The Torah says: "the scall is healed, he is clean. The priest shall declare him clean" (v. 37). But does the man become "clean" by the disappearance of the scall or by the declaration of the priest? The second problem concerned the appropriate sacrifice on Passover. While the Book of Exodus (12:5) says: "from the sheep or goats shall you take them," only a small animal; the Book of Deuteronomy (16:2) says it may be "from the flock or herd," either a small or large animal. Can this seeming contradiction be resolved? The third difficulty also involved the observance of Passover, and a contradiction between two verses. According to the Book of Exodus (13:6) "seven days you shall eat *matzah*," but the Book of Deuteronomy (16:8) ordains "you shall eat *matzah* for six days." Which is right – six or seven? Here is the text:

> Hillel went up from Babylonia because of three matters [of *halachah*]. (1) The verse says "He is clean" [the man who had the scall]. Does this mean that if the symptoms disappear he does not need the priest? No, for the verse continues "the priest shall declare him clean." But what if a priest said "clean" to one

who was really unclean, does he thereby become clean? No, for the verse says "he is *clean* [the symptoms are gone]. The priest shall declare him clean." For this Hillel went up from Babylonia.

(2) One verse says "You shall offer the Passover sacrifice from the flock or herd," and another says "from the sheep or goats shall you take them." How explain the contradiction? Small animals are for the Passover sacrifice itself, and small or large animals for the festival sacrifice [an additional offering made on all festivals].

(3) One verse says "You shall eat *matzah* for six days," and another says "seven days shall you eat *matzah*." How explain the contradiction? Six days of the new crop and seven days of the old crop.

Hillel interpreted [the Torah] and his conclusions agreed [with the received traditions]. He then went to Israel and accepted it as law (*Y. Pesahim* 6:1, 33a).

Hillel resolved the three halachic problems through Torah interpretation. As for the first, he explained that the two parts of the relevant verse indicate that both disappearance of the disease symptoms and the ritual declaration of the priest were required.

Hillel's second problem concerned the kind of animal to be offered on Passover. One verse prescribes small or large animals, the other only small animals. Hillel propounded a rule of interpretation for all such cases: "Whenever two verses contradict each other, search for a third verse to clarify the difficulty." Hillel said that the third verse in this case is Exodus 12:21, "Moses called to all the Elders of Israel and he said to them, 'Take for yourselves *sheep* for your families and offer the Passover sacrifice.'" Thus, small animals are for the Passover sacrifice, small or large ones for the festival sacrifice.

Hillel resolved the third problem by means of the same rule about finding a third verse when two verses seem to contradict each other. One verse speaks of eating *matzah* seven days, another six days. The third verse? Leviticus 23:9–14 ordains the ritual offering of a sheaf (an *omer*) of the *new harvest*. The rabbis understood this to take place on the *second* day of Passover. Therefore, Hillel concluded that permission to eat *matzah* of the new harvest of grains begins only on the *second* day of Passover, after the offering of the sheaf. So one may eat *matzah* of the *old* crop for all seven days of Passover, but of the *new* crop for only six days.

The final sentence of the text, that explains the nature of Hillel's journey in more detail, requires special attention. "Hillel interpreted [the Torah] and his conclusions agreed [with the received traditions]. He then went to Israel and accepted it as law"–*Darash vehiskim ve'alah vekibeil halachah.* The meaning of this sentence is obscure, but studying a similar case involving Rabbi Akiba will help to clarify it.[1] When Rabbi Akiba (after the Temple's destruction) taught that the priests who blew the trumpets in the Temple had to be without physical blemishes, his older master, Rabbi Tarfon, strongly opposed him, saying that he had himself seen his own lame uncle, a priest, blowing the trumpet in the Temple. When Akiba suggested that perhaps he had seen him blowing in a different circumstance, and that his memory was faulty, Tarfon realized that Akiba was correct. He then exclaimed, "By the Temple service! You did not invent this. . . . Tarfon saw and forgot, but Akiba interpreted it on his own, and his interpretation agreed with the *halachah*. . . ."[2] – *Tarfon ra'ah veshachah, Akiba doreish mei'atzmo u'maskim lahalachah.*

Another version states that Tarfon had not only seen, but had also heard the tradition. He says: "I heard the tradition and was not able to understand it, but you arrived at your conclusions by interpreting the Torah and your decision agrees with the tradition"[3] – *Ani shamati velo hayah li lefareish ve'atah doreish u'maskim shemuah.*

The language is similar to that used about Hillel. With Akiba and Tarfon, one rabbi received a tradition handed down from earlier authorities, while the other, who did not, had to make a ruling from a careful study of the relevant Torah verses. But the rabbi who expounded from the Torah came to a conclusion that agreed, as it turned out, with the tradition received by the other. This indicates that the first part of the final sentence of the text about Hillel means that his Torah interpretation of the three problems agreed with the received tradition.

But did he go to Jerusalem to learn or to teach?[4] Certainly the text gives his answers to the three problems. But the difficulty is that it *first* says that Hillel's answers agreed with the traditions, *then* that he went to Israel. If he knew while in Babylonia that his interpretations agreed with the traditions, why did he go to Israel? Or, if he had not heard traditions about these matters and was going to Israel to find out if his interpretations conformed with their traditions, how can the text say that his conclusions "agreed" with the traditions before he had gone to Israel? The end of the text is also difficult: "and he accepted the *halachah*." If his interpretative conclusions agreed with the received traditions, what had to be accepted, by him or by those in Israel? Perhaps the text is faulty.[5] Regardless, these are some possible explanations for the final sentence: (1) Perhaps Hillel had to interpret the Torah to arrive at conclusions. But he wanted to check his conclusions with the scholars in Jerusalem – who might have received traditions. He went up – to learn – and found that his conclusions agreed with the traditions others had received. He then accepted that as the *halachah*. (2) Another possibility is that, like the story about Hillel with the Sons of Bathyra, he had *both* the received traditions and the interpretations that agreed with them, and he went to Israel to teach the scholars there how to interpret the Torah. In the story of Hillel's encounter with the Sons of Bathyra, he first attempted to establish the *halachah* from conclusions he arrived at by Torah interpretation – but they would not accept the *halachah* on that basis. Only when he announced that he had also received a tradition about it from Shemaya and Avtalyon did they accept his position. There, too, there were parallel lines of Torah interpretation and received tradition. (The same combination is found in a story discussed elsewhere in this volume (chapter 7), about another halachic matter brought to Hillel when he was *Nasi*. In that instance, he and other scholars not only remembered differently the traditional ruling, but even what they had seen of the acted-out *halachah*. Arriving at an impasse, they supported their conflicting positions by Torah interpretation.)

That Hillel went to Jerusalem because of these three difficult halachic issues – after having interpreted them from the Torah – is not the act of a "beginner." On the other hand, the story of Hillel on the roof, an impoverished student unknown to Shemaya and Avtalyon, is not about an advanced scholar, but a fiery young man.[6] Probably Hillel went to Jerusalem twice.[7] He first went as a young man to study with Shemaya and Avtalyon, but then returned home. At a later time, already a great Torah scholar in Babylonia, he returned to Jerusalem a second time, perhaps for Passover, because of these three halachic problems.

Hillel's encounter with the Sons of Bathyra and his elevation to the office of *Nasi* may have happened on a later third visit, or on this same second visit. Hillel had come because of these three questions, and his help was needed on an urgent fourth one: whether the Passover sacrifice overrode the Sabbath or not. Thus, in the story about the Sons of Bathyra, when one of the sages says: "There is a man who has come up from Babylonia, called Hillel the Babylonian, and he attended upon the two great men of the generation, Shemaya and Avtalyon," it would mean that Hillel had recently returned to Jerusalem after having studied there in his earlier years. He had contacted the Jerusalem scholars for his own reasons (perhaps coming to the attention of those who knew him as "Hillel the Babylonian"), and when they found that his Torah knowledge, both in received traditions and expertise in interpretation, surpassed them all – they made him *Nasi*.[8]

The theory of Hillel's absence from Israel during the period of Herod's rise to power (Herod became king three years before Hillel became *Nasi*), when Herod massacred many of the rabbis, would explain how Hillel had escaped that scourge (although even if he had been in Israel then he might simply have been overlooked due to his lack of prominence). His journey to Jerusalem a few years later would have been when the consequences of that decimation of the community's religious leadership was being felt. As the tradition says: When the Torah was again forgotten in Israel, Hillel the Babylonian came up and reestablished it.

Appendix 5

His Heart Is Firm, Trusting in the Lord – Another Interpretation

When Hillel the Elder was once on the road approaching the city and heard a loud outcry, he said to his disciples and those with him: "I am certain that this is not coming from my house." About him, and such as him, does the verse say: "He will not be afraid of threatening news, his heart is firm, trusting in the Lord" (Psalms 112:7) (*Berachot* 60a).

In chapter 31 I interpreted this story to mean that Hillel trusted God to spare him from any disaster. An alternative interpretation is that Hillel was so humble and pious, and so confident of the similar religious qualities of his family, that when he heard cries of distress or, perhaps, the shouts of an argument, he was certain it could not be from them: If a disaster had struck they would accept it calmly, without hysteria; and they would not engage in raucous arguments among themselves or with neighbors.

Let us consider the support for this interpretation. The rabbis taught that a man should be humble even with his own family and household[1] and that if he was humble, they would learn humility from him. A pair of rabbinic teaching-stories illustrate the saying, "Teach the members of your household humility," and one seems to have a direct relation to the Hillel story. There are two versions of this pair of stories (in *ARN-A* and *ARN-B*) and we will cite both. Some significant phrases are underlined.

ARN-A, chap. 7:

" 'Teach the members of your household humility' – If a man

297

is himself humble and *those of his household are humble (anvatanin)*, when a poor man comes and stands at the door of his house asking, 'Is your father home?' they answer, 'Yes, please come in.' They quickly set the table for him, and he enters to eat and drink, making a blessing on the food and thanking God. When the father learns of their fine behavior, he is gratified. But if a man himself is not humble, and *the members of his household are ill-tempered (kapdanin)*, when a poor man comes and stands at the door, asking, 'Is your father at home?' they answer harshly, 'No!' and chase him away by their surly manner.

"Another meaning of 'Teach the members of your household humility' – If a man is humble and the members of his household are humble, when he travels abroad he says, 'I thank You, O Lord my God, that my wife and children do not get involved in strife with others.' *His heart is not afraid* and his mind is at ease all the time he is away and *until he returns home.* But if a man is not himself humble, and the members of his household are bad-tempered, when he goes abroad he prays, 'May it be Your will, O Lord my God, that my wife and children not cause strife with others while I am away.' His heart is afraid, and his mind unsettled until the time of his return home."

Here is the second version, from *ARN-B*, chap. 14[2]:

"When a man is humble, then his wife, his children, and the rest of his household are also humble – even his dogs will not harm anyone! But when he is bad-tempered, they too will treat other people badly. When someone comes to the door of a man who has an irritable[3] wife and asks, 'Is the master at home?' she answers sharply, 'No!' and chases him away by her nasty manner. But when a man has a humble wife and someone comes to visit, asking, 'Is the master at home?' she says, 'Yes,' invites him in and offers him food. He enters, is served with some bread and wine, makes a blessing, and eats. . . .

"When someone whose wife is humble leaves on a journey, his mind is at ease, *his heart trusting in her. And when he returns home, he finds everything peaceful.* But when someone whose wife is irritable leaves on a journey, he is anxious and fearful. And when he returns home, he finds her quarreling."

The second story of each pair seems to relate to the Hillel story. It teaches that when a man who has a "gentle" family leaves home, he is not anxious about their behavior in his absence. Thus, when Hillel was returning home and heard the cries, he was not afraid that it was his family. In describing the humble man, *ARN-B* says that his heart "trusts" (*batuah*) his humble wife; although the translation must differ in English, the Hebrew is the same as in the *Y. Berachot* version of the Hillel story, which teaches that a person should say "I'm *certain* (*batuah*) that these cries are not from my house."[4] We can also compare the motif of a man trusting his wife to the other Hillel story where he trusted his wife's character – when she gave the poor man at the door the meal she had prepared for Hillel's guest – and judged that all her deeds were for the sake of heaven.[5] Indeed, that story also has a common motif with the first of the pair of *ARN* stories, that a humble wife receives and feeds a poor man or anyone else who comes to the door.

The story of Hillel returning to the city and hearing a loud outcry could be interpreted along the lines of the *ARN* story – about the man trusting his family not to argue with others while he was away – that Hillel trusted his family and was certain they would not be making an outcry. The *ARN* story is concerned about quarreling with neighbors when the man is away from home. That could be the case with the Hillel story or, perhaps more likely, the outcry would have been at some domestic disaster. If it was the former, note that one of the *ARN* versions says the man found everything "peaceful" on his return; peace and avoiding quarrels was of course very important to Hillel.

Additional similarities between the first of each pair of *ARN* stories and other Hillel stories also lend some support to the interpretation that Hillel trusted his family. The language used in *ARN* to contrast how humble and irritable family members receive a beggar or any caller at the door is similar to the language contrasting how Hillel and Shammai received potential converts. This is clearer in the Hebrew, for both texts use the same terms *anvatan* and *kapdan* and also share some quite distinctive language about speaking harshly and chasing someone away.[6]

Thus, all these similarities between the *ARN* stories and the Hillel story would lead us to interpret Hillel's returning home and his confidence when hearing the outcry as his certainty it could not be from his house, since he completely trusted his wife and children not to loudly argue among themselves or with neighbors, or if some disaster had occurred, not to scream in distress and know how to accept misfortune from the hand of God.

There is a serious problem, however, with this interpretation, since it does not account for the Psalm verse that concludes the story:

"He will not be afraid of threatening news, his heart is firm, trusting in the Lord" (Psalms 112:7). When the story is read together with the verse, Hillel's remark that he is "certain" means – because of his trust in the Lord. This is different from interpreting his certainty as due to his trust in the character of his wife and children. A number of traditional commentators understand the Hillel story as being about his trust in his family (although none mentions the supporting evidence from ARN), but they have a difficult time explaining the contrary indication of the Psalm verse.[7] The Psalm verse could conceivably be the later addition of an editor, who misunderstood the story; in the Babylonian Talmud version it is part of an editorial comment at the end. On the other hand, the Jerusalem Talmud version puts the verse in Hillel's mouth. And we also know that Hillel certainly often uttered *another* Psalm verse to express his trust in God – "Blessed is the Lord day by day."[8] Thus, Hillel might have had a habit of uttering *this* verse also, to strengthen his trust in God when he heard "threatening news." This makes me reluctant to dismiss the Psalm verse in this story as editorial.

On the one hand, the associated Psalm verse and the Talmud context (particularly in the Jerusalem Talmud) about "empty prayer," and so on, suggest that the story is about Hillel firmly trusting God in the face of threatening "news." (Even with this interpretation he *also* must have trusted in his family, but the story cannot have two "primary" meanings.) On the other hand, the ARN stories suggest that Hillel trusted his wife and family.[9] Although it is difficult to choose between these two competing interpretations, I believe the weight of the evidence supports the view that the story is about Hillel's trust in God, and that is the interpretation I included in the text.

Appendix 6

In Remembrance of the Temple, like Hillel

Every Passover, Jews eat the ritual *seder* meal and recite the *Haggadah* (the traditional account of the Exodus from Egypt and its religious meaning). At one point, the destroyed Temple is commemorated. Some *matzah* and bitter herbs are first eaten separately; then after reciting the following passage, they are wrapped into a "sandwich" and eaten together.

> In remembrance of the Temple, we do as Hillel did in Temple times: He made Passover lamb, *matzah*, and bitter herbs into a sandwich and ate them together, to fulfill what is written in the Torah (Numbers 9:11): "they shall eat it [the Passover lamb] with *matzot* and bitter herbs."

The Talmud[1] explains that Hillel and some other rabbis disagreed about how to eat the three Passover foods. Hillel said they should be eaten all at once, wrapped together; the other rabbis said they could also be eaten separately. Since the *halachah* did not decide which opinion was correct, both are followed.

But why is Hillel's custom a remembrance of the Temple? Perhaps even while the Temple stood it became a pious custom to fulfill both rulings. But once the Temple was destroyed and there were no Passover sacrifices, the ruling to eat the foods separately was not affected; one merely left out the Passover lamb. But what point was there in continuing to fulfill Hillel's custom, since his whole point was that one must eat all three together? If one is left

301

out, what is accomplished? His custom could be fulfilled only in Temple times. However, for that very reason the rabbis decided to continue Hillel's custom, even without the lamb, as a remembrance of the Temple. The *Shulchan Aruch*[2] says: "After the destruction of the Temple, the sages, of blessed memory, ordained that on every joyous occasion we must remember the destruction of the Holy Temple." Therefore, although one could no longer eat an actual "Hillel sandwich" as in Temple times – because there was no Passover lamb – it was ordained that as much as was possible should be done so as to remember not only the Temple, but also, it would seem, Hillel, the great *Nasi*, who so loved the Temple that his feet carried him there again and again.

Notes

Chapter 2: Historical Setting and Family Background

1. Hillel's dates of birth and death are uncertain. Rabbinic legends suggest he died at the age of 120 around 10 C.E.. (see pp. 43-44). He probably lived to an advanced old age. Beyond that, one can merely guess how long he lived. Jacob Neusner, *From Politics to Piety*, p. 13, says the dates commonly assigned to him are 50 B.C.E. to 10 C.E., that is, 60 years. I prefer to give the tradition more credence and speculate that he lived to the age of 90. If so, his dates would be 80 B.C.E. to 10 C.E..

2. "Sadducees," *Encyclopaedia Judaica*, vol. 14, 620.

3. See "Herodians," *Encyclopaedia Judaica*, vol. 8, 388. Due to the paucity of references to them, the nature of this sect is in doubt. The Christian Gospels (Mark 3:6, 12:13, Matthew 22:16) mention them together with the Pharisees as opponents of Jesus. Some scholars associate them with Herod the Great, and it seems likely they existed in Hillel's time. See the following p. 50.

4. Joachim Jeremias, *Jerusalem in the Time of Jesus*, trans. F. H. and C. H. Cave (Philadelphia: Fortress Press, 1969), p. 252 n. 26.

5. Judges 12:13–15.

6. R. T. Herford, *The Ethics of the Talmud: Sayings of the Fathers*, p. 36.

7. *Y. Erubin* 10:1, 26a.

8. A unique manuscript of the fourteenth-century book *Menorat Ha Ma'or*, ed. H. G. Enelow, says that the "early *hasidim*" valued working for a living and states: "Abba Hilkiah, the son of Hillel's sister, worked for hire digging fields and vineyards . . . Hillel the Elder chopped wood – although he was a *Nasi* of Israel, the leader of his generation, and

descended from the kings of Judah–he nevertheless chopped wood" (Perek Talmud Torah, p. 303). Abba Hilkiah was a famous first-century C.E. *hasid*. Other than this note, no other source indicates his relation to Hillel or that Hillel had a sister.

9. *Genesis Rabbah* 98:8 on Genesis 49:10; cf. *Y. Taanit* 4:2, 68a.

10. Compare the negative evaluation by Jeremias in *Jerusalem in the Time of Jesus*, pp. 284–289. See also Israel Levi, "L'Origine Davidique De Hillel," *Revue des Etudes Juives* 31 (1895): 209ff.

    Ketubot 62b says that Rabbi Judah the Prince (second century C.E.), a descendant of Hillel, was from the tribe of Benjamin on his father's side and from King David (of the tribe of Judah) on his mother's side, from Shefatiah, David's son by his wife Avital. However, the same genealogical scroll that states Hillel was from David states that it was Rabbi Hiyya the Great (not Rabbi Judah) who was descended from Shefatiah (*Genesis Rabbah* 98:8 and *Y. Taanit* 4:2, 68a). In *Genesis Rabbah* 33:3 and *Kelaim* 9:3 Rabbi Judah, who was the *Nasi*, the leader of the Jewish community in the Land of Israel, admits that the lineage of Rabbi Huna, the exilarch, the leader of the Jewish community in Babylonia, is superior to his own: "he [Rabbi Huna] is descended from Judah, while I am from Benjamin; he is descended [from King David] on the male side, while I am so descended only on the female side." See also *Tosefot* on *Sanhedrin* 5a. Commentators regularly transfer Rabbi Judah's statement about his lineage to Hillel, saying that Hillel was from the tribe of Benjamin on his father's side and from Judah and King David, from Shefatiah, on his mother's side (Isaac Weiss, *Dor Dor v'Dorshav* [Jerusalem: Ziv, 1904], p. 146; Joseph Klausner, *Historiah Yisraelit*, vol. 3 [Tel Aviv: Yahadut v'Enoshiyut, 1924)] p. 101; Aaron Hyman, *Tannaim v'Amoraim* [Jerusalem: Kirya Ne'emana, 1964], p. 363). The genealogical scroll said Hillel was from David, and Rabbi Judah's comment about his ancestry comes right after a remark he makes about his "ancestor Hillel." So he might be referring to Hillel's father and mother. However, when he says he descends from David on his mother's side, he would more likely be referring to his own mother, not to Hillel's. Although there is possibly some connection with Hillel, it is unclear.

11. *Kiddushin* 75a.

12. Compare how not one but two utterly irreconcilable Davidic lineages were produced for Jesus in the Gospels of Matthew and Luke.

Chapter 3: Shebna

1. See Appendix 3.

2. See Appendix 3 for an interpretation of this story different from the one offered in this chapter.

3. See the story about Hillel's joking conversation with a Jerusalem donkey driver on p. 165. Hillel's comment there means that a person is rewarded for the difficulties he surmounts in his religious life.

4. See *Avot* 6:4 about the reward for this struggle.

5. *Avot* 1:13.

6. See *Avot* 4:7.

7. Compare the Grace after Meals: "We beseech Thee, O Lord our God, let us not be in need either of the gifts of flesh and blood or of their loans, but only of Thy helping hand, which is full, open, holy, and ample. . . ."

8. See the following, p. 184.

9. See Appendix 3.

10. The heavenly voice in the story may be historical, legendary, or literary. I accept the phenomenon of a heavenly voice as historical, but the rabbis also used it as a literary device in stories, that is, when they made up stories or creatively added elements to true stories in order to enhance their religious meaning. (See, for example, the comment of Rabbi Isaac in *Sanhedrin* 39b on the conversation between Ovadiah and King Ahab.) In the same way that a historian, when describing events, might create the conversations he imagined must have occurred, so the rabbis occasionally creatively imagined God's "conversations" with people–by means of the heavenly voice. It is therefore difficult to know when the report of a heavenly voice is intended to be historical and when not. Here my surmise would be that it was known that Hillel had refused an offer of help by his brother and why, and the tradition supplied the heavenly voice and the verse. The *Midrash* (*Yalkut Shimoni* on Song of Songs 8:7) speaks of other rabbis *whose generations applied this same verse to them* (with the meaning that they gave all their wealth for God and Torah); having the verse *uttered by a heavenly voice* is roughly equivalent.

Chapter 4: Hillel on the Roof

1. Hillel traveled on foot (*ARN-B*, chap. 27; see the following p. 166), probably as part of a caravan for protection. His journey would have taken several weeks (Jeremias, *Jerusalem*, pp. 59, 242).

2. *Pesahim* 66a.

3. *Pesahim* 70b.

4. However, see chap. 12, p. 481.

5. *Avot* 1:10; *Hagigah* 2:2.

6. A late tradition–found in the Rambam's interpretation of *Avot* 4:5 and in *Hovot HaLevavot*, Shaar HaPerishut, chap. 5–says he chopped wood

for a living (Hyman, *Toldot*, p. 364; Klausner, *Historiah Yisraelit*, vol. 3, p. 101). However, they do not cite any source, and this is nowhere stated in the Talmud or *Midrash*. Perhaps they confused Hillel with Akiba, who in his days of poverty sold wood (*Avot d'Rabbi Natan*, chap. 6).

7. See Matthew 20:1–7.

8. See the following p. 114.

9. Y. L. Katznelson, "Hillel u'Veit Midrasho" (Hebrew), *HaTekufah*, p. 272, suggests that Hillel worked during the day and learned Torah at night, but I wonder if that is the schedule an ardent disciple would choose. Would he wear himself out first by manual labor and then study? Moreover, the study opportunities available for laborers in the evening after work were not primarily what Hillel needed; he was a young scholar who needed to hear the sages' discussions of the *halachah*. I assume that Hillel's earning only a half wage was due to his having to fit his work to the requirements of his study schedule, not the reverse; therefore, he was limited in the amount of time he could work and when he could work.

10. Katznelson, "Hillel u'Veit Midrasho," p. 272, pointedly comments that Hillel was unwillingly made a "witness for the prosecution" against the poor in the Heavenly Court. A similar story about how Rabbi Akiba studied Torah in great poverty, with the same "lesson" to the poor, is in *Avot d'Rabbi Natan*, chap. 6.

11. The Hillel story and its lesson are part of a larger framework, where there are two other stories and related lessons for the rich and for ladies' men. This framework is clearly later and editorial: Three separate stories have been collected to illustrate three similar lessons. Therefore, the lesson for the Hillel story was most likely added to it later.

12. *Avot* 1:4.

13. *Avot* 2:8.

14. That a God-intoxicated person can be so immersed in Torah study as to be unaware of the outer world, with his physical senses "turned off," is proved by innumerable stories from ancient times to the present. Rabbi M. Brover, *Pe'er Yitzhak* (Jerusalem, 1968), p. 14, tells how when Rabbi Yitzhak Isaac of Ziditchov was once studying Torah aloud in the House of Study during the winter, Rabbi Hayim of Tzanz came near the building and was so entranced by the sweet sound that he could not move. He leaned against the door to listen and his earlocks and beard became frozen to the doorknob and he became stuck. In an echo of the Hillel story, he later said that he was mesmerized by the sound of the "words of the living God." M. Tzitrin, *Shivhei Tzaddikim* (Jerusalem, 1959), p. 48, tells how Rabbi Jonathan of Prague went out to his garden in the winter to be alone for Torah meditation and was found by his disciples covered with snow,

like Hillel. They woke him and brought him inside. Skeptics would dismiss such stories as being based on the Hillel legend. Certainly pious stories have been fabricated according to the patterns of ancient legends, but I have no doubt that such events do actually occur.

15. Years later (75, according to Aaron Blumenthal, *If I Am Only for Myself*, p. 4), when the Hillelites overcame the restrictive policies of the Shammaites, they removed the doorkeeper from the *Beit Midrash* (*Berachot* 28a).

Chapter 5: His Great Torah Knowledge

1. Yohanan ben Zakkai learned from both Hillel and Shammai (as Hillel had learned from both Shemaya and Avtalyon; cf. *Avot* 1:12 and 2:9), but Hillel was his spiritual master (see the following, p. 265), whom he refers to in the quote as "my rabbi."
2. This tradition is discussed at length in chapter 37 (Disciple of Ezra).

Chapter 6: Hillel Becomes Nasi

1. See Appendix 4.
2. The text is not clear if Hillel had come from Babylonia many years earlier as a young man or recently to celebrate this Passover festival. It seems that Hillel had returned to Babylonia after completing his studies as a young man in Jerusalem and had recently come back for the festival. This is supported by another tradition about his motives for coming to Jerusalem (see Appendix 4) and by the fact that in this story he seems to be unknown to the Sons of Bathyra.
3. In the story of his ascent to be *Nasi*, Hillel is called "Hillel the Babylonian." Elsewhere, the rabbis say that "when the Torah was forgotten in Israel, Hillel the Babylonian came up and reestablished it." It is possible that when in Israel, before he became famous, he was known as "Hillel the Babylonian." However, in both these cases his having come up from Babylonia is directly relevant to the matter under discussion, and it is not clear if he was ordinarily referred to that way.
4. See the next note.
5. His basic argument was to compare the Passover sacrifice to the daily burnt offerings: Since the latter are offered on the Sabbath, so should the former be. Thus, when asked if the Passover sacrifice took precedence over the Sabbath, he said: "Do we have only one Passover offering that supersedes the Sabbath? Don't we have more than 200

Passovers throughout the year that supercede the Sabbath?" Hillel meant that throughout the year many sacrifices were offered on the Sabbath, for example, the two daily sacrifices, morning and evening, and the two special Sabbath sacrifices. These four, for each of the fifty Sabbaths of the year, equals his "two hundred 'Passovers.' " He then proceeded to argue for this comparison between the daily offerings and the Passover sacrifice by using various rules of Torah interpretation. For example, he began with the rule of inference from a similarity of phrases (*gezerah shavah*), which states that two different situations can be compared if an identical word is used in both places in the Torah where they are referred to. Hillel said: "Since the word *bemo'ado* ("at its appointed time") is used in connection with both the Passover and also the daily sacrifices, it indicates that just like the daily sacrifices are to be offered 'in their appointed time,' even on the Sabbath, so is that the case with the Passover sacrifice."

6. In the Talmud discussion, the rabbis ask how Hillel could have approved making profane use of consecrated animals to do the work of carrying the knives to the Temple. They answered that a tradition said:

> "As long as Hillel lived, no man ever committed trespass through his burnt-offering. But he brought it unconsecrated to the Temple Court, consecrated it, laid his hand upon it, and slaughtered it" (*Pesahim* 66a).

7. See also *Tosefta Pesahim* 4:1–2.
8. Blumenthal, *If I Am*, p. 31. Explanations for this seeming anomaly can be imagined, for example, that for a few generations Temple procedures were controlled by Sadducean or priestly groups whose authority was not accepted by the sages, so that none of the sages could remember in practice anything of value for the problem. Or perhaps the priestly oral traditions that had previously governed these matters in the Temple lost their validity in the eyes of the sages for some reason, and Temple procedures had to be reevaluated based exclusively on traditions the sages had in their possession or on halachic *midrash* interpretations from the Torah. Therefore, I would not be so strong as Blumenthal and say that the report is "impossible"; perhaps some missing fact would explain the situation. Katznelson ("Hillel," pp. 286–287) suggests a possible scenario involving Sadducean control of Temple practice to explain the situation.
9. Klausner, *Historiah Yisraelit*, p. 116.
10. The story of Hillel's becoming *Nasi* shows a contrary instance, where the sages in Israel did not know and Hillel the Babylonian did.

However, Hillel had been a student of the great sages of Israel, Shemaya and Avtalyon, and, as we will see later in the text, there is reason to believe that a massacre of leading sages in Israel by Herod had caused a decline in the level of scholarship.

11. Blumenthal, *If I Am*, pp. 32–38, has a good discussion of this. See also George Foot Moore, *Judaism in the First Centuries of the Christian Era*, vol. 1, p. 78.

12. Since the rules of interpretation became an accepted part of the tradition, it is more likely that earlier opposition to them was removed rather than later invented.

13. In the Jerusalem Talmud, Hillel ignores the question of the Sons of Bathyra –"Have you ever *heard* [a tradition] whether the Passover sacrifice, etc."– and proceeds to argue his case according to his rules of interpretation. In the Babylonian Talmud version, where there is no conflict between him and them, they merely ask, "Do you *know* . . .?"

14. Ephraim Urbach, "Hillel," *Encyclopaedia Judaica*, vol. 8, 482: "It is not to be assumed that Hillel was the first to formulate these hermeneutical rules, but it does seem that he was one of the first to apply them for the determination of practical *halachah*."

15. See the preceding p. 16. Blumenthal, *If I Am* , pp. 36, 52, 55, speaks of Shemaya and Avtalyon as Hillel's "fellow Babylonians" (although they were of gentile descent) and claims that they had brought "the new Babylonian method" of Torah interpretation to Israel. He says that although they were the *Nasi* and *Av Beit-din*, the majority of the scholars in Israel refused to accept their method. This is certainly an interesting thought, but there are also reasons to question it. Shemaya and Avtalyon were descended from Sennacherib, the Assyrian and Babylonian king, but we do not know how many generations back their families converted to Judaism, where they grew up, or if they had any connection with Babylonia. It was said that when the Torah was forgotten from Israel, Hillel came up from Babylonia and restored it – not Shemaya and Avtalyon. The rules were called Hillel's seven rules of interpretation, not theirs. To conclude, we simply do not have much information about the development of the midrashic rules. Nahum Glatzer, *Hillel the Elder*, p. 46f., discusses the possible influence of the Essenes in the development of the technique of *midrash*. Others have suggested influence from Greek philosophy and logic.

16. An example of how midrashic interpretations can be used to promote change can be seen from Hillel's enactment of a legal device called the *prosbul* (see chapter 13, this volume), which radically reversed the Torah's position and allowed people to cancel the debt release in a Sabbatical year. Hillel's motive for instituting the *prosbul* was "the welfare of the community" (Hebrew *mipnei tikkun ha'olam*), but he still

needed scriptural justification to support the change; he obtained it by Torah interpretation (*Sifre* Deuteronomy 113). See chapter 13 n. 3.

17. However, see Rabbi Eliezer's deathbed scene in *Avot d'Rabbi Natan*, chap. 25, where he tells the sages, Akiba among them, that he fears they will be punished by death from heaven for not having attended upon him.

18. *Avot* 1:10.

19. *Baba Metzia* 84-85.

20. *Avot d'Rabbi Natan*, chap. 12.

Chapter 7: *The* Nasi *as Scholar*

1. In later generations it was written down and became the *Mishnah* and *Gemara*, which together comprise the Talmud.

2. *Hagigah* 9b. See the following, p. 163.

3. Joshua ben Perahya's approximate date is the second half of the second century B.C.E. Since Hillel was born in the beginning of the first century B.C.E. he cannot have seen this. Either the name of the *Nasi* or the statement that Hillel said he saw the ritual is mistaken.

4. Eleazar performed the first sacrifice of the red heifer, but "in later times it was usually – though not always – the high priests who officiated" (Hertz *Chumash* on Numbers 19:3).

5. The text itself does not say that the original answers of Hillel and his interlocutors were their versions of traditions. Perhaps their comments were based solely on what they remembered having seen. However, because of Hillel's final words, I understand the text as I have indicated by bracketed remarks. Another version of this story elsewhere (*Sifre* Hukkat 123 and *Tosefta Parah* 4:6) notes a difference of opinion as to whether it was about Hillel or Yohanan ben Zakkai. The discussion there is between Hillel and his disciples, who correct him and remind him that his answer contradicts what he had taught them earlier. Hillel then says that if he could forget what his eyes had seen, he could certainly forget what he had heard and learned (and taught them). An editorial comment reflecting on the point of the story claims that Hillel knew the correct answer, but pretended otherwise to sharpen his disciples' minds (*Sifre*: *lehadeid*) or stimulate them to greater efforts (*Tosefta*: *lezareiz*). Thus, Hillel is said to have pretended not to know in order to keep his disciples on their toes, to test them to see if they remembered that he had taught them differently, or to encourage them to go over their traditions many times to prevent forgetfulness. The version I used in the text seems preferable to this one, which is more likely a later version interested in protecting the great man.

6. *Menahot* 99a.
7. *Avot* 4:3.

Chapter 8: *The* Nasi *as Judge*

1. The final words, "according, etc." have been added from the *Tosefta* version. The Soncino Talmud on *Baba Metzia* 104a, p. 595 n. 4 comments: "It is suggested that the clause inserted by the Alexandrian Jews was mainly designed to free the husband from all obligations until actual marriage, v. Epstein, M. *Jewish Marriage Contract*, p. 295."
2. Also *Y. Ketubot* 4:8, 28d and *Tosefta Ketubot* 4:9.
3. Blumenthal, *If I Am*, pp. 112–113, notes a number of possibilities regarding the circumstances and location of this case. "(A) . . . The sages in Alexandria wanted to declare them *mamzerim*, which meant that they could not marry other Jews. Such an important case may have been referred to Jerusalem for review and Hillel's decision was given in Jerusalem. (B) The grown children may have moved to Jerusalem and appealed to Hillel to clarify their status. (C) As head of the Sanhedrin, Hillel may have gone on a visit to a number of communities, Alexandria among them, and cases probably were presented to him for review during such visits."
4. *Toldot*, p. 372.

Chapter 9: *Hillel's Views on Leadership*

1. It became standard rabbinic practice that whenever the *halachah* was unknown or unclear, the court observed how the people acted, and ruled likewise (*Y. Maaser Sheini* 5:3, 56b). Another interesting example of the humility of Hillel and the other great rabbis is found in *Eduyot* 1:3. "Hillel says: 'A full *hin* [= 12 *logs*] of drawn water renders a *mikveh* (ritual bath of purification) unfit.' [The term 'full' is quoted] only because a man must employ the style of expression of his teacher. Shammai says: 'Nine *kabs* [= 36 *logs*].' But the sages say: 'The *halachah* is not according to either of their views, but when two weavers came from [their homes near] the Dung Gate in Jerusalem and testified in the name of Shemaya and Avtalyon that three *logs* of drawn water render the *mikveh* unfit, the sages identified with their report." The next *mishnah* (1:4) asks why the views of Hillel and Shammai were even recorded, since they were not followed, and answers: to teach future generations that a person should not stubbornly persist in his views, for great teachers like Hillel and

Shammai accepted another opinion, even though it came from two lowly weavers. This story in the *mishnah* has a number of other interesting aspects. The text states that Hillel said a "full" *hin*, although that word would seem to be superfluous, because a man must exactly reproduce his teacher's words. This has given rise to much speculation: Hyman, *Toldot*, p. 363, suggests that Hillel reported the exact language of his original Babylonian teacher (Hillel's source for this tradition is not likely to have been Shemaya and Avtalyon, since his view differed from theirs). This would show Hillel's devotion to the Torah from another angle: His scrupulousness in preserving the exact language of his teacher. However, perhaps this sentence in the *mishnah* refers to the reason the compiler of the *Mishnah* reported these words of Hillel – because that is how *he* heard them. Otherwise, it is interesting that Hillel had a different tradition from Shemaya and Avtalyon and that they had students who were lowly weavers.

2. *Tosefta Pesahim* 4:1–2.
3. *Mateh Ephraim* 610:11.
4. *Baba Kamma* 8:6; *Baba Metzia* 7:1.
5. *Shabbat* 67a.
6. 1 Samuel 28:19. Note the two *gams* in the verse.
7. Hillel's midrashic comment is on 1 Samuel 15 and 28, particularly 28:18, 19.
8. Hillel perhaps intended to imply that one sin led to another that was even worse; compare 1 Samuel 15:23 with 28:8.

Chapter 10: Years and Dates

1. The connected tradition that he lived to 120 (obviously adding up the three 40s consecutively) would then be a later addition that misunderstood the original, where the 40s "overlapped."
2. See the following, p. 248 for another instance of his being compared with Moses.
3. Urbach, "Hillel," *Encyclopaedia Judaica*, vol. 8, 483, remarks about these dates: "These are only approximate figures, however, and it is more likely that the period of Hillel's activity is to be placed at the end of Herod's reign, from about the year 10 B.C.E. to about 10 C.E."
4. *Avodah Zarah* 9a.

Chapter 11: Hillel the Pharisee

1. Although Christian anti-Semitism has historically given a negative connotation to the designation "Pharisee," I rely on the readers of this

book being free of that prejudice. Familiarity with Hillel, a leader of the Pharisees, should make the pejorative usage of "Pharisee" even more unacceptable.

2. See the next note.
3. *Antiquities of the Jews* XV.1.1; 10.4. See chapter 15 n. 7 this volume.
4. 5:34.
5. *Life* 38.

Chapter 12: Hillel, Menahem, and Shammai

1. *Avot* 1:12.
2. Adolph Buchler, *Types of Jewish-Palestinian Piety from 70 B.C.E. to 70 C.E.: The Ancient Pious Men*, p. 117, identifies Shemaya and Avtalyon as Shammai's masters. I do not think that *Avot* 1:12 implies that he was their disciple – although that is perhaps likely – but simply that he was the next leader in the line of tradition.
3. Many theories try to reconcile the conflicting evidence about the Sanhedrin. In Josephus and the Christian scriptures the high priest is head of the Sanhedrin, while in rabbinic literature the head of the Sanhedrin is the Pharisee leader, the *Nasi*, such as Hillel. Some scholars think there was more than one Sanhedrin and that Hillel, as *Nasi*, was the head of a Sanhedrin that dealt exclusively with religious, and not political, matters. Others think he was the head of such a committee of the one Sanhedrin. Klausner, *Historiah Yisraelit*, vol. 3, pp. 103–104, for example, suggests the latter opinion and cites Adolph Buchler for the former (see p. 120 there for other opinions). See the next note.
4. Bacher, "Hillel," *The Jewish Encyclopedia*, vol. 6, p. 397: "According to tradition, Hillel thereupon became head of the Sanhedrin with the title of '*Nasi*' (prince), but this is hardly historical. All that can be said is that after the resignation of the *Bene* [Sons of] Bathyra Hillel was recognized as the highest authority among the Pharisees and the scribes of Jerusalem."
5. *Shabbat* 31a; see the following, p. 153.
6. Note that the title "Elder" does not refer to age.
7. As mentioned in chap. 6 n. 3, he may have been called Hillel the Babylonian before he achieved position and fame.
8. See Urbach, "Hillel," *Encyclopaedia Judaica*, vol. 8, 482; Bacher, "Hillel," *The Jewish Encyclopedia*, vol. 6, p. 397; and Katznelson, "Hillel," *HaTekufah*, p. 271.
9. Both the Babylonian and the Jerusalem Talmud have a second opinion about why Menahem "left." The former says that he "left" to

become a heretic or irreligious (*tarbut ra*), the latter (essentially the same) that he "left" one religious path for another. This other view is not incompatible with the one that he left to enter King Herod's service.

10. *Kiddushin* 31a describes Dama ben Netina, a politically important person (a council president [*Encyclopaedia Judaica*]) of Hillel's time, "wearing gold-embroidered silk robes and sitting among Roman noblemen." The Herods were famous for their grand and ostentatious clothing.

11. P. 13. Some scholars have speculated that Menahem was the same person as an Essene of that name mentioned by Josephus, but there is little to support that view. See "Menahem the Essene," *Encyclopaedia Judaica*, vol. 11, 1308.

12. See Aaron of Apt, *Keter Shem Tov* (Jerusalem, Israel, 1968), 16b.

13. See the following, p. 237.

14. Once chosen, a high priest who was not already wealthy was enriched by his fellow priests. Perhaps there was a similar arrangement for the *Nasi*. As for gifts from wealthy supporters, see the story about Hillel's disciple, Yonatan ben Uzziel, following on p. 140, and *Nedarim* 50a and *Avodah Zarah* 10a for Rabbi Akiba's receiving a gift from a Roman proselyte.

Chapter 13: The Prosbul

1. Ephraim Urbach, *The Sages: Their Concepts and Beliefs*, p. 580.

2. Judah Goldin, "Hillel the Elder," *The Journal of Religion*, p. 264, speaks of how the country and the people were desperately impoverished by: "the long succession of wars conducted first by the Hasmoneans and later the revolts and seditions; the tribute which Rome imposed and the plunderings and the upkeep of the lavish Herodian household; the revenue Herod extorted to bribe Rome or to make provisions available to his imperial superiors when they required assistance; the cost of a frenzied building program; famines and pestilence and an earthquake. . . ."

3. Hillel used Torah interpretation to allow people to cancel the debt release. *Sifre* Deuteronomy 113 has his scriptural justification for the legal device of the *prosbul*. Deuteronomy 15:3 says that whatever of "yours" that is with your brother, namely, the loan, must be released. Hillel interpreted this literally, to mean that if the debts were transferred even verbally to the court, they were no longer "yours" and could be collected.

4. *Sifre* Deuteronomy 113 on Deuteronomy 15:3.

5. The quoted *mishnah* (*Shevi'it* 10:3) also states that Hillel instituted various ordinances beside the *prosbul*, but we know of only one other. "The second *takkanah* was with regard to the houses of the walled cities which, according to biblical law (Lev. 25:29), could be redeemed by the seller only within the year of the sale. In Hillel's time the buyer who desired to acquire the house permanently would disappear until the last day of the year, so that the seller would be unable to redeem his house. Hillel's *takkanah* provided for the seller to deposit the proceeds of the sale in the Temple treasury, to enable him later to acquire the title to his house (Ar. 9:4)" ("Hillel," *Encyclopaedia Judaica*, vol. 8, 484). Goldin, "Hillel" p. 264, suggests that this relates to the *prosbul*. He says that in terrible economic conditions, the poor found it difficult to obtain loans and therefore the *prosbul* was necessary, and that some, "hoping that some ready cash, at least for a year, might solve their immediate problems, were . . . compelled to sell their homes."

6. See in chapter 20 that this vision allowed Hillel to say that the whole Torah was based on the principle of the Golden Rule.

Chapter 14: Hillel and Herod: Religion and Politics

1. *Baba Batra* 3b–4a.
2. *Baba Batra* 3b–4a.
3. *Antiquities of the Jews* XV.11.1.
4. "Bathyra, Sons of," *Encyclopaedia Judaica*, vol. 4, 324: "According to Halevy the Sons of Bathyra carried out the functions of the patriarchate [the *Nasi*] when the Sanhedrin was not operative (possibly at the beginning of Herod's rule)."
5. In the Talmud story, Baba ben Buta equates the two in his conversation with Herod, telling him that since he destroyed the rabbis, who are the light of the world, he should occupy himself with the light of the world – the Temple.
6. See *Avot d'Rabbi Natan*, chap. 12.
7. *Betzah* 20a,b; *Tosefta Hagigah* 2:11, p. 236; *Y. Betzah* 2:4.
8. See Isaiah 60:7.
9. *Y. Betzah* 2:4, 61c.
10. *Midrash HaGadol* on Deuteronomy 14:23.
11. Hillel's disciple, Rabban Yohanan ben Zakkai, taught that a person should make peace not only between individuals, but between cities, nations, and kingdoms (*Mechilta* Yitro, 20).
12. Leo Baeck, *The Pharisees and Other Essays* (New York: Schocken Books, 1966), p. 47; Glatzer, *Hillel the Elder*, pp. 63–64.

13. *Baba Batra* 3a.
14. "Nasi," *Encyclopaedia Judaica*, vol. 12, 835.
15. *Sanhedrin* 5a.
16. Note that the Torah teachers are the inheritors, so to speak, of the mantle of kingship.
17. However, see my speculation on p. 42.
18. Josephus also mentions Hillel's disciple and his great-grandson – Yohanan ben Zakkai and Simon ben Gamaliel.
19. That Menahem was or became a Herodian would explain why he and Hillel agreed in permitting burnt offerings on a festival, since Herodians would also have wanted to encourage attendance at "Herod's" Temple.

Chapter 15: Hillel and Herod: Religion and Politics – Continued

1. Something so bizarre as a floating skull, indicating – it would seem – a beheading, suggests that the death was not the result of an ordinary murder or drowning.
2. Exodus 18:11.
3. *Midrash HaGadol* on Exodus 18:11; also *Yalkut Shimoni* on Exodus 1:10.
4. When an armed crowd came to arrest Jesus and one of his disciples attacked them, Jesus told him to stop, since "all who live by the sword, die by the sword" (Matthew 26:47–52). This is essentially the meaning of Hillel's saying about those who drown others being drowned.
5. *Antiquities of the Jews* XVIII.i.16.
6. The young Herod, who was then military governor of Galilee, had put an anti-Roman rebel to death without authorization from the Sanhedrin. See "Hezekiah," *Encyclopaedia Judaica*, vol. 8, 455.
7. *Antiquities of the Jews* XV.1.1 – where the names Shemaya and Avtalyon are graecized as Sameas and Pollio. For the identification of Shemaya and Avtalyon with the figures in Josephus, see Katznelson, "Hillel," 273–274, particularly note 3; Louis Feldman, "The Identity of Pollio the Pharisee in Josephus," *Jewish Quarterly Review* 49 (1958–1959): 53–62.
8. *Antiquities of the Jews* XIV.9.4; XV.1.1.
9. Jacob Bosniak, "The Life of Hillel," pp. 80–82.
10. *Antiquities of the Jews* XV.10.4.
11. The talmudic account in *Baba Batra* 3a says that Herod slaughtered the Hasmoneans and "the rabbis." Other historical evidence indicates that the murdered Sanhedrin members were mostly Sadducean supporters of the Hasmoneans and that the Pharisaic leaders Shemaya and Avtalyon were spared. See Katznelson, "Hillel," p. 273.

Chapter 16: Disciples of Aaron

1. *Yoma* 7:4.
2. It was considered dangerous to enter the awesome chamber of the Holy of Holies, and exiting safely was a cause for rejoicing.
3. *Yoma* 71b.
4. *Avot* 1:10.
5. *Tamid* 32a.
6. See, for example, *Pesahim* 57a and the popular ditty reported in the name of Abba Joseph ben Hanin.
7. See the following teaching from *Derech Eretz Zutta* on p. 83.
8. *Gittin* 57b; *Sanhedrin* 96b.
9. Note the progression from *ger toshav* to *ger tzedek* to teaching children to teaching multitudes (of adults).
10. Compare the Gospel of John 8:39, where Jesus says: "If you were Abraham's children, you would do what Abraham did!" See also the Gospel of Luke 3:8.
11. *Avot* 5:22.
12. *Yebamot* 79a.
13. *Erubin* 86a.
14. *Tanna d'Bei Eliyahu Rabba*, chap. 25, beg.
15. *Tanna d'Bei Eliyahu Rabba*, chap. 9.
16. *Horayot* 3:8.
17. "Herod I," *Encyclopaedia Judaica*, vol. 8, 379.
18. *Baba Kamma* 38a.
19. Although in Malachi these words are spoken of Levi (2:4), since they were addressed to the priests (2:1), they were understood to be about Aaron, who represents the priests, the elite of the tribe of Levi.
20. The verse was not the lone source of Hillel's saying, for as we have seen, the basic ideas are already present in the words of Shemaya and Avtalyon to the high priest. Presumably they also had reflected on this verse.

Chapter 17: Loving Peace

1. *Avot d'Rabbi Natan*, chap. 12.
2. *ARN-B*, chap. 24.
3. *Berachot* 64a.
4. See the following, chapter 19, for a discussion of this saying.
5. As is well known, "peace" is the traditional Jewish greeting of blessing exchanged at meeting and parting.
6. *Mechilta* Yitro, 20.
7. *Gittin* 59b.

8. This motive was used, for example, when the rabbis attempted to reconcile some of the same tensions with the priests that we saw reflected in the story of Shemaya, Avtalyon, and the high priest. They ruled that "priests who fail to donate the half-*shekel* Temple-tax are not forced to pay" (*Y. Shekalim* 1:3, 46a). The rabbis held that the priests, like all others, were obliged to pay this tax for support and upkeep of the Temple. The priestly leadership, however, and many priests considered themselves exempt. Normally, if someone failed to give the half-*shekel* the rabbis would force payment. With the priests, however, "because of the ways of peace," they did not press the issue so as not to cause strife in Israel. For other rabbinic applications of the principle of "the ways of peace," see *Gittin* 5:8 and *Gittin* 61a.
9. *Avot d'Rabbi Natan*, chap. 12.
10. *Avot d'Rabbi Natan*, chap. 12.
11. Rabbi Pinhas of Koretz and Rabbi Rafael of Bershad, *Midrash Pinhas* (Jerusalem, 1971), p. 38a, no. 16.
12. *Avot d'Rabbi Natan*, chap. 12.
13. *Derech Eretz Zutta*, chapter on peace, end.
14. *Derech Eretz Zutta*, chap. 4.
15. *Berachot* 17a.
16. *Derech Eretz Zutta*, end.
17. *Sanhedrin* 6b.
18. *Midrash HaGadol* on Exodus 4:27.
19. See Y. K. K. Rokotz, *Tiferet HaYehudi* (a hasidic book), p. 20, and the *Zohar* Metzora.

Chapter 18: Being "Mixed-in" with Others

1. *Derech Eretz Rabba*, chap. 7.
2. *Derech Eretz Rabba*, chap. 7.
3. *Derech Eretz Zutta* 5:5.
4. That Hillel was not teaching conformity can be seen from some of his other teachings, such as: "In a place where there are no men, try to be a man!" (see chapter 22, this volume).
5. See Hillel's saying about joining groups organizing to do deeds of kindness, on p. 194.
6. P. 233.

Chapter 19: Charity and Peace

1. Compare *Yalkut Psalms* 711: "Great is the peace bestowed on those who give *tzedakah*, as it says: 'And the work of *tzedakah* shall be peace' " (Isaiah 32:17).

2. *Leviticus Rabbah* 34:16.
3. See chapter 39 for more about this saying.
4. Compare also the *Yalkut* saying in note 1.
5. Martin Buber, *Hasidism and Modern Man*, ed. and trans. Maurice Freedman (New York: Harper & Row, 1966), p. 157.

Chapter 20: Loving People

1. Hillel was not the first to promulgate the Golden Rule. It is already found in one of the books of the Apocrypha, the Book of Tobit. However, Hillel did declare its centrality to the whole Torah and made that view the possession of the Jewish people.
2. Of course, specifically personal feelings – likes and dislikes – are not intended here.
3. *Sifra* on Leviticus 19:34.
4. The quote from *Sifra* on Leviticus 19:34 (preceding, p. 96) takes the view that Leviticus 19:18 applies to Jews and the similar quote in 19:34 applies to gentiles in the Land of Israel. However, this may not have been the original intent of those verses. It is likely that 19:34 is a later clarification of 19:18 – the commandment to love your neighbor – for those who excused themselves from proper behavior by claiming that the stranger was not their "neighbor." Compare the relation of Exodus 23:4, 5 to Deuteronomy 22:1–4.
5. Claude G. Montefiore, *Rabbinic Literature and Gospel Teachings* (New York: Ktav, 1970), p. 72: "After all, the man was a heathen, and it is very cumbersome and improbable if we have to argue that what Hillel meant was, 'When you *have become* a Jew, the whole Law that you will have to observe is to love your fellow-Jew.' It is surely more natural to suppose that Hillel meant something far more general: something which applied to the man as heathen no less than it would apply to him if he became a Jew."
6. See *Avot* 4:20 and the story about Yohanan ben Zakkai on p. 85, preceding.
7. Rabbi Eleazar Azikri (Jerusalem, 1984), chap. 8.
8. This is also the view of Rabbi Arye Levin as recorded in Simha Raz, *A Tzaddik in our Time*, trans. Charles Wengrove (New York: Feldheim, 1978), p. 413: "Why did Hillel not teach this [the positive commandment to love] to the would-be convert? – because so exalted a concept a non-Jew was not yet ready to understand." Rabbi Levin also claimed that since Hillel recognized how difficult it was for people to love their neighbors in the full sense, he used the negative form, meaning "If you

cannot love him, at least do not hate him." However, he says that Hillel himself loved others fully (*ibid.* p. 417).

9. See the following, p. 167, for Hillel's teaching that an ignorant person cannot be truly pious.

10. "Hillel, Shammai and the Three Proselytes," *Conservative Judaism* 21:3 (Spring 1967): 33.

11. The saying about being disciples of Aaron by drawing others to Torah was primarily but not exclusively directed to leaders. Compare the saying about Abraham on p. 126 of my text. Unlike Abraham, however, Aaron was specifically a model for a leader.

12. *ARN-B*, chap. 26.

13. A teaching of Rabbi Akiba's found elsewhere is directly related to this Golden Rule story: "'You shall love your neighbor as yourself' (Leviticus 19:18)–Rabbi Akiba says: This is a great principle of the Torah" (*Sifra; Genesis Rabbah* 24:7). As said, Hillel's Golden Rule was the practical form of the commandment to "love your neighbor as yourself." If we compare the Akiba Golden Rule story with this related teaching, we see that in the story, like Hillel, he identified the Torah's essential principle as being the Golden Rule; but in this teaching, the great principle is "love your neighbor as yourself." This again shows the relation between the Golden Rule and the commandment to love in Leviticus 19:18–the same as in the *Targum* paraphrase.

14. *Sifra* on Leviticus 19:18; *Genesis Rabbah* 24:7.

Chapter 21: Love and Judging Others

1. Rabbi Elijah deVidas, *Reishit Hochmah*, ed. H. Y. Waldman (Jerusalem, 1984), Shaar HaAnavah, chap. 5, number 10 comments on Hillel's saying "Judge not, etc.": "This is an important principle to follow for the continuance of peace and love between people, since most disputes result from people judging themselves one way and others a different way. So he [Hillel] cautioned: 'Judge not your fellowman until you come into his place,' until you *put* yourself in his place. For example, if someone verbally abused you, because of something you did to him, do not answer back until you consider how you would act if places were reversed. Would you have yelled at him even worse than he did at you?"

2. *Kiddushin* 81a.

3. *Sanhedrin* 102a–b.

4. *Derech Eretz Zutta* 3, beg. Hillel was not the first to teach about judging others favorably. The teaching is found in *Avot* 1:6, in the name of

Joshua ben Perahya, who lived in the second half of the second century B.C.E.

5. *Lehapeich bezchut* (*Shabbat* 119a; *Kiddushin* 76b).
6. *Shabbat* 119a.
7. *Ketubot* 105b.
8. The story of Hillel and his wife gave us a brief look into Hillel's home life. A lone saying in the tradition from his son allows us another such peek: "Simon, his son, said: 'All the time I was growing up, I was among the sages, and I never found anything better for a person than silence'" (*Avot* 1:17). We can picture how Hillel's house was constantly full of Torah sages, both before he became *Nasi* and even more so afterward. Before Hillel's time, the rabbis had taught: "Let your house be a meeting place for the sages" (*Avot* 1:4), and "Let your house be open wide to the poor; and treat them like members of your household" (*Avot* 1:5). The former saying relates to the words of Hillel's son, about the constant presence of sages in his home, and the latter saying to the story of Hillel's wife giving food to the poor man at the door. Although the comment of Hillel's son Simon has its own spiritual and religious meaning – in teaching the value of silence – it is interesting for what it tells us about Hillel's family life. From that viewpoint, it would not be unusual if Simon, growing up among the sages and surrounded by older, greater men, became retiring and accustomed to silence. Although it is disputed whether the reference in *Avot* 1:17 to "Simon his son" is to Hillel's son or another Simon, a number of important commentators, such as Louis Ginzberg, *On Jewish Law and Lore*, p. 91 n. 9, and Herford, *Ethics*, pp. 36–37, support the view that this Simon was Hillel's son.
9. Compare how some men and women today call a spouse or lover "baby."
10. Rabbi M. Machir (Bnei Brak, Israel, 1973), p. 23.
11. *Yalkut Shimoni*, Numbers 33.
12. Although that saying is from the *Zohar*, it accurately expresses the attitude that motivated Hillel.
13. I think there is a strong likelihood that on such a basic issue the views of the House will reflect those of its founder. Note the text of *Betzah* 16a on p. 184, following, where a difference between Hillel and Shammai, about preparing for the Sabbath, is reported in a second tradition as between their two Houses.
14. *Berachot* 133b.
15. Deuteronomy 11:22.
16. Deuteronomy 4:24; Exodus 34:17.
17. See "Eliezer ben Hyrcanus," *Encyclopaedia Judaica*, vol. 6, 621. Note also that Rabbi Eliezer cites the same verse – Micah 7:19 – with a similar

purpose as the Shammaites in the following quote from *Pesikta d'Rav Kahana* in my text.

18. *Pesikta d'Rav Kahana* 61b.

Chapter 22: Under the Wings of the Divine Presence

1. See *Avot* 4:22 and 6:4. The terms and the contrasts used by Hillel are common in rabbinic literature. See for example *Betzah* 15b, *Shabbat* 10a and 33b, and *Taanit* 21a. The usual contrast is between the temporal "life of the hour" and eternal life, the "life of the [eternal] world." But another contrast is between the "life of the hour," meaning the hand-to-mouth existence of a poor person, with the "life of this world," the good life of the rich person. Hillel makes clear that eternal life, the "life of the world," includes eternal life now in this world as well as in the next world. So even in this world these laborers would gain.

2. Torah gives life and its rejection makes one deserving of death. Thus, Hillel taught: "He who does not study, deserves death" (*Avot* 1:13). The expression "deserving death" is, of course, figurative and hyperbolical. Another version has: "Whoever does not attend upon the sages deserves death" (*Avot d'Rabbi Natan*, chap. 12). Attending on the sages – meaning regular attendance at their lectures and constantly seeking their company – was expected of disciples rather than of householders; perhaps the two versions of the saying were for these different groups.

3. Buchler, *Types of Jewish-Palestinian Piety*, p. 27.

4. *Mishnat Rabbi Eliezer*, chap. 4, the section about peace.

5. *Mishnat Rabbi Eliezer*, chap. 4, the section about peace.

6. See also the teachings about Jethro in chapter 25, this volume.

7. See also the very end of the story in *Shabbat* 31a, following on p. 132.

8. Compare *Baba Kamma* 60b: "Our rabbis taught: When a pestilence is raging in the city, stay indoors (literally: gather your feet) . . . If there is a famine, leave town (scatter your feet)." Also, *Sifre* Deuteronomy 321: "During wartime stay inside (gather in the foot); during famine flee (scatter the foot)" (Klausner, *Historiah Yisraelit*, vol. 3, p. 110). Hillel's saying leaves out "the foot" in the scattering clause, but it is understood, i.e., "When others are scattering (the foot), gather in the foot!"

9. The *Tosefta Berachot* version has antithetic parallelism: "When others are scattering, gather; when others are gathering, scatter." Here there is just "one half," and also the idiomatic use of "scatter or gather the foot."

10. *Tanhuma* Mishpatim 5, 41a.

Chapter 23: A Mission to All Men

1. According to tradition, Abraham was not only the first "proselyte," the first "gentile" who became a Jew, but also the first person to make others proselytes. See *Tanhuma* Lech Lecha 6. Abraham as the "father of proselytes" comes from Genesis 17:5's derivation of Abraham's name, where God tells him: "I shall make you the father of many nations" (*goyim*) or gentiles.
2. The Hebrew behind "urging men until he wins them over" is one word, *mikapei'ah*, which more literally means "compels," not in the negative sense of "forcing," but idiomatically of "urging," "persuading," men and "winning them over."
3. *Avot d'Rabbi Natan*, chap. 12, end.
4. *ARN-B*, chap. 26, end.
5. *Midrash HaGadol* on Genesis 25:27.
6. *Avot* 1:1.
7. This seems to me what is meant by the Hebrew *hacham ve'anav*.
8. Note the typical, inclusive Hillelite phrase, about greeting or teaching "all men," which I mentioned earlier on p. 87.
9. The texts have *shanah*, not *lamad*, meaning that the issue, as in the original dictum, is about raising disciples, not merely general teaching for the public.

Chapter 24: Three Proselytes

1. It seems that a word – perhaps *lifnei* – has fallen out of the text in *Shabbat* 31a. The Hebrew now says: "can someone *be made* a king if he does not, etc." The original was undoubtedly like that in the other two versions (*ARN-A*, chap. 15, and *ARN-B*, chap. 28), where the idea is whether someone can *attend on* a king without knowing the court ceremonials.
2. Literally, that he drew a conclusion "from major to minor," that is, if the Israelites were not permitted, how much less he.
3. Note the characteristic phraseology we have seen elsewhere. Compare the phrases used at the end of the story of Hillel at the Gate of Jerusalem (earlier, p. 115).
4. This version has a few differences that should be noted. It has only two stories: the one about the two Torahs and the alphabet – and there that story is about a returning Jew, not a gentile – and the one about the high priest's clothes; the Golden Rule story is missing. Since the man in the Two Torahs story is a Jew, the details are correspondingly different: The man knows the Hebrew alphabet already, but Hillel points out to him that the Jews received the alphabet from their

ancestors and therefore should also accept the rest of the oral Torah that came down from them. Neither does it have the unifying conclusion, with the three (or even two) proselytes meeting.

5. "Sadducees," *Encyclopaedia Judaica*, vol. 14, 621.
6. *Life* 2.
7. *Yebamot* 47a.
8. *Sifre* Numbers 78.
9. *Tosefta Demai* 2:5.
10. Rashi comments on the story about The Two Torahs, where Hillel converts the man despite his refusal to accept the Oral Torah: "He [Hillel] relied on his wisdom, that in the end he would bring the man to accept [the Oral Torah]. And this does not fall under the category of 'a gentile who has committed himself to adhere to all the teachings of the Torah except one is not received,' because the man did not actually deny the Oral Torah, he simply did not believe it was from the mouth of God. And Hillel was certain that after he taught him, the man would rely on him [and accept it]." In an article entitled "Righteous Converts," Rabbi Samuel Turk writes: "Suspicion of an applicant's sincerity is enough reason to reject him or her for conversion (Achiezer, II:26). However, if the judicial panel feels that the convert will ultimately accept Judaism sincerely, it may accept the candidate even if presently his motives are questionable (Tur, Beth Joseph, Y. D. 268; Shach, Y. D. 268:23). This is borne out by the man who came to Hillel the Elder to be converted and said, 'Convert me in order that you may appoint me high priest' (T. B. *Shabbat* 31a)" (*The Jewish Press*, Feb. 26, 1988, p. 10C).
11. Shammai had claimed that there were already priests who could serve in the high priesthood, and a proselyte was not needed for this. The man finally realized that the Torah forbade even Jews who were not priests from becoming high priest, therefore, how much less eligible was he, a proselyte.
12. See earlier, p. 82.
13. *Yebamot* 65b.
14. The Talmud (*Yebamot* 65b) cites the teachings to alter the truth for the sake of peace and not to correct someone who will not accept it together because both are ways to avoid strife and foster peace. Hillel, who was a lover of peace, followed and perhaps was the source of both teachings.
15. See earlier, p. 86.
16. The obligation to refrain from saying something that will not be heeded is associated in *Yebamot* 65b with Proverbs 9:8 – "Do not rebuke a scoffer lest he hate you, but rebuke a wise man for he will love you." Otherwise, Hillel was fond of Ecclesiastes 3:4 (see earlier, p. 90),

which speaks of the wisdom of knowing when and when not to speak: "there is a time to keep silent and a time to speak."

17. *Baba Batra* 133b.

18. *Arachin* 16b.

19. Possibly, this was originally a mere metaphor, since at that time "pushing someone away with a reed" meant getting rid of a questioner with a weak answer (*Numbers Rabbah* 19:8). "Pushing someone away with a builder's cubit" might have meant: to get rid of a questioner with a harsh rebuke.

20. *Sanhedrin* 107b.

21. See the procedure described in *Gerim* 1.

22. Beshtian hasidic literature typically speaks approvingly of drawing people in with two hands.

23. *Tanna d'Bei Eliyahu Rabba*, chap. 6.

24. For another example of the way this kind of compromise could take place, see the following, p. 179, where the Hillelites argue that it is better for a person to have been created, and the Shammaites argue that it is better for him not to have been created. The "compromise" decided upon was that it is better for a person not to have been created, but once created he should weigh all his actions carefully.

Chapter 25: Receive All Men

1. *Avot* 1:15.

2. This is the opinion of Blumenthal, *If I Am*, p. 71.

3. That such a thing is not impossible can be seen from a story in *Taanit* 20b: Rabbi Simon ben Eleazar acted arrogantly and rudely when he met a certain man, was rebuked and learned his lesson, and went into the House of Study and taught: "A person should always be soft like a reed and never hard like a cedar." Moreover, this story is closely related to stories comparing Hillel's softness to Shammai's hardness, which are introduced by the saying: "A person should always be humble and patient like Hillel and never quick-tempered and irritable like Shammai."

4. That sayings could be misattributed between Hillel and Shammai can be seen from two examples: (1) A teaching about permission to continue a military operation even on the Sabbath is given in *Shabbat* 19a as Shammai's (which seems correct), and in *Tosefta Erubin* 3:7 as Hillel's; (2) The saying attributed to Hillel (here, p. 10) in *Y. Erubin* 10:1, 26b, about wearing his grandfather's *tefillin*, is attributed to Shammai in *Mechilta* Bo, xvii, p. 69. See Urbach, *The Sages*, p. 956 n. 95 about this.

5. See the story of The 400 *Zuz* Bet in chapter 26 (this volume), where Hillel warmly *receives* a difficult man who asks him questions.
6. *Midrash HaGadol* on Numbers 25:11.
7. *Y. Erubin* 5:1, 22b.
8. *Mechilta* on Exodus 18:12.

Chapter 26: Hillel's Personality

1. This does not contradict what we said earlier, on p. 107, about Hillel's judging even an opponent like Shammai favorably – that he, too, was acting for the sake of heaven – for Shammai's temper was not "for the sake of heaven" and impeded his ability to teach Torah.
2. The story that follows in the text is used in *Avot d'Rabbi Natan*, chap. 15, to illustrate *Avot* 2:15. However, I've given the version found in *Shabbat* 31a.
3. So the reader should not be confused: This sentence contrasting Hillel and Shammai appears before this story, which is then followed by the stories of the three proselytes, that we have already discussed. The sentence is more closely connected to the proselyte stories; perhaps an editor inserted the tale of the 400 *zuz* bet between them. Since the Shammai part is not relevant here, I have left it out.
4. Compare the story on p. 174 following for Hillel's religious attitude to cleanliness.
5. This detail is found in the versions in *ARN-A* and *B*.
6. Tadmor was also known as Palmyra. In *Shabbat* 31a it is incorrectly called Tarmod.
7. *ARN-B*, chap. 41.
8. "Coins," *Encyclopaedia Judaica*, vol. 5, 719. The *ARN-B* chapter 29 version of the Hillel story has *dinars* and the *ARN-A* version, like *Shabbat* 31a, has *zuzim*.
9. Although a wager would usually involve each party taking an opposite position – for example, one saying Hillel could be angered and the other disagreeing – that does not seem to be the case here, although the Hebrew can be understood in different ways. My reading is that both of them felt that Hillel could be angered – although it might be very difficult – and that one bet the other he could accomplish the feat.
10. In *ARN-A* the man each time tells Hillel that he has to ask about a matter of *halachah*, but then asks the foolish question, as if he did not even know what *halachah* meant. However, Hillel responds, at least once, "My son, you've asked an important halachic question," perhaps repeating the mistake so as not to embarrass the man about his lack of knowledge.

11. In the *ARN-B* version, the repeated motif is that Hillel is sleeping: When the man yells, he gets up from bed, comes down, opens the door, lets him in; when the man says he wants to ask a question, Hillel solemnly wraps himself in his cloak and sits down to hear and to answer. Each time, the man disturbs Hillel with his request to ask a question, but to provoke him further, when asked what it is, says at first, "I forgot." And each time Hillel acts as if the man is nervous or shy and says "Calm yourself," to help him remember. Also, after answering each question, Hillel asks him if he has any more questions. The man says no, but when he leaves, and Hillel goes back upstairs to sleep, the man returns and the cycle is repeated.

12. *Erubin* 64b.

13. *Hagigah* 14b.

14. *ARN*, chap. 41; cf. *Taanit* 20a.

15. See *Baba Kamma* 8:6 and *Berachot* 20a.

16. *Berachot* 20a.

17. Chapter 5.

18. *HaTekufah* 3 (1918): 267–301.

19. *Avot d'Rabbi Natan*, chap. 29.

20. Yehudah Leib Levine, *Hasidim Mesaprim,* vol. 2 (Jerusalem: Mosad HaRim Levine, 1979), p. 123.

21. *Kallah Rabbati*, chap. 3.

22. In the next *baraita*.

23. *ARN-B*, chap. 32.

24. See his insightful reflection on that saying, earlier, on p. 82.

25. *Midrash Pinhas*, p. 32a, no. 34.

Chapter 27: Hillel the Hasid

1. Adolph Buchler already perceived this. The first chapter of his excellent book *Types of Jewish-Palestinian Piety* is "Hillel the *Hasid*." Similarly, the third chapter of Nahum Glatzer's fine book *Hillel the Elder* is "The Ways and Beliefs of the *Hasid*," the *hasid* being Hillel. In his *Historiah Yisraelit*, Klausner says "Hillel was the founder of Hasidism in Judaism" (p. 122).

2. "Act from love [of God] and act from fear [of God]" (*Y. Sotah* 5:7, 20c).

3. "Greater is he who serves God from love than he who serves from fear" (*Sotah* 31a).

4. Bar He He is also called Ben He He. *Bar* (Aramaic) and *ben* (Hebrew) both mean "son."

5. See the other question that Bar He He asks Hillel on p. 194 following. Bar He He – son of He He (a most unusual name) – may have been a

disciple of Hillel and a proselyte converted by him (see *Encyclopaedia Judaica* under "Ben He He").

6. *Sotah* 31a.

7. *ARN-B*, chap. 10.

8. Although the *parush* serves from fear, it is a fear based in love. Thus, the hasidic devotion to Torah study that Hillel commends is shared by the *parush*.

9. Compare "He who does not increase, will decrease" with Hillel's saying in *Avot* 2:8 about always increasing Torah study, charity, etc. That teaching has sayings of the form: increasing possessions, increases anxiety. Hillel was interested in and perceptive about spiritual causality, the spiritual consequences of people's actions. See following p. 237 for a discussion of that other saying.

10. Y. K. K. Rokotz, *Nifla'ot HaYehudi* (Jerusalem), p. 66.

11. Presumably, Hillel paused so the donkey driver would think he was seriously inquiring about prices, and not merely responding to his jibe. That way the man would answer straightforwardly.

12. Emmaus, Lud, and Caesarea were approximately 15, 25, and 55 miles from Jerusalem. Since a *dinar* equals a *zuz*, the price here is slightly different from what Hillel said to Bar He He, where the charge became 2 *zuzim* at 11 miles. In this story, up to 15 miles is still only 1 *dinar*. Of course, prices may have changed over time.

13. In a comparable story, Rabbi Yohanan told how he learned to "increase reward" from a widow, who always went to his synagogue rather than a nearer one. When he asked, "Why don't you go to the synagogue in your own neighborhood?" she answered, "But, Rabbi, won't I receive an added reward for walking the extra distance?" (*Sotah* 22a).

14. *Avot d'Rabbi Natan*, chap. 12. However, in the confused story there, others quote the proverb to Hillel and not he to them.

15. Undoubtedly the meaning of this term varied in different times and locations.

16. See *Sotah* 22a, for example.

17. *Tosefta Berachot* 7:18.

18. *Avot d'Rabbi Natan*, chap. 12.

19. *Derech Eretz Zutta*, chap. 8.

20. See *Baba Kamma* 81a. By saying that Akiba "shed innocent blood," the rabbis meant that he dishonored the man with each step.

Chapter 28: A Hasid from Love

1. *Avot*, chap. 5, has four teachings about the nature of the *hasid* – 5:13, 14, 16, and 17 (the first pair is separated from the second by 5:15). In my

view, the importance of the first pair far exceeds that of the second, and I am inclined to think that the second was formulated along the lines of the first and added at a later time.

2. *Avot* 5:14.
3. Pp. 151–152 preceding.
4. *Avot* 5:13.
5. The saying I have ascribed to Hillel is found in a section of Hillel's teaching in the text, and begins with הא, which means "behold." Later commentary on Hillel's sayings is mixed in throughout this section, and this saying might or might not be from Hillel. But I believe it to be his for two reasons: (1) It is followed in the text by two other sayings beginning הה"א, the abbreviation for: "he [Hillel] used to say." It seems likely that the הא is a scribal error for הה"א; (2) The language of the saying is similar to other sayings of Hillel.

    Klausner, *Historiah Yisraelit*, p. 103, ascribes this saying to Hillel. Buchler, *Types of Jewish-Palestinian Piety*, p. 38 n. 3, comments: "If it might be assumed that the sentence in 2 ARN. 27, 28a top, 'Since that which I possess is not mine, what for do I require that which belongs to others?' was Hillel's (see Schechter's note and G. Klein, *Der alteste christl. Katechismus*, 87), the beautiful principle would account for his unselfishness."

6. Hillel's saying: "What is mine is not mine; what need have I of what belongs to others?" reflects the attitude of some of the *hasidim*, of whom it was said that they hated their own money and certainly that of others (*Mechilta* on Exodus 18:21).
7. See preceding, pp. 157–159.
8. *Avot* 3:8.
9. *Derech Eretz Zutta* 2:11.
10. The rabbis taught that a person should imitate God's Thirteen Attributes of Mercy: "Be like Him: as He is merciful and giving, so must you be merciful and giving" (*Shabbat* 133b). Being "giving" (or "gracious") means: "Give freely to all – even to those who are unworthy – expecting no return" (*Sifre* Deuteronomy 49 and *Berachot* 7a). A *hasid*, whose attitude is "what is yours is yours and what is mine is yours," is able to fulfill this exalted teaching.
11. *ARN-B*, chap. 27. Compare *Derech Eretz Zutta* 2:6: "Know the difference between today and tomorrow and also between what is yours and what is not yours, for if what is yours is not yours, what need have you of what belongs to others?" The parts of this saying are related thusly: A person should concern himself with today, which is "his," not tomorrow, which is not. Compare Ben Sira, quoted in the Talmud (*Sanhedrin* 100b): "Do not worry about tomorrow's troubles, because you do not know what tomorrow will

bring. Perhaps you will be dead and gone and will have worried about a world which is not yours."
12. See n. 10.

Chapter 29: *The* Hasid *and* Hesed

1. See following, p. 184.
2. See preceding, pp. 105–106.
3. *Shabbat* 50b. Rabbi Judah bar Ilai (mid-second century C. E.) washed his face, hands, and feet in hot water every Friday in honor of the Sabbath (*Shabbat* 25b).
4. In the *Leviticus Rabbah* version of the text, Hillel speaks of the statues gentiles set up in their theaters and in the buildings they used for chariot races. A (Roman?) philosopher once asked Rabban Gamaliel (Hillel's grandson?) why he bathed in the public bath in Acco, since there was an idol (statue) of the Greek goddess Aphrodite there (*Avodah Zarah* 3:4). Perhaps Hillel was on his way to a similar Roman-style bath, decorated with statues, and this parable naturally came to mind.
5. *Types of Jewish Palestinian Piety*, p. 20.
6. In discussions of this story about Hillel, it is frequently said that the "kindness" Hillel was doing was eating. This is nowhere stated in the text, however. Perhaps this detail is unconsciously added because kindness to a guest would often mean offering him a meal. However, eating would actually be more "kind" to the body than the soul. Hillel said he was being kind to the *soul* and his meaning was broader than what this other interpretation suggests.
7. This understanding of Proverbs 11:17 was probably suggested by the full verse, which is: "The kind man does good to his own soul; but he that is cruel troubles his own flesh."
8. Glatzer, *Hillel the Elder*, p. 37, mentions that "Seneca [the Roman Stoic philosopher], in part a contemporary of Hillel, spoke of the God who dwells as a guest in the human body; the Stoics often compared the soul to a guest in the body." Compare, for example, Seneca: "The body is not a permanent dwelling, but a sort of inn (with a brief sojourn at that), which is left behind when one perceives that it is a burden to the host." After speaking of men's bodily troubles, sicknesses, and so on, and how this shows that the soul is uncomfortable in the body: "Now this troubles us, now that, and bids us move away: It is just what happens to those who dwell in the house of another" (*Epistles* 120, 14). The difference between the Roman Seneca and the Jewish Hillel is that while Seneca felt that bodily suffering made this world uncongenial for the

soul, Hillel most likely felt that the "poor" soul suffered here because of the lack of Godliness and because of worldly temptations to sin.

9. *Wars* II. 8. 11.

10. *Erubin* 13b.

11. *Taanit* 11a–b.

12. *Sifra.*

13. See Solomon Schechter's *Aspects of Rabbinic Theology* (New York: Schocken Books, 1961), pp. 201, 205, about this.

14. *Sifra* on Leviticus 19:2.

15. *Shabbat* 133b.

16. Similar teaching is found, for example, in the words of Jesus in Luke 6:36 and in the *Targum* of Yonatan ben Uzziel on Leviticus 22:28. Jesus antedates Abba Shaul; the date of the *Targum* is uncertain.

17. See chapter 28 n. 10 (this volume).

18. See the following, p. 263.

19. Jesus, a younger contemporary of Hillel, told a parable critical of a Pharisee who, thanking God for his piety, said, "I fast twice a week, I give tithes of all I get" (Luke 18:12). Biweekly fasting on Mondays and Thursdays was a traditional custom of Pharisaic piety. The basic conditions for membership in the Pharisaic Order were special ritual purity in food and meals and strict adherence to the laws of tithing. Note the parallel to the words of the Pharisee in the parable, about being ritually rigorous regarding food (or fasting from it) and tithes. Jesus's teachings have much in common with Hillel's, and his criticism of "Pharisees" was primarily directed to the Shammaites. Note then the emphasis on fasting by the (Shammaite) Pharisee of the parable.

20. Resh Lakish (third century C.E.), who especially appreciated Hillel and his teaching, compared Hillel to Ezra, saying he had restored the Torah when it had been forgotten. See the quote following on p. 223.

21. In *Taanit* 11a–b.

22. In *Taanit* 11a–b.

23. See p. 187 following about the limits on Shammai's asceticism.

24. See p. 195 following.

25. See, for example, Dan Ben-Amos and Jerome Mintz, *In Praise of the Baal Shem Tov* (Bloomington, IN: Indiana University Press, 1970), story 49, and Martin Buber, *Tales of the Hasidim*, vol. 1 (New York: Schocken Books, 1947), p. 52. In the latter, the Baal Shem Tov alludes to *Taanit* 11a–b, that everyone who fasts overmuch is called a sinner.

Chapter 30: A Different Way

1. *Pesikta Rabbati*, chap. 23, p. 115b.

2. Another version of this teaching, in *Pesikta Rabbati* 115b, specifically

discusses Shammai's practice as being a way to look forward to the Sabbath.

3. *Shabbat* 119a.

4. In the *Pesikta Rabbati* 115b version of this story, Shammai did not choose the animal but would "get wood," presumably for the Sabbath cooking.

5. *Avodah Zarah* 3a.

6. Similarly, the saying that all Hillel's deeds were for the sake of heaven also has a general significance.

7. The Torah's lesson of trusting God for sustenance, receiving what He gives each day, and not worrying about the next, is taught particularly in the story about the manna. See *Exodus Rabbah* on 16:4, where the rabbis linked the verse that Hillel used, Psalm 68:20–"Blessed is the Lord day by day," and Exodus 16:4–"And the people should go out and shall gather a day's portion [of manna] day by day [i.e. every day]."

8. *If I Am*, p. 81.

9. However, note that the *baraita* at the end of *Betzah* 16a does not contain the saying about all Hillel's deeds being for the sake of heaven.

10. See preceding, p. 106.

11. See preceding, p. 107 and following, p. 215.

12. The *Pesikta Rabbati* 115b version of this material says explicitly that Hillel's way was superior *midah aheret yiteirah*.

13. In the text, the two aspects – one represented by "let all your deeds be for the sake of heaven" and the other by Psalm 68:20 – are connected by the phrase "as it is said." This is unclear and should be noted when considering my interpretation.

14. See, for example, *Baba Kamma* 30a.

Chapter 31: His Heart Is Firm, Trusting in the Lord

1. *Hillel the Elder*, p. 34.

2. The story in *Berachot* 60a uses the word *muvtah*, which could mean that Hillel says he is "promised" by God that such a thing will never happen to him. But it would be strange for him to rely on his great merits; and it is hard to see what the point of his comment to others would be. And does not evil befall even saintly people? The correct understanding is not that, as an exceptional person, he claimed to be "promised" by God, but that he trusted in God even when tested by this situation and was certain that the cries were not from his house. The Jerusalem Talmud version uses the word *batuah*, from the same root, which more clearly and simply means: "I am certain." The Psalm verse also has *batuah* ("trusting"). *Muvtah* expresses an intense form of certainty. In another story, where Hillel detects a sign of purity of

character in a disciple, he says: "I am certain" (*muvtah ani*) that he will one day be a great teacher in Israel (*Pesahim* 3b; see following p. 220).

3. See Appendix 5 for a different interpretation of this Hillel story.

Chapter 32: Hasid and Parush

1. *Dead Sea Scrolls*, Community Rule VIII.
2. The Sadducees are also included in *Rosh HaShanah* 17a among those who separated from the community; cf. *Avot d'Rabbi Natan*, chap. 16.
3. See preceding, p. 89.
4. See following, pp. 198–201, for other comments about this saying of Hillel.
5. *Erubin* 103a.
6. The hasidic desire to influence others for good appears in *Avot* 5:16, where, in comparing the four dispositions in giving *tzedakah* (charity), the *hasid* is the one who gives and wants others to give.
7. The rabbis use the same expression as Hillel when they speak of the importance of not "separating from the community" in the time of their difficulty and suffering, specifically when a public fast is called in response to some communal distress (*Taanit* 11a).
8. *Tosefta Yom HaKippurim* 5(4):2.
9. Women are traditionally exempt from all commandments that have a time specified for their observance and that might impede them in their performance of their home and family responsibilities, which take priority.
10. *Shulchan Aruch*: "Children too are exempt from dwelling in a *sukkah*; nevertheless, if a boy is five years or over, his father should train him to eat in the *sukkah*" (135:15).
11. *Sukkah* 2:8.

Chapter 33: The Way of Hesed

1. *Berachot* 32b.
2. *Pirke d'Rabbi Eliezer*, chap. 15.
3. The Hebrew is literally that Samuel was "in goodness (favor) with God and also with men." The traditional understanding of this phrase is that "goodness with God" is being good to God, the way of righteousness; "goodness with men" is being good to people, the way of love (note the preceding verse, 1 Samuel 2:25). See the commentaries on *Pirke d'Rabbi Eliezer* of Rabbi David Luria (Hebrew) and Gerald Friedlander (English version p. 103 n. 1).

4. *Pesikta Rabbati,* chap. 23, p. 115b. See chap. 30 n. 12.

5. *Avot* 2:6.

6. *Avot* 2:5.

7. Although the second part of the teaching, about Abraham's fear of having slain a righteous person, is found elsewhere (*Midrash Lekach Tov* on Genesis 15:1) in the name of a later rabbi, Rabbi Levi (third cent. C.E.), there are reasons to believe that the attribution to Hillel is correct.

8. It is not clear if Hillel is referring specifically to the people captured, to Abraham's fighters, or both.

9. Hillel's comment is not clear, but the main point seems to reside in the "and not even one person was lost." A similar phrase is found in an incident with King David in 1 Samuel 30:19.

10. Since the two parts of the *midrash* are connected to the two clauses of Isaiah 41:3 (see my discussion of this in the text), it seems likely that Hillel intended to say that just like Abraham returned from his expedition without having lost one person, he was afraid that he had slain one (righteous) person.

11. Genesis 11:28, 31.

12. I have paraphrased Isaiah 41:3 according to Hillel's words.

13. *Tanhuma* Hukkat 25, where examples – similar to what Hillel said about Abraham – are given about Jacob and Moses.

14. Cf. *Yoma* 38b: "When a person has lived out most of the years of his life without sinning, he will sin no more, for it is said, 'He will protect the feet of His *hasidim*' (1 Samuel 2:9)."

15. Is it a coincidence that the other *midrash* from Hillel in *Pirke d'Rabbi Eliezer* – about the prophet Samuel and King Saul – which we quoted and discussed earlier (pp. 41–42), was also about a military expedition? There, Hillel taught that Israel's defeat by the Philistines was due to the sins of their leader Saul.

16. *Y. Sotah* 5:7, 20c; *Y. Berachot* 9:7, 14b.

17. A story in the Jerusalem Talmud actually tells of a *hasid* sitting and repeating for himself aloud, as was the practice, his Torah traditions, which included this saying of Hillel. However, he was an older man and had kept himself from sin for so long that he now felt secure. He trusted in himself that he was no longer susceptible to temptation and consequently went so far as to alter Hillel's teaching, about "until the day of your death," to: "Do not trust in yourself until *the days of your old age*"!

     "A certain *hasid* of advanced age was once sitting and reciting his Torah traditions to himself. He went over the saying [of Hillel's, which, however, he altered]: 'Do not trust in yourself until your old age' – remarking to himself, 'like me.' Just then a spirit disguised as a beautiful woman appeared and tempted him by offering herself to him. He began to lust after her, but then came to his senses and started to withdraw, shocked at his own behavior. The 'woman' then said to him: 'Do not despair, for I am a spirit sent to teach you a lesson, and not a real woman. Go now, and from this time on consider yourself as no more than equal to others. And repeat the saying correctly: "Do not trust in yourself until the day of your death"!' " (*Y. Shabbat* 1:3, 3b).

18. See chap. 27 n. 1 (this volume).

Chapter 34: The Humble Man

1. *ARN*, chap. 15.
2. 1:122, 3:168.
3. *Leviticus Rabbah* 1:5.
4. *Da'anan bah man bah* (Aramaic). The *Y. Sukkah* 5:4, 55b version has *da'anan hachah man hachah*.
5. In the Hebrew text, Hillel does not actually utter the sayings. The text has first (from the editor) "If we are here, who is here," and the first half of the story, illustrating that. Then (from the editor) there is the second half of the saying, "If we are not here, who is here?" and the second half of the story, illustrating that. This editorial form is a little difficult to follow, so I have adjusted the translation to make Hillel speak the words of the saying. They were certainly sayings that he frequently used, and it is peculiar that he does not actually utter them here. In the *Y. Sukkah* 5:4, 55b version, however, Hillel does indeed speak these words to the people.
6. The language here alludes to Daniel 7:10.
7. The story says that *gavah libam* and Hillel's saying *hagbahati*.
8. Hillel's comparison of humans and angels is an interesting sidelight of this story. Although he does not say so directly, it is understood that if Israel serves God as they should, they and their worship are superior to the angels; but if they fall short somehow, they are inferior to the angels. A lovely hasidic parable about God's pleasure in the praises of Israel, more so than in those of the angels, compares it to a king who has large choirs to sing for his entertainment, but most enjoys hearing the songs of a pet canary (*Keter Shem Tov*, p. 52a). Hillel's view was that humans are placed above or below the angels depending on their level of spiritual attainment.

But there is another view about this: In a moment of exaltation and wonderment, the psalmist could only bring himself to marvel that God had created man "a little lower than the angels" (Psalms 8:6). In biblical times many people thought that even seeing an angel was fatal. Such awe of the holy angels did not "disappear" in rabbinic times. Some religious people were more impressed with the virtues of men and others with the virtues of angels. The difference in attitudes is ancient. After all, Jacob won his name Israel by struggling with and overcoming an angel: implicit therein is the idea that the lower "Jacob" is below the angels, while the higher "Israel" is above them. In rabbinic stories the angels are often in competition with humans. Putting humans – at their best – above the angels, as Hillel does, seems to me a sign of his *humanistic* attitude. Those rabbis who wanted to put humans above angels are also those who put repentant sinners above the righteous (the "angels" on earth; *Berachot* 34b). And certainly those rabbis are the ones who tried to bring sinners to repentance.

Although there is no hard evidence for this, I would speculate that the stricter school, among whom I would expect to find Shammai, would not agree to exalt humans at the expense of angels. The angels, as God's messengers and close to Him, would be considered by them so awesome, sharing God's luminosity, that sinful men could rarely reach their level or surpass them; only patriarchs such as Jacob or prophets (already called angels in the Torah) such as Elijah (called "My angel," *malachi*) could compare to the heavenly beings.

The Talmud (*Hagigah* 12a) reports that the House of Hillel and the House of Shammai disputed for years whether heaven or earth was created first: Shammaites said the heaven, Hillelites the earth. The argument seems to have been over where God's "primary" dwelling was: with humans on earth or with the angels in heaven? The Hillelites claimed that the earth was His house, the heavens only the upper story; the Shammaites said that the heavens were His throne, where He actually "sat," the earth only His footstool (presumably, this argument occurred while the Temple, God's House on earth, still stood). It might be surmised that there would have been a parallel difference between the two Schools about who had precedence: the heavenly "community," the angels, or the earthly "community," Israel. This is supported by one of the verses the Hillelites used to argue their position: "Who builds His upper chambers in the heavens and establishes *His community* (*agudato*) on the earth" (Amos 9:6).

9. See the following p. 212, for the tradition that the House of Hillel attained primacy over the House of Shammai because they "were gentle and bore insult," and this fulfilled the saying that God lowers the proud and exalts the humble. This tradition about the House of Hillel shows that this is the more generalized, third-person form of Hillel's saying.

Chapter 35: Hillel and the Once-Rich Poor Man

1. The Hebrew text calls the man an *ani ben tovim*: a poor person from a "good"–wealthy or noble–family. Although not said explicitly, it is likely he had recently *become* poor and was particularly distressed by his situation.

2. The *Midrash HaGadol* (on Deuteronomy 15:8) version of this story states that the man needed a horse and servant because "he was not able to eat unless he had first exercised [by horseback riding], and then the servant would serve him his meal." *Tosefta Pe'ah* 4:10 has a similar addition, without the remark about his not being able to eat otherwise. These explanations seem to be later additions that detract from the original meaning: the man's need for the honor and prestige. That interpretation is supported by the story of how Elijah ran before the chariot of King Ahav (1 Kings 18:44–46), as Rashi says (following the teaching of Rabbi Yohanan in *Zevachim* 102a), to give honor to the king.

3. See the preceding note.

4. The story about Hillel is paired with another story in *Ketubot* 67b that tells how the inhabitants of the upper Galilee bought for a poor man from a good (wealthy or noble) family from Sepphoris a pound of meat each day. *Shekalim* 5:6 tells how special care was taken to give charity secretly to poor people from good families.

5. See the preceding, p. 53.

6. 1 Kings 19:44–46.

Chapter 36: Gentle and Bearing Insult

1. This occurred after the destruction of the Temple, in the days of Rabban Gamaliel II of Yavneh, who was five generations removed from Hillel. He convoked all the scholars of his time to Yavneh, where after debating for three years whether the rulings of the House of Hillel or Shammai should be accepted, they heard the heavenly voice (Gershom Bader, *The Encyclopedia of Talmudic Sages*, p. 112; "Gamaliel, Rabban," *Encylopaedia Judaica*, vol. 7, 296, and "Bet Hillel and Bet Shammai," vol. 4, 740–741).

2. *Avot d'Rabbi Natan*, chap. 15.

3. *Taanit* 20a.

4. Preceding, p. 158.

5. "Be patient (*noah*) under oppression" (*Avot* 3:16).

6. *Avot d'Rabbi Natan*, chap. 23.
7. *Midrash Aggadah* on Numbers 12:3.
8. *Midrash Psalms* 16:11.
9. *Kallah Rabbati*, chap. 3.
10. *Shabbat* 88b.
11. As mentioned earlier (p. 49), this was a long-standing dispute between succeeding pairs in the dual leadership.
12. "The reason is that the person who lays his hands on an animal places his weight upon it, and one may not make use of animals – even to such an extent – on the festival day, the law of which is like that of the Sabbath in that it required one's animals to enjoy rest. One therefore lays on hands on the preceding day [that is, for the peace offering, which the Shammaites allowed]" (Neusner, *From Politics to Piety*, p. 107). See also Shemuel Safrai, *Pilgrimage at the Time of the Second Temple* (Hebrew) (Tel Aviv: Am HaSefer, 1965), p. 176.
13. *Keritot* 6:3; *Tosefta Keritot* 4:4. This does not only relate to fear of sin because it seems that the *hasidim* of that time were so enthusiastic about the rebuilt Temple that they sought any slight excuse to bring an offering (*Y. Nedarim* 1:1, 36d; *Tosefta Pe'ah* 3:8).
14. Preceding, p. 85.
15. Hillel's lying for the sake of peace has no relation to the "peace offering."
16. Laying on of hands was the symbolic issue between what we can call the right and left wings of the Pharisaic movement. The left wing was lenient and allowed the sacrifices, the right wing was strict and would not allow them. *Hagigah* 2:2 lists how the pairs of the dual leadership split on this issue and states that the first mentioned was the *Nasi*, the second the Head of the Court. In the first three pairs, the right wing position is taken by the *Nasi*, in other words, the right wing was on top, and the leader of the left wing was in the secondary office as Head of the Court. But with Shemaya and Avtalyon, Hillel's teachers, the positions are reversed: the left attained power. With Hillel and Menahem (Hillel's first co-leader) that situation continues. But when Menahem is replaced by Shammai, Shammai's position is reported first, before Hillel's. This shows that the situation with Hillel and Shammai was unstable. Hillel was the *Nasi*, but then Shammai temporarily displaced him. The story where Baba ben Butta supports Hillel against the Shammaite zealots in the Temple shows the struggle between the two camps. That Shammai, for a while at least, overcame Hillel is seen in another story, in *Shabbat* 17a (following, p. 218). See Ginzberg, *Jewish Law and Lore*, pp. 91–101, for an interesting discussion of laying on of hands and its place in the conflict between the parties.

17. The note on this in the Soncino Talmud: "This was the practice when a vote was taken upon any question; Halevi, *Doroth* I, 3, p. 585 n. 18."

18. Compare the legendary scene described in *Yalkut Shimoni, Ve'et'hanan* 3, 821, where Moses allows himself to be replaced as head of the *yeshivah*, so to speak, by Joshua, and their roles are reversed, Moses becoming the disciple: "Moses bent himself over" while "Joshua sat at the head."

19. After the reference to that being as grievous a day as the one on which they made the Golden Calf, the text in *Shabbat* 17a ends: "Shammai and Hillel enacted [this measure], but they would not accept it from them; later their disciples enacted it, and it was accepted from them." The people would not accept the enactment Hillel unwillingly approved (note that the text mentions Shammai first, before Hillel, in referring to the joint enactment). The Soncino Talmud commentary notes that the disciples enacted it at the assembly in the house of Hananiah ben Hezekiah ben Garon. (That event is described in *Y. Shabbat* 1:4, 3c and *Tosefta Shabbat* 1:16–17.) At that meeting, which took place after the death of Hillel and Shammai, the Shammaites outnumbered the Hillelites and passed eighteen measures that increased the barriers between Jews and gentiles. Presumably those same measures were originally passed when Shammai overcame Hillel, but the people refused to accept them. Later, however, they accepted them from Shammai's disciples. Opinions differ as to when this occurred; some scholars believe it took place shortly before the destruction of the Second Temple ("Bet Hillel and Bet Shammai," *Encyclopaedia Judaica*, vol. 4, 738). One tradition about the eighteen measures of the Shammaites says that "it was as grievous a day for Israel as the day on which they made the Golden Calf," and another that the Shammaites threatened the Hillelites with swords and spears. This echoes what is said about the earlier conflict when Shammai defeated Hillel, and a sword was planted in the House of Study, that being as grievous a day, etc. It is impossible to tell, however, which tradition was original and influenced the other.

20. See its use in *Soferim* 1:7 with regard to the translation of the Torah into Greek, the famous Septuagint.

21. Compare the comment of the hasidic *rebbe*, Rabbi Mendel of Vorki: "The sin of the Golden Calf was that our teacher Moses was delayed for a mere six hours and they already began to seek another leader" (N. Benari, *HaTzaddik HaShotek* [Bnei Brak, 1965], p. 100).

22. See *Yebamot* 13a about the relations between the two Houses.

23. *Tosefta Sanhedrin* 7:1. Ginzberg suggests that although two wings of the Pharisaic movement had been represented in the dual leadership for generations, the split became more serious in the generation of Hillel and Shammai, resulting in the formation of separate schools or

Houses – the House of Hillel and the House of Shammai (*Jewish Lore and Law*, p. 96).

24. The text here states that some say the teacher was not Hillel but Rabbi Judah the Prince and the disciple was one of his disciples. See the next note.

25. See preceding, p. 218. The English translation there is different, to make the meaning clear, but the Hebrew is exactly the same. That the disciple's words are exactly the same as Hillel's to Shammai in *Shabbat* 17a seems to indicate that this story was about Hillel and his disciple, Yohanan ben Zakkai (see preceding note).

26. Buchler, *Types of Jewish-Palestinian Piety*, p. 42 n. 1 (from a version of Rabbi Pinhas ben Yair's famous sentence about the rungs on the ladder of spiritual attainment).

Chapter 37: Disciple of Ezra

1. *Soferim* 16:9 lists the esoteric subjects known to Hillel and follows with a similar section about his disciple, Yohanan ben Zakkai. In *Sukkah* 28a another list of Yohanan's accomplishments in Torah says he knew: "the language of angels and the language of demons, and the language of palm trees; parables of the laundrymen and fox parables." This is quite similar to what is said about Hillel, except that it has the language of angels as well as demons; the language of palm trees rather than "trees and grasses"; specifies two kinds of parables; and leaves out the language of mountains, hills, and valleys, and the language of animals.

2. See the following, p. 229. Various biblical figures – such as Moses, Joseph, and Mordechai – were said to have known all the seventy languages.

3. *Sanhedrin* 17a.

4. This is reported in *Sotah* 49b by his son, Rabban Simon ben Gamaliel, who elsewhere (*Esther Rabbah* 4:12) was so enthusiastic about Greek that he claimed it was the only language into which the Torah could be perfectly translated.

5. *Midrash Psalms* 92:8.

6. *Avodah Zarah* 17a.

7. *Avot d'Rabbi Natan*, chap. 12.

8. "Solomon," *Encyclopaedia Judaica*, vol. 15, 106, refers to *Song of Songs Rabbah* 1:1 no. 9; *Tanhuma-B* Introd., 157.

9. *Y. Demai* 1:3, 22a.

10. Buber, *Tales of the Hasidim*, vol. 2, p. 228. Compare the following words of Swami Brahmananda, a nineteenth-century Hindu saint who was

a disciple of an even greater Hindu teacher, Sri Ramakrishna: "There is nothing outside. Everything is inside. People are fond of music, but they do not realize that the music we hear with our ears is trivial compared to the music within. How sweet and soothing it is! During his meditation in the Panchavati [a sacred garden], Sri Ramakrishna used to listen to the melody of the vina [a stringed instrument] within. Once I was meditating in the Panchavati at noon while the Master was talking about the manifestation of Brahman [God] as sound [*Shabda-Brahman*]. Listening to that discussion, even the birds in the Panchavati began to sing Vedic [scriptural] songs and I heard them" (Swami Chetandanda, ed. and trans., *Ramakrishna as We Saw Him* [St. Louis: Vedanta Society of St. Louis, 1990], p. 75). Although such statements seem incredible, I personally have not the slightest doubt about the truthfulness of its author. If one will compare this with the almost identical story about the Baal Shem Tov in Ben-Amos and Mintz, *Praise of the Baal Shem Tov*, no. 237, one will see that such stories should not be dismissed.

11. *Hagigah* 14b.
12. See *Gittin* 68a, where the rabbis connected this with some uncertain Hebrew in Ecclesiastes 2:8.
13. *Gittin* 68a.
14. *Antiquities of the Jews* VIII.ii.5.
15. *Antiquities of the Jews* II.viii.7.
16. Angels and demons were not quite "opposites"; demons were not considered uniformly evil. Whereas Hillel was said to have known the language of the demons, the similar list for Rabban Yohanan ben Zakkai, his disciple, has the languages of angels and demons. See note 1.
17. *Sanhedrin* 101a.
18. *Sanhedrin* 17a. The Hebrew translated "know about magic" could imply (and Rashi so takes it) that the knowledge is not merely theoretical. Most rabbis of that time did not doubt the efficacy of magic, and the point here could be that a member of the Sanhedrin must know about magic or be able to use countermagic when necessary.
19. See preceding, p. 41.

Chapter 38: Hillel's Teaching Style

1. *Avot* 2:6.
2. *Avot* 2:5.
3. *Soferim* 16:9. See preceding, p. 20.
4. *Hagigah* 9b. See preceding, p. 163.
5. See preceding, p. 165.
6. Glatzer, *Hillel the Elder*, p. 51.

Chapter 39: Hillel and the Rich

1. *Niddah* 70b.
2. Preceding, p. 165.
3. Compare, for example, the related and independent saying in *Avot* 2:6, quoted earlier in the text.
4. See also his words to the donkey driver in the preceding story, on p. 165: "I see that as I increase the distance, you increase the price," and the lesson he drew from that.
5. Another shorter version of this saying may support this interpretation: "The more you eat, the more you excrete; the more meat [flesh], the more worms and maggots. But the more good deeds, the more you establish peace within your body" (*ARN-A*, chap. 28). The two halves of the first sentence may be linked: the more you eat parallels the more meat, and the more excreta parallels the more worms and maggots that feed on it. Otherwise, Hillel seems to be contrasting filling one's body with food and excreta and filling it with the inner peace that comes from good deeds. See also p. 93 preceding about the second sentence of the saying.
6. "Monogamy," *Encyclopaedia Judaica*, vol. 12, 259, says that polygamy was more common among Hellenistic Jews. Jeremias, *Jerusalem in the Time of Jesus*, pp. 93–94, presents evidence for polygamy among the rich and the aristocracy.
7. *Sanhedrin* 67a. Rabbi Simon ben Yohai: "In earlier generations the daughters of Israel were not steeped in magic, but in these later generations they are" (*Erubin* 64b, end).
8. Klausner, *Historiah Yisraelit*, vol. 3, p. 112.
9. In *Leviticus Rabbah* 9:5 a rabbi complains about masters who "act as if sexual promiscuity with their female servants was permitted."
10. Hillel may in a sense have "used" the social prejudices of his audience to make his case.
11. *Sanhedrin* 6:6.
12. See preceding, pp. 18, 92–94, 236, 239.
13. *Avot* 6:1. Compare *Midrash Psalms* 1:19.
14. *Avot* 1:15.

Chapter 40: A Good Name versus a Great Name

1. Compare: "Happy is he who has grown up with the Torah, who labors in the Torah and gives pleasure to his Creator; who has grown up with a good name, and passed away with a good name. About him

did Solomon, in his wisdom, say: 'A good name is better than precious ointment' (Ecclesiastes 7:1)" (*Berachot* 17a). Note the parallelism between what is said about Torah and about a good name, the same pair as in Hillel's saying. By devotion to the Torah and following its ways of peace, one gives pleasure to God and has a good name with men, for a person must please both God and men.

2. *Ecclesiastes Rabbah* 7:1.

3. Compare Hillel's saying with the words of Munbaz, the Jewish convert and king of Adiabene (first century C.E.), in the famous talmudic story. During years of famine, when Munbaz distributed large amounts of money from his treasury to the poor so they could buy food, his relatives protested that he was dissipating the family wealth. In answering them, he repeated Jewish teaching, saying: "My ancestors stored up treasures *for others*, but I've stored up treasures *for myself*. . . . My ancestors stored up treasures *for this world*, but I've stored up treasures *for the World-to-Come*" (*Baba Batra* 11a).

4. See Appendix 1, p. 280f.

5. *Midrash Proverbs* on 22:1.

6. This epithet also alludes to his being a *baal shem*, a master of divine names and a miracle worker, of good repute.

7. See *Avot* 4:8 and note the sayings of Rabbi Tzadok and Hillel that precede in 4:7 about the crown.

8. *Avot* 4:17.

9. Genesis 12:2.

10. Genesis 23:6.

11. See an application of this saying to Hillel's own life on p. 30 preceding.

12. *ARN-B*, chap. 27.

13. See preceding p. 176.

Chapter 41: The Holy Spirit

1. Hillel – along with Rabban Yohanan ben Zakkai and Rabbi Akiba – is compared to Moses in another tradition (preceding, p. 44). He is also, of course, compared to Ezra in the eulogy here.

2. The *Y. Sotah*-9:13, 24b, version of this story is found together with a parallel story about two other rabbis who lived after Hillel, which ends that after hearing the heavenly voice praising the rabbis, the assembled elders rejoiced that "their own view had agreed with that of God."

3. See preceding, chap. 3 n. 10.

4. "Elders" in another version.

5. Gadya in another version. The gathering convened in the favored location for meetings, the upper room.

6. I have stated on p. 13 earlier that, although no location is given, the story about Hillel and Shebna took place in Babylonia.

7. The *ARN-B* version adds: "but their generation was not worthy," making the parallel with what is said about Hillel even closer.

8. Cf. *ARN-B*, chap. 28, *ARN-A*, chap. 14.

9. *Baba Batra* 75a.

10. *Taanit* 19b–20a. During the time of a pilgrimage festival, the wealthy and saintly Nakdimon ben Gurion saw that there was not sufficient water available for the multitude of pilgrims who had come to Jerusalem. A Roman general had large quantities of water at his disposal and Nakdimon arranged to borrow it, agreeing that if he did not return the same amount of water by the end of a year, he would pay a very large sum of money. The whole year passed without enough rain falling to make up for the borrowed amount, but just hours beyond the time limit, after nightfall of a year to the day, there were torrential rains. The Roman general would not bend the conditions of the agreement and so Nakdimon went to the Temple and prayed that God perform a miracle "to show that He loves His people." In answer, the sun turned back in its course and day-time returned; thus the rain had fallen during the day and the water collected was returned to the Roman general within the required time.

11. The Hebrew *katan* can refer either to status, size, or age. The parallelism with Yonatan ben Uzziel would suggest that if Yonatan was the "greatest" in ability and status, Yohanan must have been the "least." However, that seems unlikely considering Yohanan ben Zakkai's later eminence and fame, predicted by Hillel on his deathbed (see the following, p. 265). Yohanan was undoubtedly the youngest disciple of Hillel. It might be that the "greatest" is illogically perhaps compared to the youngest, or it might be that Yonatan was the oldest. But if so, why would he merit being mentioned? And we know he was a great man. The matter remains unclear.

12. *ARN-B*, chap. 28. See the quote following on p. 265.

13. *Megillah* 3a.

14. *Sukkah* 28a.

15. Compare the rabbinic legend of a snake so poisonous that when it bit even the shadow of a flying bird, the bird would fall, dead, out of the sky!

16. A version of this tradition is quoted earlier, on p. 20.

17. *Peirush HaKoteiv* commentary in *Ein Yaakov, Sukkah* 28a, referring to the Jerusalem Talmud. It gives a quaint answer, that while the effect of Yonatan's fiery holiness was restricted to the "four *amot* (cubits)" of his personal space, Hillel's extended even farther.

18. *Sotah* 9:15.

19. *Avodah Zarah* 20b.
20. Thus, the combination of the holy spirit (or mystic visions) and a paradigm of miracles (raising the dead) parallels the tradition about Hillel's eighty disciples, where the descent of the *Shechinah* is paired with the ability to do miracles, the paradigm there being the sun's stopping for Joshua.
21. Hillel, as well as other great rabbis who had the holy spirit, could and did actually prophesy on rare occasions, but they were not, for all that, prophets. Yohanan ben Zakkai, his disciple, prophesied the destruction of the Temple years beforehand (*Y. Yoma* 6:3, 43c; *B. Yoma* 39b.). And Hillel prophesied about Yohanan ben Zakkai's illustrious future as a sage (see the following p. 265). Note also Hillel's words when he did not remember about the sacrificial knives on a Passover that fell on the Sabbath and said to look at the custom of the people: "The holy spirit is on them; if they are not prophets, they are the sons of prophets." He was not talking about the holy spirit of prophecy, but of the holy spirit that guides the customs and ways of Israel, the People of God.
22. *Baba Batra* 12b.
23. The rabbis say that "a sage is superior to a prophet" (*Baba Batra* 12 a).

Chapter 42: The Rejoicing of the Water-drawing

1. The joyous water-drawing took place each day of *hol ha'mo'ed* (except on the Sabbath), not on *yom tov* ("Sukkot," *Encyclopaedia Judaica*, vol. 15, 499). The nightlong vigil that preceded each water-drawing took place on *motza'ei yom tov* of the first day of Sukkot and the succeeding nights of *hol* (Louis Finkelstein, *The Pharisees*, vol. 2 [Philadelphia: The Jewish Publication Society, 1966], II, p. 701; Shemuel Safrai, *Pilgrimage*, p. 195).
2. *Rosh HaShanah* 16a; *Tosefta Sukkah* 3:18.
3. *Sukkah* 5:1.
4. *Sukkah* 5:3; *Sukkah* 51a.
5. *Sukkah* 53a; *Sukkah* 5:4.
6. *Y. Sukkah* 5:4.
7. *Sukkah* 53a.
8. *Sukkah* 48b; Josephus, *Antiquities* XIII.13.5. See also Finkelstein, *The Pharisees* 1:102–115, 2:700–708.
9. *Ruth Rabbah* 4:9; cf. *Genesis Rabbah* 70:8.
10. *Shabbat* 30b.
11. 2 Kings 3:15.

12. *Y. Sukkah* 5:1, 55a.

13. *Ruth Rabbah* on 2:9.

14. One can determine that it was said at the Rejoicing of the Water-drawing from the context in *Tosefta Sukkah* and from the explicit mention in the related story in *ARN-B*, chap. 27, which was discussed earlier on p. 205.

15. *Tosefta Sukkah* 4:3. See preceding, p. 56.

16. *Leviticus Rabbah* 35:1.

17. *Sukkah* 53a.

18. In order not to confuse the reader, it should be noted that a saying similar to this was discussed earlier, in the context of Hillel's teaching about humility (p. 205), and will be discussed below (pp. 261f). This saying is placed at the beginning of a version of the teaching about one's feet carrying one, and so on. It seems to be unconnected with that teaching, however, and I am considering it separately here.

19. This saying appears separately in *Avot d'Rabbi Natan*, chapter 12, and is surely a saying of general relevance that Hillel used often and on many occasions. However, one such occasion specifically recorded – in *Sukkah* 53a – was at the Rejoicing. In that version, however, it seems to be joined with the saying about "where my heart loves, there my feet, etc." as if they belonged together; but that seems not to be the case, although we could force an interpretation that held them together. The *Tosefta Sukkah* 4:3 version of "where my heart, etc." (also set at the Rejoicing, in 4:1) hasn't this line about "if I am here, etc." There is another pair of sayings of a similar nature to "if I am here, etc.": "if we are here, who is here? and "if we are not here, who is here?" These are also set at the Rejoicing, which seems to confirm that setting for the other one also. Thus, *Sukkah* 53a seems to be correct in having "if I am here, etc." said at the Rejoicing, but wrong in joining it to the other sayings.

20. Another possible interpretation of this would be: "If I am here, all are here," that is, "if I am here" in the inner sense, with my heart directed to God, then "all are here," the presence of the multitude of other worshipers means something to me and can benefit me spiritually. But "if I am not here, who is here?" that is, if I am not truly present, with my heart directed to God, then what is the significance to me of all the great crowd? It is as if they were not here at all. Compare this interpretation to another saying of Hillel: "If I am not for myself, who will be for me?" See the following, p. 268. Note also that this different interpretation would change the relation of this saying to the other similar pair of Hillel sayings: "If we are here, who is here?" and "If we were not here, who would be here?"

21. The point is not that all teaching in the holy spirit must use the "I" and

"My" of God, or that any aggadic teaching that uses them was uttered with the holy spirit, but that Hillel's unusual usage, in this setting, together with the other information about the Rejoicing, indicates that these sayings were spoken with divine inspiration.

22. *Pesikta Rabbati*, chap. 1.
23. *Pesikta Rabbati*, chap. 1: "We used to go up to the Temple three times a year at the pilgrimage festivals to see the Divine Presence. Said Rabbi Yitzhak: 'Just as they came to be seen, so did they come to see, as it says: "When will I come and see [the face of God (Psalms 42:2)]," with the holy spirit. Rabbi Joshua ben Levi said: 'Why did they call the celebration the Rejoicing of the Water-drawing? Because they would draw up the holy spirit.' "
24. "The early *hasidim* would tarry an hour before prayer in order to direct their hearts to God" (*Berachot* 5:1).
25. See the preceding, p. 205.
26. The Talmud reports that excessive revelry at *Simhat Beit HaSho'evah* led to increased separation of the sexes within the Temple. At first the men and women were together in the Court of the Women, where the celebration took place, but when the rabbis saw that there was frivolity, they put the women inside – in the Court of the Women – and the men outside – in the Temple Square – but the problem continued. Then the men were put inside and the women outside, but that still did not resolve the situation. So finally they had galleries built around the courtyard where the women sat above while the men remained below (*Sukkah* 51b). This was the origin of the separate seating arrangement in synagogues. (See *"Mehizah," Encyclopaedia Judaica*, vol. 11, 1234.) Considering that Hillel cautioned the people about uncontrolled gaiety in the Temple on *Simhat Beit HaSho'evah*, it seems likely that he had a part in this rearrangement. This should not be taken to reflect a negative attitude to women, however. In fact, originally the sexes were mixed and no one considered that problematical, until problems arose. And the rabbis' first reaction was to put the women on the inside and the men on the outside. The reason that the joyous celebration of *Simhat Beit HaSho'evah* led to this seating change is that just as religious exaltation can degenerate into pride (as in the Hillel story), so can overflowing love for God degenerate into sexual love and frivolity.
27. The first is in Hebrew, the second in Aramaic.
28. Compare another teaching. "Resh Lakish said: It is written in the Scroll of the *Hasidim*: If you forsake Me for one day, I will leave you for two. A pair of parables will explain this. It is like two men who set out, one from Tiberias and the other from Sepphoris, and after meeting midway between the two Galilean cities passed on in opposite directions, each continuing separately on his journey. When this one went one mile in

one direction, the other went one mile in the opposite direction, and they were already not one but two miles apart. Or it is like a woman who is staying at home, waiting for a certain man who wants to marry her. As long as his intention is to marry her, she will continue to sit and wait; but as soon as he loses interest, she goes immediately and marries someone else" (*Y. Berachot* 9:8, 44d; cf. *Sifre* Deuteronomy 48).

This thought applies to prayer too: If a person turns his attention from God during prayer, God also turns away. There is reciprocity and mutuality in the relationship between a person and God. The teaching in the Scroll of the *Hasidim* seems similar to Hillel's mystical and hasidic perspective in the sayings we are considering. Note also the similarity of "forsake me for one day and I will leave you for two" to the form and content of "if you come to My House, I will come to yours."

29. Even his teaching that God returns a person's love and comes to those who visit Him ("To the place my heart loves, there my feet, etc. If you come to My House, etc.") has a general significance of this nature–of mutuality and reciprocity, of love answering love, of presence answering and reflecting presence–beyond its immediate application to the Temple and pilgrimage. Hillel used the verse, "In every place where I cause My name to be mentioned, I will come to you and bless you" (Exodus 20:21). In *Avot* 3:7 this verse is used to teach that the Divine Presence comes not only to those in the Temple, but to whoever mentions God's name in Torah study or prayer. Compare also *Pirke d'Rabbi Eliezer*, chap. 33, that in every place where the righteous are, God is with them, for, "In every place where I cause My name to be mentioned, I will come to you and bless you"; and Rabbi Meir's words in *Berachot* 17a, that if a person seeks God with all his heart, He promises "I will be with you in every place," which sounds like an allusion to the same verse. Adolph Buchler remarks that Rabbi Meir's goal was "the attainment of the continuous presence of God with man, wherever he happens to be . . . His religious ideal . . . merely applies Hillel's concept of the presence of God in the home of every God-fearing Jew" (*Studies in Sin and Atonement in the Rabbinic Literature of the First Century* [New York: Ktav, 1967], p. 357).

Chapter 43: Hillel's Death

1. See chap. 2 n. 1.
2. *Genesis Rabbah* 90:3.
3. Compare, for example, how at his departure from this world the prophet Elijah gave his disciple Elisha a double portion of his spiritual inheritance, like a firstborn son (2 Kings 2:9ff.).

4. A version of this list of Yohanan ben Zakkai's Torah accomplishments appears together with a parallel list for Hillel in *Soferim* 16:9. We discussed that list about Hillel in chaps. 9 and 37, this volume.
5. See the preceding, p. 20. In *Soferim* 16:9 Yohanan ben Zakkai speaks of his "rabbi," and then the text says that he received his Torah knowledge from Hillel and Shammai. It then gives a list of Hillel's Torah accomplishments. That both Hillel and Shammai were Yohanan's masters is possible, since Yohanan was young, and it seems that Shammai outlived Hillel. However, this tradition in *Soferim* could be based on *Avot* 2:9 – "Rabban Yohanan ben Zakkai received the tradition from Hillel and Shammai" – which may simply mean he was the authorized successor to that pair, and not that he studied under both teachers. Regardless, in *Soferim* Yohanan refers to Hillel as "my rabbi," as if Hillel was the major influence on him, and he has a prominent part in Hillel's deathbed story.
6. *Soferim* 16:9.
7. For example, when Yohanan ben Zakkai was on his deathbed, his disciples asked him to bless them (*Berachot* 28b).
8. Compare the words of Samuel the Small in *Sanhedrin* 11a and what Rabbi Eliezer said about Akiba in *Avot d'Rabbi Natan*, chap. 25.

Chapter 44: If I Am Not For Myself

1. The Hebrew of Hillel's saying is also very poetic and alliterative, adding to its power.
2. See the preceding, p. 260, and n. 18 there.
3. Compare the "tactic" in Hillel's maxim, that he who acquires a good name acquires it "for himself," discussed in the preceding on p. 244.
4. *Avot* 2:5.

Chapter 45: In Favor of Shammai

1. *Historiah Yisraelit*, vol. 3, p. 124.

Chapter 46: A Unique Balance

1. *Avot* 6:1.
2. This homiletic comment of the rabbis is based on a fanciful interpretation of the word for "heaven," *shamayim*, as being made up of the words *eish* (fire) and *mayim* (water).

3. Compare, for example, the relation between Simon ben Shetah the leader of the sages and Honi HaMaagal the *hasid* in *Taanit* 23a, and between Yohanan ben Zakkai the sage and Hanina ben Dosa the *hasid* in *Berachot* 34b and the difference between the sages and the *hasidim* about killing snakes and scorpions on the Sabbath in *Shabbat* 121b. In the early days of the Baal Shem Tov's movement, there was a similar tension between his *hasidim* and the "sages," their scholarly opponents.

4. Rabbi Moshe David Gross, *Otzar HaAggadah* (Jerusalem: Mosad HaRav Kook, 1977), "Kehunah," no. 169, quoting *Zohar Bereishit* 256.

5. *Avot* 2:6.

6. "Hillel," *The Jewish Encyclopedia*, vol. 6, p. 397 (photograph); "Meron," vol. 8, p. 501: "Benjamin of Tudela [twelfth century C.E.], who visited [Meron], describes a cave there containing the tombs of Hillel and Shammai and many of their disciples."

Appendix 2: From Which Hillel Are the Sayings in Avot 2:5–8?

1. "Hillel (third century C.E.)," *Encyclopaedia Judaica*, vol. 8, 486, and Hyman, *Toldot*, p. 373.

2. Hyman, *Toldot*, p. 373.

3. Klausner, *Historiah Yisraelit*, pp. 106–107; Weiss, *Dor*, p. 151 n. 2; Herford, *Ethics*, p. 44. Klausner suggests that although teachings from another Hillel may have entered this block of sayings, the majority are from Hillel the Elder. Glatzer and Blumenthal do not address this subject explicitly, but since they use Hillel sayings from this block without comment (*Hillel the Elder*, p. 35 n. 4, pp. 48–50; *If I Am*, pp. 106–109) they must consider them to be from Hillel the Elder.

4. See Herford, *Ethics*, p. 44.

Appendix 3: Hillel and Shebna – Another Interpretation

1. Compare this 1,000 versus 200 to the rabbinic teachings about the rewards for people who serve God from love or from fear, as 2,000 generations versus 1,000 (*Sotah* 36); or, two portions versus one (*Tanna d'Bei Eliyahu Rabba*, chap. 28); or a single versus a doubled reward (*Sifre Deuteronomy* 32).

Appendix 4: Why Hillel Went up to Jerusalem from Babylonia

1. See Urbach, *The Sages* 1:621–622.

2. *Sifre* Numbers 75.

3. *Y. Horayot* 3:5, 47d; also *Tosefta Zevahim* 1.
4. Bosniak, "The Life of Hillel," p. 47, notes: "For Babylonian Jewry these questions were only of theoretical value. Because in 'hutz la'aretz' the kohen exercised no such function; nor were there any sacrificial offerings made on any occasion; nor were the laws of 'yashan and hadash' [old and new crop] applied in life."
5. The text begins: "Hillel went up from Babylonia [to Israel] because of three problems." Then, for no apparent reason, at the end of the paragraph about the first problem – the priest and the skin disease – it says: "For this Hillel went up from Babylonia." Finally, at the very end, it says: "Hillel interpreted the problems and arrived at conclusions that agreed with the received traditions. He then went to Israel and accepted it as law." The second unexpected reference to Hillel's traveling from Babylonia to Israel may indicate that that was the conclusion of an originally separate tradition and that the two problems relating to Passover were also a separate tradition. Perhaps an editor in joining two somewhat contrary sources produced an unclear text.
6. See the preceding, p. 16.
7. He may have traveled to Jerusalem on other occasions also. Since Hillel as *Nasi* encouraged pilgrimage to the rebuilt Temple (see the preceding, pp. 56–59), he probably had made regular pilgrimages when living in Babylonia.
8. In the story of Hillel's encounter with the Sons of Bathyra he is questioned about the Passover sacrifice, presumably after having just made the pilgrimage to Jerusalem for the festival. And of the three questions that brought him to Jerusalem, two are about the Passover. This suggests that these latter three questions and the one presented to him by the Sons of Bathyra were all dealt with on the same fateful trip Hillel made to Jerusalem on that Passover.

Appendix 5: His Heart Is Firm, Trusting in the Lord – Another Interpretation

1. *Derech Eretz Zutta*, chap. 1; *Kallah Rabbati*, chap. 3.
2. To facilitate comparison I have reversed the order of the two stories in the *ARN-B* text to match that in *ARN-A*.
3. A *kapdanit*; like Shammai, who was a *kapdan*.
4. The Hebrew of *ARN-B* speaks idiomatically of the man's "heart trusting" his wife, similar to the Psalm verse of the Hillel story, that "his heart is firm, trusting in the Lord."
5. See the preceding, p. 105.

6. *Hotzi binzifa.*
7. The *Ein Yaakov* commentator *Anaf Yosef* on *Berachot* 60a says that some earlier commentators "interpreted the story to be about the patience Hillel instilled in his household, to be like him, not crying out at afflictions, but receiving them calmly. But although that is certainly true, I don't know how it fits the verse, 'He will not be afraid of threatening news, etc.' "
8. See the preceding, pp. 184, 186.
9. The context in the Babylonian Talmud is loose enough so that the Hillel story could be considered essentially independent and a talmudic digression on the topic of the great trust someone like Hillel can have in his family.

Appendix 6: In Remembrance of the Temple, like Hillel

1. *Pesahim* 115a.
2. Chap. 126, where there are other observances to commemorate the Temple's destruction.

Glossary

Aggadah (adj. aggadic)   Those sections of Talmud and *Midrash* containing homiletic exposition of the Bible, stories, legends, folklore, parables, anecdotes, or maxims. In contradistinction to *halachah*.

Am-haaretz   An ignorant person; a religious person of limited Torah education or an antireligious person of the lowest sort.

Anvatan (pl. *anvatanin*)   Humble, patient.

Av Beit-din   "Vice-president" of the Sanhedrin; head of the supreme religious court. Part of the dual leadership and subordinate to the *Nasi*.

Baal Shem Tov   Rabbi Israel, son of Eliezer, the founder of the modern hasidic movement. *Baal Shem Tov*, which is an epithet, not a name, literally means "Master of the Good Name"; it is often shortened to "Besht" (adj. Beshtian).

Baraita   A teaching from the time of the *Mishnah*, but not included in the final edition.

Beit Midrash   House of Torah study.

Dinar   Silver coin equal to a *zuz*.

Edomite   Idumean. From the land of Edom (Idumea), a country on the southern border of Judea. At the end of the second century B.C.E., the Judeans, under John Hyrcanus, conquered Edom and forcibly converted the Edomites to Judaism. Thenceforth they became a section of the Jewish people ("Edom," *Encyclopaedia Judaica*, vol. 6, 378). Herod the Great was an Edomite.

Essenes   A religious party or sect during the time of the Second Temple; they were a pious brotherhood of separatists who lived in isolated monastic communities.

Halachah (adj. halachic)   Jewish religious law.

Hasid (pl. *hasidim*)   A pious person. Or, specifically, a member of the hasidic movement of the Baal Shem Tov, which began in the eighteenth century (adj. hasidic).

Hasidism   Piety; can specifically refer to the hasidic movement of the Baal Shem Tov.

Hasmoneans   Maccabees. Jewish priestly family that led the fight for a Jewish state independent of the Seleucid Greek Empire and ruled it, once established, from the mid-second to the mid-first century B.C.E..

Hesed   Love, loving-kindness, compassion.

Josephus, Flavius   Jewish historian who lived during the first century C.E..

Kapdan (f. *kapdanit*; pl. *kapdanim*)   Irritable, impatient.

Maccabees   See Hasmoneans.

Midrash (pl. *midrashim*; adj. midrashic)   Exposition or exegesis of the Scriptures, often including parables, sayings, and stories. The term can refer to the act or product of interpretation. The *Midrash* is the book or body of literature, *midrash* a particular teaching.

Mishnah   Ancient collection of legal decisions of the sages; the earliest part of the Talmud, it is the text to which the *Gemara*, the other part, is the commentary. A *mishnah* is one teaching from the *Mishnah*.

Mitzvah (pl. *mitzvot*)   A divine commandment.

Nasi   "Prince" or president; exact nature of the office is unknown: perhaps leader of the Sanhedrin, Pharisees, rabbis, or the popular religious community. Senior dual leader, together with the *Av Beit-din*.

Parush (pl. *parushim*)   An ascetic; holy man. Can also mean a Pharisee (see next entry).

Pharisees   A popular religious party or sect during the time of the Second Temple, led by rabbis, that emphasized the centrality of the Torah; its members observed ritual purity in food and meals and scrupulously observed the laws of tithing.

Prosbul   A rabbinic legal device instituted by Hillel to allow creditors to collect debts, despite the release of the Sabbatical year, by transferring them to the court.

Rabban　A title of supreme distinction conferred on the heads of the central academy or the Sanhedrin, after Hillel, including Rabban Yohanan ben Zakkai and Hillel's descendants, Gamaliel I, II, III, and Simon ben Gamaliel III ("Titles," *Encyclopaedia Judaica*, vol. 15, 1163).

Rav　A title for a Babylonian Jewish teacher; equivalent to "rabbi."

Rebbe　A hasidic rabbi and sect leader of the movement of the Baal Shem Tov.

Sadducees　A conservative religious party or sect in the time of the Second Temple that represented the views of the priesthood, the aristocracy, and the wealthy.

Sanhedrin　The supreme Jewish political, religious, and judicial body during the time of the Second Temple.

Scribe　Scriptural expert and teacher; the precursor of the rabbi.

Shechinah　The Divine Presence in this world; God as immanent.

Shulchan Aruch　The main code book of Jewish religious law and behavior.

Simhat Beit HaSho'evah　An especially joyous Temple celebration during the festival of Sukkot.

Talmud　After the Bible, the most authoritative text in Judaism. It is comprised of the (earlier) *Mishnah* and the (later) discussion and commentary, based on the *Mishnah*, called the *Gemara*. The Talmud was originally exclusively oral, but later was written down as a compendious series of volumes. There are two versions that came into being in different locations: the Jerusalem Talmud and the Babylonian Talmud.

Targum　The Aramaic translation and paraphrase of the mostly Hebrew Torah. Aramaic was the spoken language of most Jews in Hillel's time.

Tefillin　Phylacteries. Leather boxes containing scriptural verses inscribed on parchment; following Deuteronomy 11:18, two separate *tefillin* (pl.) are bound by straps onto the head and arm by males. In Hillel's time they were often worn the whole day. Today they are worn during the morning prayer service and by some pious people while studying Torah.

Tzaddik (pl. *tzaddikim*)　A righteous or holy person. Also, a charismatic leader of a Beshtian hasidic group; a *rebbe*.

Zealots　An anti-Roman Jewish religious party after Hillel's time.

Zuz (pl. *zuzim*)　Silver coin equal to a *dinar*.

Bibliography

(Only major sources and those that contain information about Hillel have been included.)

Bacher, Wilhelm. "Hillel." In *The Jewish Encyclopedia*. Vol. 6. New York: Funk and Wagnalls, 1912, pp. 397–400.

Bader, Gershom. "Hillel." Chap. 13 in *The Encyclopedia of Talmudic Sages*. Northvale, Jason Aronson, 1988, pp. 94–106.

Blumenthal, Aaron. *If I Am Only for Myself: The Story of Hillel*. New York: United Synagogue Commission on Jewish Education, 1963.

Bosniak, Jacob. "The Life of Hillel." Ph.D. diss., The Jewish Theological Seminary, 1933.

Buchler, Adolph. "Hillel the Hasid." Chap. 1 in *Types of Jewish-Palestinian Piety from 70 B.C.E. to 70 C.E.: The Ancient Pious Men*. New York: Ktav, 1968, pp. 7–67.

Encyclopaedia Judaica. Jerusalem: Keter, 1972.

Flusser, David. "Hillel's Self-awareness and Jesus." *Immanuel* 4 (Summer 1974): 31–36.

Frankel, Yaakov. "Torat HaNefesh Shel Hillel HaZaken u'Mashma'uta HaPsichalogit." *Niv Midrashia* (Spring 1931): 147–163.

Gershfield, Edward. "Hillel, Shammai and the Three Proselytes." *Conservative Judaism* 21:3 (Spring 1967): 29–39.

Ginzberg, Louis. *On Jewish Law and Lore*. New York: Atheneum, 1970.

Glatzer, Nahum. *Hillel the Elder: The Emergence of Classical Judaism*. New York: Schocken Books, 1966.

Goldberger, Yisrael. "HaMekorot b'Davar Aliyat Hillel l'Nesiut." *HaTzofeh l'Hochmat Yisrael* 10 (1926): 69–76.

Goldin, Judah. "Hillel the Elder." *The Journal of Religion* 26:4 (1946): 263–277.

Graetz, Heinrich. *History of the Jews.* Vol. 2. Philadelphia: The Jewish Publication Society, 1927, pp. 96–101, 130–132.

Halevy, Yitzhak Isaac. *Dorot HaRishonim.* Vol. 1, part 3. London: Express, 1923, pp. 89–143, 668–72.

Herford, R. T. *The Ethics of the Talmud: Sayings of the Fathers.* New York: Schocken Books, 1962.

Hyman, Aaron. "Hillel HaBavli o'HaZaken." In *Toldot Tannaim v'Amoraim.* Jerusalem: Kirya Ne'emana, 1964, pp. 362–373.

Kaminka, Armand. "Hillel's Life and Work." *The Jewish Quarterly Review,* New Series, 30 (1939–1940): 107–122.

Katznelson, Y. L. "Hillel u'Veit Midrasho." *HaTekufah* 3 (1918): 267–301.

Klausner, Joseph. "Hillel v'Shammai." In *Historiah Yisraelit.* Vol. 3, gate 2, chap. 1. Tel Aviv: Yahadut v'Enoshiyut, 1924, pp. 101–124.

Levi, Israel. "L'Origine Davidique de Hillel." *Revue Des Etudes Juives* 31 (1895): 202–211.

Moore, George Foot. *Judaism in the First Centuries of the Christian Era.* Vol. 1. New York: Schocken Books, 1971, pp. 77–84.

Neusner, Jacob. "Hillel." Chap. 2 in *From Politics to Piety.* Englewood Cliffs, N J: Prentice-Hall, 1973, pp. 13–40, 104–111.

_____ . "Hillel" and "Hillel and Shammai." Chaps. 9, 10 in *The Rabbinic Traditions About the Pharisees Before 70.* Leiden: E. J. Brill, 1971, pp. 212–340.

S'vara, vol. 2, no. 2, 1991, "Prozbul: Was Hillel True to Tradition?" (symposium).

Unterman, Isaac. *The Talmud.* New York: Bloch, 1952, pp. 158–172.

Urbach, Ephraim. "Hillel." In *Encyclopaedia Judaica.* Vol. 8. Jerusalem: Keter, 1972, 482–486. (Source: *Encyclopaedia Hebraica*).

_____ . *The Sages: Their Concepts and Beliefs.* Trans. Israel Abrahams. Jerusalem: Magnes Press, 1975, pp. 339–342, 576–593.

Weiss, Isaac Hirsh. *Dor Dor v'Dorshav.* Vol. 1. Jerusalem: Ziv, 1904, pp. 146–167.

Sayings and Stories Index

Entries in this index are arranged in five categories: (1) Hillel's Sayings and Parables; (2) Hillel Quotes or Interprets Torah Verses; (3) Sayings about Hillel; (4) Stories about Hillel; (5) Teachings of or about the House of Hillel. Entries are usually listed according to the order they first appear in the text. Generally, minor references and items in the Notes are not listed. Numbers are pages numbers and those where the item is most fully discussed are in boldface.

HILLEL'S SAYINGS AND PARABLES

STORIES ABOUT HILLEL

TEACHINGS OF OR ABOUT THE HOUSE OF HILLEL

General Index

365

About the Author

Yitzhak Buxbaum is a *maggid*, an inspired and inspiring teacher and storyteller, who teaches at synagogues, Jewish community centers, and colleges. He graduated from Cornell University and has an advanced degree from the University of Michigan. The author of *Jewish Spiritual Practices*, he resides in New York City.